How Congress Works

R

How Congress Works

THIRD EDITION

CONGRESSIONAL QUARTERLY INC.
WASHINGTON, D.C.

1414 22nd Street, N.W., Washington, D.C. 20037

Cover design by Paula Anderson

Book design and production by Kachergis Book Design,
Pittsboro, North Carolina

Printed in the United States of America

The paper used in this publication meets the minimum requirements of the American National Standard for Information Science—Permanence of Paper for Printed Library Materials, ANSI Z39.48-1984.

Illustration credits and acknowledgments: 3 Scott J. Ferrell, Congressional Quarterly 9 Library of Congress 11 National Portrait Gallery, Smithsonian Institution 15 Library of Congress 17 no credit 19 Associated Press 24 Reuters 29 Douglas Graham, Congressional Quarterly 34 Reuters 39 Library of Congress 43 R. Michael Jenkins, Congressional Quarterly 45 Scott J. Ferrell, Congressional Quarterly 54 Reuters 64 C-SPAN 66 Scott J. Ferrell, Congressional Quarterly 77 Douglas Graham, Congressional Quarterly 82 Warren K. Leffler, *U.S. News and World Report* 87 Scott J. Ferrell, Congressional Quarterly 96 Douglas Graham, Congressional Quarterly 103 Douglas Graham, Congressional Quarterly 112 R. Michael Jenkins, Congressional Quarterly 118 Douglas Graham, Congressional Quarterly 125 Congressional Quarterly Scott J. Ferrell, Congressional Quarterly 138 Douglas Graham, Congressional Quarterly 142 Douglas Graham, Congressional Quarterly 146 Scott J. Ferrell, Congressional Quarterly 152 Scott J. Ferrell, Congressional Quarterly 157 R. Michael Jenkins, Congressional Quarterly

LIBRARY OF CONGRESS CATALOGING-IN-PUBLICATION DATA
How Congress Works.—3rd ed.
p. cm.
Includes bibliographical references and index.
ISBN: 1-56802-391-X (alk. paper)
1. United States. Congress. I. Congressional Quarterly, Inc.
JK1021.H69 1998
328.73—dc21 98-29616

Table of Contents

Introduction vii

CHAPTER 1 Party Leadership in Congress 1

- Congressional Leadership Structure 2
- The House Speaker 7
- House Leadership: A Hierarchy of Support 26
- Leadership in the Senate: "We Know No Masters" 36
- Party Support Structure in the Senate 46

CHAPTER 2 The Legislative Process 51

- Importance of Rules 51
- Developing Legislation 57
- House Floor Action: Structured Efficiency 67
- Senate Floor Action: Flexibility, Informality 89
- Final Action: Resolving Differences 102

CHAPTER 3 The Committee System 115

- Committees in Transition 115
- Evolution of the System: Growth and Reform 119
- The Committee Structure 141
- Committee Assignments 146
- Committee Procedures 152
- Jurisdictional Conflicts 153
- Oversight Mandate 157

Reference Materials 161

- How a Bill Becomes Law 163
- Political Party Affiliations in Congress and the Presidency, 1789–1997 164
- Speakers of the House of Representatives, 1789–1998 166
- Leaders of the House since 1899 167
- Leaders of the Senate since 1911 169
- Recorded Votes in the House and the Senate, 1947–1996 171
- Attempted and Successful Cloture Votes, 1919–1996 172
- Vetoes and Overrides, 1947–1996 173
- Congressional Information on the Internet 174

Index 177

Introduction

IN THE SEVEN YEARS SINCE *How Congress Works* was last published, in 1991, the legislative branch of the federal government has experienced some of the most noteworthy developments since the far-reaching changes that followed in the wake of the Watergate scandals and ensuing elections of the 1970s. By far the most prominent event was the Republican Party's capture of a majority of House seats in the 1994 elections, the first time the GOP had won control of that chamber in four decades. The Republicans also won control of the Senate that year, regaining a majority they had enjoyed for six years in the 1980s. Together these victories gave the party complete congressional control for the first time since 1955.

Although the Republican margins were not overwhelming, they were adequate to allow the party—primarily in the House—to set the legislative agenda, make important procedural changes, and reorganize committees and jurisdictional powers. In the process the Republicans recentralized leadership in the Speaker in a form unseen since the first decade of the century.

And yet for all the apparent change, and the tumult that accompanied it beginning in 1995, much more did not change. Committees still developed and reported legislation, though they possessed less power than in the past. Procedures and rules still were employed to maintain order and set priorities, even though some traditional practices were altered. Leaders still had to make sensible decisions and lead their followers in wise strategic and tactical ways, or risk paying a heavy political price. The institution of Congress still mattered.

How Congress Works explains how the institution really works. In clear and nontechnical language, the editors describe the core elements in the functioning of this branch: the leadership of each chamber, the legislative process, and the committee operations. Because Congress is a continuing institution that has functioned for more than 200 years in a generally beneficial way for a changing nation, in spite of being the brunt of endless jokes and criticism, the volume includes extensive history that is essential to understanding its operations and purpose. The chapters are structured to allow readers to obtain as much, or as little, detail as they need through use of section titles and a detailed index at the end of the volume. But even with the background and the details of procedures, rules, committees, and leaders, the essential focus is on Congress as the twenty-first century approaches: how its role fits in today's world of government, how its gears mesh and turn—or sometimes do not—as it conducts the public's business, and how its leaders direct it to address national issues.

The chapters are supplemented by an appendix that contains important reference information about Congress over the years, such as recorded votes, leaders in the House and Senate, party affiliations, and presidential vetoes and congressional overrides. The appendix also includes an up-to-date listing of Internet sites about Congress and congressional action that readers may find useful for additional research on the institution, its actions, and its members. All of the Web sites listed are accessible without charge.

How Congress Works is the product of many Congressional Quarterly staff writers over the years. The current edition was revised and updated by Matt Pinkus, a former CQ reporter, longtime congressional staffer, and acknowledged authority on legislative process and procedures. Congressional scholar and author Walter Oleszek gave generously of his time to review the manuscript and make suggestions on updating content.

David Tarr
Executive Editor

CHAPTER 1

Party Leadership in Congress

THERE HAS BEEN a substantial change in the role of party leaders in Congress in the closing two decades of the twentieth century. Leaders must still fulfill their traditional responsibility of managing the internal affairs of the institution, coordinating a legislative schedule, and maintaining personal relationships with colleagues anxious for advancement and sensitive to any perceived slight. But in addition modern party leaders must be able to coordinate and implement massive national fund-raising campaigns, serve as party spokespeople on controversial issues in the era of constant television reporting and Internet communication, search constantly for popular programs and ideas to use in the next campaign, and develop the ability for instant response to the opposing party's efforts to do the same things.

The traditional venues of a party leader—the floors of the House and Senate, the cloakrooms and hideaways surrounding them, and even the congressional press galleries—can seem isolated and limiting in the face of these ever-increasing demands and expectations that leaders seize control of an agenda for their party's future. In an era of narrow margins separating the two major parties in both the House and Senate, success or failure in these tasks can mean the difference between national prominence with the power to legislate as a majority, as opposed to a minority's bitterness from ineffective dissent.

The political parties themselves have also changed. Republicans, moving decisively in the 1990s out of their status as a seemingly permanent minority party in Congress, have established centralized leadership around conservative values and issues. House Republicans were indebted to their leader, Rep. Newt Gingrich of Georgia, for devising a strategy that brought them to power. As Speaker beginning in 1995, Gingrich attempted, with decidedly mixed results, to redefine the traditional institutional role of the House's presiding officer into a "transformational leader" of a revolution in American society, sometimes at the risk of his power base in the House Republican Conference. Sen. Bob Dole, R-Kan., a more traditional institutional leader, became the first Senate majority leader to win a party's presidential nomination, and attempted to juggle both of these roles simultaneously. His successor as majority leader, Trent Lott, R-Miss., a longtime conservative activist in the House, had first forced his way onto the Senate's leadership ladder to become majority whip and saw the Senate change rapidly with the addition of younger conservatives from the House who had long suffered, along with him, from the frustrations of minority status.

Democrats, who ruled the House continuously from 1955 to 1995 and the Senate for nearly as long (1955–1981; 1987–1995), have had greater difficulty developing a new identity as their southern base of support collapsed. They were relegated to minority party status in the 1994 elections even as a so-called "New Democrat" from Arkansas, Bill Clinton, occupied the White House, took issues from the Republicans' agenda, and moved the party even further away from its New Deal roots. Democrats elevated younger, telegenic leaders such as Rep. Richard Gephardt, D-Mo., and Sen. Tom Daschle, D-S.D., who were skillful at adapting to the new demands of the information society and constant fund-raising requirements. But the congressional Democratic Party had difficulty defining itself as an entity separate from its president, with whom many members had serious policy and personal disagreements. Democratic committee chairs, who had long been rivals of party leaders, were no longer in these positions of power after Republicans took House control in the 1994 election, seemingly opening the door to a more centralized leadership style.

But Democrats have been notoriously difficult to lead, sometimes rebuffing ambitious policy activists such as former House Speaker Jim Wright, D-Texas, while criticizing the quieter, consensual styles of longtime Senate majority and minority leader Robert C. Byrd, D-W.Va., and former House Speaker Thomas S. Foley, D-Wash., for lack of dynamism. Democrats often seemed unsure of what they wanted, and even if they were, appeared unwilling to allow party leaders free rein to get them there. In complete minority status after the 1994 elections, with the need for political survival and the search even for relevance taking the place of traditional concerns over chairmanships and perks, Democrats were faced with developing new priorities, including the importance of exploiting mistakes and seizing opportunities given to them by the new majority, a critical first step on the road back to power.

In the face of all these changes, party leaders in Congress in the twenty-first century will be judged by criteria far different from their predecessors. Some things remain immutable, however: power comes from majority status and leaders who can help their parties obtain, or retain, that status will have more influence than those who cannot. While Democrats ran Congress for nearly forty years, they did not credit their party leaders with that achievement. And even in the case of acknowledged successful campaign strategists such as Gingrich, the most powerful Speaker in nearly a century, the old political adage "what have you done for us lately?" still applies, as Gingrich had to face down an intraparty coup attempt from his leadership colleagues in the summer of 1997, only two years after leading his party out of the wilderness of four decades of minority status.

Organizational structures evolved over 200 years have made today's House and Senate leaders a critical link between the two political parties and the nation's legislative business, between legislators and the president, and between Congress and the voters.

Since the last half of the nineteenth century, when the two-party system became firmly entrenched on Capitol Hill, Congress has been organized on the basis of political party, with each party's congressional leaders seeking to facilitate enactment of the party's legislative program and to enhance the party's national image and electoral fortunes. Congressional party leaders of today, even though they seem in many ways so different from their predecessors in personality and ideology, represent a long-standing institutional imperative. Congress cannot run itself.

In this partisan struggle the majority party has a distinct advantage, since it controls not only the top leadership posts in both the House and Senate, but the legislative committees and subcommittees as well. Through its party leaders and its majorities on the various committees and subcommittees, the majority party is in a position to determine what legislation Congress will consider and when.

The minority party is not powerless, however; depending on its numbers and its unity, the minority can substantially influence both the shape of legislation and the operation of Congress.

The extent to which each party's leadership actually is able to exercise control over its rank and file depends on a multitude of factors, among them the personalities and abilities of the individual leaders, the institutional authority at the leadership's disposal, party unity, party strength, the willingness of the rank and file to be led, the extent of the president's involvement, and the mood in the country. In the past, particularly in the House, a few party leaders have been able to dominate the chamber. Speaker Gingrich achieved even greater influence using resources outside Congress, including tax-exempt entities, political action committees, skillful manipulation of media, policy ideas created to generate public appeal, and overarching theories of leadership.

A series of reforms both inside and outside Congress has changed it markedly from the seniority-driven, hierarchical institution of the 1950s, when House Speaker Sam Rayburn and Senate Majority Leader Lyndon B. Johnson, both Texas Democrats, exercised legendary control over their chambers.

Widespread turnover has brought into both chambers younger members, less bound by tradition, who object to being closed out of the process. New rules and procedures have made the institution more democratic. Power that had resided almost exclusively with committee chairmen has been parceled out to subcommittees, and the seniority system has been weakened. At the same time election law reforms, the advent of television campaigning, and the increasing role of political action committees in financing campaigns have made individual members of Congress much less dependent on the political party apparatus for their electoral survival.

Leaders must take care to lead in the direction the rank and file wants to go and to involve members in the decision-making process along the way. "In Mr. Rayburn's day," Wright once commented,

> about all a majority leader or Speaker needed to do in order to get his program adopted was to deal effectively with perhaps twelve very senior committee chairmen. They, in turn, could be expected to influence their committees and their subcommittee chairmen whom they, in those days, appointed. . . . Well, now that situation is quite considerably different. There are, I think, 153 subcommittees [in Congress]. . . . We have relatively fewer rewards that we can bestow or withhold. I think that basically about all the leadership has nowadays is a hunting license to persuade—if we can.[1]

In more recent times, even as a Republican-controlled Congress has changed the style of operation of the institution, particularly in the House, leadership power is still the power to persuade others to follow.

Congressional Leadership Structure

Although the strategies of leadership have changed substantially in recent years, the basic leadership structure has remained the same. In the House the leadership consists of the Speaker, who is both the chamber's presiding officer and the majority party's overall leader; the majority and minority floor leaders, who are responsible for handling legislation once it reaches the floor; the assistant floor leaders or whips, who try to convince party members to follow the leadership's program and who serve as the communications nerve center for the parties; and several party committees that develop party strategy, assign party members to the standing committees, assist the leadership in scheduling and keeping track of legislation, and provide campaign assistance to House and Senate candidates.

The Senate has no institutional or party official comparable in power and prestige to the Speaker. The Constitution designates the vice president of the United States as the president, or presiding officer, of the Senate, as well as the president pro tempore, who presides in his absence. Neither office, however, has been endowed with any commanding legislative or political authority, and neither has ever played much of a leadership role in the Senate. *(See box, The Senate's Presiding Officers, p. 36.)*

The remainder of the Senate leadership apparatus is similar in structure and function to that of the House.

Of all the party leadership positions in Congress, the only one that has functioned continuously since 1789 is that of Speaker—a post established by the Constitution. Although various members assumed the roles of floor leader and whip from time to time, the positions were not made official in the House until 1899, during a period when parties and partisanship were strong, both in Congress and throughout the country. Formal party leadership positions began to develop in the Senate in the

House Republican leaders speak at a 1997 news conference in front of the Capitol to outline plans for a tax cut. From left are GOP Conference Chairman John A. Boehner, Majority Leader Dick Armey, and Speaker Newt Gingrich.

early 1900s, but majority and minority leaders were not officially designated by the party caucuses until the 1920s.

The top leaders of both parties in both chambers are elected by their respective party caucuses, or conferences as three of the four are formally named. (Today only House Democrats refer to their partisan gathering as a caucus.) Factors such as personal style, geographical balance, and length of service traditionally play an important role in the selection of the leadership. In an age of television news and the "thirty-second sound bite," the leaders' ability to serve as effective national spokespeople for their party and legislative program has taken on new importance, as has their ability to use the media adroitly.

Ideologically, leaders tend to represent the center of their party. In this, as well as in their role as mediators, they usually occupy the "middle ground" as the various factions of the party try to draft legislative compromises that the party and Congress will accept. "As a member of the leadership," said Senate Majority Whip Byrd in 1976, "it is my duty to bring North and South, liberals and conservatives together; to work out compromises. . . . I think it takes a centrist to do that."[2] A conservative when he entered the Senate in 1959, Byrd had moved considerably leftward by the time he was first elected majority leader after the 1976 elections.

But ideological perceptions are often deceiving and can be a product of a specific point in time, and can change rapidly with the shifting political orientation of the parties. For example, Gingrich, often branded a right-wing extremist by Democrats and even by some moderate Republicans when the party was a minority in the House, was later criticized as too centrist by some of the conservative firebrands he helped elect in 1994. In 1998 Senate Majority Leader Trent Lott, who might have been considered on the far right of his party just a few years before, made a comfortable fit with the Republican Conference that had moved toward him politically and added many like-minded legislators. And the demands of institutional leadership and majority responsibility changed these leaders as well, along with their approach to politics.

LEADERSHIP FUNCTIONS

The powers the leaders may exercise and the ways the leadership functions differ in the House and Senate. In essence House rules allow a determined majority to lead, while Senate rules protect minority rights. Yet House and Senate leaders have the same fundamental job: "to bring," as political scientists Roger H. Davidson and Walter J. Oleszek have written, "coherence, direction, and efficiency to a decentralized and individualistic legislative body."[3]

The job has two overlapping, sometimes competing, parts. Leaders, Davidson and Oleszek observe, must constantly balance the needs of Congress as a lawmaking institution against Congress as a representative assembly:

> In their 'inside' role, party leaders guide institutional activities and influence policy. . . . Good communications skills, a talent for coalition building, tactical and strategic competence, intelligence, parliamentary expertise, and sensitivity to the mood of the membership and of the electorate are important attributes of an effective leader. . . . In their 'outside' role, party leaders not only help recruit candidates and assist them in their campaigns. Leaders also serve as the party's link to the president, the press, and the public.[4]

In their inside role, leaders organize each chamber and each party within the chamber, setting and reviewing committee jurisdictions and assignments and institutional and party rules.

PARTY CONTROL OF CONGRESS AND PRESIDENCY IS NO GUARANTEE OF LEGISLATIVE SUCCESS

The stalemate and gridlock that so often characterized executive-legislative relations in the 1980s and 1990s were blamed in large part on divided government. With the Republicans in control of the White House and the Democrats in control of one or both houses of Congress between 1981 and 1993, and with a Democratic president and Republican Congress beginning in 1995, conflicts between the branches were inevitable.

But control of Congress and the presidency by the same party does not always guarantee cooperation between the two branches. There have been numerous occasions in American history in which determined lawmakers resisted the proposals of their own presidents, and strong-willed presidents disregarded their party leaders in Congress.

LINCOLN, WILSON, THE ROOSEVELTS

Many of the conflicts between the White House and Congress when both were controlled by the same party have come at times of strong presidential leadership. Abraham Lincoln, Woodrow Wilson, and the two Roosevelts—Theodore and Franklin Delano—all had difficulties with their party's congressional leaders, although all four men were largely successful in winning enactment of their programs.

The first important clash of this kind arose during the Civil War, when Republican extremists dominated Congress. In 1861 Congress created a Joint Committee on the Conduct of the War, which went so far as to intervene in military operations. In 1864 Congress sought to undermine Lincoln's liberal reconstruction program by transferring responsibility for reconstruction from the president to Congress. Lincoln pocket-vetoed that bill and, so far as possible, ignored the extremists. He used executive orders to maintain the upper hand, but after Lincoln's assassination Congress achieved the supremacy it was seeking and retained it for more than thirty years.

Theodore Roosevelt was the next strong president to experience difficulty with his party's congressional leadership. Roosevelt clashed sharply with Sen. Nelson W. Aldrich, R-R.I., the unofficial but acknowledged leader of the Senate's Republicans. Aldrich, for example, refused to support the president's bill to regulate railroad rates in exchange for Roosevelt's agreement to drop tariff reform. After relying primarily on Democrats to report the rate bill from the Senate committee, Roosevelt won agreement from William B. Allison of Iowa, the other most influential Republican in the Senate, on judicial review of rate adjustments. This maneuver split the opposition and led to passage of the bill by an overwhelming vote. Aldrich, however, continued to oppose administration measures and occasionally won important concessions from the president.

Although relations between President Wilson and the Democratic congressional leadership generally were good, party leaders sometimes deserted the president on foreign policy issues. On the eve of the opening of the Panama Canal in 1914, both Speaker Champ Clark, Mo., and House Majority Leader Oscar Underwood, Ala., opposed Wilson's request to repeal a provision of a law exempting American vessels traveling between U.S. ports from having to pay canal tolls. The exemption, which Great Britain said violated an Anglo-American treaty, was eventually eliminated despite the opposition of the House leadership.

In 1917 Rep. Claude Kitchin, D-N.C., who had replaced Underwood as majority leader, opposed Wilson when the president asked Congress to declare war on Germany. Later, Speaker Clark opposed Wilson's request for military conscription. Near the end of Wilson's second term, relations between Clark and the president were nearly nonexistent.

Although Franklin Roosevelt's overall relations with Congress were as good as or better than Wilson's, he still had problems with his own congressional leadership. During his third term (1941–1945) the Democratic leadership deserted Roosevelt on major domestic issues. In 1944 Senate Majority Leader Alben W. Barkley, Ky., resigned the post when FDR vetoed a revenue bill. The Democrats promptly reelected Barkley, and the bill was passed over the president's veto.

MADISON, JOHNSON, MCKINLEY

Congressional leaders also frequently clashed with less aggressive presidents of their own party. These conflicts usually occurred when Congress attempted to dominate the president by initiating its own legislative program and directives. One of the earliest examples came during the administration of James Madison when Speaker Henry Clay forced the president into the War of 1812 against Britain. Another was Clay's successful attempt to pressure James Monroe into a series of unwanted postwar measures including a revision of the tariffs.

After the Civil War, the Radical Republicans in Congress were able to push through their reconstruction policy over President Andrew Johnson's opposition. In the process they almost managed to remove the president.

The next major clash came in 1898. Speaker Thomas Brackett Reed, R-Maine, a strong isolationist, sought but failed to block three controversial aspects of President William McKinley's foreign policy: war with Spain, annexation of Hawaii, and acquisition of the Philippine Islands. Reed's failure to stop McKinley, which led to his retirement from Congress, was due largely to the popularity of the president's policies, not to the successful application of pressure on congressional leaders by McKinley.

MODERN PRESIDENTS: JOHNSON, CARTER, CLINTON

In the mid-1960s President Lyndon B. Johnson demanded congressional support of his military policies in Southeast Asia. Although the Democratic Congress generally went along with Johnson's conduct of the war, his majority leader in the Senate, Mike Mansfield, D-Mont., actively opposed the president's military venture virtually from the beginning.

Congress was overwhelmingly Democratic throughout the four years Democrat Jimmy Carter was president (1977–1981). Nevertheless, many of Carter's proposals and the way they were formulated and presented to his party received less than enthusiastic support from the leadership in Congress. Said Majority Leader Robert C. Byrd, D-W.Va., in 1980: "At the leadership meetings, he [Carter] urges certain action and says he hopes he'll have our support. But he can't force it. The president is expected to make his proposals, and we have a responsibility to him and the country to weigh them and act on them only if, in the judgment of the Senate, we should."

President Bill Clinton failed to receive support from both ideological wings of his party on several highly contentious issues during the 103rd Congress, which contributed to loss of Democratic control of both houses for the first time in forty years in 1994. Clinton was distrusted by liberals for his campaign as a "new Democrat" willing to reassess traditional party orthodoxy, while more conservative members worried about his administration's initial liberal policy proposals, such as his support for the rights of gays to remain in military service. However, it was Clinton's controversial plan for a new system of national health insurance that most deeply divided the party and angered the public; it failed to receive floor consideration in either house and undermined Democratic claims that its unified control of both major branches of government would lead to substantial achievements. Many House liberals also deserted Clinton on major crime control legislation in 1994, forcing the president to deal with individual Republicans to assemble a majority for a more conservative bill.

SUCCESS THROUGH BIPARTISANSHIP

Cases in which a party's congressional leadership has cooperated in a substantial way with a president of the other party are less frequent and have dealt mainly with national security and related issues. One example is Republican President Dwight D. Eisenhower, who worked with a Democratic Congress for six of his eight years in office. Yet Democratic congressional leaders cooperated actively and willingly with the White House most of the time. Speaker Sam Rayburn, Texas, who often described himself as a Democrat "without prefix, without suffix, without apology," generally acted as the president's man in the House. During Eisenhower's second term, Rayburn's liberal critics, dismayed over his seeming inattention to traditional Democratic Party causes, began referring to him as an "Eisenhowercrat."

As Senate majority leader, Lyndon Johnson was a firm believer in the bipartisan conduct of foreign policy. In 1980 House Minority Leader John J. Rhodes, R-Ariz., recalled Johnson sitting in on foreign aid conference committee meetings: "He was there, not to ensure the Democratic position would win, but to ensure the administration position would win. He was acting as a broker for the Eisenhower administration. . . . It was often said at that time that 'the president proposes while Congress disposes.' The philosophy is not very popular today, but the people running Congress then were pretty much dedicated to that idea, no matter who the president was."

Ronald Reagan's first year in office was marked by a Republican Senate and a Democratic House more conservative than it had been during Carter's presidency. Working closely with Senate and House Republicans and with conservative Democrats in the House, Reagan was able to put together a string of dramatic victories, including the deepest budget cuts and largest tax reductions ever considered by Congress and a controversial arms deal with Saudi Arabia. In 1986 the Republican president and a divided Congress produced a landmark tax reform bill, largely because both parties saw political gain in passing the bill, and neither wanted to advantage the other party by blocking the reform.

President George Bush won bipartisan support from Congress to use force in the Persian Gulf crisis but it came over the objections of Democratic leaders in both the House and Senate. Bush worked effectively with Democratic leaders in both houses to push through long-delayed legislation in 1990 to strengthen the Clean Air Act.

Clinton won bipartisan support for a number of foreign policy initiatives, including passage of the North American Free Trade Agreement (NAFTA) in the Democratic-controlled House in the 103rd Congress but with Republicans providing the majority of votes; the expansion of NATO; and ratification of a chemical weapons treaty with substantial help from Senate Majority Leader Trent Lott, R-Miss. Congress denied Clinton controversial "fast track" trade negotiating authority in 1997, which was supported by many Republicans, but the president failed to obtain enough support within his own party.

But Republican congressional leaders repeatedly refused to defer to the tradition that politics stops at the water's edge. Clinton's personal difficulties with a variety of scandals intruded on his foreign policy efforts, as when House Majority Whip Tom DeLay, R-Texas., denounced Clinton's alleged behavior in a sex scandal as the president was touring African countries in 1998. And later in that year, House Speaker Newt Gingrich, R-Ga., visiting Israel, made several provocative remarks that were denounced by the administration as disruptive of its efforts to encourage peace negotiations in the region, including a statement that Secretary of State Madeleine Albright was acting like an agent of the Palestinians.

On domestic issues, Clinton vetoed much of the Republicans' ambitious domestic policy agenda in the 104th Congress and resuscitated himself politically by taking advantage of the missteps of the inexperienced new House majority. But he also embraced and reshaped a number of major Republican initiatives, resulting in enactment of a 1996 law repealing the long-standing federal welfare program and a 1997 law that balanced the federal budget the following year for the first time since 1969. Republicans took the lead in enacting a 1996 law making Clinton the first president to exercise a "line item veto" over certain new spending and tax provisions. However, the Supreme Court declared the law unconstitutional in 1998. *(See box, Line-Item Veto Experiment Ended by Supreme Court, p. 110.)*

Leaders of each party also work together and with their members, usually through the party caucuses, to develop the party's stand on policy issues. Leaders assign individual bills to the appropriate committee or committees and decide how best to handle each bill as it comes to the floor. Once a bill is on the floor, the leadership is responsible for monitoring the debate and using the rules and procedures in ways that will help the party's chances of legislative success. Throughout, establishing and maintaining party unity is an important goal.

Scheduling business on the floor—deciding what will come to the floor when, under what conditions, and in what order—may be the majority leadership's most important institutional task, and it is a forceful tool in realizing the party's policy agenda. "The power of the Speaker of the House is the power of scheduling," Speaker Thomas P. "Tip" O'Neill Jr., D-Mass., declared in 1983.[5]

The leadership often schedules floor action for the convenience of members; little business is scheduled in the House on Mondays and Fridays, for example, so that members can return to their districts for long weekends. The leadership may delay action on a controversial bill until it is sure that it has the winning votes, or it may bring a controversial bill to the floor quickly to prevent opposition from building.

In the Senate, where bills are open to nearly unlimited amendment and debate, the majority leader generally consults with the minority leadership, the floor managers of the bill, and other interested senators to draw up unanimous consent agreements governing floor action on major legislation. These agreements can be quite complicated, stipulating which amendments will be offered, how long they will be debated, and when they will be voted upon. Because a single member can block a unanimous consent agreement, the leaders must take care to ensure an opportunity to speak to all senators who want to be heard on the issue. The procedure is quite different in the House, where all but the most routine bills typically receive a rule for floor consideration. *(See "Major Legislation and the Rules Committee," p. 76, in Chapter 2.)*

Building winning coalitions is also essential to effective leadership. In the House this leadership function is aided by expanded whip organizations in both parties, which poll party members on specific issues, inform them of upcoming votes, help persuade them to support the party's cause, and ensure that they show up to vote. Ad hoc task forces also are used in both chambers to build support for specific issues important to the leadership. And for all the partisan rhetoric and real philosophical differences, leaders of both parties try to win support from members of the opposing party on most major legislation and amendments.

In their outside roles, congressional leaders of both parties meet periodically with the president to discuss his legislative agenda, letting him know how their respective memberships are likely to respond to his proposals. The leaders of the same party as the president also generally serve as his spokespeople in the House and Senate, although they remain independent of the president. "I'm the president's friend," Senate Majority Leader Byrd said of President Jimmy Carter. "I'm not the president's man."[6]

MESSAGES THROUGH THE MEDIA

In both inside and outside roles, skilled use of the media has become a prerequisite for success and even for selection as a leader. Despite his relatively short tenure in the Senate when he ran for majority leader in 1988, George J. Mitchell of Maine won the support of many Democrats who thought he would be a more articulate and appealing public spokesperson for Senate Democrats than his opponents.

Leaders in both chambers are routinely available to the news media. The Speaker of the House for many years until 1995 held a press conference before each House session began. The Senate majority and minority leaders gather with journalists on the Senate floor prior to Senate sessions, to announce the schedule and answer questions. Party leaders in both the House and Senate routinely respond to presidential addresses such as the State of the Union message or other speeches calling for legislative action.

Use of the media goes beyond simply articulating party positions. Public opinion is one of the main influences on a legislator's vote and fights on the House and Senate floor can be won not only by appealing to members of Congress but also by appealing to their constituents. "Being a good legislator means you have to do both," future House Majority and Minority Leader Richard A. Gephardt, D-Mo., once said. "If you are going to pass important legislation, you have to both deal with members and put together coalitions in the country."[7] Tactics both parties use to influence public opinion include floor speeches meant to be picked up by the television news networks, newspaper opinion page pieces written by senior members of key committees, and carefully scheduled appearances on the Sunday morning TV talk shows. Party leaders and members generally in recent years have set up Web sites on the Internet to post their views.

One of the most adroit congressional manipulators of the media was Gingrich, a conservative Republican who arrived in the House in 1979, the same year the national cable network C-SPAN began televising House proceedings. Using that medium to attack and confront the Democratic leadership, and on occasion moderate Republicans, Gingrich soon became a visible presence in the national media and a favorite of conservatives throughout the country. "Conflict equals exposure equals power," the future Speaker told a reporter.[8]

The strategy paid off. Gingrich's Conservative Opportunity Society had a significant impact on the shape of the 1984 Republican platform. In 1988 Gingrich filed the formal ethics complaint against Speaker Wright that forced him to resign his seat a year later. The following year Gingrich was elected minority whip over the preferred candidate of the minority leader. The ultimate victory came after the Gingrich-led GOP won control of the House in the 1994 elections and he was elected Speaker.

TOOLS OF PERSUASION

Although the greater independence of individual members means leaders in both chambers must rely heavily on persuasion and negotiation, they are not without inducements and a few punishments to help coax their colleagues into line. A legislator who votes with his party might be rewarded with a better committee assignment or a visit by party leaders to his district during his reelection campaign. A pet program might be handled by a sympathetic committee or attached to an important bill heading for the floor. Leaders can see that a loyal member gets benefits for her district or state—a tax break for a key industry, a new flood control project, or an exemption from clean air rules. Campaign appearances and funds are also distributed judiciously to encourage loyalty.

In addition there are many services the leadership can offer individual members, what Speaker Thomas P. O'Neill, D-Mass., called the "little odds and ends":

> You know, you ask me what are my powers and my authority around here? The power to recognize on the floor; little odds and ends—like men get pride out of the prestige of handling the Committee of the Whole, being named Speaker for the day. . . . [T]here is a certain aura and respect that goes with the Speaker's office. He does have the power to be able to pick up the telephone and call people. And members oftentimes like to bring their local political leaders or a couple of mayors. And often times they have problems from their area and they need aid and assistance. . . . We're happy to try to open the door for them, having been in the town for so many years and knowing so many people. We do know where a lot of bodies are and we do know how to advise people.[9]

Punishment for disloyal behavior can be subtle. A member's bid for a local dam or scheme to revamp national education grants could languish in an unresponsive committee. A request to switch committees, add another staff member, or move to a bigger office could be denied. Sometimes the threat of punishment may be enough to induce a member to fall into step. In the 104th Congress, Speaker Gingrich threatened to refuse to appoint members to a conference committee and to deny permission for foreign travel as a penalty for supporting a former member who opposed abortion and was running in a primary against a proabortion Republican incumbent. In the 105th Congress he endorsed a proposal that threatened to discipline members holding chairmanships who opposed the GOP position on key procedural votes, such as ordering the previous question or rules from the Rules Committee and sustaining rulings of the chair. In rare cases legislators are stripped of committee seniority or a committee post for repeatedly betraying the party position. After Democratic Rep. Phil Gramm, Texas, masterminded enactment of budgets proposed by Republican President Ronald Reagan, Democratic leaders in 1983 stripped him of his seat on the House Budget Committee. Gramm resigned his House seat, won reelection as a Republican, and soon rejoined the committee as a GOP member.

Divided government—a president of one party and a Congress of another—was a significant factor in the difficulties political leaders faced in Congress but by no means the only one. Partisan differences were exacerbated by forces within Congress and the country that had been gathering for years. Many were the direct and indirect results of the reforms that Congress had put in place in the 1970s. By 1990 Congress was filled with politicians who had never known the era in which backbenchers took care to be seen but not heard. They owed their seats and careers not to the party apparatus but to their constituents, their campaign consultants, and their political contributors. Gone were the days when their votes were there to be "delivered"—especially on issues they considered dangerous.

The rise of negative campaign tactics and the thirty-second sound bite made this new generation of politicians see more and more votes as perilous. Many members also felt that party leaders no longer offered them political cover. "There is a sense that they are out there all by themselves," said Foley, "that if they are not careful, no one will be careful for them."

That undertow of political vulnerability, combined with the diffusion of power that resulted from the 1970s reforms and the leadership's lack of effective tools to keep the rank and file in line, made it difficult to impose the discipline needed to legislative effectively, especially on huge federal budget deficits that overshadowed almost all other considerations until the mid-1990s.

The House Speaker

Widely regarded as the most powerful figure in Congress, the Speaker is the presiding officer of the House of Representatives as well as the leader of the majority party in the House. Since 1947 the Speaker has also been second in line, after the vice president, to succeed the president. "No other member of Congress possesses the visibility and authority of the Speaker . . . ," Davidson and Oleszek have written. "As the 'elect of the elected,' the Speaker stands near the president as a national figure."[10]

The speakership has not always been endowed with such prestige. For the first two decades of Congress, the Speaker was largely a figurehead; not until Henry Clay was elected to the office in 1811 did a Speaker exercise any real leadership in the House. After Clay left the House in 1825, the authority of the Speaker ebbed and flowed, but no Speaker wielded as much influence as Clay until 1890, when Republican Thomas Brackett Reed of Maine used his personal and institutional authority to ensure that the minority could no longer frustrate the legislative actions of a unified majority. *(See "Speakers of the House, 1789–1998," p. 166, in Reference Materials.)*

"Czar" Reed was soon followed by Joseph G. Cannon, R-Ill., the Speaker from 1903 to 1911, whose autocratic control over the House led to a revolt against him in 1910. Ultimately the Speaker's powers as presiding officer were limited. Changes in the caucus rules of the two political parties also served to lessen the Speaker's authority.

Cannon's tyrannical rule and the rebellion against it had a lasting effect on the office and the men who have held it. Until the mid-1970s power in the House was concentrated in the hands of the chairmen of the legislative committees. The reforms of the 1970s restored many of the Speaker's powers. Yet every Speaker since Cannon who has been an effective House leader has achieved influence chiefly through personal prestige, persuasion, brokerage, and bargaining.

That is not to say that Speakers do not use their authority to achieve their goals. "Tradition and unwritten law require that the Speaker apply the rules of the House consistently, yet in the twilight zone a large area exists where he may exercise great discrimination and where he has many opportunities to apply the rules to his party's advantage," wrote future Senate parliamentarian Floyd M. Riddick in 1949—a statement as true today as it was then.[11]

But in the modern era a Speaker must take care to ensure that his actions have the continued support of a majority of his party. Democrat Jim Wright pushed his leadership close to the limits of its powers and caused resentment by acting without first consulting other party leaders or the rank and file. That exclusion, coupled with his aggressive and sometimes abrasive style, left him politically vulnerable when a challenge to his personal ethics arose. The crisis eventually forced Wright to resign both the speakership and his House seat. Republican Newt Gingrich, the most powerful speaker since Cannon, surmounted political difficulties and personal ethics problems because he enjoyed support from a united party and from colleagues who valued strong leadership.

FRAMERS' INTENTIONS

The framers of the Constitution were silent on the role they intended the Speaker to play in the House. The Constitution's only reference to the office is in Article I, Section 2, clause 5, which states, "The House of Representatives shall chuse their Speaker and other Officers. . . ." There is no evidence that the Founding Fathers debated this provision.

Two respected authorities on the speakership, Mary P. Follett and Hubert Bruce Fuller, have suggested that this absence of any discussion indicated that the framers thought the Speaker would act as both presiding officer and political leader. "Surely," wrote Follett in *The Speaker of the House of Representatives,* the Speaker could not have been thought of "as a non-political moderator, as a mere parliamentary officer whom it was necessary to dissociate from politics. What [was] intended must be inferred from that with which [the framers] were familiar. . . ." Follett's book, published in 1896, is still widely regarded as the authoritative study of the early development of the office.[12]

What the framers knew were the colonial Speakers. In most cases these Speakers were active politicians who not only presided over the legislatures but also used their positions to further their own or their faction's legislative aims. This concept of the office differed sharply from that of the speakership of the House of Commons. The British Speaker was, and still is, a strictly nonpartisan presiding officer. (The term "Speaker" first appeared in the Commons in 1377, when Sir Thomas Hungerford assumed the post. Until the late seventeenth century, the Speaker in England was directly responsible to the Crown. The term was derived from the fact that it was the duty of the presiding officer to interpret the will of the House of Commons to the Crown.)

In any event, because political parties had not yet been formed, the first Speaker, Frederick A. C. Muhlenberg, Pa., was nonpartisan. His duties, as spelled out by the House on April 7, 1789, were to preside at House sessions, preserve decorum and order, announce the results of standing and teller votes, appoint select committees of not more than three members, and vote in cases of a tie, a practice referred to as the Speaker's "casting" vote. By the Second Congress, clearly defined party divisions had begun to develop, and Muhlenberg's successor, Jonathan Trumbull of Connecticut, displayed definite leanings toward President George Washington's legislative program. In 1796 Speaker Jonathan Dayton, a Federalist, twice voted to produce ties that resulted in the defeat of Jeffersonian motions that would have undermined the Federalist-backed Jay Treaty with Britain.

Party affiliation, although weak and more diffuse than in modern times, also became the basis for choosing the Speaker. In 1799 the Federalists elected Theodore Sedgwick of Massachusetts over Nathaniel Macon of North Carolina to the Speaker's post by a vote of 44–38, a margin that reflected that of the Federalists over the Jeffersonians in the Sixth Congress. Sedgwick, according to Follett, "made many enemies by decided and even partisan acts," so many that the Jeffersonians in the Sixth Congress refused to join in the customary vote of thanks to the Speaker at adjournment. At the beginning of the Seventh Congress, the Jeffersonians, now in commanding control of Congress, elected Macon to the speakership by a wide margin.

But throughout the early years, and particularly during Thomas Jefferson's presidency, it was the executive, and not the Speaker, who was the real political and legislative leader in the House. As Washington's Treasury secretary, Alexander Hamilton dominated the Federalist majority even during the First Congress by operating through supporters in Congress who formed what might be considered the first party caucuses. "Instead of being a forum, where every member was a peer and no man led, where great principles of government were evolved through the give and take of unrestricted discussion, Congress as such had become in effect a mere ratifying body," wrote Ralph V. Harlow in 1917. "The real work of legislation was put in shape, not in the legislature, but in secret session of the majority party."[13]

Jefferson's secretary of the Treasury, Albert Gallatin, soon became as adept as Hamilton in guiding administration measures through the party caucus and the House. Jefferson, moreover, carried his control over the legislative branch one step further, picking his own floor leader, who was named chairman of the Ways and Means Committee at the same time. One of these leaders, William B. Giles of Virginia, was actually referred to as the "premier" or "prime minister." As Ronald M. Peters notes, there was little room under Jefferson's shadow for a Speaker to carve out an independent leadership role.[14]

CLAY AND THE SHIFT OF POWER

Executive domination of the House came to an end under Jefferson's successor, James Madison. Although nominally supported by the Democratic-Republican (Jeffersonian) majorities throughout his two terms, Madison soon lost control of the party to a band of young "war hawks," who, affronted by British interference with American trade and shipping, advocated war with England. Henry Clay of Kentucky, who had served brief stints as a senator in 1806–1807 and 1810–1811, entered the House in 1811 as spokesperson for the war hawks who had swept seventy House seats in the elections of 1810. Although only thirty-four and a newcomer, he was elected Speaker on his first day in the House. He would soon become the first Speaker of national prominence and the first to use the position to achieve his own ends.

Clay's great success as presiding officer lay in his personal magnetism. "All testify," wrote Follett, "to the marvelous charm of his voice and manner, which attracted attention, awakened sympathy, and compelled obedience. He had a bold and commanding spirit, which imposed its will upon those around him. He carried all before him with his imperious nature to give him complete ascendancy over his party, and the easy leadership of the House."[15]

Employing to the full his power as Speaker to select committee chairmen and appoint members to committees, Clay immediately filled key positions on the Foreign Affairs, Military Affairs, and Naval Affairs committees with fellow war hawks. On November 29, 1811, less than four weeks after Congress had convened, the Foreign Affairs Committee issued a report recommending that the nation begin immediate preparations for war. President Madison, a leader of the Constitutional Convention and a strong secretary of state under Jefferson, proved to be a weak president. Although he sought a peaceful settlement with England, he was subjected to continuous pressure for war from Clay and the war hawks. Finally, on June 1, 1812, Madison sent Congress a war message. The House voted 79–49 for war three days later.

As congressional historian George Rothwell Brown wrote, in this episode, "Clay had lifted the Speakership of the House to a point of new power and responsibility, the Speaker to a place in the state where, backed by party organization . . . he could present to the President a program determining national policy and involving a declaration of war . . . against the pacifist sentiment of the President and most of the Cabinet."[16]

According to Peters, Clay was not a particularly good parliamentarian. Another Speaker, Robert Winthrop, said of him that "he was no painstaking student of parliamentary law, but more frequently found the rules of his governance in his own instinctive sense of what was practicable and proper than in Hatsell's Precedents or Jefferson's Manual."[17] Yet Clay was widely respected for his ability to maintain order on the House floor and to bring into line some of the chamber's more unruly members.

A notable example of these talents occurred during the debate on the proposed declaration of war, when John Randolph,

Henry Clay was chosen as Speaker on the day he entered the House of Representatives in 1811. A formidable presiding officer, he exerted firm control over the House.

a Virginia Democrat who for years had intimidated House members with his rhetoric, sought to take the floor to oppose the war policy. Clay ruled that Randolph could not speak unless he submitted a motion to the House. Randolph did so, whereupon Clay ruled that he still could not speak until the House considered the motion. The House refused to consider it, and Randolph was denied the floor. Clay frequently resorted to such tactics on important issues. In his six terms as Speaker, none of his rulings was overturned, though many were sustained only by strict party-line votes.

In addition to establishing new standards of order for the conduct of business on the House floor, Clay also helped to establish the committee system. There were ten standing committees in the House in 1810, the year before Clay entered the chamber. When he left the House in 1825 there were twenty-eight.[18] Historians and political scientists disagree about whether Clay fostered the committee system primarily to solidify and advance his own position or to improve the efficiency of the House.

Unlike previous Speakers, Clay remained a vigorous spokesperson for the interests of his congressional district. He was the first Speaker—and one of the few in history—to vote in instances when his vote could make no difference in the result. Clay's voting practices and his participation in debate set the precedent that Speakers forfeit none of their normal privileges as members.

Clay remained Speaker as long as he was in the House. Although he left his seat twice—in 1814, to help negotiate an end to the War of 1812, and in 1820—he was reelected Speaker as soon as he returned to the House in 1815 and again in 1823. He is the only early Speaker members elected repeatedly "irrespective of their partisan or factional allegiances, their geographic loyalties, or their views."[19]

FROM CLAY TO COLFAX

For the next four decades, as the issue of slavery grew to dominate the national agenda, factional allegiances and geographic loyalties would divide both the country and Congress. In the House the speakership rarely stayed in one man's possession for more than a single term. Of the fourteen Speakers who presided between 1825, when Clay left the House, and 1861, only three—Andrew Stevenson of Virginia, James K. Polk, the future president from Tennessee, and Linn Boyd of Kentucky—served for more than one Congress. Many election contests for the speakership were marked by multiple ballots; it took sixty-three ballots, for example, before Howell Cobb, a proslavery Democrat from Georgia, was elected Speaker in 1849 by a two-vote margin. *(See box, Heated Contests for Speakership: Lively but Rare in House History, p. 12.)*

Given the brief periods that most of these Speakers served, it is little wonder that none of them achieved the stature and influence of Clay. Stevenson, who served between 1827 and 1834, may have come the closest. Although he lacked Clay's magnetism, he was an able politician, actively promoting Andrew Jackson's program in the House. "No Speaker," wrote Follett, "except perhaps Macon, has been so distinctly the president's man. . . ."[20]

Two men, both Republicans, presided over the House during the Civil War, Galusha Grow of Pennsylvania (1861–1863) and Schuyler Colfax of Indiana (1863–1869). But the real leader of the House during this period was Thaddeus Stevens, the leader of the Radical Republicans, who engineered the impeachment of President Andrew Johnson.

Grow was clearly in thrall to Stevens, and Colfax, while personally popular, was not a forceful Speaker and was, like Grow, regarded by many as Stevens's man. "Colfax possessed neither will nor mind of his own," said historian Fuller. "Thaddeus Stevens furnished him with these mental attributes."[21]

RISE OF MINORITY OBSTRUCTIONISM

While the speakership may have been a position of little real authority by the time the Civil War began, the emergence of the modern two-party system and a new partisanship in the House was soon to produce two of the most powerful Speakers in history. The first Speaker after the Civil War to add any new authorities to the post was James G. Blaine, R-Maine, one of the founders of the Republican Party and Colfax's successor. As Speaker from 1869 to 1875, Blaine was the first leader since Clay to organize the House in a way that favored his party's program. Blaine successfully manipulated committee assignments to produce majorities favorable to legislation he desired.

As partisan as he was, Blaine nonetheless refused to use the powers of the speakership to stop the variety of obstructionist tactics that the Democrats used to block action on legislation they did not support but could not defeat through the regular procedures. Chief among these tactics were constant demands for roll-call votes and use of the "disappearing" or "silent" quorum, in which members of the minority party refused to answer to their names even though they were present on the floor. Blaine's reluctance to restrict the rights of the minority party may have stemmed in part from his realization that the Republican Party would some day find itself in the minority and wish to avail itself of the same tactics.

When the Democrats won control of the House with the elections of 1874, they elected as their Speaker Michael C. Kerr of Indiana, who died in 1876. They then chose Samuel J. Randall of Pennsylvania, who served as Speaker until 1881 when the Republicans regained control of the House. Randall too refused to curb minority (this time Republican) obstructionism, but he did initiate a thorough revision of the House rules designed "to secure accuracy in business, economy in time, order, uniformity and impartiality."[22] Perhaps the most significant of these revisions, which were adopted in 1880, made the Rules Committee a standing, instead of a select, committee. The Speaker retained chairmanship of the committee, a privilege he had enjoyed since 1858.

Republicans controlled Congress for one term (1881–1883), and when Democrats regained control of the House in 1883, they passed over Randall (who opposed the party's low-tariff policy) and elected instead John G. Carlisle of Kentucky, who served as Speaker until 1889. Carlisle was a strong Speaker, deriving much of his authority from his willingness to use his power of recognition to forestall motions he opposed. By asking "For what purpose does the gentleman rise," Carlisle could withhold recognition from any member whose purpose opposed his own.

But like Blaine and Randall before him, Carlisle was reluctant to do anything about minority obstructionism, making him what one commentator called "the slave of filibusters." By the end of his speakership, the minority's use of delaying tactics, coupled with a disappointing legislative record, opened the House to public criticism and demands that the rules be modified "to permit the majority to control the business for which it is responsible," to quote one editorial in the *New York Tribune*.[23]

REED'S RULE

Reform was to come in the person of Thomas Brackett Reed, Republican of Maine. Reed—a physically imposing man at six feet, three inches and nearly 300 pounds, dressed always in black—was Speaker from 1889 to 1891 and again from 1895 to 1899. In his rulings from the chair in his first months in office, later formally incorporated into the rules and procedures of the House, Reed expanded the powers of the office more than any other Speaker except Clay, in essence establishing the absolute right of the majority to control the legislative process.

Thomas Brackett Reed was one of the most powerful Speakers in House history. Known as "Czar" Reed, he established the "Reed Rules" to curb Democratic obstructionism in the 1890s.

Even as minority leader, Reed had deplored minority obstructionism. "The rules of this House are not for the purpose of protecting the rights of the minority," he had said, "but to promote the orderly conduct of the business of the House."[24] The minority's rights were preserved in their right to debate and to vote, Reed argued. The dilatory tactics the minority used controverted the essential function of the House, which was to legislate. Once elected Speaker, he determined to do something about the situation.

The Speaker's decision was risky—his Republicans commanded only a seven-vote majority in the House, 166 to the Democrats' 159—not only to his role as Speaker but also to his future political ambitions. Like Clay and Blaine before him, Reed aspired to the presidency. According to historian Barbara Tuchman, Reed confided his decision to attack the silent quorum to no one, not even to Cannon, his closest lieutenant, in part because no one else would have thought he had any chance of success, in part because he was not sure his own party, including Cannon, would support him.

On January 21, 1890, Reed took his first major step against obstructionism by refusing to consider a member's demand for a teller vote on a motion to adjourn. A few days later he announced his intention to disregard all motions and appeals, even if procedurally correct, if their purpose was simply to delay House business.

Then, on January 29, Reed made his assault on the silent quorum. When the Republicans called up the first of several contested election cases, Charles F. Crisp of Georgia, the Democratic leader who would succeed Reed as Speaker in the next two Congresses, objected to considering the Republican motion. The yeas and nays were ordered, and the vote came to 161 "yeas," two "nays," and 165 not voting—mainly Democrats who while not voting were nonetheless present. When the vote was announced, the Democrats immediately claimed that it was invalid because a quorum (165) had not voted, whereupon Reed ordered the clerk to enter the names of those present who had refused to vote. He then ruled that a quorum was present and that consideration of the question was in order.

The House erupted into pandemonium when the quorum count began. Republicans applauded the Speaker. Democrats, wrote historian Tuchman, "foamed with rage. A hundred of them 'were on their feet howling for recognition,' wrote a reporter. 'Fighting Joe' Wheeler, the diminutive former Confederate cavalry general, unable to reach the front because of the crowded aisles, came down from the rear 'leaping from desk to desk as an ibex leaps from crag to crag.' As the excitement grew wilder, the only Democrat not on his feet was a huge representative from Texas who sat in his seat significantly whetting a bowie knife on his boot."[25]

An appeal from the ruling was tabled by a majority of those voting (again with a quorum present but not voting). The following day, the Speaker declined to reconsider the ruling and declared that he would refuse to recognize any member rising to make a dilatory motion. The debate, angry and strident, continued for several more days. At one point, it appeared that a group of irate Democrats were preparing to pull the Speaker out of the Chair. At another point, Democrats decided to leave the chamber, in an effort to deny the Republicans a quorum, but Reed ordered the doors locked, forcing Democrats to hide under their desks and behind screens. Reed was called tyrant, despot, dictator—the epithet that stuck was czar. Throughout it all he remained calm and implacable, and on the fifth day the Democrats conceded, unable to muster a majority to overturn the Speaker's decision.

On February 14, 1890, the House formally adopted new rules incorporating Reed's rulings and other new procedures. The new code, reported by the Rules Committee chaired by Reed, provided that all members must vote unless they had a pecuniary interest in the issue at hand, motions to recess or to fix a date of adjournment would not be entertained when a question was under debate, 100 members would constitute a quorum in the Committee of the Whole, and the Speaker would entertain no dilatory motions. The House adopted the "Reed Rules" after bitter debate. The most controversial of them—counting present but nonvoting members to make a quorum—was upheld by the U.S. Supreme Court in an 1891 test case (*U.S. v. Ballin*, 144 U.S. 1).

The Democrats regained control of the House in 1890 with such a convincing majority that they were able to reject the Reed Rules. But Reed had not had his final word on the subject. Though the Democrats after the 1892 elections reverted to the

HEATED CONTESTS FOR SPEAKERSHIP: LIVELY BUT RARE IN HOUSE HISTORY

At the beginning of every two-year term each party caucus nominates a candidate to be Speaker of the House and the candidate of the majority party wins the office, normally on a straight party-line vote on the House floor. The Clerk of the House from the previous Congress presides until a Speaker has been chosen. The Speaker is elected by a majority of members-elect voting by surname, a quorum being present. Traditionally, the members nominated for Speaker vote "present" rather than for themselves. The Constitution does not require that the Speaker be a member of the House, but he always has been. Any member who desires to may run for the speakership.

But pro forma elections of the Speaker have not always been the case. Before the two-party system became entrenched on Capitol Hill, factions sometimes so splintered the majority party that the election of a Speaker turned into a battle royal. On two occasions, the House departed from precedent and, using special rules, chose Speakers by a plurality vote; but in each case the House by majority vote subsequently passed a resolution declaring the result.

Regional disputes, mainly over slavery, produced at least eleven hotly contested races for the speakership before the Civil War. The first was in 1809, when none of the Democratic-Republican candidates was able to achieve a majority on the first ballot. The election finally went to Joseph B. Varnum of Massachusetts after the South's candidate, Nathaniel Macon, N.C., withdrew because of poor health.

Other battles occurred in 1820, when an antislavery candidate, John W. Taylor, D-N.Y., won on the 22nd ballot; in 1821, when Philip P. Barbour, D-Va., won on the 12th; in 1825, when Taylor recaptured the post on the second ballot; in 1834, when John Bell, Whig-Tenn., won on the tenth vote; in 1847, when Robert C. Winthrop, Whig-Mass., won on the third; and in 1861, when Galusha A. Grow, R-Pa., won on the second.

In four other pre–Civil War instances the House became deadlocked for weeks or months over the election of the Speaker.

1839: NEW JERSEY CONTROVERSY

The first of these prolonged battles began on December 2, 1839, when election of the Speaker hinged on the outcome of five contested House seats in New Jersey. Excluding the five New Jersey members, the party lineup in the House was 119 Democrats and 118 Whigs. Democrats sought to organize the House (and elect the new Speaker) before the contested elections were decided; the Whigs wanted to wait until the elections were resolved.

After much debate the House on December 14 agreed with the Democratic proposal to vote for Speaker before the contested seats were decided. But Democratic leaders were then unable to hold a sufficient number of members in line to name a Speaker. On December 16, Robert M. T. Hunter, D-Va., who had declared himself an independent, was elected Speaker on the 11th ballot.

1849: FREE-SOIL DISPUTE

The next major contest for the speakership developed in 1849, when neither the Whigs nor the Democrats could achieve a majority because the so-called Free-Soil factions in both parties decided to act independently. The resulting deadlock lasted for three weeks and sixty-three ballots.

The Free-Soilers, who opposed expansion of slavery into the territories, wanted to ensure that certain House committees were controlled by antislavery legislators. They thus opposed the election of the leading candidates for Speaker in both parties: Robert C. Winthrop, Whig-Mass., who they felt had been lukewarm on the issue as Speaker from 1847 to 1849, and Howell Cobb, D-Ga., a strong proponent of slavery. Each faction put up its own candidate—at one time there were eleven—preventing either Winthrop or Cobb from winning a majority.

At various points compromise solutions were considered and rejected, including proposals that the Speaker be chosen by lottery and that members receive no salary or mileage reimbursement until a Speaker was elected. Finally, after the 59th vote, the House agreed to elect the Speaker by a plurality, provided that it be a majority of a quorum. On the 60th vote, Cobb led; on the 61st, Winthrop; and on the 62nd, the vote was tied. The issue was decided on the 63rd vote, when Cobb won a plurality of two votes. "The choice of a very pronounced pro-slavery and southern man at this crisis undoubtedly aggravated the struggles of the following decade," Mary P. Follett noted in her authoritative 1896 book on the speakership.

1855: KANSAS AND SLAVERY

Six years later another multifaction battle stemming from the slavery issue delayed election of a Speaker. The specific concern was who would be appointed to the committee investigating the admission of Kansas into the Union: Would the Speaker choose committee members who favored its entry as a free state or as a slave state?

Although antislavery forces held a majority of House seats, their ranks were so split by factions—mostly the new Republican Party and various Free-Soil groups—that they could not unite behind a single candidate. After 129 ballots, the House decided that the candidate receiving the largest number of votes on the 133rd ballot would be declared the winner. On February 2, 1856, Nathaniel P. Banks, American-Mass., was elected with 103 out of the 214 votes cast.

Banks met the expectations of the antislavery forces by giving them a majority on the Kansas investigating committee. The practical effect of that action, Follett observed, "delayed the settlement of the Kansas episode until after 1857, and this gave time for the antislavery forces to organize."

1859: IMPENDING CRISIS

The last of the great pre–Civil War contests over the speakership occurred in 1859. The tone was set on the first day of the session, December 5, when slavery advocates proposed a resolution that anyone who endorsed the sentiments of *The Impending Crisis of the South: How to Meet It,* a book hostile to slavery, was not fit to be Speaker.

The resolution and another introduced the next day were directed at John Sherman, R-Ohio, who had endorsed the book. "The ball thus set rolling," Follett wrote, "the discussion of slavery began, bitter and passionate on one side, eager and vehement on the other. The state of the country was reflected in the struggle for Speaker. The House was the scene of a confusion and uproar which the clerk could not control. . . . Bitter personal invectives nearly led to personal encounters. . . . It seemed as though the Civil War was to begin in the House of Representatives."

Sherman led in the early voting, falling only six votes short of a majority on the third ballot. By the end of January, however, Republicans saw that Sherman could not be elected and shifted their support to William Pennington, Whig-N.J., a new and unknown member. On February 1, 1860, after forty-four votes and two months into the session, Pennington was elected with 117 votes, the minimum needed to win. Pennington was the only Speaker other than Henry Clay ever elected to the speakership during his first term. But he did not share Clay's skill. Pennington was defeated for reelection to the House in 1860.

1923: PROGRESSIVE INSURGENCY

The only deadlock over the speakership since the Civil War occurred in 1923, when twenty Progressive Republicans held the balance of power in the House. They put up their candidate, Henry A. Cooper, R-Wis., as a protest against House procedures. After eight inconclusive votes, Nicholas Longworth, R-Ohio, the GOP majority leader, made an agreement with the progressives to liberalize the rules. The next day they threw their support to the Republican candidate, Frederick H. Gillett, R-Mass.

OTHER LEADERSHIP FIGHTS

Since 1923 there have been no floor battles for the speakership. One party has always held a clear majority and has been able to elect its choice on the first ballot. But there have been fights in the party caucuses. In 1933 Democratic Majority Leader Henry T. Rainey of Illinois faced four candidates in his bid to win the nomination in the caucus, which was tantamount to election since the Democrats controlled the House. A northerner and a liberal, Rainey was opposed by the southern establishment that controlled the Democratic Party at the time. But with three of the other four candidates from southern states, Rainey had room to maneuver. He was nominated Speaker in a deal that ensured the southern establishment would continue to be the effective ruling power in the House.

No significant battles for the speakership have developed on the Democratic side since 1933; each time a Democratic Speaker has left office and the party controlled the chamber, the Democratic majority leader has been elevated to the speakership without much ado. In several cases the Democratic Caucus has then elected the party whip to be majority leader. However, this pattern appeared to be ending in the 1970s, as Democratic whips failed to sustain long-term careers in the House. John McFall, D-Calif., lost a race for majority leader in 1976. His successor as whip, John Brademas, D-Ind., was defeated in the 1980 Republican landslide. Thomas S. Foley, the last member to be chosen as whip by appointment, then got back on the ladder, rising to become majority leader and Speaker. However, the next two Democratic whips, Tony Coelho of California and William Gray III of Pennsylvania, resigned from the House before any opportunity of advancement opened up.

The Democratic pattern of leadership succession fell apart most visibly in 1976 when deputy whip Jim Wright of Texas offered himself as an alternative to the bitterly antagonistic front-runners, Caucus Chairman Phillip Burton of California and Richard Bolling of Missouri. Whip John McFall was popular with his fellow Democrats but tainted by his association with the "Koreagate" influence-peddling scandal; he was eliminated from the race on the first ballot. Wright had seemed an unlikely winner when he announced he would enter the contest, but he eliminated Bolling by two votes on the second ballot, and Burton by a single vote on the third ballot.

House Republicans have had more contests for party leader in recent decades. In 1959 Charles A. Halleck of Indiana, a conservative, deposed the more moderate Joseph W. Martin Jr., of Massachusetts, as minority leader. Martin had served as Speaker of the House in 1947–1949 and 1953–1955. Republicans had suffered massive losses in the 1958 elections.

Similarly, Gerald R. Ford of Michigan ousted Halleck as minority leader in 1965 following landslide Democratic election victories. After the 1980 elections Robert H. Michel, the minority whip since 1974, was elected minority leader over Guy Vander Jagt of Michigan. Members apparently agreed with Michel's claims that his experience as the party's whip and his negotiating skills would serve House Republicans better than Vander Jagt's claim to be the more effective party spokesperson. Michel did not seek reelection to the House in 1994.

Minority Whip Newt Gingrich, R-Ga., then became Speaker by unanimous vote of the House Republican Conference in 1995 and was elected by a party-line vote in the House as the first Republican Speaker since Joseph Martin left office in 1955. Gingrich's political stature dropped dramatically during his first term as Speaker, and he endured a scare in 1997 as he sought reelection in the face of an ongoing ethics investigation. Despite his party's 227 members in the chamber, Gingrich received only 216 votes for Speaker, three more than the absolute majority required from among members-elect who voted for candidates by surname. Four Republicans voted for other persons, either sitting Republican House members or former Republican members. Five other Republicans voted present, but their actions did not affect the race.

SOURCES: George B. Galloway, *History of the House of Representatives* (New York: Thomas Y. Crowell, 1961), 43; Mary P. Follett, *The Speaker of the House of Representatives* (New York: Longmans, Green, 1896; reprint, New York: Burt Franklin Reprints, 1974), 56, 59, 61–62, 95.

Reed rule that set a quorum in the Committee of the Whole at 100 members, Speaker Crisp refused to count those present but not voting. In his capacity as minority leader, Reed in 1893 and early 1894 organized several Republican filibusters in an effort to force Crisp to count the quorum. These efforts were to no avail until February 1894, when Reed attacked a Democratic-supported measure by calling for one roll call after another and then using the silent quorum tactic to delay action. Despite their majorities the Democrats were unable to muster a quorum on their own, and after two months Crisp was forced to concede; the House adopted a rule allowing the Speaker to declare a quorum when a majority of members were actually present, regardless of whether they answered to their names.

Crisp's tenure is notable in the evolution of the speakership for strengthening the Rules Committee as a tool of the Speaker. Historian Fuller noted that this expanded role for the Rules Committee was a "radical departure from the long-established rules and principles of parliamentary law and practice." He added that the "tyranny of Reed seemed beneficence when Crisp ruled that not even 'the question of consideration could be raised against a report from the Committee on Rules.' "[26]

"CANNONISM"

During their reigns as Speaker, Reed and Crisp centralized power in the House. Not only was the Speaker now able to take effective command of the House, his authority to name the members and chairmen of all committees gave him the power to punish or reward his colleagues. As chairman of the Rules Committee, which had the right to immediate access to the floor, he could control the timing and content of bills to be brought before the House. And with unlimited power of recognition, he could determine in large measure what business would be taken up on the floor of the House. Though these authorities ensured that the House would run efficiently, if abused they could allow a Speaker to tyrannize the House. That is what happened when "Uncle Joe" Cannon was elected Speaker in 1903.

Regaining control of Congress in 1895, the Republicans returned Reed to the speakership. Having broken with President William McKinley over the intervention in Cuba and the annexation of Hawaii and the Philippines, Reed resigned from the House in 1899. Cannon, who had already lost races for the speakership in 1881 and 1889, hoped to succeed Reed then, but the Republicans instead chose David B. Henderson, R-Iowa, who served two ineffective terms as Speaker before retiring from the House. When he was finally elected Speaker in 1903, Cannon was the oldest representative (sixty-seven) and had served longer (twenty-eight years) than any member yet to head the House of Representatives.

Cannon's first years in office gave little indication of what would develop. The affable Speaker was one of the most popular men in Congress, and in his first term, "his natural kindliness and sense of humor fostered a spirit of amicability that influenced the mood of the House."[27] Though he would eventually rescind it, Cannon even granted authority to the Democratic leader, John Sharp Williams, D-Miss., to assign Democrats to committees, subject to Cannon's veto.

But Cannon was also a devout conservative, unsympathetic to much of the progressive legislation sought by President Theodore Roosevelt and favored by a growing number of liberal Republicans and Democrats in the House. Though he was forced to accept some of these measures—including the Hepburn Act (1905), which strengthened the power of the Interstate Commerce Commission to set railroad rates, the Pure Food and Drug Act of 1906, and the Mann Act of 1910—he also made increasingly arbitrary use of his powers as Speaker to maintain control of the House.

On days set aside for approval by unanimous consent of purely local bills of minor importance, Cannon moved arbitrarily to reward his friends and punish his enemies. "Often on the success of these bills would depend the reelection of many men in Congress," Fuller wrote. The Speaker's "smile and assent made and unmade members, accordingly, as he bestowed or withheld these powerful benefices."[28] Although the seniority system was still not firmly embedded, Cannon's flagrant disregard for it in assigning members to committees further contributed to the chamber's growing irritation with his rule.

But it was Cannon's use, or misuse, of the Rules Committee that most offended his colleagues. Before any committee could report legislation to the full House, the committee had to obtain clearance from Rules, and clearance usually was granted only for those measures that met with Cannon's favor. The Rules Committee's special terms and guidelines for bills to be considered by the House—those acceptable to Cannon—usually placed sharp limits on debate and foreclosed floor amendments. The latter practice enabled Cannon and his associates to attach legislative "riders" (nongermane amendments) in committee that might have been defeated on the floor if brought to a separate vote. But because these riders were frequently attached to annual appropriations bills, the House usually accepted them rather than kill the entire bill.

Eventually the persistent use of the Speaker's powers to obstruct the legislative will—not of the majority party itself, but of a new majority of members of both parties—sparked a revolt. In March 1909 the House adopted the Calendar Wednesday rule, setting aside time each Wednesday for committee chairmen to call up bills that their committees had reported but that had not been cleared for floor action by Rules. *(See box, Prying Loose Legislation Stuck in Committee: Use of Discharge and Calendar Wednesday, p. 70.)*

At the beginning of a special session that opened a few days later, a group of Republican insurgents joined the Democrats, led by James Beauchamp "Champ" Clark, D-Mo., in a move to curb the powers of the Rules Committee. That effort failed when several Democrats joined the Republican majority in opposition to Clark, and instead the House adopted a weak alternative that made only slight inroads into Cannon's power. Chief among these was the establishment of the Consent Calendar,

"Uncle Joe" Cannon addresses the House of Representatives. Cannon dominated the House from 1903 until 1910, when Republicans and Democrats revolted against his arbitrary rule.

which set aside two days each month on which individual members could call up minor bills of particular interest to them without prior approval from the Speaker.

In March 1910 the insurgent Republicans found another opportunity to challenge Cannon's iron rule. On March 17, George W. Norris, R-Neb., the leader of the insurgents, took advantage of a parliamentary opening to move for immediate consideration of a reform resolution that would remove the Speaker from the Rules Committee and expand the committee to fifteen members; the members would be chosen by election of the House and would then choose their own chairman. Cannon stalled for two days, while he pondered a point of order that Norris's motion was out of order, until Republican stalwarts who had gone to their districts for St. Patrick's Day returned to the capital. Finally, on March 19, Cannon ruled that Norris's motion was out of order. The returning Republicans were not enough. The House overturned Cannon's decision, 164–182, and then adopted the reform resolution, which Norris had modified, 191–156. The modification set the size of the Rules Committee at ten members, six from the majority and four from the minority.

In what has been described as one of the most dramatic events in the history of the House, Cannon then announced that he would entertain a motion to declare the chair vacant so that the House could elect a new Speaker. But though they were willing to strip him of his powers, most of the Republican insurgents were not willing to unseat him—or to help put a Democrat in the speakership—and Cannon remained Speaker until the term ended in March 1911.

DECLINE OF THE SPEAKER'S POWER

When the Democrats won control of the House in 1911, they named Champ Clark their new Speaker and chose Oscar W. Underwood, D-Ala., as majority leader and chairman of the Ways and Means Committee. They also agreed that the Democratic members of Ways and Means would serve as their Committee on Committees to draw up committee assignments for all Democrats, a move that further weakened the powers of the Speaker. (The Democrats retained that arrangement until 1974, when the power to make committee assignments was transferred to the Steering and Policy Committee. In 1917 Republicans set up their own Committee on Committees.) Both parties now call their committee assignment bodies the "Steering Committee."

The Democrats also retained the Calendar Wednesday and Consent Calendar innovations, as well as a discharge rule, adopted in 1910, which allowed a majority of House members to petition to free legislation bottled up in a committee. A special calendar for private bills was also established.

Because Clark left most of the management of party business to Underwood, the floor leader quickly became the acknowledged leader in the House. "The Speaker became a figurehead, the floor leader supreme," wrote a contemporary observer.[29] Underwood made frequent use of the party caucus to develop unity on legislative issues. Democrats in 1909 had adopted rules that bound all party members to support any party position approved by two-thirds of those Democrats present and voting at a caucus meeting, provided the vote represented a majority of the Democrats in the House. A member could vote against the caucus position only if he considered the position unconstitutional or had made "contrary pledges to his constituents prior to his election or received contrary instructions by resolutions or platform from his nominating authority."

Underwood also used the caucus to develop legislative proposals, which then would be referred to the appropriate committees for formal approval; to instruct committees as to which bills they might or might not report; and to instruct the Rules Committee on the terms to be included in its special orders governing floor consideration on major bills and proposed amendments. The power that had been concentrated in the hands of the Speaker was now transferred to "King Caucus" and the man who dominated it. "Whereas Cannon had often exercised control by keeping unwanted legislation off of the floor," observed Peters, "Underwood sought to control legislation by ensuring a majority vote on the floor. The result was despotism under two different guises."[30]

Rule by caucus worked well as long as Democrats were relatively united on the issues; during President Woodrow Wilson's first term, they were able to enact a large body of domestic legislation. But the Democrats soon began to split over foreign policy, and the effectiveness of the binding caucus had disappeared by the time the Republicans took control of the House in 1919. Once again, however, the Speaker was not the true leader of the House.

The leading contender for the speakership in 1919 was James R. Mann, R-Ill., who had been minority leader since 1911. But many Republicans feared that Mann would try to centralize power in the Speaker's office, so they turned to Frederick H. Gillett, R-Mass., who, like his Democratic predecessor, Champ Clark, declined to assert political leadership. Mann refused the position of floor leader, which was then given to Franklin W. Mondell, R-Wyo. Mann, however, retained substantial influence among House Republicans.

To further ensure decentralization, the Republicans set up a five-member Steering Committee, chaired by the majority leader. The Speaker and the chairman of the Rules Committee were barred from sitting on this committee, though Mondell invited both to attend its meetings, which were held almost daily to discuss party positions and map strategy with committee chairmen and other Republican leaders. "For the most part," Randall B. Ripley reported, "the Steering Committee carried out the wishes of the Republican leaders in the House, even when these were not in accord with the Republican administration." As example Ripley cited Steering Committee opposition that killed a bill to raise civil service pensions despite support from the Coolidge administration, the Senate, and every member of the House Civil Service Committee. Leadership under this system was so diffuse that House Republicans accomplished little during the period. House members, Ripley wrote, "including some committee chairmen, used the loose leadership structure to pursue legislative ends other than those officially sanctioned."[31]

As Speaker from 1925 to 1931, Nicholas Longworth, R-Ohio, sought to centralize power once again in the Speaker's office. Longworth held it "to be the duty of the Speaker, standing squarely on the platform of his party, to assist in so far as he properly can the enactment of legislation in accordance with the declared principles and policies of his party and by the same token to resist the enactment of legislation in violation thereof."[32] One of his first actions was to discipline Republican Progressives; those who had opposed his candidacy for the speakership, and who had also opposed a rules change that made it much more difficult to discharge a bill from committee, found themselves stripped of their committee seniority.

Despite these moves, Longworth as Speaker had few of the powers that enabled Cannon to centralize power in the speakership. He nonetheless was considered an effective Speaker, able, as Peters notes, to wield power and authority not so much by manipulating the rules but "by force of his character." Longworth's style was collegial. While he made little use of the Steering Committee, he established a small group of trusted associates to help him run the House. Though it appeared contradictory given his stand on strong party leadership, Longworth also was willing to deal with the Democrats not only on policy issues but on scheduling business. He and the Democratic leader, John Nance Garner, D-Texas, began the tradition, later made famous by Sam Rayburn, of the "Board of Education"—gatherings in a Capitol hideaway where leaders from both parties met over drinks to work out accommodations on various matters.

THE POWER OF PERSUASION: RAYBURN

Democrats regained control of the House in 1931, a position they lost only twice in the next sixty-four years, in 1947–1949 and 1953–1955. During the first ten years of this cycle, four different Democrats held the speakership. Garner was elected Speaker in 1931. When he became vice president in 1933, he was replaced by Henry T. Rainey of Illinois, who died in 1934. Rainey was followed in 1935 by Joseph W. Byrns of Tennessee, who died in 1936. Byrns's successor, William B. Bankhead of Alabama, served as Speaker until his death in 1940. None of them left a lasting

One of the most respected twentieth-century House Speakers was Texas Democrat Sam Rayburn.

mark on the office. That was to change with the election in 1940 of Majority Leader Rayburn who served as Speaker until his death in 1961, except for the two Republican Congresses when Joseph Martin of Massachusetts held the post.

Rayburn was a strong Speaker—indeed, his reputation reached near mythic proportions in the decades following his death. But the reasons for Rayburn's strength and the style with which he led the House were in sharp contrast to those in play during the Reed and Cannon speakerships.

Rayburn entered the House in 1913, just three years after the revolt against Cannon and at a time when the powers and the stature of the Speaker were at low ebb. By 1940 little real change had been made in the Speaker's powers. The seniority system was well entrenched, which meant that committee chairmen and ranking members could act with a great deal more independence than they could at the turn of the century. In 1940 and for the next two decades most of the chairmen of the major committees were southern Democrats.

At the same time most southern Democrats began to vote with the Republicans on New Deal, and eventually on civil rights, issues, forming a conservative coalition against liberal northern Democrats. Even when the conservative coalition did not form on a particular issue, the thin Democratic majorities could make it difficult for the Democratic leadership to achieve its program. As Rayburn himself put it in 1950, "The old day of pounding on the desk and giving people hell is gone. . . . A man's got to lead by persuasion and kindness and the best reason—that's the only way he can lead people."[33]

A man of great integrity who venerated the House of Representatives, Rayburn dealt with the individual rather than the party. He sought to bind individual members to him through friendship and favors; he did not force Democrats to vote against their conscience or constituency; he played down partisanship, shunning the use of the caucus and other party mechanisms that he thought divisive and working with minority leaders, even doing the occasional favor for a rank-and-file member of the minority; he cultivated younger members, advising them "to get along, go along."

Rayburn's preferences were controlling when it came to Democratic committee assignments. In 1948 he obtained the removal from the Un-American Activities Committee of three Democrats who had supported Dixiecrat Strom Thurmond in the 1948 presidential campaign. He saw to it that Democrats named to vacancies on Ways and Means were sympathetic to reciprocal trade bills and opposed to reductions in oil depletion allowances. And he turned the Education and Labor Committee from a predominantly conservative body into a more liberal one.

Despite the active presence of the conservative coalition, Rayburn was able to win House passage of an impressive amount of legislation dealing with both foreign and domestic matters, including two far-reaching civil rights bills. He accomplished his goals by working with the other power centers in the House. Rayburn, writes Peters,

> was a man carved for the role he played, yet he was also a shrewd politician who was able to create a political labyrinth in which his own skills would prove most effective. His success lay less in his ability to swing large numbers of votes than in avoiding situations in which that would be necessary. When he wanted legislation stopped, he let others stop it; when he wanted legislation passed, he worked with the committee chairman to get bills that could command a floor majority. . . . [Rayburn's] emphasis upon the virtue of honesty and his reputation for fairness in dealing with members contributed to the creation of an atmosphere of comity in the House that facilitated his leadership. . . . He did not win votes by staring people down; instead, he established a set of expectations about behavior that enabled him to deal for votes when necessary.[34]

TRANSITIONAL SPEAKERS: MCCORMACK, ALBERT

Rayburn's speakership marked the end of an era. In his later years, younger and more liberal Democrats began to demand changes that would lead to the greatest internal reforms in the history of the House. Indeed, Rayburn's last major victory, in 1961, came in a battle to make the Rules Committee, dominated by conservative southerners, more responsive to the will of the Democratic majority. *(See, "Major Legislation and the Rules Committee," p. 76, in Chapter 2.)*

Rayburn's two immediate successors, John W. McCormack, D-Mass., who served as Speaker from 1962 to 1971, and Carl Albert, D-Okla., who was Speaker from 1971 to 1977, had the ill luck to lead the House during a time both of great social and political upheaval within the nation and of great institutional change that neither man was well equipped to manage. McCormack was popular with his colleagues, and like Rayburn, based his leadership on his personal ties to members. But he lacked the persuasive skills of his predecessor and placed considerable reliance on Albert, his majority leader, and on the majority whip, Hale Boggs, D-La.

McCormack's weakness as a leader, coupled with his opposition to reform proposals in the House and his support of President Johnson's escalation of the Vietnam War, frustrated many of the younger, more liberal House Democrats. In 1968 Morris K. Udall, D-Ariz., challenged him for Speaker in the party caucus. McCormack easily won reelection, but soon announced his decision to retire at the end of the Congress.

Albert, too, was generally considered by his colleagues to be a weak leader. His low-key style did not seem suited to the requirements of the times, although any Speaker would have been hard put to guide the House smoothly and firmly through an unparalleled period of internal reform, against the backdrop of U.S. withdrawal from the Vietnam War and the Watergate crisis, which resulted in President Richard Nixon's resignation.

Relations between the Republican president and the Democratic Congress were tense throughout the Nixon presidency. Intent on expanding his power, Nixon acted with minimal consultation with and concern for Congress. His administration was committed to political and economic programs opposed by the great majority of the Democrats. Their first priority was to halt administration plans to revamp or terminate many of the Great Society programs. The prolonged congressional-executive stalemate that resulted gave rise to frustration in Democratic ranks that found expression, especially in the House, in criticism of the leadership.

Albert also drew criticism from younger and more activist House members for not supporting internal House reforms more vigorously. By the early 1970s a sharp increase in retirements and reelection defeats of much of the "Old Guard" had resulted in a significant infusion of new blood in the House. The average age of House members had crept steadily downward, and most of the new generation were liberal Democrats. With the dramatic turnover in membership—particularly the election of seventy-five new Democratic members in 1974—came pressure for changes in House rules and practices. Reforms adopted by the Democratic Caucus in the early 1970s, particularly in 1971, 1973, and 1974, were to have a substantial effect on the way the House and its leaders would conduct their business.

One set of reforms broke the grip senior members held on the House by subjecting committee chairmen to election by secret ballot. In 1975 the caucus deposed three chairmen. Committee chairmen also were forced to share their powers with quasi-independent subcommittees, some of which were led by junior members. Other changes limited House Democrats to one subcommittee chairmanship, gave the subcommittees their own staffs and budgets, and guaranteed each party member an assignment on a major committee.

A second set of reforms granted new powers to the Speaker, making that office potentially stronger than at any time since the reigns of Reed and Cannon. The Speaker was given the right to nominate the chairman and all the Democratic members of the Rules Committee, subject to caucus approval, and that panel once again became an arm of the leadership, not the independent power center it had been in the previous three decades. The Democratic Steering and Policy Committee was set up in 1973 to give coherence and strategy to the party's legislative program and was placed firmly under the Speaker's control. At the end of 1974 the committee was given the authority, formerly held by Ways and Means Democrats, to appoint the Democratic members to House committees, subject to caucus approval, and to refer bills to more than one committee. Although most of these new powers became available during Albert's tenure as Speaker, he made little use of them, leaving them to his successors to exploit.

THE MODERN SPEAKERSHIP: O'NEILL

In many respects Thomas P. "Tip" O'Neill Jr., of Massachusetts was an unlikely candidate to modernize the speakership. A New Deal liberal, he was to the political left of most of his colleagues. Intensely partisan, he was forced to work with a popular Republican president, Ronald Reagan, and a Republican Senate during six years of his decade as speaker from 1977 to 1987. A consummate practitioner of inside politics, O'Neill faced demands from rank-and-file Democrats for greater participation in the decision-making process. A less-than-commanding public speaker who reserved his public appearances for his Massachusetts constituents, the new Speaker was called upon to be the national spokesperson for his party. O'Neill once told a reporter than he was one old dog ready to learn new tricks—and he did learn some, giving many more members, especially junior members, leadership responsibilities and becoming a nationally recognized media celebrity. But his reluctance to temper both his liberal beliefs and his partisanship made coalition-building, even within his party, difficult at times.

Genial and enormously popular, O'Neill based his leadership on friendships, doing favors for loyal colleagues, taking care of what he called the "little odds and ends." But O'Neill also took some innovative steps to expand participation of the party rank and file in House affairs, enlarging the whip organization and setting up special task forces to help the leadership develop support and strategy on major legislation. One of O'Neill's most successful ploys was the creation of an ad hoc committee in 1977 to draw up comprehensive energy legislation, a top priority of the Carter administration. Although the tactic worked well in that case, policy differences and objections from the standing committees prevented the Speaker from ever using it again.

O'Neill also made use of several powers the House reforms had bestowed upon the Speaker, including the authority to name the Democratic members of the House Rules Committee.

Although O'Neill did not demand unstinting loyalty from the Democrats on Rules, he did expect them to support him on key issues. In response to the Republican minority's penchant for offering floor amendments designed to put Democrats on the spot, O'Neill also came to rely heavily on restrictive rules, those specifying which amendments could be offered on the floor and in what order, as a potent tool to maintain control of debate on the House floor. *(See "Shift Toward Restricted Rules, p. 77, in Chapter 2.)*

Another tool O'Neill used to help the leadership control the flow of legislation was the authority to refer bills to more than one committee either at the same time or sequentially. If a bill is referred to committees sequentially, the Speaker may also set time limits for committee action. This authority keeps alive bills that otherwise might die in an unfriendly committee.

O'Neill also gave the speakership unprecedented visibility. He was aided by the decision to allow House floor proceedings to be televised to the public, beginning in 1979, and later spurred on by criticisms from his colleagues that he was not effectively articulating Democratic alternatives to President Reagan's legislative agenda. Soon the Speaker's office was issuing a steady stream of press releases trying to mobilize support for Democratic party positions. Though previous Speakers had met with reporters before every House session, they usually only answered specific questions. Now O'Neill used them to volunteer information about the goals and achievements of House Democrats and to spar with Reagan on the issues.

O'Neill's attempts at public relations won mixed reviews. His sometimes garbled syntax, his physical bulk, shaggy dog appearance, and ever-present cigar were reminiscent of the stereotypical backroom pol, an image that some younger members had hoped the Democratic Party could shed. Nonetheless, O'Neill affected public attitudes on a variety of questions, some more successfully than others. Nothing the Speaker said or did could have headed off support in the nation or in the House for the 1981 Reagan economic program. But on several foreign policy issues, where there was substantial doubt about Reagan's approach, O'Neill helped solidify Democratic opposition and made it credible to the public. For example, by coming out strongly against an expensive and controversial intercontinental ballistic missile, known as the MX missile, and U.S. aid to the Nicaraguan "contras," a guerrilla force that was battling to oust the leftist government of that nation, the Speaker focused media attention on the anti-Reagan position and almost certainly locked in some Democratic votes on those closely fought issues.

Yet O'Neill's speakership was not an unqualified success. His first year in the post seemed to bear out early predictions that he could be the strongest Speaker since Rayburn. But Carter's weak presidency and new militancy on the part of House Republicans combined with O'Neill's own unyielding partisanship to his disadvantage. Unable to keep his Democrats united, he lost several key votes in his first four years.

Ronald Reagan's election in 1980 and the loss of thirty-three House seats only worsened his situation in 1981–1982. Not until House Democrats won twenty-six seats in the 1982 elections was O'Neill able to unite his party in opposition to Reagan's policies. The stalemate that often resulted and the heightened partisan rhetoric that it engendered led to accusations that O'Neill was a heavy-handed partisan and that the Democratic Party had no focus and could not govern. When O'Neill did try to exercise policy leadership on an issue, he was often deserted by one wing or another of his party, as he was in 1983, when a number of Democrats—including Majority Leader Jim Wright and Whip Thomas S. Foley, Wash.—voted against O'Neill to support funding for the MX missile.

Despite these setbacks, O'Neill's speakership was never in any jeopardy. But criticisms of his leadership and the clear frustrations among many House Democrats about the image the party was projecting may have weighed in his decision to retire at the end of 1986.

THE LIMITS OF POWER: WRIGHT

As Speaker from 1987 to June 1989, Jim Wright was determined to give House Democrats the policy leadership many of them had found lacking in O'Neill. "I think there's a creative role for the legislative branch and a leadership role for the Speaker . . . ," Wright once said. "The Congress should not simply react, passively, to recommendations from the president but should come forward with initiatives of its own."[35]

Ethics charges forced the resignation of Speaker Jim Wright in 1989. Wright, shown here offering his resignation as Speaker of the House, was the first Speaker in history to give up his post under fire.

SOME SPEAKERS FACED A TRIAL BY FIRE

Service as Speaker of the House would have to be considered the culmination of any politician's career but some leaders must survive a trial by fire to hold on to the post and emerge with their political and personal reputations reasonably intact. Some have succeeded better than others.

Speaker Newt Gingrich, R-Ga., was embarrassed during his reelection campaign for Speaker in 1997 as several Republicans cast their votes for other persons or voted present; suffered an historic formal reprimand by his colleagues for ethics violations; and repelled a group of younger conservatives who, allegedly with encouragement from other members of Gingrich's leadership team, made an effort to depose him. However, Gingrich managed to hold onto his office and much of the new authority he had brought to it when Republicans assumed control of the House in the 104th Congress. Gingrich survived because he was in the mainstream of his party conference and lacked popular rivals positioned to take over the post.

Jim Wright, D-Texas, the only Speaker to be forced out of office during his term, has often been compared to Gingrich in his desire to be a visible national leader and to use the speakership to promote a strong party agenda. But Wright never commanded strong loyalty or personal regard from his party colleagues. The link between them probably also is inevitable given Gingrich's leading role in pummeling Wright with ethics allegations for years before Wright's resignation in 1989. Wright left to avoid formal discipline by the House. Historians will no doubt argue whether the controversy that ended Wright's career was more or less serious than the reprimand, $300,000 fine, and allegations of tax law violations and misleading the ethics committee that Gingrich endured. There is broad consensus that Gingrich helped to create the political climate for use of ethics charges to demonize opponents, a tactic that his Democratic rivals then turned against him.

Gingrich and Wright were by no means the first Speakers to be embroiled in a controversy that attracted national attention and disrupted congressional leadership.

NINETEENTH-CENTURY SPEAKERS

In the early nineteenth century, Speaker Nathaniel Macon also came close to being deposed. Macon was one of Thomas Jefferson's most devoted loyalists, and was rewarded for his fealty with Jefferson's support during his election as Speaker in 1801.

But Macon later allied himself with a bitter foe of the president's, John Randolph, who broke with Jefferson over a plan to acquire Florida. Jefferson retaliated against Macon by opposing his reelection as Speaker in 1805. Jefferson's effort failed, but it was a close enough decision that Macon chose not to seek another term as Speaker.

Henry Clay went to the well of the House to defend himself against allegations of impropriety while he was Speaker in 1825. In a published letter in a newspaper, another member accused Clay of cutting a secret deal to support John Quincy Adams for president in exchange for an appointment as secretary of state. Adams had been elected by the House after the popular vote leader, Andrew Jackson, failed to receive a majority of the electoral vote. The scandal died quickly. Clay asked the House to name a special committee to look into the charges, but the member who had made the allegation refused to appear.

John White, Speaker from 1841–1843, came under fire for one of the last speeches he gave before leaving the House in 1845 to take a judgeship in Kentucky. After it was disclosed that a particularly elo-

But in pursuing his activist agenda for the House, Wright may have overstepped the limits of the speakership's powers at that time, although Speaker Newt Gingrich would later seek to expand the office far beyond anything Wright had attempted. Wright exceeded the bounds of what many Democrats were willing to accept in a leader. He certainly was not what Democrats had expected when they chose him as a balanced compromise for majority leader over the ambitious liberals Phillip Burton and Richard Bolling a decade earlier.

By his second year in the office, Republicans considered him to be the match for Cannon in his treatment of the minority. Democrats were alienated by his failure to practice the politics of inclusion that had become *de rigueur.* As allegations of financial misconduct, lodged against the Speaker by Gingrich developed into a full-blown investigation, Wright found that Democrats who were willing to support him when he—and they—were winning were not as ready to back him on a question of personal ethics. On May 31, 1989, Wright announced that he would give up the speakership effective June 6, becoming the first Speaker to be forced from office at midterm. A month later he resigned his House seat. *(See box, Some Speakers Faced a Trial by Fire, above.)*

Wright was deputy whip when he ran for majority leader in 1976, winning by a single vote. Had he lost, he would have become chairman of the Public Works Committee. Unlike his three rivals, Wright had few enemies or personal negatives. He had always compromised personal differences when possible, or disagreed gently if he had to. He also had another advantage: as a member of the Public Works Committee, he had done countless small favors, making sure a dam was put up here or a federal building there. And throughout his ten years as majority leader, Wright continued to do the little favors, devoting months of precious time to public appearances and fund-raising missions in districts throughout the country.

Favors notwithstanding, many members felt a sense of unease, even mistrust, about Wright. Private, competitive, at times aggressively partisan, Wright did not inspire the sort of personal affection that O'Neill had drawn. His reputation for oratorical skills was well deserved, but now and again his speech turned florid, his smile disingenuous. "You watch him and you know quent speech he gave had been plagiarized from former Vice President Aaron Burr, White committed suicide.

While James G. Blaine, R-Maine, was Speaker, he was cleared of wrongdoing by a special committee appointed to look into the Credit Mobilier bribery scandal, in which promoters of the Union Pacific Railroad used stock to bribe members of Congress to support federal subsidies for the railroad. But other allegations of graft surfaced in 1876, after Blaine left the Speaker's office due to a change of party control in the House.

Blaine took to the House floor to read from letters that supposedly exonerated him. That quelled efforts to censure him but the scandal did not help his unsuccessful quest for his party's presidential nomination at the GOP convention just months later. Blaine was finally nominated in 1884, but he lost the election to Grover Cleveland.

CANNON: STRIPPED OF POWER

The House in 1910 nearly deposed Speaker Joseph G. Cannon, R-Ill., for his heavy-handed use of power. The revolt against Cannon exploded in response to his spectacular use of the Speaker's powers to reward friends and punish foes. Cannon freely wielded his authority to control who sat on which committee, which bills went to the floor, and who would be recognized to speak.

Democrats made common cause with insurgent Republicans on March 19, 1910, and defeated Cannon on a procedural question that was, in effect, a referendum on his leadership.

The insurgents went on to ram through rules changes that stripped the Speaker of his right to make committee assignments and of his control of the Rules Committee.

Cannon refused to resign as Speaker, but invited a vote on deposing him. Pandemonium broke loose on the House floor, judging from the notation in the *Congressional Record:* "Great confusion in the Hall."

A resolution declaring the Speaker's office vacant was put to a vote—the only time such a vote has been taken—but Cannon survived, 155–192. It suited the political purposes of some to keep Cannon in office: that made it easier to run against "Cannonism" in the 1910 elections. This was perhaps the first time a Speaker had been a major focus in an election campaign. Cannon lost the speakership after Democrats won a majority of House seats for the first time since 1895. Cannon's resistance to political change in the country and within his party, and his increasingly arbitrary style of leadership had cost his office the influence it had long held within the House.

MCCORMACK, O'NEILL

More recently, Speaker John McCormack, D-Mass., retired in 1971 after top aides were accused of using the Speaker's office and name for fraudulent purposes, without McCormack's knowledge. McCormack, in his seventies and under pressure from a restive younger generation of lawmakers, had other reasons for leaving the House when he did.

When Thomas P. O'Neill Jr., D-Mass., became Speaker in 1977, he immediately faced questions raised in connection with the "Koreagate" influence-peddling scandal. The House Committee on Standards of Official Conduct in January 1977 began an investigation into allegations that as many as 115 members—Republicans and Democrats—had taken illegal gifts from South Korean agents. Some people suggested that O'Neill, during a 1974 trip to Korea, had asked Korean rice dealer Tongsun Park to make contributions to House members and their wives. But other members were the principal target, and in July 1978 the committee issued a statement exonerating O'Neill. The panel said the only thing of "questionable propriety" the Speaker had done was to let Park pay for two parties in his honor.

when he's going to get partisan," GOP leader Bob Michel, R-Ill., said in 1984. "The eyebrows start to rise. The voice begins to stretch out. And the Republicans say, 'Snake oil is at it again.'"[36] Though such descriptions might be dismissed because they came from the opposition, Democrats were nonetheless concerned about the image Wright might convey to the public.

Despite these misgivings, Wright was not challenged when he ran to succeed O'Neill in 1986. His assertions that he would be a strong, policy-oriented Speaker appealed to his Democratic colleagues who not only wanted to demonstrate that the Democrats could govern but also wanted a record to see them through the 1988 presidential campaign. And Wright was clearly ready. As Speaker, he seemed to suddenly unleash an agenda and a pace of activity he had kept under wraps from his colleagues, and the adjustment was sometimes difficult even for members who professed to want such activism in their leader.

In his acceptance speech Wright laid out an ambitious agenda for the 100th Congress, calling for renewal of the clean water act and a new highway bill and suggesting that the tax rate for the wealthy be frozen at 1987 levels instead of dropping as scheduled, a proposal that some said put him beyond the majority of the Democrats. By the end of the 100th Congress, not only had the clean water and highway bills become law, but Congress had overhauled the welfare system, approved the biggest expansion of Medicare since its creation, and rewritten U.S. trade law. Most of this legislation had passed the House with bipartisan support.

Although Wright's Democratic colleagues took pride in these legislative achievements, many resented being excluded from the process of achieving them. The "Lone Ranger," as Wright was sometimes dubbed, had a record of springing major decisions without consulting key colleagues. His very public involvement in trying to negotiate a peace plan between the Nicaragua government and the contra rebels not only angered the administration and Republicans in the House but unsettled Democrats who feared that they might be held accountable at the polls if the peace process failed.

Wright was also criticized for his aggressive tactics in getting legislation passed. Rules to guide floor debate grew more restrictive; no amendments, for example, were allowed on the clean water and highway bills or on a moratorium on aid to the Nicaraguan contras. Republicans complained that under Wright, many bills were never given hearings and came to the floor of the House without being reported by committee, that substantive legislation was being enacted through self-executing rules (which provide for the automatic adoption of an amendment or other matter upon adoption of the rule), and that the minority was more often denied its right to try to recommit bills.

Wright's support among Democrats was substantially weakened early in 1989 over a proposed pay raise that would have increased congressional salaries by 51 percent. The raise was to take effect if the House and Senate did not veto it by February 9. The initial strategy was to let the pay raise take effect and then to vote on legislation to curb honoraria. But public outrage at the size of the raise—and the fact that it might take effect without a vote in Congress—was overwhelming.

Wright buckled to the pressure, his colleagues believed, failing in his duty to take the heat and protect their interests. He circulated a questionnaire to Democratic members asking whether they wanted a vote scheduled. They viewed this tactic as a major blunder, focusing additional attention on the issue and creating a mechanism that could reveal members' views. Members were soon barraged with demands from the press about how they had filled out the questionnaire. As expected, the pressure proved too great and the questionnaire indicated that a majority of members had asked to have a vote on the issue, whether they really wanted one or not.

After the Senate yielded to the pressure and voted no on the pay raise, Wright scheduled a vote for February 7. When the raise, not surprisingly, was defeated, many Democrats angrily blamed Wright for changing the strategy at the last minute.

Barely a month later, the ethics committee announced that it "had reason to believe" that Wright had violated House rules on financial conduct. In the next few weeks, new allegations of misconduct surfaced, further damaging the Speaker, as did a *Washington Post* story revealing that a top aide to Wright had a criminal record for brutally beating a woman sixteen years earlier. After Wright's attorneys failed to persuade the Ethics Committee to dismiss the charges on technical grounds, the Speaker decided to resign to spare the House the embarrassment of a public investigation of its Speaker. Only days before, Democratic Whip Tony Coelho, D-Calif., had announced he would resign his House seat in the face of allegations of irregularities in his purchase of a $100,000 junk bond.

Political scientist Ronald Peters observes that "if Wright had not been vulnerable to the ethics charges brought against him, it is unlikely that his Republican opponents could have undermined his support in the Democratic Caucus. However, if Wright had led the House differently, neither Republicans nor Democrats would have had a sufficient motive to seek to unseat him."[37]

Whether a Speaker who worked more closely with his own leadership and his rank and file and who was less openly partisan would have survived the same ethics charges Wright faced is, of course, conjecture. But the Wright episode clearly shows the potential weakness of a Speaker who fails to develop an atmosphere in which consensus building and shared decision making can flourish in a Democratic Party that had grown used to broad dispersion of power and multiple independent power centers. Wright himself seemed to recognize this. "Have I been too partisan? Too insistent? Too abrasive? Too determined to have my way?" he asked in his resignation speech. "Perhaps. Maybe so."[38]

While Wright's relatively brief tenure and the circumstances of his departure may make it easy to brand his speakership a failure, a case can also be made that Wright was focused on creating legislative achievements for his party, and was ahead of his time in his willingness to recentralize leadership to respond to an increasingly aggressive partisan opposition. Ironically, the much criticized Central American peace plan, which the Republicans used to help demonize him, may be remembered as Wright's most successful and daring initiative. However, after Wright's resignation Democrats wanted a respite from what they regarded as excessive activism and controversy and a return to a quieter, more consensual leadership style.

END OF AN ERA: FOLEY

On June 6, 1989, the Democratic Caucus nominated Majority Leader Thomas S. Foley of Washington by acclamation to succeed Wright as Speaker. Better known for bringing together warring factions than for drawing up battle plans, Foley seemed well equipped to help the Democrats—and the House—put the Wright episode behind them; in his first speech as Speaker he called for debate "with reason and without rancor."

Indeed, Foley had the most impressive resume of any House Speaker in decades; he had served in each of the Democrats' major leadership positions in succession—caucus chairmanship (1976–1980), as the last appointed whip (1980–1986), and majority leader (1986–1989). He was also the first Speaker since Rayburn to have been a committee chairman—he had chaired the Agriculture Committee (1975–1981).

A thoughtful and articulate man, Foley was perhaps the first Speaker his Democratic colleagues felt comfortable putting in front of a television camera. With a knack for telling stories and a near-photographic memory that helped him to master the substance of most issues that came before him, Foley was a superb negotiator who was on good terms with most Democrats and a good number of Republicans. "Foley has a talent for listening and knowing what other people want," a veteran leadership aide said.[39] He chaired the task force that drew up the Democratic alternative to the 1985 Gramm-Rudman deficit reduction act. He also chaired the 1989 budget negotiations and was the lead negotiator on a comprehensive aid package for the Nicaraguan contras.

Endowed with a sense of detachment rare among politicians, Foley was a cautious, careful political navigator. "The reality," he said a few weeks before becoming Speaker, "is that in a modern, participatory Congress . . . the responsibility of leadership and the necessity of leadership is to constantly involve members in the process of decision and consensus."[40] He did not like to commit himself early on controversial issues, and he could be as skillful at making the case for the opposing side as for his own. "I think I am a little cursed," he said in 1984, "with seeing the other point of view and trying to understand it." Indeed, he was criticized by some for not being partisan enough, and for being indecisive. "He sees three sides of every coin," noted one observer.

Foley's honeymoon as Speaker was brief. Republicans were in no mood for an olive branch. Foley's passive leadership style—trying to avoid controversy within the caucus and allowing committee chairmen to compete among themselves, and with the leadership, for influence—allowed him to be overtaken by events at critical points. And he seemed especially ill-suited to confront the accelerating guerrilla warfare against Democrats, and against the institution of Congress itself, led by Minority Whip Gingrich.

Foley was surprised by the scandal that surrounded the House Bank throughout 1992, when it was revealed that hundreds of sitting and former House members had routinely overdrawn their accounts without penalty. Foley had argued for limited disclosure, as recommended by the Committee on Standards of Official Conduct, but could not resist overwhelming public pressure as the Republicans forced the names of members of both parties to be made public. Of the 269 sitting members with overdrafts, seventy-seven retired or were defeated in primary or general election bids for the House or other offices. The House Post Office also fell victim to allegations of embezzlement and drug dealing by postal clerks as well as revelations that some members had received special favors, including the ability to convert stamps received by their offices into cash. (Ways and Means Committee Chairman Dan Rostenkowski, D-Ill., later went to prison as a result.)

Foley said that he was not responsible for supervising these House offices, which, indeed, had long operated as quasi-independent patronage operations under the nominal control of the Democratic Caucus. Both the Sergeant at Arms, whom many members blamed for the bank scandal, and the Postmaster ultimately went to prison. The Post Office was eliminated as a separate entity, and Foley finally acceded to a caucus rules change giving him the responsibility for nominating the officers of the House, which he had previously resisted.

Nonetheless, Foley seemed well-positioned for a long career as Speaker. He acted swiftly to shore up support for his reelection in the Democratic Caucus in 1992, and no challenger emerged as a result of the scandals. In his first four years, he faced the same dynamic of a Democratic House confronting a Republican president as O'Neill and Wright had.

Many Democrats considered Foley too accommodating to the administration of President George Bush. When Democrats won the 1992 presidential election and obtained unified control of the executive and legislative branches for the first time in twelve years, the party nonetheless lost seats in the House. Foley was put in the position of having to pass an ambitious presidential program with a caucus membership that was not united either on policy or in loyalty to the new chief executive.

In pre-inauguration meetings with President-elect Clinton, Foley and other congressional leaders urged him to retreat from some of his commitments as a "New Democrat" candidate, including a promise to press campaign reform legislation on Congress. The new administration also began inauspiciously with highly visible political missteps on numerous issues, most notably President Clinton's proposed health care reform plan, which never achieved enough support even to reach the floor in the Democratic-controlled Congress. Internal divisions within the party, as well as effective opposition from a highly-unified Republican minority in both chambers, limited the ability of Congress to develop a politically popular legislative record. The widely touted benefits of unified government appeared hollow to much of the public. Clinton's unpopularity also created a backlash against Congress.

Foley himself showed serious weakness in his Washington congressional district for the first time in more than a decade, falling below forty percent of the vote in the state's all-candidate primary in September 1994. He was opposed by an attractive Republican, George Nethercutt, who was not the sort of fringe candidate who sometimes had won GOP nominations to oppose Foley. In addition to vulnerability based on his leadership post, Foley was also attacked for supporting a legal challenge to Washington's newly enacted law, passed by referendum, to impose term limits on the state's congressional delegation. (The U.S. Supreme Court later threw out the law.)

Amid the national Democratic rout in 1994, Foley lost in the general election, only the third such defeat for a sitting Speaker. The last had been Galusha A. Grow, a Pennsylvania Republican, who lost in 1862; his predecessor, William Pennington of New Jersey, had lost in 1860.

The Democratic Party surrendered fifty-two seats and control of the House shifted to the GOP after forty years of Democratic rule. Gracious in defeat, Foley offered cooperation in the transition, but Republicans responded harshly, with warnings to Democratic leaders and outgoing committee chairmen not to shred documents.

After his departure from Congress, Foley joined a law firm and, following the career path of former Senate Majority Leader Mike Mansfield and former Vice President Walter Mondale, was nominated by President Clinton to be ambassador to Japan, a post he assumed in 1997.

GINGRICH: TRANSFORMING THE HOUSE, AND BEYOND

While it is far too early by 1998 to evaluate Newt Gingrich's place in history, it had been clear for many years prior to his accession to the speakership that the former historian, conservative backbencher and rabble-rouser from Georgia was looking for one. And his mere presence as a Republican Speaker, after

After surviving a House ethics investigation, Speaker Newt Gingrich of Georgia is sworn in after being reelected by a slim margin to a second term in January 1997.

forty years of Democratic rule, guaranteed it. Gingrich's move from freshman to Speaker in only sixteen years, never having chaired a committee or subcommittee, was also unprecedented in the modern era.

Gingrich was clearly a new breed of legislative leader, although his role combined recognizable elements from predecessors of both parties. Among modern Speakers Gingrich most resembled Wright in his desire to use power. But his control of his party gave him a power unrivaled since the days of Cannon.

Gingrich was elected to the House from Georgia's 6th District in 1978 after consecutive defeats in 1974 and 1976. In the earlier races, he had campaigned as a more liberal alternative to traditional Georgia Republicans, stressing the importance of civil rights and environmental protection. But in his winning campaign he ran as a conservative promising tax cuts. For the majority of his service prior to becoming Speaker Gingrich was the only Republican in his state's House delegation. The sea change in southern politics that helped make Republican control of the House possible was illustrated by Georgia's representation in the 104th and 105th Congresses—an eight-to-three GOP advantage.

Unlike other recent leaders of both parties, Gingrich was in no sense a "man of the House," a phrase denoting a quintessential congressional insider that Speaker O'Neill had used to characterize his own service and as the title of his autobiography. It suggested someone who allowed himself to be shaped by the institution around him, by the need to establish relationships with the Senate and the executive branch, by shared personal and political accommodation with colleagues, and by the desire to pass legislation. Indeed, a substantial part of Gingrich's "apprenticeship" for the speakership consisted of demonizing Congress, its leaders, the rival political party and almost every aspect of its manner of doing business, and creating issues to use in the future.

For Gingrich, the House was the trophy in a campaign of conquest; once secured, it was to be a vehicle for transforming society, not just through enactment of the principles stated in the 1994 election platform Republicans call the "Contract with America" as well as other legislation, but for ushering in a new era and repudiating the old. Its rules and practices were subservient to this greater purpose. The House seemed almost too small to contain the revolutionary zeal that the new majority, especially its large freshman class from the 1994 election, sought to spread throughout the country.

Gingrich as Speaker conceived of himself as a visionary who could make the House not only a vehicle for passage of legislation but a forum for ideas, principles, and values. Gingrich had these goals early. "The Congress in the long run can change the country more dramatically than the president," he said in a 1979 interview with Congressional Quarterly. "One of my goals is to make the House the co-equal of the White House."[41]

Indeed, for years as a backbencher Gingrich had developed a political philosophy that he felt could lead eventually to Republican control of the House, a conservative but futuristic creed that called for replacing the welfare state with an "opportunity society" in which the rising technological tide of the Information Age would lift the poor to prosperity. Gingrich formed a group of members called the "Conservative Opportunity Society" in 1983 to foster these beliefs, mastered the use of special order speeches and other mechanisms in the House to gain public attention and to use ethics as an issue to dramatize not only disagreements with his colleagues over ideas but to condemn personally opponents who fought him, most notably Speaker Wright. In 1986, he inherited the chairmanship of GOPAC, a political action committee, and turned it into an instrument to inspire Republicans candidates with ideas and strategies for seeking office.

Gingrich was hardly a loyal follower of the House Republican leadership, which he viewed as too passive, too prone to negotiate with Democrats for scraps of influence, and too easily coopted by the collegialism of the House. Many of his colleagues, including some moderates, came to share these concerns, creating an unlikely coalition that elected Gingrich as minority whip in 1989 over the opposition of Minority Leader Robert H. Michel of Illinois. Gingrich also opposed policies of Republican presidents that he felt compromised the party's long-term goals, such as the bipartisan 1990 budget agreement between President Bush and the Democratic congressional leadership, which repudiated Bush's "no new taxes" pledge. As political scientist Barbara Sinclair has noted, "(Gingrich) was willing to pay the policy cost in order to preserve the message."[42]

Gingrich's Republican colleagues in the 104th Congress were

interested not in forming consensus or in shaping his style of leadership, which had helped elect many of them and gave them a program to run on and a list of bills to enact, but in aggressive followership. It was Gingrich's ability to inspire followership in the early days of his speakership that perhaps distinguished his role as a party leader most clearly from the Democrats, whose many factions had developed a distracting sense of self-importance that often made party unity and coherent leadership difficult. And it was the weakening of this loyalty, as Gingrich struggled with the transition from the rhetoric of revolution to the responsibility of governing, that threatened his hold on the speakership in the 105th Congress.

Gingrich united the Republican Conference around the plan of voting on all ten planks of the contract in the first 100 days of the session. The strategy focused the conference and invited a high level of party loyalty, even from less enthusiastic moderates who nonetheless welcomed the title of "chairman" preceding their names and gave Gingrich the benefit of the doubt. The contract was drafted to avoid divisive social issues like abortion and school prayer and to focus on unifying conservative themes geared toward economic policy and a reduced role for government, such as balancing the budget, reforming welfare and curbing unfunded mandates directed at the states. *(See box, Contact with America, p. 26.)*

As Speaker, Gingrich enjoyed remarkable success, at least in his first year, in passing legislation through the House and in shaping a national debate over issues based on the Republicans' message of less government, more tax cuts, and a return of power to the states. He was far less successful in reaping proportionate political credit for himself or for the Republican Party in part because the speakership contained innate limitations as a bully pulpit that no amount of revolutionary zeal could overcome and that Gingrich's often bombastic personality aggravated. It has been axiomatic in American politics in the twentieth century that the nation looks to the president as the nation's chief policy spokesperson and representative of the national values. Indeed, Gingrich became, as polls showed, perhaps the most disliked political figure in the nation, and gave President Clinton a target that helped reinvigorate a presidency some had given up for dead after the 1994 elections. Gingrich's assertiveness was often perceived by the public as arrogance, with a tendency to lecture and to appear overbearing, uncaring, and threatening. By the end of 1995, some polls gave him an approval rating hovering around 30 percent.

Congress shut down much of the government at the end of 1995, refusing to pass new versions of appropriations bills, after Clinton had vetoed the GOP leadership's ambitious domestic policy changes and tax cuts contained in a budget reconciliation bill and various spending measures. Republicans tried to blame Clinton for the ensuing disruption of vital services but it was the president who convinced the country that he was right, and the Republicans had to retreat, pass new appropriations bills, and allow government agencies to reopen. Senate Majority Leader Bob Dole, who was running for president, also appeared eager to repudiate House Republicans and present a more traditional image of responsible governance. The House revolutionaries were placed on the defensive, and the defeat forced Gingrich to reevaluate GOP tactics.

In 1996, Gingrich tried a less confrontational approach, allowing appropriations to pass with fewer controversial riders and obtaining enactment of welfare reform, a major Republican policy goal for decades that Clinton was also eager to use as a centerpiece for his reelection. The public seemed to like the more cooperative style and emphasis on bipartisan legislative achievements, retaining the status quo in the 105th Congress with a slightly reduced GOP House majority.

Gingrich's leadership style could hardly be called consistent, as he careened from one manner of doing business to another during his first three years in power. He experimented with different techniques, sometimes engaging in what his critics called micromanagement, at other times withdrawing from a direct role in the House to focus on the future and long-term political themes. He could be consultative and autocratic in rapid succession.

Part of Gingrich's need for experimentation stemmed from the Republicans' long years in the minority; they had no experience in running the House and many of their members had no significant legislative or political experience to deploy in their new roles. Many senior conservative veterans were regarded with suspicion by the freshmen as insufficiently zealous or too frequently collaborationist in earlier years with the defeated Democrats. Gingrich formed numerous task forces to develop ideas and sometimes let them draft actual legislation, although in the 105th Congress he deferred more frequently to the committee system.

The Speaker's daily press conference, a traditional event that had preceded every House session, became a major media spectacle when Gingrich opened it to television coverage after taking office. But Gingrich quickly ended the event entirely after the press became hostile, asking about his ethics problems or other potentially unfavorable matters, and his own lack of discipline in his comments threatened to shift public focus away from the GOP message.

Democrats, eager for payback against Gingrich for his attacks on Wright, filed dozens of ethics complaints against him. On December 21, 1996, the Speaker admitted, after two years of repeated denials, that he had failed to properly manage the financing of his political activities through charitable foundations. He also conceded giving the ethics committee misleading information in the course of the investigation. The admission spared the Speaker the spectacle of a trial-like proceeding to defend himself before the committee.

In 1997, the election for Speaker was held before the ethics committee submitted its final report and recommendation for punishment. Gingrich barely survived. As the election was being conducted, he was still negotiating for votes with disgruntled Republicans, four of whom defied the Republican Conference to vote for other Republicans while five others voted "present."

CONTRACT WITH AMERICA

On September 27, 1994, six weeks before the November 8 election, approximately 350 House Republican members and candidates unveiled a ten-point campaign manifesto—they called it their "Contract with America." The event, staged on the Capitol lawn and spearheaded by Minority Whip Newt Gingrich, R-Ga., was aimed at creating a high-profile national platform from which Republicans could attack the Democratic Congress and present their priorities. When the GOP won a major victory in 1994, the contract became the agenda for House Republicans' first 100 days in office in the 104th Congress. GOP leaders promised only that the House would vote on the proposals, not that all would pass or be enacted.

Following are the ten subject areas covered by the contract, as well as the changes in internal House procedures discussed in the contract's preface:

• **Congressional Process.** Require that Congress end its exemptions from eleven workplace laws; and revise House rules to cut committees and their staff, impose term limits on committee chairmen, end proxy voting, and require three-fifths majority votes for tax increases.

• **Balanced Budget Amendment, Line-Item Veto.** Send to the states a constitutional amendment requiring a balanced budget and give the president enhanced rescissions power to cancel (line-item veto) any appropriation or targeted tax break.

• **Crime.** Require restitution to victims; modify the exclusionary rule; increase grants for prison construction; speed deportation of criminal immigrants; create block grants to give communities flexibility in using anticrime funds; and limit death row appeals.

• **Welfare.** Cap spending on cash welfare, impose a lifetime five-year limit on welfare benefits, deny benefits to unwed mothers under age eighteen, and give states new flexibility, including the option to receive federal welfare payments as a block grant.

• **Families and Children.** Require parental consent for children participating in surveys; provide tax benefits for adoptions and home care for the elderly; increase penalties for sex crimes against children; and strengthen enforcement of child support orders.

• **Middle-Class Tax Cut.** Add $500-per-child tax credit; ease "marriage penalty" for filers of joint tax returns; and expand individual retirement account savings plans.

• **National Security.** Prohibit use of U.S. troops in United Nations missions under foreign command; prohibit defense cuts to finance social programs; develop a missile defense system for U.S. territory; and cut funding for United Nations peacekeeping missions.

• **Social Security.** Repeal the 1993 increase in Social Security benefits subject to income tax; permit senior citizens to earn up to $30,000 a year without losing benefits; and give tax incentives for buying long-term care insurance.

• **Capital Gains and Regulations.** Cut capital gains taxes; allow for accelerated depreciation of business assets; increase first-year deductions for small businesses; reduce unfunded mandates; reduce federal paperwork; and require federal agencies to assess risks, use cost-benefit analysis, reduce paperwork, and reimburse property owners for reductions in value as a result of regulations.

• **Civil Law and Product Liability.** Establish national product liability law with limits on punitive damages; make it harder for investors to sue companies; and apply "loser pays" rule to certain federal cases.

Gingrich received 216 votes, only three more than the majority required from among members who had voted for candidates for Speaker.

On January 21, 1997, the House for the first time formally reprimanded a Speaker, by a vote of 395 to 28. It adopted the report of the ethics committee that found that Gingrich had brought discredit on the House by failing to seek legal advice regarding the use of tax-exempt foundations for political purposes and for providing inaccurate information to the ethics subcommittee investigating the case. The House also fined Gingrich $300,000 to cover some of the costs of the investigation.

House Leadership: A Hierarchy of Support

The party leadership structure is particularly important in the House because of its size and consequent potential for unwieldiness. In his 1963 study of the House, *Forge of Democracy,* Neil MacNeil described the chamber's leadership organizations as its "priesthood." Though the younger, media savvy, sound-bite quoting, expert fund-raisers who rise to the leadership late in the century might laugh at such a description, the leadership remains a structure separate from other members.

> Indeed, over the years, a hierarchy of leaders has been constructed in the House to support the Speaker, and opposing this hierarchy has been another, created by the minority party and led by the 'shadow' Speaker, the leader of the opposition party. With the hierarchy also has been built a vast array of political and party organizations to assist the Speaker and his lieutenants in the complicated task of making the House a viable, responsible legislative body.[43]

THE MAJORITY LEADER

In the modern House, the second in command is the majority leader, whose primary responsibility is to manage the legislative affairs of the chamber. To that end, he or she helps formulate, promote, negotiate, and defend the party's program, particularly on the House floor. A majority leader was not officially designated in the House until 1899, when Sereno E. Payne, R-N.Y., was named to the post. But from the earliest days, the Speaker has appointed someone to help him guide his party's legislative program through the House. Occasionally this person was a trusted lieutenant. More often the chairman of the Ways and Means Committee also served as the floor leader, largely because until 1865 the committee handled both revenues and appropriations and thus the bulk of the legislation that came before the House. Payne, for example, was also chairman of Ways and Means. *(See "Leaders of the House since 1899," p. 167, in Reference Materials.)*

After the Appropriations Committee was established, its chairman sometimes served as majority leader. At other times, the Speaker chose a leading rival within the party, presumably either to promote party harmony or to neutralize an opponent. Thus in 1859 William Pennington, R-N.J., the only House member besides Clay to be elected Speaker in his first term, chose as his majority leader his chief rival for the speakership, John Sherman, R-Ohio. And in 1889 Reed named as his majority leader William McKinley Jr., R-Ohio, who had challenged Reed for the speakership and who, like Reed, had presidential ambitions.

The revolt against Cannon in 1910, which stripped the Speaker of many of his powers, also stripped him of the right to name the majority leader. Since 1911 Democratic majority leaders have been elected by secret ballot in the party caucus. The first two, Oscar W. Underwood, Ala., and Claude Kitchin, N.C., also chaired the Ways and Means Committee. When the GOP returned to power in 1919, their Committee on Committees named the majority leader, but since 1923 the Republican Conference, as the caucus is called, has selected the majority leader.

Franklin W. Mondell, Wyo., the Republican floor leader chosen in 1919, had been chairman of the Ways and Means Committee, but he gave up his committee assignments to help the Speaker manage the House. The first Democratic majority leader to give up his committee assignments was Henry T. Rainey, who resigned his seat on the Ways and Means Committee upon his election as majority leader in 1931. Beginning in the 1970s, Democratic majority leaders held leadership-designated slots on both the House Budget Committee and, later, on the Permanent Select Intelligence Committee, in order to be able to intervene when needed in difficult budget negotiations and maintain access to sensitive national security information. However, after the Republican takeover in 1995, the practice was not continued by the new majority; Majority Leader Dick Armey, R-Texas., held no committee assignment.

Underwood, the first elected majority leader, may also have been the strongest majority leader in the history of the House. Champ Clark, the Democrat who succeeded Cannon as Speaker, gave Underwood a free hand to manage both legislation and the party. "Although I am going to be Speaker . . . , I am going to sacrifice the Speaker's power to change the rules," he declared.[44] As a result of Clark's attitude and the limitations placed upon the Speaker's office, Underwood was able to dominate the House through the Democratic Caucus and his chairmanship of Ways and Means, which assigned members to the standing committees. "The main cogs in the machine were the caucus, the floor leadership, the Rules Committee, the standing committees, and special rules," wrote historian George B. Galloway. "Oscar Underwood became the real leader of the House. He dominated the party caucus, influenced the rules, and as chairman of Ways and Means chose the committees."[45]

But changing circumstances in the years following World War I made it more difficult for Underwood's successors to wield such power. Internal party divisions made the caucus ineffective, while strong Speakers such as Longworth, Garner, and Rayburn elevated the prestige and thus the power of the Speaker. The majority leader eventually came to give up his committee chairmanships, and between 1937 and 1975 the Rules Committee ceased to be an arm of the leadership. The majority leader under the Democrats was seen as the chief lieutenant to the Speaker, not his rival. The majority leader, Wright wrote in 1976, "must work with the Speaker, in a supportive role, and never against him."[46]

The status of any potential Republican leadership ladder remains problematic in the absence of any long-standing tradition of succession after decades in the minority. Both Majority Leader Armey and Minority Whip Tom DeLay, who assumed their positions in the 104th Congress, are conservatives from Texas, an unusual pairing that the Republican Conference may be reluctant to continue in the higher posts of Speaker and majority leader. Both leaders also sustained political damage based on differing perceptions of their roles in the alleged "coup" plotted against Speaker Gingrich in the summer of 1997 by younger conservatives dissatisfied by what they considered Gingrich's loss of focus and movement toward moderation, further aggravated by a series of tactical mistakes by the Speaker. The coup may have been more smoke than fire but it created an embarrassing spectacle of members of a now-divided party scheming to remove their leader in the middle of a session and damaged the reputations of the entire top GOP leadership, with unpredictable long-term consequences for their future advancement.

Every Speaker between 1900 and 1989, when Foley took office, advanced to that position from either the majority or minority leadership position; Gingrich effectively continued the tradition because he had been the highest-ranking sitting leader of his party—minority whip—as the Republican-controlled 104th Congress organized itself. (Minority Leader Bob Michel had retired in 1994.) Three of the six Democratic Speakers elected between 1945 and 1989 also served as whip. The exceptions were Rayburn, who was chairman of the Interstate and Foreign Commerce Committee when he was chosen majority leader in 1937; McCormack, who was chairman of the House Democratic Caucus; and Wright, who was a deputy whip and next in line to chair the Public Works Committee when he bid for, and won by a single vote, the floor leader position in 1976.

The duties of the majority and minority leaders are not spelled out in the standing rules of the House, nor is official provision made for them, except through periodic appropriations specifically made for their offices. House rules do provide preference in recognition for the party leaders to offer certain specified procedural motions on the House floor. Both leadership positions are also enumerated in their respective party rules.

HOUSE LEADERSHIP "LADDER" DEVELOPS GAPS

It used to be that ambitious House members of both parties yearned to be Speaker and plotted for years to advance their careers and position themselves more advantageously in the leadership. The post of majority leader, or "heir apparent," once attained, virtually guaranteed eventual promotion by acclamation to the speakership. All modern Democratic Speakers had advanced in this fashion. But in recent years, prominent members of both parties have attempted to leap over colleagues and move up the ladder more quickly than one step at a time. Other members have looked up the ladder and simply retired from politics instead.

REPUBLICANS

The Republicans threw out two top leaders, minority leaders Joseph Martin of Massachusetts in 1959, and his successor, Charles Halleck, in 1965, after election debacles. Martin had been Speaker in the two postwar Republican-controlled Congresses (1947–1949 and 1953–1955). The bloodletting did not continue after the 1974 Watergate election, in which the GOP lost many seats, since Minority Leader John Rhodes of Arizona had only just assumed the post in 1973 after incumbent Gerald Ford left the House to become the first appointed vice president in history.

Bob Michel of Illinois had been minority whip from 1974–1981, and assumed the top post after Rhodes stepped down in 1980. Newt Gingrich, R-Ga., had been minority whip from 1989–1995 and gradually assumed much of Michel's authority in his final term.

The race to succeed Speaker Gingrich began years in advance of any potential opening. Gingrich was limited to four terms of service by a new House rule adopted in 1995, so he had to vacate the position no later than January 3, 2003, assuming Republicans retained control of Congress. The nominal front-runner, Majority Leader Dick Armey, R-Texas, was not assumed to be a shoo-in for the top job, in part because Republicans did not have a clear leadership ladder after forty years in the minority. Before becoming leader, Armey had been chairman of the House Republican Conference, the third-ranked post in the minority.

Speculation fueled by Gingrich himself of a potential presidential run in 2000 led other candidates to assume that the Speaker would resign prior to embarking on a campaign, creating a vacancy perhaps sometime in 1999. This led to further speculation that Armey would be challenged by Rep. Bill Paxon of New York, chairman of the National Republican Congressional Committee in 1993–1997 and briefly holder of a new post, chairman of the Republican leadership, appointed by Gingrich. Paxon had been ousted by Gingrich following a reported "coup" attempt by junior conservatives in the summer of 1997 but remained widely popular for his campaign strategy and funding work in electing the GOP class of 1994. However, within days of announcing an exploratory and unprecedented campaign to oust Armey as majority leader in the 106th Congress as a means of positioning himself for the speakership upon Gingrich's hypothetical resignation, Paxon suddenly announced that he would not seek reelection in 1998 in order to spend time within his family.

While Paxon jumped off the leadership ladder, Rep. Bob Livingston of Louisiana suddenly backed away from political oblivion to seek the speakership. Having decided to retire in 1998, Livingston suddenly changed his mind and announced not only for reelection but for the speakership upon Gingrich's departure. He immediately began to line up commitments from colleagues and, as chairman of the powerful Appropriations Committee, was considered a formidable challenger to Armey.

Livingston was steeped in the culture of the Appropriations Committee, which often put governance ahead of ideology through enactment of its "must pass" appropriations bills. He had only reluctantly agreed to such ploys as the 1995–1996 federal government Christmas shutdown and the use of appropriations bills to enact controversial policy riders, which had frequently prompted presidential vetoes. His early decision to seek the speakership reinforced the movement away from a guaranteed ladder of leadership succession.

DEMOCRATS

Democrats had endured the most shocking break in their leadership ladder in 1987 when Speaker Jim Wright, D-Texas, resigned in the face of disciplinary action by the ethics committee. His successor, Speaker Thomas S. Foley, D-Wash., was defeated for reelection in 1994 as the party was losing control of the House, the first such loss by a sitting Speaker since 1862. But the other top leaders—Majority Leader Richard Gephardt of Missouri, who became minority leader, Majority Whip David Bonior of Michigan, who became minority whip, and caucus Vice Chair Vic Fazio of California, who moved up to caucus chairman to fill a vacancy caused by the party's rotation rule for that office—simply remained in place, turning back more conservative challengers who had little support. But Fazio, considered a likely aspirant for majority leader if Democrats regained control of the House, later surprised colleagues in 1998 by announcing his retirement. He faced another in a series of close reelection campaigns that had made political life difficult since an unfavorable 1992 redistricting and also wanted more time for a private life.

Other significant breaks in the leadership ladder for Democrats have occurred in the whip's position, which was frequently, though not always, the stepping stone to majority leader. Two very visible occupants, Tony Coelho of California and William H. Gray III, of Pennsylvania, resigned in 1989 and 1991, respectively. Coelho was caught up in a financial scandal and Gray accepted an offer to head the prestigious United Negro College Fund, passing up the potential opportunity to become the first African American to run a serious campaign for Speaker someday.

In practice, the majority leader's job has been to formulate the party's legislative program in cooperation with the Speaker and other party leaders, to steer the program through the House, to persuade committee chairmen to report bills deemed of importance to the party, and to arrange the House legislative schedule. The majority leader is also the field general for his or her party on the floor, coordinating with the bill's floor manager and the whip and task force organizations, anticipating and solving problems before they develop.

Like the Speaker, the majority leader is in a position to do many favors for colleagues—scheduling floor action at a convenient time, speaking in behalf of a member's bill (or refraining from opposing it), meeting with a member's important constituents, or campaigning for a member in his home district. Such favors clearly help the leadership build coalitions and maintain party unity; indeed, the opportunity to campaign for colleagues has become, in recent years, an opportunity eagerly sought after by party leaders of both parties.

THE MINORITY LEADER

Although individual members occasionally stepped forward to lead the loyal opposition against the majority position on specific bills or issues, the position of House minority leader first became identifiable in the 1880s. Since then the post has always been assumed by the minority party's candidate for the speakership. The titular head of the minority party, or "shadow Speaker" as he is sometimes called, is chosen by the party caucus.

The basic duties of the minority leader were described by Bertrand Snell, R-N.Y., who held the post from 1931 to 1939: "He is spokesman for his party and enunciates its policies. He is required to be alert and vigilant in defense of the minority's rights. It is his function and duty to criticize constructively the policies and program of the majority, and to this end employ parliamentary tactics and give close attention to all proposed legislation."[47] Snell might also have added that if the minority leader's party occupies the White House, he is likely to become the president's chief spokesperson in the House.

Because the minority's role is to counter the legislative program of the majority, or advance the president's legislative agenda if he or she is of the same party, it rarely offers its own comprehensive legislative program. However, given the success of the minority House Republicans' "Contract with America" proposals in unifying the party prior to the 1994 election, this pattern could change.

Robert Michel, who became the GOP minority leader in 1981, described his job as twofold: "To keep our people together, and to look for votes on the other side."[48] Michel's greatest success in this regard came in 1981, when Congress, aided by a Republican Senate and a popular president of the same party, passed the Reagan administration's unprecedented budget and tax-cut package, known as the Gramm-Latta bill. Large-scale defections by conservative Democrats in the House made the Republican successes possible.

But such victories are rare for the minority. "One of the minority leader's greatest problems," wrote Ripley, "is the generally demoralizing condition of minority party status."[49] Minority members want the same things majority members do—information, legislative success, patronage, and the like. When they do not get them, the minority leader is often the target of their frustrations. Throughout his term as minority leader Michel was pushed by younger, more conservative, and more aggressive colleagues who urged him to turn the House floor into a theater for all-out partisan warfare. The election of Gingrich as minority whip in 1989 greatly accelerated this trend and further eroded remaining patterns of bipartisan cooperation. *(See box, Partisan Tensions in the House: Stridency Increased in the 1980s and 1990s, p. 30.)*

Michel did grow increasingly confrontational during Wright's tenure as Speaker, when he, along with most other House Republicans, believed the Democrats were becoming more brazen in using the rules to deny them their rights. Republicans' intense personal dislike of Wright made this easy. And Michel made a Republican takeover of the House in the 1992 elections—the first to be held after the decennial redistricting—a top priority, working with various Republican groups in the House to develop Republican alternatives on issues such as child care, education, and health policy. Although some judged Michel to be one of the most effective House leaders on either side of the aisle since Rayburn, many Republicans felt a need for the strident partisanship offered by Gingrich and other members of his Conservative Opportunity Society. In 1989 Gingrich defeated Michel's friend and candidate Edward R. Madigan of Illinois, 87–85, to succeed Richard Cheney of Wyoming as minority whip.

Democratic House Minority Leader Richard A. Gephardt of Missouri, left, and Minority Whip David E. Bonior of Michigan discuss campaign finance reform at a 1997 news conference.

PARTISAN TENSIONS IN THE HOUSE: STRIDENCY INCREASED IN THE 1980S AND 1990S

Any institution that embraces members with competing ideals and philosophies is likely to break down in partisan bickering from time to time. The U.S. House of Representatives may be the premier example.

But political or personal disagreements reached a level of vituperation and nastiness beginning in the 1980s not previously seen in the modern Congress. The gloves came off. The weakening of personal relationships among members and traditions of comity on the House floor accelerated the process. And new members entering the House were less willing to recognize the legitimacy of opposing viewpoints or to allow their respective party leaderships to negotiate as readily with "the enemy."

Some referred to it as "the politics of personal destruction" as opponents were no longer satisfied simply to win an argument and move on, perhaps working together on the next issue. Instead, they sought to destroy a rival both personally and politically, using investigations, demands for special prosecutors, ethics charges, or seemingly any other technique that would garner advantage. Rep. Newt Gingrich, R-Ga., was credited, or blamed, as the case may be, for pioneering this technique and for using it successfully to publicize and escalate partisan tensions in the ethics investigation of Speaker Jim Wright, which led to Wright's resignation.

PARTISAN WARFARE

One other factor that accounted for the increased stridency was divided government—a Congress controlled by one party and a president of the other (1987–1993; 1995–1999), or a Congress split between the parties, as was the case in 1981–1987. Democrats lost control of the White House for twelve years during the Reagan and Bush administrations, and House Republicans had been in the minority from 1955 to 1994. This led to frequent clashes over policy that often left both parties frustrated by the inevitable "half a loaf" results. Members of the Republican minority concluded that they could benefit if they sharpened the conflict and demonstrated strong disagreements between the parties, ultimately forcing the public to make a choice between them, rather than engaging in compromise and bipartisanship that tended to muffle distinctions between the parties.

Partisan tensions escalated rapidly during the first term of Gingrich's speakership (1995–1997) as Democrats raged at their sudden loss of power and Republicans, including many newcomers unschooled in the mechanics of legislating, exulted at their ability to pass quickly most elements of their "Contract with America" legislative agenda that was used so effectively in the 1994 election campaign. In doing so, they sometimes ran roughshod over the minority rights that they had long complained Democrats had ignored during that party's long era of House control.

The strain on the House reached a climax during Gingrich's fight for reelection as Speaker in 1997 in the face of ethics charges filed by Democrats. A telephone strategy conference among Gingrich and other Republican leaders dealing with the ethics charges was recorded by private citizens from a cellular phone and was later leaked to the press, allegedly by Democratic House member Rep. James McDermott, D-Wash., ranking minority member of the Committee on Standards of Official Conduct, which was investigating Gingrich. McDermott recused himself from further participation in the Gingrich case. Rep. John Boehner, R-Ohio, chairman of the House Republican Conference from whose cell phone the conversation had been recorded, demanded that McDermott resign from the House and later filed a civil lawsuit seeking damages. In July 1998 a federal judge dismissed the lawsuit.

The proceedings of the Committee on Standards of Official Conduct, which were usually insulated from direct partisan intervention, broke down as the GOP leadership forced the committee to adopt a timetable for issuing its recommendations that minimized potentially embarrassing public hearings.

In the aftermath of Gingrich's narrow reelection as Speaker and subsequent formal reprimand by the House, both parties made some effort to cool tensions, with mixed results. But numerous investigations of President Bill Clinton and of allegations of campaign finance abuses in the 1996 presidential campaign further exacerbated partisan warfare. The GOP was accused of conducting a witch hunt against the president and First Lady Hillary Clinton and abusing its subpoena powers to investigate campaign violations by Democrats while virtually ignoring Republicans. Majority Leader Dick Armey, R-Texas., and Whip Tom DeLay, R-Texas., broke precedent by criticizing Clinton in highly personal terms, but the low point in the 105th Congress probably came when controversial House Government Reform and Oversight Committee Chairman Dan Burton, R-Ind., called the president a "scumbag" in a news interview.

In earlier years, House Speakers Thomas P. "Tip" O'Neill Jr., of Massachusetts, who retired from the House in 1987, and Jim Wright of Texas, who resigned in June 1989, were both highly partisan Democrats who did not feel comfortable working with Republicans on a regular basis. Republicans were outraged in the early 1980s when the Democrats under O'Neill stacked key committees to deny Republicans representation proportional to their numbers in the House. (Re-

"What that says to me," Michel told reporters immediately after Gingrich's election, "is that they want us to be more activated and more visible and more aggressive, and that we can't be content with business as usual."[50] Indeed, as minority whip Gingrich often eclipsed Michel as the Republicans aggressively attacked the majority and planned the strategy that led to the Republican takeover of the House in the 1994 elections.

The new minority leader beginning in the 104th Congress was Rep. Richard Gephardt, D-Mo., who had earlier been caucus chairman (1984–1988) and majority leader (1989–1995) in the Democratic-controlled House and had run unsuccessfully for the party's presidential nomination in 1988. Gephardt was unprepared for his greatly reduced role but had no trouble turning back a token challenge in the caucus from the more conservative Rep. Charlie Rose, D-N.C., who did not offer a strong rationale for running. Democrats, unlike Republicans after previ-

publicans adopted a similar practice when they assumed control with a substantially smaller majority.) Democrats eventually agreed to increase the number of seats on most major committees. In 1985, a drawn-out fight over a contested election in Indiana's Eighth District further embittered Republicans, who walked out of the House chamber *en masse* after the Democratic candidate, Rep. Frank McCloskey, was declared reelected by a four-vote margin. O'Neill managed to maintain cordial personal relations with many Republicans, including Minority Leader Robert H. Michel, R-Ill., which helped prevent passions from becoming too personal. His successor, Wright, however, was unable to do so.

Republicans were even more incensed at what they considered to be Speaker Wright's heavy-handed partisanship. One of the most divisive incidents occurred October 29, 1987, when Wright forced passage of a major deficit-cutting budget reconciliation bill that called for taxes Republicans opposed. The Speaker, who has sole authority under House rules to determine when to announce the result of a vote after the normal time allotment has expired, held the vote open so a Texas ally, Rep. Jim Chapman, could be persuaded to change his vote, making the result 206–205. Angry GOP House members booed Wright after the vote and accused him of stealing their victory. (After assuming the Speakership in 1995, Gingrich used this authority to extend voting time for much longer periods to persuade members to change their positions; he said he was following the "regular order" of House practice in doing so. During one such interlude, a Democrat asked Gingrich from the floor whether he was planning to apologize to Wright for the earlier criticism.)

THE GINGRICH FACTOR

Much of the partisan tension was deliberately fomented over a long period of time by a group of Republicans led by Gingrich. Younger Republican conservatives effectively demonized the Democrats not only as political and policy adversaries but also personally as "corrupt" and "evil" in their ultimately successful campaign to seize power in the chamber. Such feelings, and such language, made it virtually impossible for the parties to communicate and hamstrung those who still were willing to attempt bipartisan cooperation. Since he entered the House in 1979, Gingrich had argued that the badly outnumbered Republican House contingent should forget about compromising to improve Democratic legislation and instead use the chamber as a political forum to express opposition and build political support. To advance his strategy Gingrich and his supporters frequently criticized the Democrats during the "special order" period held after the close of regular business. Like regular business, these proceedings were televised to the nation (although the requirement at the time that the camera remain on the member speaking meant that viewers could not know the chamber was often nearly empty), and Gingrich was soon attracting regular attention not only from conservative viewers but also the national media.

The use of dilatory tactics on the House floor increased. The use of motions to adjourn, demands for roll-call votes on routine matters and other techniques to disrupt the schedule of the House proliferated. These tactics had been used in the past, usually in response to some specific event that angered the minority or to try to run out the clock for action on legislative business at the end of a session. But more aggressive conservatives like Gingrich had little concern with the majority's reaction to the frequency of these techniques; nor did they care that they could not win these votes or have significant impact on the end product of legislation. Delaying tactics helped mobilize and unite the minority, created uncertainty in the majority's otherwise firm control of the chamber, attracted the media's notice, and made bipartisan collaboration more difficult.

In 1984 Gingrich endeared himself to Republican conservatives when he humiliated Speaker O'Neill on the House floor. Addressing a nearly empty chamber during the special order period after the close of regular business one night in May, Gingrich denounced Majority Leader Wright and nine other Democrats for writing a conciliatory letter to Nicaraguan leader Daniel Ortega, addressing him as "Dear Commandante" and calling for a settlement between political factions in that country. Gingrich said the letter was undermining U.S. foreign policy. O'Neill retaliated by ordering the television cameras to pan the chamber during special order speeches so that viewers would see that Gingrich and his supporters were addressing an empty chamber.

A few days later, when Gingrich repeated his charges during regular debate, O'Neill took the floor himself to denounce the Georgian's tactics as "the lowest thing that I have seen in my thirty-two years in Congress." That remark, an obvious violation of House rules of decorum, brought a demand from GOP Whip Trent Lott, Miss., that O'Neill's words be "taken down," that is, be reread to the House and examined by the Speaker, who determines whether they should be stricken from the record. Speaker pro tempore Joe Moakley, a Massachusetts Democrat with close ties to O'Neill who was presiding at the time, had no choice but to agree with Lott—the first time the words of a Speaker had been taken down since February 12, 1797, when Speaker Jonathan Dayton of New Jersey was called to order for using "improper language" during debate on the House floor.

ous political disasters in 1958 and 1964, did not take out their anger on party leaders. In contrast to his earlier roles in developing policy and serving as a national party spokesperson, Gephardt now had to devote substantial energy just to the mechanics of obtaining committee assignments for members displaced by the election results and calming various party factions who wanted to assess blame for the election defeat. The press reported that he and Gingrich almost never spoke, inhibiting the development of a sustainable relationship between the majority and minority leaderships under the new regime.

PARTY WHIPS

The term "whip" comes from British fox-hunting lore; the "whipper-in" was responsible for keeping the foxhounds from leaving the pack. It was first used in the British Parliament in 1769 by Edmund Burke. Though neither party in the House of

Representatives designated an official whip until 1897—Rep. James A. Tawney, Republican of Minnesota, was the first—influential members played that role from the outset working to forge consensus on important issues and for particular floor fights.

Unlike the British system, where political parties are well disciplined and a whip's major concern is good party attendance, whips in the U.S. House cajole votes as well as count noses, gather information as well as impart it. "We try to keep our people . . . informed of the leadership's position on things—what they'd like, what we're seeking, what we're trying to do," a member of the Democratic whip organization said. "Not only on policy, but also on scheduling and programming. . . . We pick up static from our people and relay it to the leadership, so that they know what's going on, but we also pick up information from the leadership and convey it back. It's a two-way conduit."[51]

Specifically, whips of both parties help their floor leaders keep track of the whereabouts of party members and lobby them for their votes. Whips also serve as the party's acting floor leaders in the absence of the regular leaders. They handle the mechanics of polling members both on their views on issues and on the stands on specific floor votes, information that the majority leader uses to determine whether and when to bring a bill to the floor. Through weekly whip notices, whips inform members about upcoming floor action, including key amendments.

The whips are also responsible for ensuring that members are present for tight votes. Sometimes, whips and their assistants stand at the door of the House chamber, signaling the leadership's position on a vote by holding their thumbs up—or down. During recorded votes, a computer on the floor prints out how members have voted. If the vote is close, the whips can use that list as a guide to seek possible vote switches before the result of the vote is announced. Occasionally the whip organization goes to extremes. In 1984, for example, deputy whip Marty Russo, D-Ill., actually carried Daniel K. Akaka, D-Hawaii, onto the House floor in an effort to persuade him to change his vote.

House Republicans have always elected their whip. The Democratic whip was appointed by the Speaker and majority leader until 1986, when the Democratic Caucus elected Tony Coelho of California. In recent decades the Democratic whip position has frequently been a first step toward the speakership. The change to elective status had been demanded and passed years earlier by caucus members who did not want an appointed member to gain the advantage of such an important post, with its potential for advancement on the leadership ladder. But implementation of the new rule was delayed until a vacancy developed in the whip post, which it did when Thomas S. Foley moved up to become majority leader. Members also wanted the whip to act as a liaison between the leadership and the rank and file, and not simply as an enforcer and intelligence gatherer. Coelho shocked his colleagues by resigning suddenly in 1989 in the midst of an ethics controversy that developed simultaneously, but unrelated to, Speaker Wright's troubles. He was succeeded by the first African American to win a major leadership position, Rep. William H. Gray III, of Pennsylvania, who had previously been Budget Committee chairman (1988–1989) and moved up to whip from the chairmanship of the Democratic Caucus. Gray's career was brief, as he also stunned his colleagues by abandoning the leadership ladder in 1991 and accepting a post as head of the United Negro College Fund.

In the last years of Democratic rule in the House, the whip system was expanded into a continuous information-gathering and strategizing mechanism. Congressional scholar Sinclair notes that in the 103rd Congress, with more than ninety-five members involved, the whip system had evolved "from a sporadically active body more inclined to count than persuade . . . into a continuously active organization that perceived persuasion as its central mission."[52]

Coelho and Gingrich were the most influential party whips of the modern era, Coelho for his fundraising skills and Gingrich as a political strategist, which gave them both influence beyond the technical rank of their leadership positions. Rep. Tom DeLay, R-Texas., who became majority whip in 1995, was an aggressive conservative activist who enjoyed considerable success in the 104th Congress in passing most elements of the "Contract with America" and other items on the new majority's legislative agenda. His opposite number was Rep. David Bonior, D-Mich., who had served as majority whip from 1991 to 1995 and continued in that role for the minority.

In recent years the politics of inclusion and the need to build coalitions have induced both parties to expand and enhance their whip organizations.

By the late 1980s virtually every bill of significance was given a task force by the Democrats, made up of committee members and noncommittee members with an interest in the issue. The task force's job was to round up support for the bill. Task force members discussed which arguments would work best with which members of Congress and who was best suited to push those points with individual members. Sometimes task forces reached out to unions, trade associations, and others who were lobbying on the issue. If the votes were not there, the task force and key committee members, under the aegis of the leadership, might even tinker with the substance of the legislation to try to reach a compromise acceptable to a majority.

The tactic proved successful in getting legislation through the House and in involving more members, especially junior members, in the process. "It's helped the leadership to get to know the new members and the new members to get to know the leadership," one member told Sinclair. "And it's certainly helped the new members . . . understand the need for leadership and followership. I think the guys who have served on task forces know a lot more about the need for a party structure with some loyalty than those who haven't."[53]

Republicans in the majority also used many of these same techniques. DeLay was heavily criticized for involving outside interest groups more visibly in the process of garnering support for legislation, but Republicans countered that labor and liberal group had always been consulted by Democrats.

The whip system of both parties has expanded over time to involve more members in the process and to gather greater amounts of political intelligence. For example, in 1998 DeLay had one chief deputy whip, Dennis Hastert of Illinois, sixteen deputy whips, and forty-eight assistant whips. The whip's functions as formally defined by the leadership included floor strategy, counting votes, identifying member concerns, providing information on floor activities, an automatic call system for Republican members, a Republican job bank, and a member ombudsman program.

THE PARTY CAUCUSES

The use of party caucuses—the organization of all members in each party in the House—has waxed and waned since the beginning of Congress. In the Jeffersonian period, the Democratic-Republicans, in conjunction with the president, used the caucus to formulate their party's legislative strategy. During Clay's terms as Speaker, most important legislative decisions were still made in the Democratic-Republican caucus; less than two weeks after being seated in 1813, Federalist Daniel Webster concluded that "the time for us to be put on the stage and moved by the wires has not yet come," since "before anything is attempted to be done here, it must be arranged elsewhere."[54]

The nominees for president and vice president were chosen by congressional caucuses from 1800 to 1824. By the 1830s the importance of the caucuses had diminished, and except to nominate the party's candidate for Speaker at the beginning of each Congress, they met rarely during the next sixty years.

In the 1890s the caucus was revived as a forum for discussing legislative strategy. Speaker Reed used the Republican caucus to a limited extent to discuss policy questions. For the most part, though, the caucus under Reed functioned only to give the party's stamp of approval to decisions Reed had already made. In the early 1900s Speaker Cannon called caucus meetings occasionally but manipulated them much as Reed had. It was not until the revolt against Cannon and the return of control of the House to the Democrats that the caucus was restored to its earlier legislative significance.

The Democratic Caucus

In 1909 the Democrats adopted a party rule that the caucus, by a two-thirds majority, could bind its members on a specific vote. Throughout President Wilson's first term, the Democratic leadership used this rule and the caucus effectively, achieving remarkable party unity on a wide range of domestic legislation. But the party began to split over foreign policy issues, and the caucus fell into disuse in Wilson's second term. The binding caucus rule was used during Franklin D. Roosevelt's first term as well, but subsequently it was invoked only on procedural or party issues, such as voting for Speaker, and the rule was finally abolished in 1974.

In recent decades the Democratic Caucus has been revived. In the late 1960s younger House Democrats with relatively little seniority sought to revitalize the caucus as a means of countering the arbitrary authority exercised by committee chairmen and other senior members. The campaign, led by the House Democratic Study Group, began when Speaker McCormack established regular monthly caucus meetings in 1969, and it gained momentum in the early 1970s. The result was a basic transferal of power among House Democrats and eventually throughout the House.

The most important change modified the seniority system by making committee chairmen subject to secret-ballot election by the caucus. This modification was achieved in steps and took its final form—automatic secret votes on all chairmen—in December 1974. Early in 1975 the caucus rejected three chairmen, a clear signal that all chairmen in the future would be held accountable to their colleagues and could not expect to exercise the absolute powers they had held when the seniority system all but guaranteed them tenure as chairmen. Other chairmen were unseated in 1984 and 1990.

The Democratic Caucus instituted other changes that helped transform the House into a more open and accountable institution. It opened many of its own meetings to the public and the media between 1975 and 1980. It limited House Democrats to one subcommittee chairmanship and guaranteed each party member a seat on a major committee. It also created a "bill of rights" for subcommittees that gave them considerable independence from committee chairmen. On purely party matters it transferred the authority to make committee assignments from the Democratic members of the Ways and Means Committee to a revamped Steering and Policy Committee and placed that committee firmly under the control of the leadership.

Although the Democratic Caucus focused primarily on procedural reforms during this period, it also gave some attention to substantive issues. In 1972, for example, it forced a House vote on a nonbinding, end-the-Vietnam-War resolution. In 1975 it went on record as opposing more military aid to Indochina, and it voted to order the Rules Committee to allow a floor vote on an amendment to end the oil depletion allowance.

These forays into substantive legislation plunged the caucus into new controversy, partly because it was seen as usurping the powers of the standing committees and undermining the committee system. At least that was the argument expressed by conservative Democratic opponents of the resolutions, which were drafted and backed mainly by the party's liberal bloc. The conservatives insisted that caucus meetings, which had been closed, be opened to the public. That killed the role the caucus played as a "family council," which greatly diminished its usefulness.

Occasionally the caucus still took a stand on a legislative matter. In 1978, for example, it voted 150–57 to approve a resolution urging Ways and Means to roll back a planned Social Security tax increase. President Carter and House leaders backed the increase, however, and thwarted the rollback attempt.

The caucus elects a variety of party leaders, including the nominee for Speaker when Democrats hold a majority. Other

Members of the freshman class of the House of Representatives pose on the steps of the Capitol before the start of the 105th Congress.

elected posts in the 105th Congress were the minority leader, whip, caucus chair and vice chair, and chair of the Democratic Congressional Campaign Committee, though in practice that position is filled by appointment of the minority leader. The chair and vice chair of the caucus serve no more than two full consecutive terms, the only positions in the Democratic leadership required under the rules to rotate.

Under the chairmanship of Gillis W. Long, D-La., (1980–1984) the Democratic Caucus once again closed its meetings following substantial losses in the 1980 election. This made it easier to keep party disputes within the family.

Long also set up a Committee on Party Effectiveness early in 1981 to reassess the party's direction after its election losses in 1980; members of the committee covered a spectrum of political opinion, including several rising stars such as Richard Gephardt, who succeeded Long as caucus chairman. Gephardt ran for president in 1988 while holding the post. He was succeeded at the caucus by Gray (1988–1989), the outgoing Budget Committee chairman. (Rep. Shirley Chisholm of New York had been caucus secretary, a post at that time traditionally reserved for a woman, in the 1970s. The title was later changed to the more prestigious "vice chair," which, ironically, had the effect of eliminating the automatic claim to it by women members.) When Gray became whip in 1989 after Coelho resigned, the vice chairman, Steny Hoyer of Maryland, was elected to fill the vacancy and was then reelected twice for full terms, ultimately holding the post for five and one-half years. When Democrats lost control of the House in 1994, the party did not hold it against Vic Fazio of California, who was both vice chairman of the caucus and chairman of the Democratic Congressional Campaign Committee. It elevated him to caucus chairman until his retirement from the House in 1998.

The Republican Conference

The counterpart of the Democratic Caucus, the Republican Conference, is the umbrella organization for House Republicans. Like its Democratic counterpart, the conference sets party rules and elects the leadership. In the majority, it chooses its nominee for Speaker, and also elects a majority leader, whip, conference chairman, vice chair, and secretary. Other than the Speaker, who is limited to four terms under House rules used by the GOP majority, the other positions are not term limited.

The conference builds party unity through retreats and other meetings of the rank and file, and helps to identify campaign issues. The conference also produces legislative status reports and research information on issues pending before the House, coordinates use of talk radio, and provides training sessions for members and staff on efficient use of House resources.

The Republican Conference rarely served as a policy-setting body, although in the 1965–1969 period it was used occasionally to develop policy positions for consideration by the party's leadership. Although he did not try to make it an active arm of the leadership, Minority Leader Michel used the conference as a sounding board to determine the party's position on substantive matters and to communicate the viewpoint of House Republicans to the Republican administration.

The conference occasionally passed resolutions stating House Republican views on particular issues. In what was widely seen as a slap at Republican President Bush, the conference in 1990 approved a resolution opposing any new taxes; Bush had recently renounced his "no new taxes" campaign pledge in an effort to reach agreement with the Democrats on a budget deficit reduction measure.

The Republican Conference was revitalized by Gingrich and often served as the vehicle pressing the GOP leadership to implement the "Contract with America" and other items on its legislative agenda. Rep. John Boehner of Ohio was elected chairman in the 104th Congress. There were frequent policy discussions, including votes on strategy, such as when a conference majority urged continuation of the controversial government shutdown at the end of the 1995 session.

Gingrich also summoned members to conference meetings to explain votes at variance with party policy, such as when defections resulted in defeat of the 1997 committee funding resolution. The most dramatic conference event of Gingrich's tenure as Speaker was a session in the summer of 1997 at which various party leaders were asked to explain their roles in a reputed coup aimed at toppling the Speaker.

Gingrich set up task forces to develop legislation, and allowed Conference Chairman Boehner a major strategic role. Boehner was later accused of participating in the coup discussions but his position in the leadership was not challenged. One problem with the new Republican leadership structure since the party achieved its majority has been the absence of clear lines of authority on some matters, as Gingrich experimented with different strategies and combinations of party personnel. For example, to reward Rep. Bill Paxon, R-N.Y., who had led the campaign committee successfully to achieve the majority, Gingrich in 1997 created the title of "chairman of the Republican leadership" to give Paxon continuing status among the top leadership. However, several months later Paxon was forced to resign, and the new post was abolished, when his loyalty to the Speaker was questioned in the aftermath of the coup discussions.

MAKING COMMITTEE ASSIGNMENTS

After the House revolt against Cannon in 1910, the power to appoint members of standing committees was taken from the Speaker and vested in the party caucuses. In 1911 the Democratic Caucus delegated the authority to choose the party's committee members to a special Committee on Committees, which was composed of all Democrats on the Ways and Means Committee.

The reforms of the 1970s also affected the committee assignment process. In 1973 the Democratic Caucus expanded the Committee on Committees to include the Speaker, who served as chairman, the majority leader, and the caucus chairman. In December 1974 the caucus transferred the assignment power to the Steering and Policy Committee, which is composed of the Democratic leaders and their appointees and regionally elected members. The Steering and Policy Committee's recommendations were subject to ratification by the caucus, as were those of Ways and Means, but ratification, particularly of committee chairmen, is no longer perfunctory. The policy functions were later split off into another body and the committee assignment function is now performed by the Steering Committee.

In 1917 the Republican Conference also established a Committee on Committees, which traditionally is chaired by the GOP House leader. Committee chairmanships when in the majority, or ranking minority positions otherwise, as well as committee assignments, are subject to approval by the conference. In 1989 Republicans gave their minority leader the same authority to appoint the GOP members of the Rules Committee that Democratic Speakers had obtained for their Rules members in 1974. When Republicans took control of the House in 1995, the committee on committees was called the Steering Committee and was chaired by Speaker Gingrich.

Speakers often have exercised great influence on committee assignments, even when they were not on the panel making the choices. In the late 1920s, for example, Speaker Longworth had four uncooperative members of the Rules Committee replaced with his own choices. In the 1940s and 1950s Speaker Rayburn intervened frequently to influence the makeup of the Ways and Means Committee, which he insisted be stacked with members opposed to reductions in the oil and gas depletion allowance. Rayburn was from Texas, one of the largest oil-producing states. Rayburn also led the effort in 1961 to increase the size of the Rules Committee, which allowed him to engineer the selection of two additional Democrats more amenable to his leadership.

Speaker Gingrich made sure that members of the aggressive and conservative 1994 freshman class received assignments to the most important committees, both to cement their loyalty and spread their activism.

POLICY AND STRATEGY COMMITTEES

During the twentieth century both parties established groups called "steering committees" to assist the leadership with legislative scheduling and party strategy (not to be confused with the entities with similar names in the 1990s that now handle only committee assignments). The Republican Steering Committee, established in 1919, dominated the business of the House until 1925, when power again shifted to the Speaker. Speaker Longworth largely ignored the Steering Committee. In 1949 the committee was expanded and renamed the Policy Committee. The Policy Committee was considered the chief advisory board for the minority leader from 1959 to 1965, when it was replaced in the role by the Republican Conference. In its role after the Republicans assumed majority status in 1995, the Policy Committee issues and disseminates policy statements on issues of concern to the conference, considers policy resolutions, issues reports, and conducts policy forums. It helps develop the legislative agenda for House Republicans.

Conference Democrats established a Steering Committee in 1933, abandoned it in 1956, and reconstituted it in 1962. Its duties and role in the party structure were vague. In 1973 the Democratic Caucus voted to create a new Steering and Policy Committee to give coherence and direction to the party's legislative strategy. In 1974 the caucus gave the new Steering and Policy Committee the authority to make Democratic assignments, removing that power from the Democratic members of the Ways and Means Committee. However, this and other periodic efforts by Democrats in later years to create a separate leadership entity to deal with policy floundered due to opposition both by party leaders, who thought a new structure hampered their flexibility, and committee chairs who did not want a potential rival intruding on their turf.

The size of the Steering and Policy Committee expanded over time as additional members of the leadership were added to it. The Speaker was also given the right to make additional appointments of members of his choice, the number of which also increased. The caucus membership at large could seek elective seats from geographic regions.

In 1992, the caucus created a "Speaker's Working Group on Policy Development" to satisfy demands for a separate, smaller entity to deal with policy matters, since the Steering and Policy Committee focused on little besides committee assignments and that was the reason members sought to be on it. Speaker Foley promptly expanded the size of the "Working Group," which made the new entity unwieldy, and it exercised little influence. After becoming the minority in 1995, Democrats created a new, separate Policy Committee.

The Democratic Study Group (DSG), created in 1959, functioned as the primary source of research on legislative issues for the Democrats and exercised considerable influence, particularly during the height of the reform period. It was one of many Legislative Service Organizations (LSOs) that hired staff and used office space in the House funded by members from their office allowances. DSG's legislative reports, which explained the content of bills, and its more political special reports that often had a partisan slant, were widely read even by Republicans. But the DSG and similar entities were effectively abolished in 1995 when the new Republican majority eliminated LSOs and the ability of members to pool resources. This action damaged the Democrats' ability to gather and coordinate legislative information and weakened the party's ability to compete effectively with the Republican Conference, which published similar legislative materials for its own party members. Some of the LSOs lingered in name only, without offices or staff, or reconstituted themselves as entities outside the House relying on other sources of funding.

Leadership in the Senate: "We Know No Masters"

Sen. Daniel Webster in 1830 described the upper chamber as a "Senate of equals, of men of individual honor and personal character, and of absolute independence. We know no masters, we acknowledge no dictators. . . ."[55] At the time and for several

THE SENATE'S PRESIDING OFFICERS

The only two Senate leaders mentioned by the Constitution have little effective leadership power. Article I, Section 3 provides that the vice president "shall be President of the Senate, but shall have no vote, unless they be equally divided." It also provides that the "Senate shall choose . . . a President pro tempore, in the absence of the Vice President, or when he shall exercise the office of President of the United States."

DUTIES OF THE PRESIDING OFFICER

As presiding officer, the principal function of the vice president and the president pro tem is to recognize senators, but this is rarely significant since Senate rules usually require the presiding officer to recognize the senator who first seeks recognition. The presiding officer also decides points of order, subject to appeal to the full Senate; appoints senators to House-Senate conference committees (although it is customary for the presiding officer to take the recommendations of the floor manager of the bill in question); enforces decorum; administers oaths; and appoints members to special committees. The president pro tem may appoint a substitute to replace him in the chair; the vice president may not.

As a senator, the president pro tem may vote on all matters; the vice president may vote only if the Senate is evenly divided on a question, as stipulated by the Constitution, and then only if he is available and chooses to participate.

Such votes may be widely separated in time. Between 1945 and 1997, when twelve different vice presidents served, only thirty-four such votes were cast; of these, Vice President Albert Gore Jr., D-Tenn., cast three votes, the last in 1994. Four other modern vice presidents, Lyndon B. Johnson, D-Texas, (1961–1963), Gerald R. Ford, R-Mich., (1973–1974), Nelson A. Rockefeller, R-N.Y. (1974–1977), and Dan Quayle, R-Ind., (1989–1993), did not cast any.

THE VICE PRESIDENT AS PRESIDING OFFICER

It is little wonder that the Senate has not placed any real power with the vice president, who is not chosen by the Senate, may not be a member of the majority party in the chamber, and may not be sympathetic with the aims of its majority. Precedent was established by John Adams, who, although in agreement with the majority of the Senate during his terms as vice president (1789–1797), perceived his role simply as that of presiding officer and made little effort to guide Senate action. His successor, Thomas Jefferson (1797–1801), could not have steered the Federalist-controlled Senate even if he had wanted to.

A few vice presidents have attempted to use their position as presiding officer to achieve a partisan purpose, with varying degrees of success. John C. Calhoun, vice president to John Quincy Adams, was hostile to the Adams administration. Taking advantage of an 1823 rule change giving the presiding officer the right to appoint committee members, Calhoun placed supporters of Andrew Jackson on key committees. But he refused to use the authority exercised by earlier vice presidents to call senators to order for words used in debate.

Nelson A. Rockefeller, vice president to Gerald R. Ford, once used his authority to refuse to recognize a senator who wanted to mount a filibuster against a Ford administration bill. Senators from both parties were incensed at Rockefeller's action and made it very clear that the president's program would suffer if Rockefeller did not desist immediately.

Most vice presidents preside only upon ceremonial occasions or when a close vote on a bill or amendment of interest to the administration is likely to occur. But as president of the Senate, the vice president is well positioned to lobby on behalf of the president's program. Walter F. Mondale, D-Minn., who left his Senate seat to become Jimmy Carter's vice president, proved to be an effective decades thereafter, the Senate had no structured leadership apparatus. Not until the early twentieth century did either party formally designate a leader to oversee and guide its interests in the Senate. Now both parties name a leader and an assistant leader and have a number of party committees to help them formulate policy and strategy and win reelection.

But Webster's words still hold true; the Senate is essentially a collection of individuals, each of whom is a leader in his or her own sphere. The independence of each senator is further ensured by Senate rules, which protect the rights of the minority against the will of the majority. As Ripley has observed, Senate floor leaders are not "automatically invested with a specific quota of power; they still must create much of their own."[56] Effective leadership in the Senate, even more than in the House, thus depends on the leaders' personal and negotiating skills.

EVOLUTION OF SENATE LEADERSHIP

As with the House, the Constitution did not offer much direction about Senate leadership. Its two references to leadership posts and responsibilities in the Senate (Article I, Section 3) stipulate that the vice president shall be president of the Senate and that the Senate shall choose a president pro tempore to preside in the vice president's absence. Neither of these offices has ever been a very effective leadership position.

Thus legislative leadership was left to individual senators. Here, as in the House, Alexander Hamilton acted much like a stage manager, controlling floor action through his many friends in the chamber. Jefferson and his Treasury Secretary Albert Gallatin exercised as much control over the Senate as they did over the House. Jefferson, wrote Thomas Pickering of Massachusetts, tries "to screen himself from all responsibility by calling upon Congress for advice and direction. . . . Yet with affected modesty and deference he secretly dictates every measure which is seriously proposed."[57]

The first significant move toward party organization did not occur until 1846, when the parties began to nominate members of the standing committees. Until 1823 the Senate had chosen committee members by ballot. That year the Senate turned over

spokesperson for the White House on numerous occasions and tried to fill part of the gap caused by Carter's lack of experience in Washington and the absence of any long-standing political or personal relationships with congressional leaders. Vice President Al Gore wielded even more influence during the Clinton administration, exercising significant power over federal appointments and several key areas of government policy, most notably on government reorganization, technology, and the environment.

THE PRESIDENT PRO TEMPORE

The first president pro tempore, John Langdon of New Hampshire, was elected on April 6, 1789, before John Adams appeared in the Senate to assume his duties as presiding officer. When the first vice president took his seat on April 21, Langdon's service as president pro tem ended. For the next 100 years, the Senate acted on the theory that a president pro tempore could be elected only in the vice president's absence and that his term expired when the vice president returned. (Unlike modern practice, the vice president frequently presided over the Senate in the nineteenth century.) By 1890 the Senate had elected presidents pro tempore on 153 occasions. In the 42nd Congress alone (1871–1873), ten such elections, all of the same senator, were held.

In 1890 the Senate gave the president pro tem tenure of a sort by adopting a resolution stating that ". . . it is competent for the Senate to elect a president pro tempore, who shall hold the office during the pleasure of the Senate and until another is elected, and shall execute the duties thereof during all future absences of the vice president" until the Senate otherwise orders. That practice was still in use in 1998.

By law, the president pro tem is third in line, behind the vice president and the Speaker of the House of Representatives, to succeed to the presidency. Like the Speaker, he is a member of the majority party, and election is usually by a straight party-line vote. By custom the most senior member of the majority party in terms of Senate service is elected president pro tem. Only one of those elected since 1945 did not follow this pattern: Arthur H. Vandenberg, R-Mich., was the second-ranking Republican when elected in 1947.

Before 1945 there were some notable exceptions to the custom. George H. Moses, R-N.H., ranked only fifteenth in party seniority when he was elected president pro tem in 1925, and Willard Saulsbury, D-Del., was still in his first term when elected to the post in 1916.

Strom Thurmond, R-S.C., was considered the most senior Republican when he was elected president pro tem in 1981 even though John Tower of Texas had served longer as a Republican. Thurmond, a former Democratic governor, began his Senate service in 1955 after winning election as a write-in candidate, the only senator ever to do so. He resigned the following year and was absent from the Senate for most of 1956 in order to run again, and win, as a Democrat. Thurmond became a Republican in 1964; the Republican Conference agreed to base his seniority on the date he entered the Senate, not the date he switched parties. Thurmond resumed the president pro tempore post when Republicans regained Senate control in 1995.

Few presidents pro tem in the twentieth century have had much influence on the Senate. One who did was Vandenberg, who was also chairman of the Foreign Relations Committee. Vandenberg "no doubt exerted as much influence in what was done and not done as the Speaker of the House," Floyd M. Riddick, who would later become Senate parliamentarian, wrote in 1949. When Robert C. Byrd of West Virginia became president pro tempore (1989–1995), he liked to preside over complicated procedural situations. As chairman of the Appropriations Committee and a former majority and minority leader, Byrd brought far more stature to the position than could accrue simply through seniority.

the appointment process to the presiding officer. Initially this officer was the president pro tempore, but in 1825–1827 Vice President John C. Calhoun assumed the power. Hostile to the administration of John Quincy Adams, he used the power to place supporters of Andrew Jackson in key positions. In 1828 the Senate amended its rules to return the appointment power to the president pro tem, who, of course, was selected by the Senate itself. In 1833 the Senate reverted to selection by ballot.

By this time the seniority system had begun to develop, and chairmanships of Senate committees rotated less than they had in the past. Parties began to control assignments, committees began to divide along ideological lines, and minority reports began to appear. By 1846 the routine was formalized. When the second session of the 29th Congress met in December, the Senate began balloting for committee chairmen. Midway through the process the balloting rule was suspended, and on a single ballot the Senate accepted the list of committee assignments that had already been agreed upon by the majority and minority. For the most part, that routine has been followed since.

Immediately before and during the Civil War, party authority extended to substantive as well as organizational matters. In 1858, for example, the Democratic Caucus removed Stephen A. Douglas as chairman of the Committee on Territories, despite his seniority, because he had refused to go along with President James Buchanan and the southern wing of the party on the question of allowing slavery in the territories.

With the end of the Civil War, however, party influence on substantive matters declined. By the time Ulysses S. Grant entered the White House in 1869, political parties required unity only on organizational matters. Disputes over committee assignments were settled in the party caucuses, and pressing issues were discussed there, but there was no way to enforce caucus decisions against senators who refused to be bound by a vote of the majority of their caucus. "I am a senator of the United States," Charles Sumner, R-Mass., once declared. "My obligations as a senator were above any vote in a caucus."[58]

Beginning in the 1870s, Republicans sought to strengthen party control of the Senate by appointing a caucus chairman, who was considered to be the party's floor leader, and setting up a Committee on Committees to recommend committee assignments to the caucus and then to the full Senate. But the power of the caucus chairman, then Henry Anthony, R-R.I., was overshadowed by a Republican faction led by Roscoe Conkling of New York, that held sway for roughly ten years. Though the faction generally controlled the Committee on Committees, it never controlled the Senate's proceedings. Eventually in the early 1880s, it dissolved as a consequence of a series of unsuccessful feuds with Republican presidents over patronage in New York state.

EMERGENCE OF REPUBLICAN LEADERS

The emergence of another Republican faction in the 1890s led to establishment of a permanent leadership organization in the Senate. The leader of this faction was Nelson W. Aldrich of Rhode Island, who worked in close alliance with William B. Allison of Iowa, Orville H. Platt of Connecticut, and John C. Spooner of Wisconsin. Aldrich had, in the words of one historian, "made himself indispensable to the party organization [in the Senate], rising step by step as the elders passed out, until in the end he made himself the dictator of the cabal which for a time was the master of the government."[59] Already an influence in the Senate, this group took complete control after Allison, as the member with the longest period of Senate service, was elected chairman of the Republican Caucus in March 1897.

Previous caucus chairmen had not seen the office as a vehicle for consolidating party authority, an oversight that Allison and Aldrich were quick to correct. Since the mid-1870s the Republicans had appointed a Steering Committee to help schedule legislative business. Unlike previous caucus chairmen, Allison assumed the chair of this committee and filled it with his allies. For the first time a party organization arranged the order of business in minute detail and managed proceedings on the Senate floor.

Allison also controlled the Committee on Committees. By this time committee chairmanships were filled through seniority, and Allison and Aldrich made no attempt to overturn this practice (to which they owed their committee chairmanships—Allison of Appropriations, Aldrich of Finance). But seniority did not apply to filling committee vacancies, and here the two found an opportunity to reward their supporters and punish their opponents. "Realizing the potentialities for control in the chamber," wrote historian David J. Rothman, Allison and Aldrich "entrenched and tightened personal leadership and party discipline. Their example would not always be emulated. . . . Nevertheless, they institutionalized, once and for all, the prerogatives of power. Would-be successors or Senate rivals would now be forced to capture and effectively utilize the party post."[60]

Like Speaker Cannon, who dominated the House for much of the same period, Allison and Aldrich were largely successful in imposing their conservative political views upon the chamber. Defeats were rare until President Theodore Roosevelt was able to push a part of his legislative program through Congress. The group retained much of its power even after Allison's death in 1908. Though Allison had held the formal positions of power, Aldrich exercised power through the sheer force of his personality; he was considered by many to be the most powerful man in the Senate. But as the number of Republican insurgents in the Senate increased, the once all-powerful group began to weaken, and it quickly disintegrated after Aldrich retired in 1911.

EMERGENCE OF DEMOCRATIC LEADERS

A centralized Democratic organization in the Senate developed in the same period. Under the leadership of Arthur P. Gorman of Maryland, who served as chairman of the Democratic Caucus from 1889 to 1899, the Democratic power structure was very similar to that put together by Allison and Aldrich. Gorman consolidated his power by assuming all of the party's top leadership posts himself, including floor leader and the chairmanship of both the Steering Committee and the Committee on Committees. He further solidified his control by appointing his political allies to positions of influence.

Historian Rothman has concluded that the Democratic Party structure under Gorman may have been more conducive than the Republican structure to the emergence of an effective and energetic leadership. Rothman notes that Gorman was elected chairman of the caucus not on the basis of seniority, but because of his standing among his colleagues. And Gorman eventually came to appoint the same group of men to the Steering Committee and the Committee on Committees, concentrating power over the party organization in a relatively small number of Democrats. For all but two of his ten years as caucus chairman, however, Senate Democrats were in the minority, and they were often badly divided on substantive issues. As a result Gorman never attained the same degree of power and authority as the Allison-Aldrich team.

EARLY EFFECTIVE LEADERS

Few of the Senate leaders in the twentieth century were particularly effective. One of the stronger leaders was Democrat John W. Kern of Indiana, whose election as caucus chairman in 1913, after only two years in the Senate, was engineered by progressive Democrats after they first deposed conservative Thomas S. Martin of Virginia. The Democratic Steering Committee, appointed by Kern and dominated by the progressives, assigned members sympathetic to President Woodrow Wilson's programs to key committees. The Steering Committee also recommended, and the caucus adopted, rules that permitted a majority of committee members to call meetings, elect subcommittees, and appoint conferees. Thus party authority was augmented, and the power of committee chairmen curbed, in a movement that somewhat paralleled the rise of the caucus in the House. *(See "Leaders of the Senate since 1911," p. 169, in Reference Materials.)*

Kern worked hard to push Wilson's progressive program through the Senate, achieving passage of a steep reduction in import duties and imposition of the first income tax under the Sixteenth Amendment, establishment of the Federal Reserve and the Federal Trade Commission, and enactment of antitrust laws, among others. Kern served as leader for only four years (he was defeated for reelection to the Senate in 1916). Yet until the 1950s few other floor leaders of either party attained the effectiveness he had achieved.

Massachusetts Republican Henry Cabot Lodge, who served as majority leader from 1919 to 1924, managed twice (in 1919 and 1920) to mobilize the Senate to oppose the Treaty of Versailles, which embodied the Covenant of the League of Nations and which Wilson strongly backed. But on other matters, Lodge was not a particularly effective leader, nor were the other Republicans who served in the 1920s.

President Franklin D. Roosevelt was fortunate in having Joseph T. Robinson of Arkansas as the Senate majority leader from 1933 to 1937. Robinson revived the Democratic Caucus, and won agreement from Senate Democrats to make caucus decisions on administration bills binding by majority vote. There is no evidence that Robinson ever made use of the binding rule, but nonbinding caucuses were frequently held to mobilize support. In his four years as majority leader, Robinson pushed through the Senate most of the president's controversial New Deal legislative program, including measures he personally opposed.

Alben W. Barkley of Kentucky, who was elected majority leader after Robinson died of a heart attack in 1937, was also influential with his colleagues, but, like a growing number of Senate Democrats, he did not always support Roosevelt on domestic issues. In 1944 Barkley resigned his leadership post when FDR vetoed a revenue bill. He was promptly reelected by the Democrats, and the bill was passed over the president's veto.

THE JOHNSON YEARS

In the decades immediately after World War II two Republicans were widely acclaimed as effective Senate leaders. "Mr. Republican," Robert A. Taft of Ohio, was the majority leader for only a few months before he died in 1953, but he had been the de facto Republican power in the Senate since the early 1940s, just as Richard B. Russell, Ga., was the real leader of the Senate Democrats. Everett McKinley Dirksen of Illinois, known as the "wizard of ooze" for his florid style, was one of the more colorful personalities to grace the modern Senate. A conservative, he served as minority leader from 1959 until his death in 1969.

Taft and Dirksen employed two different styles—Taft won unity through his intellectual command of the issues; Dirksen won it through negotiation and compromise. Both men centralized the Republican leadership apparatus, controlling the formulation of Republican policy in the Senate and taking an active part in scheduling and setting floor strategy.

Taft and Dirksen may have had great influence among their Republican colleagues but their leadership talents were eclipsed by those of Lyndon Baines Johnson. Johnson, wrote political scientist John G. Stewart, "set for himself no less an objective than *running* the Senate, in fact as well as in theory. . . ."[61] Elected minority leader by the Democrats in 1953 after only four years in the Senate, Johnson became majority leader when the Democrats regained control of the Senate after the 1954 elections and served in that position until his resignation to become John F. Kennedy's vice president in 1961.

As a leader Johnson quickly became famous—some would say notorious—for his power of persuasion and his manipulative skills. Johnson was adroit at doing favors for and extending courtesies to his colleagues, their families, and staffs, at maneuvering his supporters onto desired committees and keeping his opponents off. He revitalized the Senate Democratic Policy Committee and modified the seniority system to ensure freshman Democrats at least one major committee assignment, a practice the Republicans also eventually adopted. On the floor he exploited to the fullest the majority leader's right of first recognition by the chair to control what was debated and under what terms. He was the first majority leader to make extensive use of unanimous consent agreements to control debate on legislation. He also used night sessions to wear down senators who might, if fresher, choose to engage in extensive floor debate. Perhaps most important, Johnson kept himself informed about the views and positions of his Senate colleagues through an active intelligence operation headed by Robert G. "Bobby" Baker, secretary to the Senate Democrats.

Johnson, whose entire tenure as both minority and majority leader was spent with Republican President Dwight D. Eisenhower in the White House, was also a master of compromise. He made sure to have allies among conservative southern Democrats and Republicans as well as among northern liberals. Similar to his mentor, House Speaker Sam Rayburn, Johnson worked to pass those elements of Eisenhower's legislative program that did not challenge basic tenets of Roosevelt's New Deal or Harry S. Truman's Fair Deal. As a result Johnson presided over some of the most productive years in Senate history.

The future president was renowned for what came to be known as the "Johnson Treatment," a tactic he carried with him into the White House. Rowland Evans and Robert Novak gave a vivid description in their book, *Lyndon B. Johnson: The Exercise of Power:*

> The Treatment could last ten minutes or four hours. It came, enveloping its target, at the LBJ Ranch swimming pool, in one of LBJ's offices, in the Senate cloakroom, on the floor of the Senate itself—wherever Johnson might find a fellow senator within his reach. Its tone could be supplication, accusation, cajolery, exuberance, scorn, tears, complaint, the hint of threat. It was all of these together. It ran the gamut of human emotions. Its velocity was breathtaking, and it was all in one direction. Interjections from the target were rare. Johnson anticipated them before they could be spoken. He moved in close, his face a scant millimeter from his target . . . his eyes widening and narrowing, his eyebrows rising and falling. From his pockets poured clippings, memos, statistics. Mimicry, humor, and the genius of analogy made The Treatment an almost hypnotic experience and rendered the target stunned and helpless.[62]

Johnson's effectiveness lost some of its edge after the 1958 elections added substantially to the Democrats' majority in the Senate. Members began to lose patience with Johnson's intensity; as one observer said, "After eight years of Lyndon Johnson, a lot of senators were just worn out."[63] An influx of liberal Democrats rejected the long-standing notion that junior senators were to be seen and not heard, and they began to chafe under Johnson's centralized leadership. In response Johnson stepped up the number of caucus meetings and named some freshmen to the Policy Committee. But calls from younger liberal members for greater inclusion in party matters continued to build.

By all accounts, Johnson was the most effective leader the Senate had ever seen, if not always the most liked. ("I know he comes off with high marks for getting things done, but he was repugnant to me," one senator recalled. "When I dealt with him I always had the feeling that I was standing on a trap door that was waiting to be sprung."[64]) Like the strong leaders before him, he derived his power primarily from his own force of personality, aided by his skill at finding out what his colleagues needed and wanted. As one observer put it, Johnson "worked at being better informed than anyone else, and that information then made him better equipped than anyone else to broker many agreements."[65]

Although he made innovative use of a number of institutional tools, such as unanimous consent, Johnson left the structure of the Senate itself largely untouched. When he left, Evans and Novak wrote, it was as though the leadership system he had constructed had never existed.

THE AGE OF COLLEGIALITY

Meanwhile other factors were changing the Senate substantially. Between the 1950s and the mid-1970s, southern domination and the seniority system gave way to a more decentralized, more democratic institution, in which junior members played a greater role. Party leaders on both sides of the aisle eschewed the arm-twisting tactics that Johnson used so effectively and engaged in a more collegial style of leadership, dependent for its success not on the leader's ability to bend the Senate to his will but on his ability to meet the expectations of his colleagues and to facilitate the conduct of Senate business.

Johnson's successor, Mike Mansfield, D-Mont., could not have provided a greater contrast in leadership styles. Known as the "gentle persuader," Mansfield, who served longer than any other majority leader in Senate history (1961–1977), was a permissive, at times even passive, leader. "I rarely asked for votes on specific legislation," Mansfield told political scientist Robert L. Peabody in 1972. "I assumed that these people are mature, that they have been sent back here by their constituents to exercise their own judgment. I will say that if on an issue they are doubtful I would hope that they will give the administration, if it's a

Democratic administration, the benefit of the doubt. Or if it's a party matter, that they will give the party the benefit of the doubt. But I don't believe in being pressured myself and I don't pressure other senators. I treat them as I would like to be treated myself."[66]

Though Mansfield was criticized for not being sufficiently partisan and for sometimes failing to provide direction, he was working with a larger, more liberal, and less cohesive group of Senate Democrats than Johnson had led. As congressional scholar Roger Davidson noted, "Most senators flourished under Mansfield's regime, for its very looseness gave them the leeway they needed to pursue their increasingly diverse legislative and career goals."[67]

When Mansfield retired from the Senate at the end of 1976, Democrats chose Robert Byrd of West Virginia as his successor for the first of two cycles as majority leader (1977–1981; 1987–1989). Byrd had been whip from 1971–1977, taking the post on a dramatic secret ballot away from Edward Kennedy, D-Mass., who had been distracted by the consequences of a 1969 accident at Chappaquiddick in Massachusetts, which resulted in the death of a passenger in a car driven by the senator. Byrd was in many ways an old-style Senate personality, but he also had to contend with a rapidly changing body that was more partisan, less patient, and with younger and more independent colleagues even more willing to employ the Senate's rules to press their interests and less susceptible than ever to party discipline. More significantly, Byrd also had to survive and adapt a leadership style to a Senate no longer with a firm Democratic majority, as the Republican Party took control from 1981–1987 and relegated him to minority leader.

While other senators built their careers on national issues and oratorical flair, Byrd was the quintessential insider, working quietly and diligently to build support through a combination of service to his colleagues and knowledge of Senate rules and procedures, skills he honed to near perfection during his six years as Democratic whip. As majority leader he so disadvantaged his opponents through the artful use of his parliamentary talents that the Republicans later hired the parliamentarian Byrd had fired, Robert B. Dove, to improve their procedural strategies. (Dove became Senate parliamentarian again in 1995).

A more activist leader than Mansfield, Byrd emphasized the need for strong party loyalty and said he wanted to bring about a resurgence of party spirit. He did not see his role as forcing an unpopular measure on his colleagues, who probably would not have accepted such a role in any event, but as trying to find consensus. Byrd tended to go to his colleagues with only the hint of an objective. If a consensus could be found that would attract the necessary number of votes, he would take the bill under his wing. "I talk to senators. I have meetings with senators, I try to stimulate a consensus for a party position on issues where one is necessary," he explained. "By getting a consensus first, senators are more likely to support the leadership."

Byrd had an uneasy relationship with President Carter, who came to the White House in 1977, the year Byrd became majority leader. Byrd seemed to regard Carter as an amateur with little aptitude for the exercise of power. Nonetheless, he repeatedly saved the Democratic administration in difficult legislative situations. Byrd played an indispensable role in the passage of Carter's energy policy package and in the extension of the deadline for ratification of the Equal Rights Amendment, among other matters. He successfully commanded the floor, with Vice President Walter Mondale in the chair to deny recognition to any other senator, to sweep dilatory amendments out of the way and successfully break a postcloture filibuster against the energy legislation by Senate liberals. Perhaps his most dramatic rescue operation came in 1978, when he amassed enough votes to ratify the Panama Canal treaties—giving canal ownership to Panama—through nonstop negotiation with wavering senators, personal diplomacy with Panamanian officials, and last-minute language changes.

Byrd also took steps to help the Senate conduct its business more smoothly, perfecting a track system that allowed noncontroversial measures to be dealt with while controversial legislation was being debated, and instituting periodic scheduled recesses, known as "nonlegislative work periods." Along the way he found time to write and deliver a series of Senate speeches—later published as a book—chronicling the history of the Senate from 1789 to 1989.

Despite his obvious love and respect for the Senate, Byrd was a private man, withdrawn from his colleagues; a former aide once noted that "Byrd was most comfortable in a room by himself."[68] His inability to develop a personal rapport with fellow senators combined with his emphasis on Senate procedures and prerogatives meant that though he was respected, Byrd was regarded by some as more of a technician than a leader. Dissatisfaction grew louder after the 1980 elections, when Republicans took control of the Senate and Byrd was relegated to what for him was the uncomfortable role of minority leader.

Byrd worked hard to reunite the party, scheduling weekly luncheon meetings of the Democratic Caucus, which had rarely met during the Carter years, and holding a series of weekend retreats in West Virginia where Democratic senators could work through many of their disagreements. He also set up several task forces to propose Democratic alternatives to President Reagan's legislative proposals.

But perceptions lingered that Byrd was too stilted and old-fashioned to be the Senate Democrats' national spokesperson in the age of television. After the 1984 elections Lawton Chiles, of Florida, challenged Byrd for the leadership post, but lost, 36–11. Never before had anyone challenged an incumbent Democratic leader in the Senate, and it was a sign of simmering discontent that Chiles, a cautious, moderate-to-conservative figure, had chosen to undertake it. J. Bennett Johnston, La., spent much of 1986 preparing to challenge Byrd, but when the Democrats regained control of the Senate, and by a much wider margin than had been expected, he quietly dropped his plans.

In his second tour as majority leader Byrd played the partisan spokesperson that his party seemed to want, rallying the

LEADERSHIP FIRSTS

From the very first, when Oliver Ellsworth of Connecticut exercised "more practical leadership in the day-to-day activities" of the Senate, the upper chamber has had unofficial leaders. But congressional scholars disagree as to who were the first official Senate floor leaders.

Some scholars, among them Randall B. Ripley, hold that the position of floor leader emerged around 1911. The chairmen of the Democratic Caucus—Thomas S. Martin of Virginia from 1911 to 1913 and John W. Kern of Illinois from 1913 to 1917—were clearly the party's leaders in the Senate, although it is unclear that the term "floor leader" was formally applied to either man.

In a 1988 pamphlet on the origins of Senate leadership, Senate parliamentarian emeritus Floyd M. Riddick wrote that neither party's caucus minutes used the term "leader" until 1920, when the Democratic minutes referred to Oscar W. Underwood, D-Ala., as "minority leader." (Underwood had also served two terms as majority leader in the House before being elected to the Senate.) According to Republican Caucus minutes, the first GOP Senate floor leader was Charles Curtis of Kansas (1924).

SOURCE: Walter J. Oleszek, "John Worth Kern," in *First Among Equals*, ed. Richard A. Baker and Roger H. Davidson (Washington, D.C.: CQ Press, 1991), 9–10.

Democrats behind an ambitious legislative agenda meant to show that the Democrats could govern. But criticisms of his leadership style and his media image continued, and in the spring of 1988 Byrd announced that he would retire from the leadership post at the end of the year to take up the chairmanship of the Senate Appropriations Committee and to become president pro tempore, where he was more active than previous occupants, sometimes choosing to preside over complex parliamentary situations where his knowledge of Senate rules was especially valuable. And on the Appropriations Committee, Byrd was in an even better position to direct billions of dollars to his home state. Even in the minority after 1994, Byrd remained an aggressive institutionalist, leading opposition to the enactment of the line-item veto in 1996 and challenging it in the Supreme Court. He was ultimately vindicated in 1998 when the Supreme Court, in a case brought by other persons, declared the law unconstitutional. *(See box, Line-Item Veto Experiment Ended by Supreme Court, p. 110.)*

THE MODERN LEADERSHIP: MITCHELL

The winner in a three-way race to succeed Byrd as majority leader was George J. Mitchell of Maine, unsuccessful Democratic nominee for Maine governor in 1974 and former federal judge. Mitchell was appointed to the Senate to fill the vacancy caused in 1980 by President Carter's appointment of Sen. Edmund Muskie as secretary of state, and did not have to run for election in that year. He quickly caught the notice of his colleagues with his keen memory for detail and his command of facts, particularly on environmental issues. Mitchell further impressed his fellow senators with his political skills when he came from thirty-six points behind to win election to a full term in 1982 with 61 percent of the vote.

Chosen to chair the Democratic Senatorial Campaign Committee for the critical 1986 elections, Mitchell was instrumental in helping the party regain control of the Senate with a wider-than-expected margin. As a reward he was made deputy president pro tempore, a post created for Hubert H. Humphrey, D-Minn., in 1977 and not occupied since. Appointed in 1986 to the joint committee investigating the Iran-contra scandal, involving the illegal transfer of arms by the Reagan administration to Nicaraguan rebels, Mitchell proved himself to be an able performer before national television cameras, a factor considered crucial to his election as majority leader over Louisiana's Bennett Johnston and Daniel K. Inouye of Hawaii.

Mitchell's background left him flexible enough for a variety of tasks awaiting the leader of a rapidly changing body that had just endured two shifts of partisan control. "The role of party leaders has changed so that . . . they have become conciliators who must set broad goals and then prepare themselves for incremental progress that may yield both policy change and eventual political support," *National Journal* reporter Richard E. Cohen has written.[69]

In his first year in the position, Mitchell won high marks for his legislative savvy and administration of the Senate. Toward the end of the session, he managed almost single-handedly to kill a capital gains tax cut sought by the Bush administration, which had passed the House when nearly a quarter of the Democrats there defected from the party position to support it. Early in 1990 he demonstrated the effectiveness of negotiation and persistence, working out a comprehensive compromise with the White House on a clean air bill when it became clear that the committee version could not overcome a filibuster and then fighting to protect the compromise from major amendment. The bill was assembled over a month of extraordinary closed door meetings just off the Senate floor run by Mitchell, who assembled key senators and administration representatives to thrash out details for a package that could be protected by a bipartisan majority coalition. Mitchell attributed his victory on the floor to direct, personal, face-to-face talks with his colleagues, urging them to stick with the compromise or see the entire bill collapse under the weight of controversial amendments. Mitchell also cemented his leadership by successfully staring down his predecessor, Byrd, whose efforts to protect coal miners threatened to unravel the bill. Byrd's key floor amendment was defeated by a single vote.

Republicans considered Mitchell partisan but his judicial demeanor often served to mask that aspect of his leadership. His more matter-of-fact debate style was a far cry from the sometimes emotional, florid performances of Johnson, Dirksen, and Byrd. Nonetheless, Mitchell often found the Senate as frustrating as they had. His announcement that he would not seek reelection in 1994 shocked colleagues. He quickly became the front-runner for a vacancy on the Supreme Court in that year,

Senate Majority Leader George Mitchell (left) meets with President-elect Bill Clinton and House Speaker Thomas Foley in 1993.

but Mitchell issued a statement asking that he not be considered and noting the importance of his presence as majority leader in trying (ultimately unsuccessfully) to push health care legislation through the Senate.

The result of Mitchell's departure, for Democrats, was loss of his Senate seat to the GOP and another hotly contested leadership fight.

The contest to succeed Mitchell as Democratic leader began as a contest between younger senators close to Mitchell and more senior traditionalists, although like any struggle by secret ballot in a highly personalized body the alliances did not always follow obvious or expected patterns. Mitchell's mantle fell on Sen. Thomas A. Daschle of South Dakota, elected in 1986, who had been made cochairman of the Policy Committee. Because the original senior contender for majority leader, Budget Committee Chairman Jim Sasser of Tennessee, appeared a likely loser in his reelection race, his supporters switched quickly to Christopher Dodd of Connecticut. When the Democrats lost control of the Senate in the 1994 elections, the battle became one over who would become minority leader. Dodd, elected in 1980, had substantial seniority over Daschle. But he lost to Daschle by one vote, 24–23, indicating, as did Mitchell's election, that senators had different criteria than seniority in mind in choosing leaders.

Daschle had served in the House and was attuned to the needs of a media-conscious Senate to develop a united party message. From 1995 to 1998, Daschle enjoyed considerable success as Senate minority leader. Although his Democratic colleagues in the Senate were further reduced to forty-five at the start of the 105th Congress—which was also the party's low-point in strength during the 1980s—Daschle was able to keep the Democrats together during many cloture votes.

MODERN REPUBLICAN LEADERSHIP

Republican leadership styles in the age of collegiality paralleled those of the Democrats. Hugh Scott of Pennsylvania, who was narrowly elected to succeed Dirksen in 1969, was less assertive but perhaps even more flexible than Dirksen. His leadership of compromise and accommodation was very much like Mansfield's, but Scott was considered a rather ineffective leader. His moderate-to-liberal politics sometimes made it difficult for him to serve as a spokesperson for the Nixon and Ford administrations, and his support, first of U.S. action in Vietnam long after many of his colleagues and constituents had turned against it, and then of Nixon well into the Watergate crisis, further undermined his standing.

Scott, who retired at the end of 1976, was succeeded by Dirksen's son-in-law, Howard H. Baker Jr., of Tennessee. Baker had sought the post twice before, running unsuccessfully against Scott in 1969 and 1971. Baker was best known for adopting an aura of bipartisanship during the televised 1973 hearings of the Senate Watergate Committee, where he served as the ranking Republican to folksy Chairman Sam Ervin, D-N.C., and for asking the famous question "What did the President know and when did he know it?" In 1977 his colleagues, apparently convinced that he would be a more articulate spokesperson for the party, elected Baker minority leader over minority whip Robert P. Griffin of Michigan by a single vote. When the Republicans took over the Senate in 1981, Baker was made majority leader with no opposition.

A relaxed manner and close friendships with many of his Republican colleagues were Baker's principal assets. He was open and accessible to GOP senators of every ideology and was committed to protecting their rights. As majority leader, Baker was able to hold the disparate group of Republicans together on most issues during Reagan's first year in office. But when the economy faltered in late 1981, old divisions between moderate and conservative Republicans reopened, and unity became more difficult to achieve.

Baker's job was increasingly frustrated by the procedural chaos that gripped the Senate. His penchant for accommodation created a situation in which nearly every senator expected the schedule to conform to his or her personal needs. Floor action was delayed by senators who asked for "holds" on legislation—guarantees that a particular matter would not be taken up until the senator was present to protect his or her interests. Baker eventually announced that he would no longer consider holds sacrosanct, nor would he stack votes for the convenience of members who wanted more time to return to their home states. But there was little Baker could do to prevent individual members from tying up the Senate with filibusters and other delaying tactics.

In January 1983 Baker announced that he would retire from the Senate after the 1984 elections. To succeed him as majority leader, Republicans elected Bob Dole of Kansas over four other candidates.

DOLE: SHARP TACTICS, HARD EDGES

After four years of Baker's easygoing stewardship, Republican senators opted for a leader who they thought would restore some discipline and sense of purpose to a chamber increasingly bogged down in procedural chaos.

Five candidates entered the lists: Dole; Ted Stevens, Alaska, the majority whip; Richard G. Lugar, Ind.; Pete V. Domenici, N.M.; and James McClure, Idaho. It was the first time since 1937 that the selection of a Senate majority leader came down to a vote in a party body. On the first ballot, McClure fell out of the race, followed on subsequent ones by Domenici and then Lugar. On the fourth ballot, Dole won, 28–25.

Dole was chairman of the Republican National Committee at the time of the Watergate burglary in 1972 but was forced out of the post at the beginning of 1973 and was never associated with the scandal. "Watergate happened on my night off," he said. Dole, as the nominee for vice president on the Republican's unsuccessful 1976 national ticket, had suffered a memorable embarrassing moment in debate with the Democratic nominee, Sen. Walter Mondale, D-Minn., by referring to World Wars I and II as "Democrat (sic) Wars." It cemented the public image of Dole as a harsh and humorless partisan, which he tried with only mixed success to mellow in later years. He also ran briefly for president in 1980, but dropped out without mounting a serious effort.

However, despite his often glowering persona on national television, in the Senate Dole moved steadily into the position of insider who was willing to negotiate and valued legislative achievement. Dole had a hand in much of the important legislation of a generation, from taxes to Social Security to civil rights to protections for the disabled. He ably chaired the Finance Committee for four years (1981–1985) before ascending to the leadership, and ultimately Dole was to become the longest serving Republican Senate leader in history (1985–1996).

In addition to his image as a decisive leader, Dole was known as a superb negotiator with an ability to find compromises where others had failed. "You don't try to cram things down people's throats," he once said. "You try to work it out." Many of his colleagues, especially those up for reelection in 1986, thought he would also be willing to stand up to the Reagan White House when needed to protect their political interests. Of the candidates for majority leader, Dole was considered the least likely to toe the White House line on legislation. He had disagreed with president Reagan on issues as diverse as food stamps, civil rights, and tax policy.

That did not mean that Dole was anything less than an aggressive advocate for the administration on a broad range of issues. With a thin 53–47 Republican majority in his first term as majority leader, Dole produced significant victories, helping to pass tax revision, a new immigration law, a new farm bill, and aid to the Nicaraguan contras. Although Dole restored a modicum of discipline to the Senate, some of his methods—lengthy sessions and complicated parliamentary tactics intended to disarm obstructionists—were not popular with his colleagues and in some instances had only minimal effect. Democrats often gleefully used Dole's past image as a tough political hatchet man against him. They successfully ran against the Republicans' conservative budget priorities as well as the weaknesses of many members of the Republican's class of 1980, who proved too weak to withstand a campaign without an accompanying presidential landslide.

Dole was relegated to minority leader from 1987–1995. He ran again for the Republican presidential nomination in 1988, winning the Iowa caucuses before losing the New Hampshire primary to Vice President George Bush's better focused effort. As minority leader, Dole was considered a tough partisan who was particularly effective in mobilizing Republicans against President Clinton's 1993 economic stimulus package, which was killed by a filibuster signaling that Republicans would give Clinton no honeymoon.

In his second incarnation as majority leader in 1995 and part of 1996, Dole became the front-runner for the Republican presidential nomination, but as a congressional leader he played second fiddle to Speaker Gingrich during the first session of the 104th Congress. Known to be skeptical of elements of the "Contract with America," Dole was uncomfortable with the House's breakneck pace and what he regarded as careless legislating. However, Dole pushed aggressively for elements of the GOP plan, particularly the constitutional amendment requiring a

Republican Senate Majority Leader Trent Lott (at podium) holds a press conference with other members of the GOP Senate leadership in 1998.

balanced federal budget that had passed the House for the first time in 1995. Dole's aggressive tactics angered Democrats, who accused him of breaking an agreement by delaying a final vote that would have defeated the proposal, as he tried to secure one additional vote. However, the defection of Sen. Mark Hatfield, chairman of the Appropriations Committee and the only Republican to oppose the amendment, killed any chance of it passing and deeply embarrassed Senate Republicans.

After Speaker Gingrich was badly weakened following the fiasco of the two government shutdowns during the winter of 1995–1996, Dole took the initiative to force an end to the controversy and to repudiate conservative House members who wanted to continue the shutdown.

Democrats in 1996 successfully tied down Dole in the Senate, blocking legislation and making him appear frustrated and ineffective. Realizing that trying to run the Senate was incompatible with his ambitions for the White House, Dole surprised his colleagues by resigning not only from the leadership but the Senate itself in the spring of 1996. After losing the presidential election to Clinton overwhelmingly, Dole joined a law firm.

LOTT: PRAGMATIC IDEOLOGUE

Sen. Trent Lott, R-Miss., had crashed his way into the GOP leadership in 1994 by defeating the combative, but less conservative incumbent Alan Simpson of Wyoming for majority whip by a single vote. In his new role, there was speculation that Lott would push Dole to the right but the two leaders moved to put aside their initially uneasy relationship.

Lott became majority leader in mid-1996 after squashing a campaign by his senior Mississippi colleague and longtime rival, Thad Cochran, 44–8. Lott seemed well suited to lead the most conservative Senate since the 1920s, with a 55–45 Republican majority in the 105th Congress. He came into office with high expectations. Once considered a sharp-edged ideologue from his days in the House as minority whip from 1981 to 1989, Lott did not use the Senate's top post, as some thought, to transform the chamber into an engine of conservative activism similar to the House. That perception may have been buttressed by an increasing number of conservative Republican senators who had served in the House and agreed with many of the views of Gingrich and the 1994 GOP freshman class.

However, Lott had broad legislative experience that characterized House leadership. He also had an accommodating personal style, unlike the often harsh tones Gingrich took in the House. The nature of the Senate itself made such a strategy impractical. Like many Senate leaders, Lott found that a more successful approach was to accommodate a leadership style to the institution of the Senate than it was to change that body to suit outside constituencies. "Senate majority leaders are so highly constrained by institutional arrangements, the variations we see among them in strategy and tactics are very small," notes political scientist Steven Smith.

The challenge of mustering votes from the minority side in the House gave Lott formidable training for his whip role in the Senate. And it gave him valuable ties to colleagues of both parties, many of whom had since been elected to the Senate.

Lott has been very effective at the sort of member-to-member, retail politics that have traditionally sustained cooperation and inoculated leaders from assault in the Senate. The smiling, affable demeanor of Lott, a former cheerleader at the University

CAMPAIGN AID: PRIORITY ROLE FOR PARTY LEADERS

Helping their members win reelection and wresting seats away from the other party are top priority jobs for party leaders in Congress. Given the ever-mounting cost of House and Senate election campaigns, fund-raising is probably the most valuable service the leadership can provide. In addition to attending fund-raising dinners and receptions in members' home districts or states, many leaders in both parties have established their own political action committees (PACs) that solicit money from unions, corporations, and other contributors, which the leaders then channel to candidates. Commonly referred to as "leadership PACS" or "congressional PACS," these fund-raising tools are formed by ambitious members to help party candidates win seats, expand party representation, and establish a sense of gratitude among beneficiaries when leadership positions are decided.

The major campaign efforts, however, are handled by special party committees set up expressly for the purpose: the Democratic Congressional Campaign Committee (DCCC) and the National Republican Congressional Committee (NRCC) in the House; and the Democratic Senatorial Campaign Committee (DSCC) and the National Republican Senatorial Committee (NRSC) in the Senate. Chaired by members of Congress, these committees help identify candidates to challenge incumbents of the other party or to run for open seats. They brief candidates on the issues and help them with all phases of campaigning, advising—even supplying—campaign managers, finance directors, and press secretaries. They also play an increasingly important role in recruiting candidates.

These committees also raise and disburse millions of dollars. For the 1996 elections, the Democratic committees raised nearly $57 million on behalf of their candidates; the Republican committees nearly $139 million.

The party campaign committees are important to candidates not only as sources of money but also because they attract funding from other contributors. Given the high cost of campaigns and the limits on campaign contributions, a commitment from a congressional party entity can help a candidate cross an important threshold of credibility with other potential sources of funding. The party committees almost invariably give to an incumbent of their party if there is a challenge in the primary, except in unusual circumstances. For example, in 1998, the NRCC worked aggressively to shore up Rep. William Goodling of Pennsylvania, chairman of the House Committee on Education and the Workforce, in a primary against an opponent who had won 45 percent of the vote against him two years earlier. Goodling won the rematch easily. But at the same time, it refused to support Rep. Jay Kim of California for renomination in 1998 after he had pleaded guilty to campaign finance law violations in earlier campaigns, was sentenced to house arrest, and was forced to campaign from Washington, where he had been required to wear an electronic monitoring device. Kim lost in the primary.

Incumbents are routinely asked to contribute to the party committee in their chamber, and also for special purposes, such as hotly contested special elections that may arise in the House.

of Mississippi, provided a stark contrast with the dour, acerbic Dole, generating praise even from Democrats.

Lott did not often employ the all-or-nothing tactics employed by House Republicans in 1995. Faced with an opportunity for legislative achievement at the expense of ideological purity, Lott grabbed it eagerly, disposing of major legislation to raise the minimum wage, improve the safety of drinking water, guarantee health insurance coverage for displaced workers, and overhaul the nation's welfare system. The fact that some of these initiatives were favored by Democrats and passed over the opposition of conservatives did not prevent Lott from claiming credit for substantial legislative accomplishments and increasing the GOP majority by one in the 1996 election even as the President Clinton was trouncing his predecessor, Dole. Lott's impeccable conservative credentials enabled him to strike deals with Democrats without arousing the mistrust of Republicans, who, he told a reporter, "know where my heart is."

As the 105th Congress neared its end, Lott had not yet become a high-profile national figure, as had Gingrich. With the Speaker weakened politically, it had been anticipated that Lott, with a larger GOP majority in his chamber—at least in percentage terms—would assume a more prominent role as party spokesperson. However, Lott demonstrated no rush to fill such a role. And when he did step forward as a party spokesperson, Lott sometimes was too open for his troops' tastes, as when early in 1998 he called on special prosecutor Kenneth Starr to wrap up his investigation of the Clinton presidency, when many Republicans considered the variety of alleged presidential scandals ripe for lengthy political exploitation.

Party Support Structure in the Senate

The leadership hierarchy in the Senate is not as strong as that in the House, but the apparatus follows a lot of the same patterns. The party support structure is composed of party whips, the party conference, and other party committees.

PARTY WHIPS

The first whips appeared in the Senate about the same time the floor leader positions were being institutionalized. The Democrats designated J. Hamilton Lewis of Illinois their first whip in 1913; in 1915 James W. Wadsworth Jr., R-N.Y., was named the first GOP whip.

Although the duties of Senate whips are essentially the same as those of their House counterparts, the whip organizations are much less prominent in the Senate than in the House. For one thing, their functions and duties are less institutionalized, and their organizations much less elaborate. The majority and mi-

The party committees often decline to support candidates for an open seat that is being contested in a primary. But if one candidate is believed to be visibly stronger for the general election early intervention can help that candidate win the primary and begin an earlier focus on the general election. With party control of Congress closely divided, especially in the House, such intervention may become much more common. Recruitment activities by the party committees can also be expected to intensify.

To help attract additional funding, the party committees work on selling their candidates to PACs through meetings with the candidates, briefings, even newsletters. Party committees can also play a crucial role by giving a promising challenger money to get his or her campaign off the ground or by channeling funding into a sagging campaign.

Raising campaign funds for one's colleagues is not new. In his book *The Path to Power,* Robert A. Caro writes that in 1940 Lyndon B. Johnson, then in his third year in the House, tapped into Texas oil money, directing it to Democratic colleagues. His endeavors are credited with saving thirty to forty Democratic seats, which kept the House from going Republican. Of course, campaign finance laws, and the amounts of money potentially available, have changed dramatically since then but the leadership's interest has not.

In more recent times, House Majority Whip Tony Coelho, D-Calif., and Senate Majority Leader George J. Mitchell, D-Maine, won their leadership positions in part because of their success in directing their respective campaign committees. Mitchell ran the committee for the 1986 election cycle, when Democrats regained control of the Senate. Similarly, Rep. Bill Paxon, R-N.Y., used his success running the NRCC before the 1994 election, when the Republicans gained control of the House, to position himself for a run for higher office in the GOP leadership before suddenly announcing his retirement in 1998 to spend more time with his family. Indeed, fund-raising for colleagues seems to have become a prerequisite for anyone who wants to join the party leadership. Mitchell's two challengers for the post of majority leader in 1988 both set up PACs to direct campaign funds to colleagues. Mitchell did not set up a PAC but indirectly channeled money to colleagues when asked for advice from other PACs and contributors.

Today, campaign aid is one of the services that leaders are expected to provide their rank and file. It is a service that can also benefit the leadership when the time comes to ask for support for the parties' legislative programs in Congress. More disturbingly, however, the money chase has filtered down to other levels of leadership activities, such as the assignment of members to committees. It is not uncommon for members on the leadership panels making such assignments to examine how financially supportive an applicant for an important legislative committee has been to other, more vulnerable, colleagues.

nority leaders in the Senate also generally assume some of what the whip's responsibilities would be in the House.

Senate whips at times have openly defied their own party leaders. Both parties elect their whips in the Senate, and the political maneuvering entailed in running for the office has sometimes led members to back certain senators for reasons that may have little to do with leadership effectiveness.

A serious breach occurred between Majority Leader Mansfield and Russell B. Long, La., the Democratic whip from 1965 to 1969. The two first clashed in 1966 over Long's proposal for federal subsidies for presidential election campaigns. Long exacerbated the dispute in 1967 by sending a newsletter to constituents in which he listed his disagreements with President Johnson (and Mansfield) on the issue. Mansfield sought to circumvent Long's influence by appointing four assistant whips. Long was defeated for whip by Edward Kennedy in 1969 (although Long eventually won the policy battle in 1971, when Congress finally approved public financing legislation).

Long lost his bid for reelection perhaps as much because he had been insufficiently attentive to the day-to-day details of the whip's job as because of any lingering ill-feeling between him and Mansfield. His successor, Kennedy, who was neither a particularly active nor effective whip, and was crippled early in his tenure by the auto accident at Chappaquiddick. In 1971 he lost his bid for reelection to Robert C. Byrd, then secretary of the Democratic Conference.

Alan Cranston, of California, who was elected Democratic whip when Byrd became majority leader, was particularly effective in that post. A liberal able to build bridges to Senate moderates and conservatives, he demonstrated a remarkable ability to sense shifts in sentiments as legislation moved toward the Senate floor and through the years put together numerous winning coalitions.

Senate whips do not move up the leadership ladder as regularly as House whips do. Although Johnson, Mansfield, and Byrd all did so, Cranston did not even seek the leadership spot when Byrd announced he would vacate it in 1989. When Cranston left the Senate in 1993, he was succeeded by the more conservative and low-key Wendell H. Ford of Kentucky, who did not run in the 1994 race to replace George Mitchell. On the Republican side the whips who moved up to floor leader in recent times have been Dirksen, Scott, and Lott, with Robert Griffin and Ted Stevens trying and losing.

PARTY CONFERENCES

The development of party caucuses (now called conferences) in the Senate paralleled that of the House. In 1846 the party caucus increased in importance by acquiring the authority to make committee assignments. During the Civil War and Reconstruction era, Republicans used the caucus frequently to discuss and adopt party positions on legislation.

In the 1890s Republican leaders Allison and Aldrich used the caucus extensively and effectively. As Rothman observed, "The Republican caucus was not binding, and yet its decisions commanded obedience for party leadership was capable of enforcing discipline. Senators could no longer act with impunity unless they were willing to forego favorable committee posts and control of the chamber proceedings."[70]

It is unlikely that any Senate Democrats ever were penalized for not abiding by a binding caucus rule adopted in 1903. But they used the rule to achieve remarkable unity in 1913–1914 in support of President Wilson's legislative objectives. Twenty years later, charged with enacting Franklin Roosevelt's New Deal, Democrats readopted the rule. It was not employed, but frequent nonbinding caucuses were held to mobilize support. Since that time neither party has seriously considered using caucus votes to enforce party loyalty on legislative issues.

Both party conferences elect the various party leaders and ratify committee chairmanship and ranking minority member posts and other committee assignments. After resuming control of the Senate in the 104th Congress, Republicans amended their conference rules to limit service in elected party leadership posts, except floor leader and president pro tempore, to no more than three Congresses. The affected positions would be majority whip, conference chairman and conference secretary, chairman of the policy committee, and chairman of the National Republican Senatorial Committee (NRSC), though that post has traditionally rotated. In recent years both parties have used the conference to collect and distribute information to members, to perform legislative research, and to ratify decisions made by the policy committees. Each conference meets weekly for luncheons to discuss scheduling and strategy. Administration officials sometimes attend their party's sessions.

OTHER PARTY COMMITTEES

The two Senate parties each have a policy committee, a committee on committees (called the Steering Committee by the Democrats), and a campaign committee. Traditionally the Democratic leader chaired the party conference as well as the Policy and Steering committees, giving him significant potential power to control the party apparatus. Breaking with that custom, George Mitchell gave responsibility for the Steering Committee to Inouye and made Daschle cochair, with Mitchell, of the Policy Committee. The Republican Conference and party committees traditionally are chaired by different senators, thus diffusing power among Senate Republicans.

The first of the party committees to be created was the Committee on Committees, which originated during the Civil War era, when Republicans, then in the majority, used a special panel appointed by its party caucus to make both Republican and Democratic committee assignments. Senate Democrats set up a Committee on Committees in 1879. Committee assignments made by each of these committees are subject to ratification by the respective party conference and the full chamber.

What was, in effect, the first Senate Steering Committee was established in 1874, when the GOP Conference appointed a Committee on the Order of Business to prepare a schedule for Senate floor action. That committee was replaced in the mid-1880s by a Steering Committee appointed by the caucus chairman. Democrats established a Steering Committee in 1879 but abandoned it when the Republicans regained control of the Senate and the legislative agenda. They did not set up another Steering Committee until 1893 when the Democrats once again controlled the Senate.

In 1947 both parties created policy committees that were assigned the scheduling functions of the old Steering committees. At the same time the Democratic Steering Committee, while retaining its name, was reconstituted as the party's committee on committees. The Policy committees—which prepare material on issues and legislation and discuss broad questions of party policy—have been more or less active, depending on the needs of the party leadership and whether the party was in or out of the majority.

Under Daschle's leadership, for example, the Democratic Policy Committee stepped up its analysis of the issues and put together an ambitious policy agenda for Senate Democrats.

NOTES

1. Christopher J. Deering and Steven S. Smith, "Majority Party Leadership and the New House Subcommittee System," in *Understanding Congressional Leadership,* ed. Frank B. Mackaman (Washington, D.C.: CQ Press, 1981), 288–289.
2. Roger H. Davidson and Walter J. Oleszek, *Congress and Its Members,* 6th ed. (Washington, D.C.: CQ Press, 1998), 174–175.
3. Ibid., 175.
4. Ibid., 156.
5. Ibid., 175.
6. Richard E. Cohen, "Byrd of West Virginia: A New Job, A New Image," *National Journal,* August 20, 1977, 1295.
7. Richard E. Cohen, "Taking Advantage of Tax Reform Means Different Strokes for Different Folks," *National Journal,* June 22, 1985, 1459.
8. Howard Fineman, "For the Son of C-Span, Exposure Equals Power," *Newsweek,* April 3, 1989, 23.
9. Michael J. Malbin, "House Democrats Are Playing with a Strong Leadership Lineup," *National Journal,* June 18, 1977, 942.
10. Davidson and Oleszek, *Congress and Its Members,* 157.
11. Floyd M. Riddick, *The United States Congress: Organization and Procedure* (Washington, D.C.: National Capitol Publishers, 1949), 67.
12. Mary P. Follett, *The Speaker of the House of Representatives* (New York: Burt Franklin Reprints, 1974), 25–26 (reprint of 1896 edition).
13. George B. Galloway, *History of the House of Representatives* (New York: Crowell, 1961), 20.
14. Ronald M. Peters Jr., *The American Speakership: The Office in Historical Perspective* (Baltimore: Johns Hopkins University Press, 1990), 31.
15. Follett, *The Speaker of the House of Representatives,* 82.
16. George Rothwell Brown, *The Leadership of Congress* (New York: Arno Press, 1974), 37–38 (reprint of 1922 edition).
17. Peters, *The American Speakership,* 35–36.

18. Steven S. Smith and Christopher J. Deering, *Committees in Congress,* 2nd ed. (Washington, D.C.: CQ Press, 1990), 28.

19. Peters, *The American Speakership,* 36.

20. Follett, *The Speaker of the House of Representatives,* 84.

21. Hubert B. Fuller, *The Speaker of the House* (Boston: Little, Brown, 1909), 26.

22. Galloway, *History of the House of Representatives,* 51.

23. Ibid., 132.

24. Ibid., 133.

25. Barbara W. Tuchman, *The Proud Tower: A Portrait of the World before the War: 1890–1914* (New York: Macmillan, 1966), 127.

26. Fuller, *The Speaker of the House,* 244.

27. Peters, *The American Speakership,* 77.

28. Fuller, *The Speaker of the House,* 257.

29. Robert Luce, *Congress: An Explanation* (Cambridge, Mass.: Harvard University Press, 1926), 117.

30. Peters, *The American Speakership,* 94.

31. Randall B. Ripley, *Party Leaders in the House of Representatives* (Washington, D.C.: Brookings Institution, 1967), 101.

32. Galloway, *History of the House of Representatives,* 144.

33. *U.S. News & World Report,* October 13, 1950, 30.

34. Peters, *The American Speakership,* 140–141.

35. John M. Barry, *The Ambition and the Power* (New York: Viking Penguin, 1989), 4.

36. Alan Ehrenhalt, ed., *Politics in America: Members of Congress in Washington and at Home, 1986* (Washington, D.C.: CQ Press, 1985), 1507.

37. Peters, *The American Speakership,* 280.

38. Phil Duncan, ed., *Politics in America, 1990* (Washington, D.C.: CQ Press, 1989), 2.

39. Christopher Madison, "The Heir Presumptive," *National Journal,* April 29, 1989, 1036.

40. Ibid., 1035.

41. *1995 Congressional Quarterly Almanac* (Washington, D.C.: Congressional Quarterly, 1996), I-21.

42. Barbara Sinclair, "Transformational Leader or Faithful Agent? Innovation and Continuity in House Majority Party Leadership: The 104th and 105th Congresses," paper presented at 1997 meeting of the American Political Science Association, Washington, D.C., 9.

43. Neil MacNeil, *Forge of Democracy: The House of Representatives* (New York: McKay, 1963), 87.

44. Peters, *The American Speakership,* 92.

45. Galloway, *History of the House of Representatives,* 108.

46. Barbara Sinclair, *Majority Leadership in the U.S. House* (Baltimore: Johns Hopkins University Press, 1983), 46.

47. Floyd M. Riddick, *Congressional Procedure* (Boston: Chapman & Grimes, 1941), 345–346.

48. Irwin B. Arieff, "Inside Congress," *Congressional Quarterly Weekly Report,* February 28, 1981, 379.

49. Ripley, *Party Leaders in the House of Representatives,* 29.

50. Duncan, ed., *Politics in America, 1990,* 470.

51. Sinclair, *Majority Leadership in the U.S. House,* 57.

52. Sinclair, "Transformational Leader," 20.

53. Barbara Sinclair, "Majority Party Leadership Strategies for Coping with the New U.S. House," in *Understanding Congressional Leadership,* ed. Frank H. Mackaman (Washington, D.C.: CQ Press, 1981), 202.

54. Galloway, *History of the House of Representatives,* 130.

55. Sinclair, *Majority Leadership in the U.S. House,* 96–97.

55. George H. Haynes, *The Senate of the United States: Its History and Practices,* (Boston: Houghton Mifflin, 1938), vol. 2, 1003.

56. Randall B. Ripley, *Power in the Senate* (New York: St. Martin's Press, 1969), 24.

57. W. E. Binkley, *The Powers of the President* (New York: Russell & Russell, 1973), 52.

58. David J. Rothman, *Politics and Power: The United States Senate 1869–1901* (Cambridge, Mass.: Harvard University Press, 1966), 19.

59. Charles O. Jones, *The Minority Party in Congress* (Boston: Little, Brown, 1970), 48.

60. Rothman, *Politics and Power,* 44.

61. John G. Stewart, "Two Strategies of Leadership: Johnson and Mansfield," in *Congressional Behavior,* ed. Nelson W. Polsby (New York: Random House, 1971), 61–92.

62. Rowland Evans and Robert Novak, *Lyndon B. Johnson: The Exercise of Power* (New York: New American Library, 1966), 104.

63. Roger H. Davidson, "The Senate: If Everyone Leads, Who Follows?" in *Congress Reconsidered,* 4th ed., ed. Lawrence C. Dodd and Bruce I. Oppenheimer (Washington, D.C.: CQ Press, 1989), 280.

64. Ross K. Baker, *Friend and Foe in the U.S. Senate* (New York: The Free Press, 1980), 203.

65. Barbara Sinclair, "Congressional Leadership: A Review Essay," in *Leading Congress: New Styles, New Strategies,* ed. John J. Kornacki (Washington, D.C.: CQ Press, 1990), 141.

66. Robert L. Peabody, "Senate Party Leadership: From the 1950s to the 1980s," in *Understanding Congressional Leadership,* ed. Frank B. Mackaman (Washington, D.C.: CQ Press, 1981), 59.

67. Davidson, "The Senate: If Everyone Leads, Who Follows?" in *Congress Reconsidered,* 281.

68. Janet Hook, "Mitchell Learns Inside Game; Is Cautious as Party Voice," *Congressional Quarterly Weekly Report,* September 9, 1989, 2294.

69. Richard E. Cohen, *Washington at Work: Back Rooms and Clean Air* (Needham Heights, Mass.: Allyn and Bacon, 1995), 96.

70. Rothman, *Politics and Power,* 60.

SELECTED BIBLIOGRAPHY

Alexander, De Alva Stanwood. *History and Procedure of the House of Representatives.* Boston: Houghton Mifflin, 1916.

Baker, Richard A., and Roger H. Davidson, eds. *First Among Equals: Outstanding Senate Leaders of the Twentieth Century.* Washington, D.C.: Congressional Quarterly, 1991.

Baker, Ross K. *Friend and Foe in the U.S. Senate.* New York: The Free Press, 1980.

——. *House and Senate.* 2nd ed. New York: Norton, 1995.

Baldwin, Louis. *Hon. Politician: Mike Mansfield of Montana.* Missoula, Mont.: Mountain Press Publishing, 1979.

Barry, John M. *The Ambition and the Power.* New York: Viking Penguin, 1989.

Bolles, Blair. *Tyrant from Illinois: Uncle Joe Cannon's Experiment with Personal Power.* New York: Norton, 1951.

Bolling, Richard W. *House Out of Order.* New York: Dutton, 1965.

——. *Power in the House: A History of the Leadership of the House of Representatives.* New York: Dutton, 1968.

Brown, George Rothwell. *The Leadership of Congress.* New York: Arno Press, 1974.

Burns, James MacGregor. *Leadership.* New York: Harper and Row, 1978.

Busbey, L. White. *Uncle Joe Cannon.* New York: Henry Holt, 1927.

Byrd, Robert C. *The Senate, 1789–1989: Addresses on the History of the United States Senate.* 2 vols. Washington, D.C.: Government Printing Office, 1988.

Chiu, Chang-Wei. *The Speaker of the House of Representatives since 1896.* New York: Columbia University Press, 1928.

Clancy, Paul, and Shirley Elder. *Tip: A Biography of Thomas P. O'Neill, Speaker of the House.* New York: Macmillan, 1980.

Clark, Joseph S. *The Senate Establishment.* New York: Hill & Wang, 1963.

Cohen, Richard E. *Washington at Work: Back Rooms and Clean Air.* Needham Heights, Mass.: Allyn and Bacon, 1995.

Connelly, William F., and John J. Pitney Jr. *Congress' Permanent Minority? Republicans in the U.S. House.* Lanham, Md.: Rowman and Littlefield, 1994.

Davidson, Roger H., and Walter J. Oleszek. *Congress and Its Members.* 6th ed. Washington, D.C.: CQ Press, 1998.

Dodd, Lawrence C., and Bruce I. Oppenheimer, eds. *Congress Reconsidered.* 6th ed. Washington, D.C.: CQ Press, 1997.

Evans, C. Lawrence, and Walter J. Oleszek. *Congress Under Fire: Reform Politics and the Republican Majority.* Boston: Houghton Mifflin, 1997.

Evans, Rowland, and Robert Novak. *Lyndon B. Johnson: The Exercise of Power.* New York: New American Library, 1966.

Fiorina, Morris P., and David W. Rohde, eds. *Home Style and Washington Work: Studies of Congressional Politics.* Ann Arbor: University of Michigan Press, 1989.

Follett, Mary P. *The Speaker of the House of Representatives.* New York: Longmans, Green, 1896. Reprint. New York: Burt Franklin Reprints, 1974.

Fuller, Hubert Bruce. *The Speakers of the House.* Boston: Little, Brown, 1909.

Galloway, George B. *History of the House of Representatives.* New York: Crowell, 1961.

Gillespie, Ed, and Bob Schellhas, eds. *Contract with America.* New York: Times Books, 1994.

Hardeman, D. B., and Donald C. Bacon. *Rayburn.* Austin: Texas Monthly Press, 1987.

Haynes, George H. *The Senate of the United States: Its History and Practice.* 2 vols. Boston: Houghton Mifflin, 1938.

Hinckley, Barbara. *Stability and Change in Congress.* 4th ed. New York: Harper and Row, 1988.

Jones, Charles O. *The Minority Party in Congress.* Boston: Little, Brown, 1970.

Koopman, Douglas L. *Hostile Takeover: The House Republican Party, 1980–1995.* Lanham, Md.: Rowman and Littlefield, 1996.

Kornacki, John J., ed. *Leading Congress: New Styles, New Strategies.* Washington, D.C.: CQ Press, 1990.

Loomis, Burdett A. *The New American Politician.* New York: Basic Books, 1988.

Mackaman, Frank H., ed. *Understanding Congressional Leadership.* Washington, D.C.: CQ Press, 1981.

MacNeil, Neil. *Dirksen: Portrait of a Public Man.* New York: World Publishing, 1970.

——. *Forge of Democracy: The House of Representatives.* New York: McKay, 1963.

Mann, Thomas, and Norman J. Ornstein, eds. *The New Congress.* Washington, D.C.: American Enterprise Institute, 1981.

O'Neill, Thomas P. Jr., with William Novak. *Man of the House: The Life and Political Memoirs of Speaker Tip O'Neill.* New York: Random House, 1987.

Peabody, Robert L. *Leadership in Congress: Stability, Succession and Change.* Boston: Little, Brown, 1976.

Peters, Ronald M. Jr. *The American Speakership: The Office in Historical Perspective.* Baltimore: Johns Hopkins University Press, 1990.

——, ed. *The Speaker: Leadership in the U.S. House of Representatives.* Washington, D.C.: Congressional Quarterly, 1995.

Ranney, Austin. *Channels of Power.* New York: Basic Books, 1983.

Reedy, George E. *The U.S. Senate: Paralysis or a Search for Consensus?* New York: Crown, 1986.

Riddick, Floyd M. *The United States Congress: Organization and Procedure.* Manassas, Va.: National Capitol Publishers, 1949.

Ripley, Randall B. *Congress: Process and Policy.* 4th ed. New York: Norton, 1988.

——. *Majority Party Leadership in Congress.* Boston: Little, Brown, 1969.

——. *Party Leaders in the House of Representatives.* Washington, D.C.: Brookings Institution, 1967.

——. *Power in the Senate.* New York: St. Martin's Press, 1969.

Robinson, William A. *Thomas B. Reed: Parliamentarian.* New York: Dodd, Mead, 1930.

Rothman, David J. *Politics and Power: The United States Senate, 1869–1901.* Cambridge, Mass.: Harvard University Press, 1966.

Sinclair, Barbara. *Majority Leadership in the U.S. House.* Baltimore: Johns Hopkins University Press, 1983.

——. *The Transformation of the U.S. Senate.* Baltimore: Johns Hopkins University Press, 1989.

——. "Transformational Leader or Faithful Agent? Innovation and Continuity in House Majority Party Leadership: The 104th and 105th Congresses." Paper presented at the meeting of the American Political Science Association, Washington, D.C., August 1997.

Steinberg, Alfred. *Sam Rayburn.* New York: Hawthorne Books, 1975.

Stewart, John. "The Strategies of Leadership: Johnson and Mansfield." In *Congressional Behavior,* edited by Nelson W. Polsby, 61–92. New York: Random House, 1971.

Tuchman, Barbara W. "End of a Dream." In *The Proud Tower: A Portrait of the World before the War: 1890–1914.* New York: Macmillan, 1966.

U.S. Congress. House. *The History and Operation of the House Majority Whip Organization.* 94th Cong., 1st sess., 1975. H Doc 94-162.

U.S. Congress. Senate. *Majority and Minority Leaders of the Senate: History and Development of the Offices of the Floor Leaders.* Prepared by Floyd M. Riddick. 94th Cong., 1st sess., 1975. S Doc 94-66.

——. *Majority and Minority Whips of the Senate: History and Development of the Party Whip System in the United States Senate.* Prepared by Walter J. Oleszek. 92nd Cong., 2nd sess., 1972. S Doc 92-86.

——. *Policymaking Role of Leadership in the Senate* (papers compiled for the Commission on the Operation of the Senate). "Party Leaders, Party Committees, and Policy Analysis in the United States Senate." Prepared by Randall B. Ripley. 94th Cong., 2nd sess., 1976.

Wilson, Woodrow. *Congressional Government: A Study in American Politics.* Boston: Houghton Mifflin, 1885. Reprint. Cleveland: Meridian, 1956.

CHAPTER 2

The Legislative Process

NOWHERE ARE policy and process more intertwined than in the Congress of the United States. They interact at many stages of the legislative drama as skillful senators and representatives use the rules of procedure—fashioned to ensure orderly consideration of legislative proposals—to advance their policy goals.

Bill sponsors tinker with wording to ensure the proposal goes to a sympathetic rather than a hostile committee. The Senate may attach major tax legislation to a House revenue bill, circumventing a constitutional requirement that all revenue bills must originate in the House. Wording of a House rule for consideration of a bill on the floor may greatly constrict the ability of opponents to alter the substance. Senators may seek to end or continue debate on a proposal in order to position themselves to force action on an entirely unrelated matter. All of these things, and many more, routinely go on in a session of Congress.

On the surface, the actions of Congress appear fairly straightforward. To become law proposed legislation must be approved in identical form in both the House and the Senate. Most legislative proposals are first considered in subcommittee and committee. After reaching the floor legislation is debated, possibly amended further, and approved by the full House or Senate. After both chambers have acted, any differences in the two versions of the legislation must be resolved and the final version sent to the White House for the president's signature, which completes the process. If the president vetoes the legislation, Congress may enact the measure into law by overriding the veto.

Both chambers use procedures to expedite minor and noncontroversial legislation, but negotiating this lawmaking course for controversial measures is complicated and time-consuming. Throughout the process Congress must consider the opinion of the executive branch, constituents, and special interest groups. At any point the bill is subject to delay, defeat, or substantial modification. At each step of the way the bill's proponents must assemble a majority coalition through continual bargaining and compromise. "It is very easy to defeat a bill in Congress," President John F. Kennedy once observed. "It is much more difficult to pass one."[1]

Importance of Rules

Reinforced by more than two centuries of precedent and custom, congressional rules and procedures can speed a bill to final passage or kill it, expand the policy alternatives or narrow them, disadvantage the minority or thwart the will of the majority. *(See box, House and Senate Rules, p. 56.)*

Legislators who know the rules and procedures are better able to influence the legislative process than those who do not. "If you let me write the procedure," Rep. John D. Dingell, D-Mich., once said, "and I let you write the substance, I'll [beat] you every time."[2] Dingell may have exaggerated. No amount of procedural wizardry is ultimately a substitute for having the votes needed to win.

In the House of Representatives, a majority can always find a way to work its will. But in both houses skillful use of the rules can allow a majority to achieve its objectives more quickly, bargain with the other chamber and with the president from strength, and reap maximum political advantage. Ineffective use of the rules, on the other hand, can splinter a potential majority, require unwelcome concessions to opponents, create a potentially damaging record of controversial and divisive votes, and portray a chamber in disarray.

House and Senate rules and procedures differ significantly. Because House actions are intended to mirror the will of a national majority, its procedures are intended to ensure that the majority of the nation's representatives prevail. Because the Senate was designed to check what Thomas Jefferson called the "irregularities and abuses which often attend large and successful legislative majorities," its procedures are intended to ensure that the voice of the individual will be heard. This tradition survived the Senate's radical transformation from a body whose members were originally selected by state legislators to one elected directly by popular vote, starting in 1913. "Senate rules are tilted toward not doing things," Speaker Jim Wright, a Texas Democrat, said in 1987. "House rules if you know how to use them are tilted toward allowing the majority to get its will done."[3]

The sheer size of the House—with 435 members it is more than four times larger than the Senate—requires it to operate in a more orderly, predictable, and controlled fashion than the Senate. Thus the House is more hierarchically organized and has more rules, which it follows more closely. Because debate is restricted and the amending process frequently limited, the House is able to dispose of legislation more quickly than the Senate.

By comparison, the Senate's smaller size allows it to be more personal and informal in its operations. Although the Senate has an elaborate network of rules and procedures, it may ignore or override them to suit the political needs of the moment, often increasing the difficulty of predicting how the Senate may operate at any particular time. However, it most often conducts business (such as deciding what legislation to call up, the length of time for debate, or the number of amendments) by unanimous consent. Each member, even the most junior, is accorded a deference rarely seen in the House, and failure to recognize this could result in paralysis of the chamber's business. The privileges of engaging in unlimited debate—the filibuster—and offering nongermane amendments are cherished traditions in the Senate that are not permitted under House rules. Thus, it is not surprising that the Senate may spend days or weeks considering a measure that the House debates and passes in a single afternoon.

EVOLUTION OF RULES

Congressional rules and procedures are not static, but evolve in response to changes within Congress. In the modern era several external developments and internal reforms have led to significant changes in the ways the two chambers conduct their business.

A major change in the 1970s was a new openness in congressional proceedings. For the first time many committees, including Senate-House conference committees, were required to open their meetings to the public; outsiders could sit in as committee members bargained over provisions and language to be included or deleted from bills and resolutions.

Magnified further by the antipolitical atmosphere fostered by the Watergate scandal, which led to the resignation of President Richard Nixon, the emphasis on openness even extended to the traditionally secret meetings of the House Democratic Caucus, the organization of House Democrats. The Caucus, which met in the House chamber, opened the public galleries to visitors and to the press from 1975 to 1980 for certain types of business.

A rules change in the House in 1971 made it possible to record how each individual voted on floor amendments considered in the Committee of the Whole, one of the procedures used to consider legislation. Formerly, the House only recorded the total number voting for or against such an amendment. The rules change meant that members could not vote one way while telling their constituents they voted another. Many of these changes were favored by more liberal members of both parties, who correctly believed that a more open process would weaken long-established power centers in congressional committees where conservative committee chairmen wielding immense power often frustrated their legislative goals. *(See box, Methods of Voting in the House and Senate, p. 78.)*

Another major development in the 1960s and 1970s was an increase in the number of amendments offered on the floor of each chamber. Several factors contributed to this development. Constituents and special interest groups pressured individual members to take specific stands on issues of concern to them. Members, with one eye always on reelection, responded in ways to gain them wide recognition with their constituents and in later years with organizations that donated money to their reelection campaigns. Increased opportunities to obtain recorded votes in the House made it much easier to be visibly on the public record. In addition, gradually increasing partisanship in Congress since the 1960s has broken down political norms of earlier eras—exemplified by Speaker Sam Rayburn's admonition to "get along, you have to go along"—which had tended to discourage members who wanted to be considered serious legislators from presenting issues and seeking confrontation solely to score political points.

Within Congress, reductions in the authority exercised by committee chairmen and the rise in importance of subcommittees also contributed to increased amending activity. "Weaker full committee chairmen were less able to mold consensus positions in their committees, making it more likely that disputes among committee members would spill onto the floor," political scientist Steven S. Smith wrote. "Subcommittee chairmen, who assumed more responsibility for managing legislation on the floor, often lacked the experience and political clout" to anticipate and divert floor amendments.[4] Increased coverage of congressional activities by the media, the televising of congressional floor and committee sessions, and members' desire to use this visibility led them to exploit such opportunities through speeches and the amendment process. This combination of diminished committee authority and more assertive members meant that lawmakers in both chambers began to offer more amendments during floor action.

In response leaders in each chamber began to develop ways to limit amendments. In the House that meant writing more restrictive rules to limit amendments that could be offered to some legislation, raising concerns among the minority party that it was being closed out of the debate. In the Senate it meant developing complicated agreements for each major piece of legislation that would reduce the likelihood the Senate would bog down in filibuster and delay, unable to act on important issues in timely fashion.

The number of amendments brought to the House and Senate floors decreased somewhat in the 1980s, partly because of these new strategies and partly because massive federal budget deficits meant that fewer new programs—and therefore fewer amendments to them—were being initiated.

By the mid-1980s the deficit itself—and the special process Congress had devised for dealing with it—had become by far the single most time-consuming issue before Congress. It had also led to the increased use of omnibus bills, the packaging of many, often unrelated, proposals in a single, massive piece of legislation. So-called budget reconciliation measures, for example, revised existing laws touching every aspect of government to bring government programs into conformity with the overall budget plan for the year. In addition it became common practice to package all or most of the year's appropriations bills in a single piece of legislation. The opportunities to debate and amend these bills were often severely limited.

Rank-and-file House members were particularly affected by this narrowing of their opportunities to influence legislation.

TERMS AND SESSIONS

The two-year period for which members of the House of Representatives are elected constitutes a Congress. Under the Twentieth Amendment to the Constitution, ratified in 1933, this period begins at noon on January 3 of an odd-numbered year, following the election of representatives the previous November, and ends at noon on January 3 of the next odd-numbered year. Congresses are numbered consecutively. The Congress that convened in January 1997 was the 105th in a series that began in 1789.

Prior to 1935, the term of a Congress began on March 4 of the odd-numbered year following the election and coincided with the inauguration of the president (also changed by the Twentieth Amendment to January 20 beginning in 1937), but Congress often did not actually convene until the first Monday in December.

Under the Constitution, Congress is required to "assemble" at least once each year. The Twentieth Amendment provides that these annual meetings shall begin on January 3 unless Congress "shall by law appoint a different day," which it frequently does. For example, before the first session of the 105th Congress adjourned it passed a law, later signed by the president, to reconvene for the second session on January 27, 1998. Each Congress, therefore, has two regular sessions beginning in January of successive years.

The Legislative Reorganization Act of 1970 stipulates that unless Congress provides otherwise the Senate and House "shall adjourn *sine die* not later than July 31 of each year" or, in nonelection years, take at least a thirty-day recess in August. The provision is not applicable if "a state of war exists pursuant to a declaration of war by the Congress." Congress routinely dispenses with this restriction by passing a concurrent resolution. In practice the annual sessions may run the entire year.

Adjournment *sine die* (literally, without a day) ends a session of Congress. Adjournment of the second session is the final action of a Congress and all legislation not passed by both houses expires. However, following adjournment there may still be some delay before legislation that has passed near the end of the session is enrolled and formally presented to the president for action. Members frequently include in the adjournment resolution language to authorize their leaders to call them back into session if circumstances require it.

The president may "on extraordinary occasions" convene one or both houses in special session, or threaten to do so to achieve a political or legislative objective. For example, in 1997 President Bill Clinton threatened to delay the adjournment of the first session of the 105th Congress by calling a special session to consider campaign finance reform legislation. The Senate quickly took up the major legislation but the proposal succumbed to a filibuster.

Within a session either house of Congress may adjourn for holiday observances or other brief periods of three days or less. In a typical week, for example, the Senate or House may meet through Thursday and then, by unanimous consent or by motion, convene on the following Monday. By constitutional directive neither house may adjourn for more than three days without the consent of the other, which they give through passage of a concurrent resolution.

The third session of the 76th Congress was the longest session in history; it lasted 366 days, from January 3, 1940, to January 3, 1941. Four other sessions have lasted 365 days: the first session of the 77th Congress (1941–1942), the second session of the 81st Congress (1950–1951), the first session of the 102nd Congress (1991–1992), and the first session of the 104th Congress (1995–1996).

"What we have now is a technique for returning to a closed system where a few people make all the decisions," said Indiana Democrat Philip R. Sharp.[5]

In the 1980s and 1990s the tough choices posed by the need to reduce the deficit, frustration over the reduced opportunities to enact new programs, the new assertiveness of individual lawmakers, and increased partisanship posed procedural challenges in both chambers. When they were in the minority, House Republicans complained, sometimes bitterly, that the Democratic leadership restricted floor debate and amendments in ways that trampled minority rights. In the minority themselves in both houses starting in 1995 in the 104th Congress, Democrats made the same claims.

Members in both houses complained that it was politically difficult to make tough decisions in open committee meetings, and majority members were reluctant to allow the minority too many opportunities for procedural and political counterattack. An uneasy balance began to evolve between the ideals of process and the realities of politics. Many members of Congress, who were reformers of the 1960s and 1970s and had risen to power as committee barons in the 1980s and 1990s by criticizing the institutions of Congress, were squirming in the limelight under multiple pressures from the public, the press, interest groups, and the opposition party; and these committee chairmen were ready to make some compromises.

A few committees began to close their doors occasionally to the public, although the vast majority of meetings remained open. Conference committees, required by rule to operate in the open unless the full House of Representatives closed them by recorded vote, often finessed the rules by holding one or two open meetings and then having closed subconferences, "caucuses" of conferees and staff negotiations to make the real decisions. These mechanisms proved essential to enact complex legislation such as omnibus budget reconciliation bills potentially involving two dozen committees and hundreds of conferees. In these cases, it was often physically impossible to squeeze all of the conferees into the same room at the same time, and any "meeting" could merely be ceremonial or procedural rather than substantive.

The procedural problems were most acute in the Senate, where individual members could, and often did, bring the chamber to a standstill. Many senators were vocal about their dissatisfaction with Senate procedures that let individual members pursue their legislative interests at the expense of the Sen-

The House of Representatives greets Speaker-elect Newt Gingrich as he arrives to take the oath of office at the start of the 104th Congress in 1995.

ate's interests. Washington Republican Daniel J. Evans, a former governor and university president, said frustration with the Senate was a major reason he chose not to seek reelection in 1988. "Somehow we must reach a happy compromise between the tyranny of autocratic chairmen and the chaos of a hundred independent fiefdoms," Evans said.

It is ironic that throughout the 1970s and 1980s, despite the emphasis on deficit reduction, balancing the budget, and the development of new procedures supposedly to enhance the ability to set priorities, little actual progress was made toward these goals. The federal budget deficit and the national debt increased substantially throughout the 1980s. It was almost as if a constant emphasis on reforming the process took the place of the substantive decision making it was meant to enhance. A major budget-reform effort, named Gramm-Rudman-Hollings after its congressional authors, was routinely waived when the political consequences of using it became clearer. Ultimately it had little impact.

Only in the 1990s, when Congress adopted a new budget ethos based on "pay as you go," which required new spending to be counterbalanced by cuts, did progress toward deficit reduction resume. These accomplishments were made possible by mechanisms and events essentially outside of process—budget "summit" deals negotiated between key executive branch and congressional leaders and then sold to a majority of both chambers as a package, and a booming economy that increased tax revenues.

CHANGE IN LEADERSHIP

Just when consistent trends and historical patterns observed over several decades in Congress seem ripe for analysis and placement in historical perspective, the political environment can change rapidly. It is often easy to forget that for all its powers, rules, and traditions, Congress is dominated by forces beyond its control, such as the shifting will of the electorate.

The evolution of congressional procedures and practices over the thirty years from the end of the 1960s reflected the emergence of a younger, more liberal Democratic congressional membership, especially in the House, who began as insurgents in the 1950s and 1960s, assumed control of both chambers in the 1970s, and became the power brokers and senior committee members of the 1980s and early 1990s. There was a period of brief conservative resurgence in the House following the presidential landslide of Ronald Reagan in the 1980s, which was complemented by Republican control of the Senate from 1981 to 1987. By the early 1990s, with the Democrats back in control of both houses of Congress, however, these GOP inroads on Democratic power seemed transitory and did not leave any fundamental changes in either body.

The Democratic dominance ended abruptly in 1995, as a new Republican majority containing large numbers of young, militant conservatives joined frustrated and angry senior GOP members who had long felt victimized and impotent in their legislative careers. Suddenly Republicans found themselves the guardians of congressional practices that many either knew little about, or had railed against for years. Although it remained to be seen whether the Republican Party would adapt the institutions of Congress to its own ends, or break the mold and create a fundamentally different House and Senate, one thing was certain: the rules and procedures that had guided Congress for more than 200 years would continue to evolve.

PITFALLS TO PASSAGE

As President Kennedy said, it is easier to defeat legislation than to pass it. And the route a bill must travel before it wins final approval allows many opportunities for its opponents to defeat or delay it. "Legislation is like a chess game more than anything else," Representative Dingell has said. "It is a seemingly endless series of moves, until ultimately somebody prevails through exhaustion, or brilliance, or because of overwhelming public sentiment for their side."[6]

The first place that a bill might run into trouble is in subcommittee or committee, where the measure is likely to receive its closest scrutiny and most significant modification. That occurs in part because committee members and staff have developed expertise in the subject areas within their areas of jurisdiction and in part because committee consideration gives opponents their first formal opportunity to state how the bill needs to be changed to be acceptable to them, if it can be.

The second place a bill may be delayed is in scheduling for floor action. When, and sometimes whether, a bill is brought to the floor of either the House or Senate depends on many factors, including what other legislation is awaiting action, how controversial the measure is, and whether the leadership judges its chances for passage to be improved by immediate action.

The leadership, for example, might decide to delay taking up a controversial bill until its proponents can gather sufficient support to guarantee its passage. In the Senate, bills often cannot be scheduled much in advance until all of the interested senators have given clearance and "holds" by individuals senators or groups of senators have been removed. (A "hold" is a request by a senator to delay action on a matter. The intent may be to delay indefinitely or postpone action until some concern is addressed. A hold carries an implicit threat that a filibuster would begin if the hold is not honored.) Even then, absent a unanimous consent agreement, filibusters are possible unless a supermajority of sixty senators intervenes to move the process forward. However, even if a bill itself is delayed or blocked, that still does not prevent controversial issues from reaching the floor unexpectedly because they can be offered as nongermane amendments to other legislation at almost any time.

The next hurdle a bill must cross is amendment and passage on the chamber floor. The amending process is at the heart of floor debate in both chambers. Amendments have many objectives. Members may offer amendments to dramatize their stands on issues, even if there is little chance their proposals will be adopted. Some amendments are introduced at the request of the executive branch, a member's constituents, or special interests. Some become tactical tools for gauging sentiment for or against a bill. Others are used to stall action on a bill. In the Senate, the majority leader, who has the choice of always being the first to be recognized, may offer amendments to prevent other amendments from being offered, which is called "filling the amendment tree." In the House, where debate is more strictly limited, a member may offer a pro forma amendment, later withdrawn, solely to gain a few additional minutes to speak on an issue.

Still other amendments may be designed to defeat the legislation. One common strategy is to try to load a bill with so many unattractive amendments that it will eventually collapse under its own weight. Another strategy is to offer a "killer" amendment, one that if adopted, would cause members who initially supported the bill to vote against it on final passage. Conversely, amendments known as "sweeteners" may be offered to attract broader support for the underlying measure. And finally, in the House, a motion to recommit the bill back to committee, either to kill it outright or send it back to the floor "forthwith" with additional amendments, gives opponents a final chance to persuade their colleagues to back away from the proposal or change it significantly.

Legislation that fails to win passage at any of these points in either the House or Senate is likely to be abandoned for the remainder of that Congress. Those bills that survive passage by both houses must still be reconciled through processes that hold a host of additional dangers and delays. The House and Senate may trade the bills back and forth like ping pong balls, adding, subtracting and modifying provisions; or the legislation may face the conference committee, a temporary panel of House and Senate members established solely to work out the differences between the two chambers on a particular bill. Sometimes known as the third house of Congress, conference committees bargain and compromise until they reach a version of the legislation acceptable to a majority of the conferees of each chamber; sometimes the legislation is substantially rewritten in conference. Occasionally conferees cannot strike a compromise, and the legislation dies.

For a small number of measures the final hurdle is approval by the president. All modern presidents have used the veto threat to persuade Congress to pay attention to the executive viewpoint as it considers specific measures. Because presidents most of the time can muster the necessary support to defeat override attempts in Congress, lawmakers usually try to compromise with the president. Sometimes, however, such efforts fail, and the bill is vetoed.

All of these steps, repeated in endless variation for dozens of major bills, must be completed within the two-year cycle of a single Congress. Any bill that has not received final approval when a Congress adjourns automatically dies and must be reintroduced in the next Congress to begin the entire procedure over again. When a Congress is drawing to a close, the pressure to act can be intense. Lawmakers, who have put off making difficult choices, often find themselves rushing to keep their bills from dying. In a sentiment as apt in the 1990s as it was in the 1820s, Davy Crockett, a legendary frontiersman who served four House terms, once said: "We generally lounge or squabble the greater part of the session, and crowd into a few days of the last term three or four times the business done during as many preceding months."[7]

Controversial and far-reaching proposals are seldom enacted in a single Congress. More often they are introduced and reintroduced, incubating in a legislative cauldron as national sentiment on the issue coalesces and the necessary compromises are struck. The comprehensive revision of the Clean Air Act finally approved in 1990 had been stalled in Congress since 1977—over such controversial issues as acid rain—before the right combination of supporters and political circumstances emerged simultaneously to free it finally. Congress enacted welfare reform in 1996, ending a sixty-one-year federal guarantee and representing the first time a major entitlement program for individuals was transformed into a block grant to states. Republicans had advocated radical changes in welfare for decades, and they revived these ideas as part of the "Contract with America," a grouping of legislative and philosophical proposals the GOP used in the 1994 elections in its campaign to win control of the House. *(See box, "Contract with America," p. 26.)*

HOUSE AND SENATE RULES

Article I, Section 5 of the Constitution stipulates that "Each House may determine the Rules of its Proceedings." In addition to the standing rules adopted under this authority, the House and Senate each have a separate set of precedents, practices, and customs that guide their conduct of business.

The standing rules of the House are set forth in the *Constitution, Jefferson's Manual, and Rules of the House of Representatives,* or the House Manual as it is commonly called, which is published with revisions during the first session of each Congress. The content is also available on Congress's web site *(See "Congressional Information on the Internet," p. 174, in Reference Materials.)*

This is the most important single source of authority on the rules and contains voluminous annotations. In addition to the written rules of the chamber, the document contains the text of the Constitution, portions of the manual on parliamentary procedure that Thomas Jefferson wrote when he was vice president, and the principal rulings and precedents of the House. The formal rules of the Senate are found in the *Senate Manual Containing the Standing Rules, Orders, Laws, and Resolutions Affecting the Business of the United States Senate.*

In the House, on the day when a new Congress convenes, the chamber has no formal rules and thus, no committees, which are created in the rules. It operates under what is called "general parliamentary law," which relies on *Jefferson's Manual* and many precedents of the House. Prior to opening day, the rules have been drafted by the majority party's conference or caucus; amendments suggested by individual majority members are considered at such party meetings.

Following the election of the Speaker and the administration of the oath of office to members, the proposed rules of the House are offered directly from the floor as a resolution, usually by the majority leader. After one hour of debate, the minority has an opportunity to offer a substitute. After it is defeated, the majority's rules package is then formally adopted, usually on a party-line vote, and becomes effective immediately. Once adopted, House rules continue in force through the Congress, unless further amended, and expire at its end.

Amendments to the rules package on the House floor are not permitted unless opponents can "defeat the previous question," the motion offered by the majority party that has the effect of cutting off debate and forcing a vote on final passage. This has not occurred since 1971, when a conservative coalition of Republicans and southern Democrats defeated the previous question and forced the Democratic leadership to drop a provision for a "twenty-one-day rule," a procedure that would have allowed legislation to reach the floor without action by the Rules Committee.

When Republicans took over the House in 1995 after forty years in the minority, they deviated from the traditional practice by splitting their rules proposal into numerous pieces to highlight what they considered major reforms in the rules. All passed, some by votes largely along party lines, others with substantial bipartisan support. However, in the 105th Congress that began in 1997, Republicans returned to a single rules package.

The Senate, on the other hand, does not readopt its rules at the beginning of a Congress. Since only one-third of the chamber turns over every two years, the Senate considers itself a continuing body. Any proposed changes in existing rules are adopted subject to provisions already in the rules, such as Rule XXII, the cloture rule requiring a supermajority to cut off debate. This interpretation of the Senate's continuing nature was challenged by liberals for many years as conflicting with Article I, Section 5 of the Constitution, but their contention that the Senate could cut off debate on proposed rules changes by majority vote at the beginning of a Congress was strongly resisted.

In the controversy leading to the most recent important change

Bill Clinton in his 1992 campaign for the presidency had promised to "end welfare as we know it." But it was only after initial presidential vetoes of Republican bills in 1995 and 1996, the intervention of the nation's governors who were greatly burdened by welfare costs, GOP fears of political reprisals from a partial shutdown of the federal government in late 1995 after a deadlock with Clinton, and Clinton's desire in his 1996 reelection bid to claim a major promise kept that efforts led to the necessary compromises to ensure enactment.

The legislative process and its various stages seem straightforward enough. Those interested in either passing or defeating legislation, will ultimately win, lose, or accept some compromise. However, as noted earlier, sometimes long-standing patterns of congressional behavior, the seemingly fixed interrelationships with other branches of government, and the comfortable access to the legislative process enjoyed by a mix of influential special interest groups can shift abruptly with the public mood.

An extraordinary modern example of the effects of a sudden radical change in the traditional approach to legislating occurred during the first few months of the 104th Congress in 1995, after the Republican Party had assumed control of both houses for the first time in more than four decades. The House Republican majority, apparently sensing a popular mandate after its landslide 1994 victory and gain of fifty-two seats, briefly appeared to be ushering in a new era of "congressional government." The House Speaker seemed to be the nation's first "legislator-in-chief." The Senate was relegated to playing second fiddle. The president was widely seen as almost irrelevant. The House worked feverishly to rush the legislative components of its "Contract with America" proposals to the floor, sometimes without even holding hearings or allowing amendments. The House seemed to be all action, but little deliberation. While most of these bills passed, action was delayed on routine but essential legislation in the congressional process, such as the appropriations bills needed to fund government activities and services.

in the cloture rule, the Senate did cast a series of votes in 1975 that appeared to support the right of a simple majority to avoid a filibuster and change Senate rules. But agreement was subsequently reached to change Rule XXII by invoking cloture first by a two-thirds vote. Before doing so the Senate cast procedural votes which, it was argued, reversed this precedent.

House precedents, unwritten rules based on past rulings of the chair, are contained in three multivolume series: *Hinds' Precedents of the House of Representatives* covers the years 1789 through 1907; *Cannon's Precedents of the House of Representatives* covers from 1908 through 1935; and *Deschler's Precedents of the United States House of Representatives,* volumes one to nine, and *Deschler-Brown Precedents of the United States House of Representatives,* volumes ten to thirteen, cover 1936 through 1996. In addition, *Procedure in the U.S. House of Representatives* is a summary of all important rulings of the chair through 1984. *House Practice: A Guide to the Rules, Precedents and Procedures of the House,* published in 1996, is a single volume by retired House Parliamentarian William Holmes Brown that discusses selected precedents and the operation of current House rules in a less intimidating format and includes material on rules changes following the shift in party control in the 104th Congress.

Riddick's Senate Procedure: Precedents and Practices, by retired parliamentarian Floyd M. Riddick and Alan S. Frumin, who was parliamentarian when the book was last revised in 1992, contains current precedents and related standing rules and statutory provisions through the end of the 101st Congress.

In addition to precedents, each chamber has particular traditions and customs that it follows—recognition of the Senate majority leader ahead of other senators seeking recognition from the chair is an example of such a practice. Moreover, each party in each chamber has its own set of party rules that can affect the chamber's proceedings (Rules of the Republican Conference of the United States House of Representatives, 105th Congress; Rules of the House Democratic Caucus, 105th Congress; History, Rules and Precedents of the Senate Republican Conference).

Many public laws also contain provisions that affect House and Senate procedures. Prominent examples are the Congressional Budget and Impoundment Control Act of 1974; the Balanced Budget and Emergency Deficit Control Act of 1985, better known as Gramm-Rudman-Hollings, after its sponsors; and so-called "fast track" legislation, enacted in previous Congresses but blocked from a House vote on renewal in 1997, which would have forced each chamber to vote on the president's proposed international trade agreements without amendments. Other examples would be numerous statutory provisions, rendered moot by the Supreme Court's 1983 *Chadha* decision, which provided for various schemes of approval or disapproval of actions by the executive branch or independent agencies by either one or both houses.

Such rulemaking statutes obviate the need for each chamber to create special procedures on an ad hoc basis whenever it takes some action on the subject matter dealt with in these laws. Without "fast track," for example, it would be extremely difficult for the president to negotiate credibly with foreign nations without the advance assurance that each chamber would not amend the agreements in potentially unpredictable ways, ultimately rendering them unacceptable to these nations. The existence of procedures set out by law is particularly significant in the Senate, where they serve to limit debate and prevent filibusters. However, such statutes, even though they are laws passed by both chambers and signed by the president, still remain subservient to each chamber's constitutional power to amend its rules at any time. (For example, the House could always adopt a special rule allowing amendments to a "fast track" trade agreement; in the Senate, which has no equivalent of the House's Rules Committee, any alterations in process would be far more difficult).

The controversies associated with the ambitious new agenda led to gridlock between the GOP-led Congress and a Democratic president, vetoes of tax and appropriations bills, two shutdowns of some government departments and agencies from December 1995 to January 1996, a near collapse of Republican control of the chamber in the 1996 election, and the easy reelection of the once seemingly crippled President Clinton.

In the 105th Congress that followed beginning in 1997, although many controversial bills were still considered, the multiple, time-consuming steps of the normal legislative process reasserted themselves without the weight of an overarching political agenda or the new theories of governance that had nearly consumed its predecessor. In other words, the more things seemed to have changed, the more they remained the same. Congress still waited for presidential proposals. Committees still mattered. Committee chairman could still exercise power. The minority could still offer its proposals and slow down the process. Members of both parties appeared relieved to fall back on a more predictable, less confrontational manner of doing business because the potential rewards of radical change that had proved so tempting two years earlier had led to excessive political risk.

Developing Legislation

Procedures for introducing legislation and seeing it through committee are similar in the House and Senate.

Legislative proposals originate in different ways. Members of Congress, of course, develop ideas for legislation. Assistance in drafting legislative language is available from each chamber's Office of Legislative Counsel. Special interest groups—business, labor, farm, civil rights, consumer, trade associations, and the like—are another fertile source of legislation. Many of these organizations and their lobbyists in Washington provide detailed technical knowledge in specialized fields and employ experts in the art of drafting bills and amendments. Constituents, either as individuals or groups, also may propose legislation. Sometimes, a member of Congress will introduce such a bill "by request," whether or not he or she supports its purposes.

Much of the legislation considered by Congress originates in the executive branch (although key members of Congress may participate in the formulation of administration programs). This is especially true if Congress and the president are of the same political party. However, the periodic emergence of an entirely separate congressional agenda, such as the GOP's 1994 contract, illustrates the ability of Congress to confront the president aggressively and push ahead independently on a vast range of issues. Although Congress may not be dependent on the executive if it wants to pass legislation, the presidential veto usually remains the ultimate arbiter of whatever is enacted into law.

Each year after the president outlines his legislative program, executive departments and agencies transmit to the House and Senate drafts of proposed legislation to carry out the president's program or ideas. These bills usually are introduced by the chairman of the committee or subcommittee having jurisdiction over the subject involved, or by the ranking minority member if the chairman is not of the president's party. The congressional leadership, especially if it is from the opposition party, may designate a group of bills as key legislative initiatives and give them low bill numbers (such as HR 1 or HR 2) to emphasize their importance.

Committees may also consider proposals that have not been formally introduced. The committee may work from its own preliminary text, called the "chairman's mark," and an actual bill is introduced at a later stage. When legislation is heavily amended in committee, all the changes, deletions, and additions, together with whatever is left of the original bill, may be organized into a new bill. Such measures, referred to as "clean bills," are reintroduced, usually by the chairman of the committee, given a new bill number and formally reported out of committee.

Some committees, such as House Appropriations, usually skip this stage because they have the special power in House rules to originate legislation directly—that is to draft bills themselves and report the final text to the floor, only at which point is the bill given a bill number.

In an ideal world, cooperation between the two branches throughout the legislative process will smooth out the rough edges in legislation and help ensure that no one is surprised either in committee or on the floor. This assumes, of course, that there is a desire for cooperation. It may appear to be to the political advantage of one branch or the other, or both, to engage in a confrontation; enactment of legislation may not be the primary goal in such circumstances, or even be desired. Someone wants to create an issue, so they pick a fight. Fights involve risks, so one side must perceive some political reward for taking them. The president often gains the advantage in such situations because of the White House's ability to present a case more clearly and consistently to the public, while Congress has many potential spokespeople of lesser stature who may not all be of the same opinion or able to command attention.

For example, President Harry S. Truman in the midst of his 1948 reelection campaign, summoned the Republican-controlled 80th Congress—which he had labeled "do nothing"—back to Washington for a special summer session that produced no legislation of substance. The president then used this inaction—in a situation he created exactly for the purpose—to bolster his campaign themes and aid his uphill reelection fight.

More recently, congressional Republicans disregarded the Clinton administration in pressing their "Contract with America" in 1995. When the president vetoed the omnibus budget reconciliation bill containing the GOP's major tax cut proposals and other key priorities, as well as a number of appropriations bills, both the GOP-controlled Senate and House adopted a strategy of shutting down government departments over the Christmas and New Year's holidays at the end of the first session of the 104th Congress to try to force him to yield and to better position themselves to retain control of Congress and regain the presidency in 1996. House Speaker Newt Gingrich became the principal spokesperson for this strategy in the public mind, but he was eventually undercut by Senate Majority Leader Bob Dole, a presidential candidate himself, who followed the more traditional precepts of congressional behavior that legislation, especially appropriations bills, were "must pass" matters.

The shutdown strategy was a major political miscalculation and disaster for the Republicans. Congress was blamed for shutting off important government services. The president won the ensuing public relations battle, and Congress had to back down and pass the requisite funding. Gingrich's popularity, as registered in numerous polls, plummeted and his political control of the House weakened.

These were examples of pure political calculation, one of which worked while the other failed. At other times, new issues suddenly emerge and catch fire, or long-standing controversies finally gain a spark and become highly visible through the media that raises them above the normal din of the legislative process.

INTRODUCTION OF LEGISLATION

No matter where a legislative proposal originates, it can be introduced only by a member of Congress. In the House, a member may introduce any of several types of bills and resolutions by handing them to the clerk of the House or by placing them in a mahogany box near the clerk's desk called the hopper. The member need not seek recognition for the purpose. The resident commissioner of Puerto Rico and the delegates of the District of Columbia, Guam, American Samoa, and the Virgin Islands, none of whom may vote on the floor, also have this right. Senators introduce legislation from the floor during the "morning hour" or other period of the day set aside for doing so, but increasingly they have gone to the House practice of leaving them at the desk. In some cases, such as the example of the House appropriations committee originating legislation, a bill is introduced by the chairman and given a bill number only after committee action has been completed and the bill is ready for floor debate; in this instance, a committee report would also be filed simultaneously.

There is no limit to the number of bills and resolutions members may introduce, nor any restrictions on the time during a Congress when they may do so. It is rare to find a day when Congress is in session when someone does not introduce something. House and Senate bills may have joint sponsorship and carry several members' names. (Before 1967 House rules barred representatives from cosponsoring legislation. Members favoring a particular measure had to introduce identical bills if they wished to be closely identified with the original proposal.) The Constitution stipulates that "all bills for raising revenue shall originate in the House of Representatives," and the House has successfully insisted that it reserves the power to originate appropriation bills as well. All other bills may originate in either chamber.

Major legislation often is introduced in both houses in the form of companion (identical) bills, primarily to speed up the legislative process by encouraging both chambers to consider the measure simultaneously. Sponsors of companion bills also may hope to dramatize the importance or urgency of the issue and show broad support for the legislation. At the beginning of a Congress, members vie to be the sponsors of the first bills introduced and to retain the same bill number in consecutive Congresses on legislation that has not been enacted. The House and Senate majority leadership typically reserve low bill numbers for measures that are key elements of their legislative program. In 1987, for example, House Speaker Wright made sure that his top-priority bills for the session were numbers HR 1 and HR 2. In 1995, Speaker Gingrich gave many "Contract with America" items the first bill numbers assigned, including designating as HR 1 the Congressional Accountability Act, which applied workplace laws in the private sector to Congress (this was S 2 in the Senate), and as H J Res 1 a proposed constitutional amendment to require a balanced federal budget.

Thousands of bills are introduced in every Congress, but most never receive any consideration, nor is consideration expected. Every lawmaker introduces measures for a variety of reasons—to stake out a stand on an issue, as a favor to a constituent or a special interest group, to get publicity, or to ward off political attack. As congressional expert Walter J. Oleszek writes, once such a bill has been introduced, the legislator can claim that he or she has taken action "and can blame the committee to which the bill has been referred for its failure to win enactment."[8]

However, in the House, a number of factors have operated to reduce the number of bills introduced substantially during the 1980s and 1990s. The most significant was a rules change at the start of the 96th Congress in 1979 that allowed an unlimited number of members to cosponsor any legislation introduced, obviating the need for members to introduce duplicate bills in order to get their names onto them. The effect was immediate, reducing the number of bills introduced from 14,414 in the 95th Congress to 8,456 in the 96th. Since then, the number continued to decline, averaging fewer than 6,000 over the next five congresses.

The modern Congress considers and enacts fewer measures than its predecessors. But it is impossible to measure congressional workload by the number of measures passed. After enactment of the Congressional Budget and Impoundment Control Act of 1974, Congress tended to package many, often unrelated, proposals in lengthy pieces of legislation known as omnibus bills. Each year the House and Senate adopt a budget resolution setting an overall plan for government spending and revenues. They often follow up with another omnibus measure—called a budget reconciliation bill—revising government programs to conform to the overall plan, but this type of legislation is not needed every year.

With the advent of massive budget deficits in the early 1980s Congress repeatedly used the practice of providing funding for most or all government departments and agencies in a single omnibus appropriations bill, known as a continuing resolution. Although Congress used continuing resolutions previously their prominence expanded as legislative delays resulted from ever-increasing complexities of the budget process, rivalries among authorizing committees, disputes between authorizing and appropriations committees, House-Senate conflicts, and the traditional use of thirteen different appropriations bills. The presence of controversy over a particular year's budget does not necessarily mean that a CR will be required or that final appropriations will not be in place when a new fiscal year begins on October 1. Congress managed to pass all thirteen appropriations bills separately and before the beginning of the new fiscal year as recently as 1994. In 1996, after passing seven appropriations bills but facing delays in six others, Congress placed the remaining ones in an omnibus appropriations bill that was completed on September 30. This was only the fourth time since modern federal budgeting began in 1974 that Congress finished all of its spending bills at the start of the new fiscal year.

During the 1980s, the number of commemorative bills—those designating commemorative days, weeks, or months, for example—increased. Commemoratives were introduced as joint resolutions, which required a presidential signature to become law and carried the possibility of a signing ceremony and media coverage. However, their sheer volume was often misrepresented by critics and by the media to ridicule the work product of a Congress whose principal achievements might actually be contained in a massive omnibus budget reconciliation bill and a continuing resolution.

When the Republicans took control of the House in 1995, they prohibited by rule the introduction of commemorative legislation or its consideration in that chamber, which also had the effect of shutting off similar Senate action. The impact of the new rule can easily be seen in the drop in the number of joint resolutions introduced in the House, from 429 in the 103rd Congress to 198 in the 104th, and in the Senate from 232 in the 103rd to 65 in the 104th. The total of public laws enacted declined from

WHEN A SUPERMAJORITY VOTE IS REQUIRED BY CONGRESS

The Constitution created two houses of Congress, each of which could act, with a quorum present, by simple majority vote except with respect to certain extraordinary matters that required support from a supermajority. *Jefferson's Manual* states: "The voice of the majority decides . . . where not otherwise expressly provided." These principles have also applied to actions taken in congressional committees, unless otherwise provided by rule or statute.

The Constitution requires a two-thirds majority vote of *both* the House and Senate to:

- Override a presidential veto
- Pass a constitutional amendment
- Remove political disabilities

The Constitution requires a two-thirds majority in the Senate to:

- Convict in an impeachment trial
- Ratify a treaty

The Constitution requires a two-thirds majority of either the House or the Senate to expel a member.

The House and Senate also have adopted supermajority requirements for various procedural actions. In the House, a two-thirds majority is required to:

- Suspend the rules and pass a measure
- Consider a report from the Rules Committee relating to a rule or special order of business on the same legislative day it is reported to the House
- Dispense with Calendar Wednesday
- Dispense with the call of the Private Calendar

The House in the 104th Congress (1995–1997) adopted rules that also require a three-fifths vote to pass a measure called up from the Corrections Calendar and to pass a federal income tax rate increase.

In the Senate, a two-thirds vote is required to suspend a rule of the Senate (a rarely used procedure) and to invoke cloture and end debate under Rule XXII on any measure to change the rules of the Senate. (Senate rules themselves may be amended by a simple majority.)

The Senate rules otherwise require sixty votes ("three fifths of the senators duly chosen and sworn," assuming no vacancies in the Senate) to invoke cloture under Rule XXII on debate on all other debatable matters including bills, nominations, and motions.

A supermajority of sixty members is also required in the Senate to override various points of order under the Budget Act and to appeal rulings of the presiding officer related to those provisions.

465 in the 103rd Congress to 333 in the 104th, a drop of more than 28 percent.

Bills not enacted die with the Congress in which they were introduced and must be reintroduced in a new Congress if they are to be eligible for further consideration. Resolutions adopted by the House affecting its operations during a Congress also expire automatically; however, similar Senate resolutions may remain in effect, as the Senate considers itself a "continuing body." (The Senate reads George Washington's Farewell Address each year pursuant to a resolution adopted on January 24, 1901.) Nominations pending in the Senate expire at the end of each session of Congress, but are usually carried over into the next session of the same Congress by unanimous consent. Treaties pending in the Senate, once submitted by the president, remain pending from one Congress to another; nominations, however, lapse under those conditions and must be resubmitted in the next Congress.

Major legislation goes through changes in nomenclature as it works its way through the legislative process. When a measure is introduced and first printed, it is officially referred to and labeled as a bill. When it has been passed by one house and sent to the other body it is reprinted and officially labeled an act. When cleared by Congress and signed by the president, it becomes a law (and also may still be referred to as an act).

Types of Legislation

The types of measures that Congress may consider and act on (in addition to treaties and nominations submitted by the president to the Senate) include bills and three kinds of resolutions (joint, concurrent, and simple). The first to be introduced is designated as number 1 of its type, and numbers increase with the chronological introduction of additional measures.

Bills are prefixed with HR when introduced in the House and with S when introduced in the Senate, followed by a number assigned to the measure. The vast majority of legislative proposals dealing with either domestic or foreign issues and programs affecting the United States government or the population generally are drafted in the form of bills. These include both authorizations, which provide the legal authority and spending limits for federal programs and agencies, and appropriations, which actually provide the money for those programs and agencies. When passed by both chambers in identical form and signed by the president (or repassed by Congress over a presidential veto), they become laws.

Joint resolutions are designated H J Res or S J Res. A joint resolution, like a bill, requires the approval of both houses and (usually) the signature of the president; it has the force of law if approved. There is no real difference between a bill and a joint resolution. The latter generally is used when dealing with a single item or issue, such as a continuing or emergency appropriations bill.

Joint resolutions also are used for proposing amendments to the Constitution. Such resolutions must be approved by two-thirds of both houses. They do not require the president's signature but become a part of the Constitution when ratified by three-fourths of the states.

Concurrent resolutions are designated as H Con Res or S Con Res. Used for matters affecting the operations of both houses, concurrent resolutions must be passed in the same form by both houses, but they are not presented to the president for his signature, and they do not have the force of law. Concurrent resolutions are used to fix the time of adjournment of a Congress or to express the "sense of Congress" on an issue. Some concurrent resolutions, such as the annual congressional budget resolutions setting Congress's revenue and spending goals for the upcoming fiscal year, set rules or other procedures for one or both houses and, as such, can have a substantial impact on all other legislation that Congress considers.

Resolutions, also referred to as simple resolutions, are designed as H Res or S Res. A simple resolution deals with matters entirely within the prerogative of one house of Congress, such as setting the spending levels for its committees, revising the chamber's standing rules, or expressing the opinion of that house on a current issue, and is acted on only by that chamber. A simple resolution is not considered by the other chamber and does not require action by the president. Like a concurrent resolution, it does not have the force of law. However, adoption of resolutions can have effects outside the chamber. For example, the Senate adopts resolutions of ratification for treaties; at the end of the 100th Congress (1987–1989) adoption of a Senate resolution had the effect of carrying over into the next Congress impeachment proceedings against a federal judge. In the House, simple resolutions embody the special orders of business, or "rules," reported by the Rules Committee that set guidelines for floor consideration of legislation.

Bill Referral

Once a measure has been introduced and given a number, it is almost always referred to committee. (Very rarely a member might ask unanimous consent that a bill be taken up for consideration on the House or Senate floor immediately. Such bills are usually either noncontroversial or of great urgency.) The Speaker of the House and the presiding officer in the Senate are responsible for referring bills introduced in their respective chambers to the appropriate committees, but the job is usually left to the House and Senate parliamentarians, respectively.

(House and Senate rules require that all bills be read three times before passage, in accordance with traditional parliamentary usage. In the House the first reading occurs when the bill is introduced and printed by number and title in the *Congressional Record.* The second reading occurs when floor consideration begins; often the bill is read section by section for amendment. The third reading comes just before the vote on final passage. Senate rules require bills and resolutions to be read twice, on different legislative days, before they are referred to committee. The third reading follows floor debate and voting on amendments.)

The jurisdictions of the standing committees are spelled out in House Rule X and Senate Rule XXV, and referrals are generally routine—tax bills go to House Ways and Means and Senate Finance, banking bills to the banking committees in both chambers, and so on. However, bills can cover a multitude of subjects that need not have any relationship to each other, which can lead to complications in the referral process.

Many issues that come before Congress cut across the jurisdictions of several committees. Three House committees—International Relations, Commerce, and Ways and Means—might all lay claim to jurisdiction over a trade measure, for example, and the Speaker might refer it all of them for consideration.

The authors of a bill often try to manipulate or anticipate the referral process to ensure it goes to a sympathetic committee or avoids a hostile one, a consideration that often figures into the manner in which legislation is drafted initially. The mechanics of this strategy have changed over the years, especially in the House, where the rules on committee referral have been modified on several occasions. Prior to 1975, measures introduced in the House could only be referred to a single committee, no matter how many subjects they might encompass. Any bill containing a tax provision, for instance, was always referred to the Ways and Means Committee.

During the reform period of the mid-1970s, in an attempt to prevent some committees from monopolizing legislation, to provide additional opportunities for a larger number of members to participate in the legislative process, and to strengthen the role of the Speaker, House rules were changed to allow the Speaker to refer legislation to more than one committee and to impose time limits on referrals. The Speaker was given several options. The Speaker could refer a bill to several committees at once, which was called a "concurrent" or "joint" referral; refer a bill first to one committee and then later to others, called a "sequential referral"; and send portions of bills to different committees, called a "split referral." As a result, some bills could be referred to numerous committees simultaneously, making it difficult to plot a path for them to the floor. Open warfare often developed among committees that sought opportunities to expand their power by claiming jurisdiction, with the Speaker placed in the middle. The Energy and Commerce Committee under the Democrats, with a mammoth portfolio and chaired by the aggressive John D. Dingell, D-Mich., from 1981 to 1995, was especially noted for its expansive, repeated, and contentious jurisdictional claims.

If necessary, legislation can be rereferred from one committee to another by unanimous consent to correct any errors that may arise.

In referring bills, the House Speaker may set deadlines for committee action. At the beginning of the 1983 session Speaker Thomas P. "Tip" O'Neill Jr., D-Mass., announced that in some multiple referrals he would designate one committee the primary committee and might "impose time limits on committees having a secondary interest following the report of the primary committee." The use of multiple referral gave House leaders greater opportunities to bargain with and bring together key legislative players and opened the process to a broader range of views. But multiple referral also created potential additional obstacles for a bill to surmount before it reached the floor. While the referral reforms of the 1970s in the House democratized the process and prevented one committee from monopolizing a particular subject matter, there were distinct negative tradeoffs in terms of increased complexity, confusion, and lack of ultimate accountability for legislation. The House-Senate conference process also was affected, as conferences grew in size to accommodate all the new participants.

Sometimes the subject matter of a bill, or the political situation surrounding it, proved to be so complex that the normal rules could not work. House rules were amended to provide that, in addition to referring bills to more than one committee, the Speaker, with the approval of the House, may set up an ad hoc committee to consider a bill. Speaker O'Neill did that in 1977 when he created a temporary committee to consider President Jimmy Carter's energy package.

When the Republicans took over the House in 1995, they had little stake in the existing system or in the various formal and informal jurisdictional accommodations that had been reached over the years to satisfy key Democrats. They reacted to complaints that the referral process was too confusing by changing the rules again and further enhancing the role of the leadership. The earlier version of the "joint" referral was abolished. Instead the Speaker was required to designate a primary committee to manage the major workload related to a bill; other committees would participate through an "additional initial referral" or through later sequential referrals at the Speaker's discretion, and under possible time limitations.

The Senate usually refers bills to more than one committee by unanimous consent. Bills may be referred to two or more committees concurrently or sequentially, or a bill may be split so that part of it is referred to one committee, part to another. Also, the majority and minority leaders or their designees, acting jointly, may offer a motion providing for a joint or sequential referral. In the Senate multiple referrals may contain a deadline for action by one or more of the committees.

Often, different committees of the House and Senate can claim jurisdiction of the same subject matter, because the committee systems of the two bodies do not coincide. The result can be a dramatically different reception for a measure, depending on the composition of the panel. A classic example of this strategy was the 1963 civil rights bill. The House version was referred to the Judiciary Committee, whose chairman supported the measure. The chairman of the Senate Judiciary Committee, however, opposed it; thus the Senate version was drafted in such a way that it would be referred to the more sympathetic Senate Commerce Committee. (The measure guaranteed minorities access to public accommodations, which fell within the commerce clause of the Constitution.)

IN COMMITTEE

Although the House and Senate handle bills in different ways when they reach the floor, the committee system in both chambers is similar. The standing committees of Congress determine the fate of most proposals. A bill comes under the sharpest scrutiny at the committee stage, in part because committee members and staff frequently are experts in the subjects under their jurisdiction. If a measure is going to be substantially revised that revision usually occurs at the committee or subcommittee level rather than during floor consideration. Committees usually use hearings as the first step of their process, to receive testimony and information. But if legislation moves forward, further revision occurs at meetings where a bill is "marked up" when amendments are offered, debated, and voted on.

Legislation may be disposed of by a committee in several ways:

• It may be ignored if the chairman never puts it on the agenda at a committee meeting, which is by far the most frequent disposition of most legislation.

• It may be approved, or "reported favorably" with or without amendments, which is the normal result for most legislation that is allowed to reach the stage of a committee markup.

• It may be reported "negatively" or "without recommendation," which might still allow full House or Senate consideration. For example, in a highly unusual action the House Rules Committee in 1996 reported a rule providing procedures for consideration of a controversial campaign reform bill "without recommendation," an indication of distaste for the House GOP leadership's decision to schedule floor action on this controversial proposal. (Thirty years earlier, when the committee was still an autonomous power center rather than an arm of the House leadership that it later became, the panel would probably have simply refused to grant a rule).

• It might be taken up and killed outright through a tabling motion, a rare event but one that occurred in 1997 in the House Judiciary Committee, which used this means to give sponsors of legislation abolishing affirmative action programs a vote while demonstrating that the proposal was not yet ripe for action.

Subcommittee Action

The full committee may decide to consider a bill in the first instance but more often the committee chairman assigns it to a subcommittee for study and hearings. The rules of many committees in the House were amended starting in the 1970s to require the referral of bills to subcommittees, and the House Democratic Caucus adopted a rule urging a greater role on the floor for subcommittees that had initiated major legislation. The Republican-controlled House of the late 1990s, while continuing to use subcommittees, subjected them to greater discipline and control by the leadership in pursuing a party agenda than was true when Democrats were in the majority.

Assigning bills to a sympathetic or unsympathetic subcommittee is one of the ways a committee chairman can influence the legislative outcome. No longer able to dictate committee activities the way they could prior to 1970s procedural reforms, committee chairmen now negotiate with committee members to work out arrangements that will accommodate as many members as possible. But the chairmen still controls the committee's funds and can hire and fire most committee staffers. Chairmen therefore are in a position either to promote expeditious action on legislation they favor or to encourage delay and inaction on measures they opposes.

Few bills reach the House or Senate floor without first being the subject of subcommittee hearings. Hearings are used to receive testimony from members of Congress, executive branch officials, policy experts, interest groups, and the general public, and are usually held at the subcommittee level. Testimony may be delivered by witnesses either in person or through written submissions that may later be published as part of the hearing transcript. Most persons who come before committees offer prepared statements, after which they may be questioned by subcommittee members and, on some committees, by staff members.

Hearings are used for a raft of purposes—to gather information, to attract media attention, to test initial reaction to a legislative idea. Full committees will sometimes hold hearings as well on subjects of major public controversy, or when witnesses from the top levels of government are called to testify. Senate hearings in 1997 on alleged campaign finance scandals were held by the full Committee on Governmental Affairs, rather than its investigations subcommittee, and a companion House inquiry was run by the full Committee on Government Reform and Oversight.

Hearings are intended as fact-finding forums to educate both members of Congress and the public about specific problems. They may also be used to assess the degree of support or opposition to a particular bill or to promote support or opposition to a bill both in Congress and among the public. Many hearings are brief and perfunctory. Because demands on legislators' time are so great only a few subcommittee members with a special interest in a subject are likely to participate.

The presence of television, along with controversial subject matter, can attract substantial interest from members even on subjects on which they might not otherwise actively participate. The creation of the Cable Satellite Public Affairs Network (C-SPAN) network, which usually televises some hearings on any day that Congress is in session, has forced Congress to accommodate the new medium. Television's powerful intrusiveness is coupled with the medium's need for interesting or dramatic events that readily provide heroes and villains and promote controversy. Members with the skill to accommodate these channels of communication to the public have a powerful force to influence the outcome of policy debates. *(See box, Televised Floor Debate Here to Stay, p. 64.)*

The Army-McCarthy hearings in the early 1950s turned public opinion against Sen. Joseph R. McCarthy, R-Wis., who had made a career of accusations of Communist penetration of the government. Senate Foreign Relations Committee hearings in the mid-1960s, under Sen. J. William Fulbright, D-Ark., mobilized opposition to the Vietnam War. Senate committee hearings in 1973 into a variety of illegal activities in the White House that came to be known collectively as the Watergate scandal, and the ensuing 1974 House Judiciary Committee impeachment proceedings against President Nixon, destroyed the remnants of popular support for Nixon and, in the process, made folk heroes of the committees' chairmen, Sen. Sam Ervin, D-N.C. and Rep. Peter W. Rodino Jr., D-N.J. Televised Senate Judiciary Committee hearings in 1987 helped fuel the controversy over the nomination of Robert H. Bork to a seat on the Supreme Court, moving public opinion decisively against him and ensuring his defeat. Explosive 1991 hearings by the all-male Senate Judiciary Committee on sexual harassment accusations against Supreme Court nominee Clarence Thomas charged a national debate that continued years later. While public opinion about Thomas was sharply divided and he was ultimately confirmed by a 52–48 vote, the most immediate impact of the hearings was to focus more attention on issues sexual harassment and gender politics in the 1992 political campaigns, contributing to the election of four additional women to the Senate in a period that their supporters called the "Year of the Woman."

In less historic or controversial circumstances, a reasonable amount of national press coverage will result from testimony by popular actors and other celebrities who are active in a particular cause, such as film stars Robert Redford on environmental issues or Elizabeth Taylor on increased AIDS research funding.

Ordinary citizens with good stories to tell can also hit a nerve, especially on subjects of broad public interest. In 1997, House hearings on allegations of abusive tactics against citizens by the Internal Revenue Service (IRS) had such a significant and swift impact that Clinton administration opposition to a reform bill sponsored by House Republicans instantly collapsed and the president endorsed the legislation. Before the president's reversal, the fight seemed to be about the structure of the IRS. With the help of television, the Republicans gained control of the issue and won a political victory far more easily than otherwise might have been possible.

During the last decade, most hearings and meetings of congressional committees occur in open session, although committees dealing with national security and other sensitive or classified information often close their meetings. The congressional Intelligence committees nearly always meet in closed session. The Senate Armed Services and House National Security committees use a combination of open and closed (executive) hearings. Until 1971 the House Appropriations Committee held all its hearings in closed session.

House rules by 1995 made it extremely difficult for most committees and subcommittees to close meetings or hearings except for a few specified reasons relating to national security, use of law enforcement information, or protection of the rights of witnesses testifying. A rules amendment in 1995 liberalized media access to open sessions and made coverage by radio, television, and photographers a right to be exercised by the press, not a privilege to be granted or withheld by committees.

Once the hearings are concluded, the subcommittee may take no action, in effect killing a bill. Or it may "mark up" the bill, considering the contents of each provision and section of

TELEVISED FLOOR DEBATES HERE TO STAY

At noon on March 19, 1979, the U.S. House of Representatives made its live television debut. That appearance was the culmination of years of hard work by proponents of the idea. First proposed in 1944 by then-Sen. Claude Pepper, D-Fla., the movement to open the chambers to television cameras took hold only slowly in a body often resistant to change. Indeed, Senate floor action has been televised only since June 1986.

Albert Gore, a Tennessee Democrat who became vice president under Bill Clinton, led the fight for television in the House, where he served from 1977 to 1985, and in the Senate, where he served from 1985 to 1993. "The marriage of this medium and of our open debate have the potential . . . to revitalize representative democracy," Gore said in the first televised speech in 1979, a one-minute address to the House before the regular legislative day began.

Since members can use television to keep up with the action, said political scientist Steven S. Smith in 1989, "(they) are not quite as reliant on a colleague at the door telling them whether to vote up or down."

DAWN OF A NEW AGE

Until the early 1970s, television was just a dream to its proponents. But the arrival in Congress of reform-minded members in the wake of political scandals in the 1970s, particularly the Watergate affair that led to President Richard Nixon's resignation, contributed to an atmosphere more amenable to openness.

In 1977 the Democratic leadership directed the House Select Committee on Congressional Operations to conduct a ninety-day experiment using closed-circuit telecasts of House floor proceedings to members' offices. The experiment was labeled a success, and on October 27, 1977, the House tentatively agreed to go ahead, although it took some time to iron out the details.

In June 1978 news organizations began broadcasting House proceedings over radio, and by March 1979 television had arrived. The Cable Satellite Public Affairs Network (C-SPAN), the private, nonprofit cooperative of the cable television industry, was launched in 1979 with the express purpose of televising Congress. House employees remain in control of the cameras.

The Senate proceeded more slowly in bringing in the cameras. Majority Leader Howard H. Baker Jr., R-Tenn., began the effort in earnest in 1981. In February 1986 the Senate passed a resolution to allow television broadcasting.

For a month the Senate permitted closed-circuit transmissions into members' offices, followed by six weeks of public broadcasts. At the conclusion of the six-week test period, the Senate voted to keep the cameras permanently. And on June 2, 1986, the Senate premiered on a second C-SPAN channel.

Senate rules are fairly strict. Cameras are operated by congressional staff and usually remain fixed on a single speaker. Initially the House rules were similar. Since May 1984, however, House cameras began to slowly pan the room during votes and special orders, a period at the end of a daily session when members may speak on various topics, usually to a mostly empty chamber.

When the Republicans took control of the House in 1995, procedures for panning the chamber changed. The camera would focus on individual members talking on benches in the chamber or reading the newspaper, practices which appeared to give some degree of "editorial control" to the camera operators and raised concerns about possible partisan abuse of the television coverage. After protests at the new intrusiveness, Speaker Newt Gingrich ordered that such close-in shots of members who are not directly participating in the business on the floor be stopped, though the cameras still have more mobility than they did under Democratic rule.

THE VIEWING AUDIENCE

The public does watch Congress on television. As of January 1998, C-SPAN had 72.5 million subscribing households who received its cable channel showing House proceedings (C-SPAN1), and 49.5 for its Senate channel (C-SPAN2).

the measure, amending some provisions, discarding others, perhaps rewriting the measure altogether. When the markup is finished, the subcommittee reports its version of the legislation, presuming it has not rejected the measure, to the full committee. In some instances, the full committee may exercise its authority to take up the bill directly, bypassing a separate subcommittee markup stage.

Full Committee Action

The full committee may repeat the subcommittee procedures, sometimes even including additional hearings. It may conduct an amending process, especially if that stage of subcommittee action has been bypassed, or it may simply ratify the action of the subcommittee. Frequently the full committee will propose additional amendments to alter the proposal. If the amendments are not extensive, the original bill is "reported with amendments." When the bill comes to the floor, the House or Senate must approve, alter, or reject the committee amendments,

If the changes are substantial and the legislation is complicated, the committee chairman or another committee member may introduce a "clean bill," which embodies the proposed amendments. The original bill is then set aside and the clean bill, with a new number, is the version voted out of committee

In a survey by Statistical Research Inc. released in January 1997, it was estimated that 22.4 million people watched C-SPAN at some point each week, with 72 percent watching congressional hearings, 67 percent the House floor, and 64 percent the Senate floor. However, the increase in the number of viewers was less than four percent from a decade earlier.

In 1988 21.6 million households reported watching C-SPAN, which commissioned the survey. The public is not C-SPAN's only audience, though. When Congress is in session it is nearly impossible to find a congressional office without its television tuned to C-SPAN.

Time is a precious commodity for members of Congress. Televised proceedings and committee hearings often allow them to gauge their time better during votes and other floor activities. Members follow the proceedings and committee hearings to keep abreast of the latest developments.

MIXED VERDICTS ON MEDIA IMPACT

Members of Congress and political scientists agree that the cameras are a fixture in the chambers and the public would not allow their removal. "The horror stories that were supposed to happen didn't happen," political scientist Larry Sabato said in 1989.

While passage of rules changes allowing television coverage of floor proceedings was probably inevitable, the ultimate effect on the legislative process at the heart of Congress remains difficult to evaluate. During the 1990s there have been widespread complaints from members about the increasing partisanship and "meanness" in debate, and some observers—both in and out of Congress—blamed the live coverage for encouraging use floor speeches to produce sound bites for the evening news. Not only television, but the advent of talk radio shows that specialized in inciting listeners, contributed to a debasement of political dialogue. A substantive and spontaneous legislative process, it is argued, has too often been sidelined by staged events.

In the House, use of one-minute speeches for this purpose has become widespread with outside political committees and interest groups sending suggested remarks for members to recite. Both parties often carefully organize their presentations in this daily forum. The use of charts and exhibits likely to be visible on a television screen has proliferated. Even opposing political candidates have gotten into the act, using excerpts of speeches by House members in campaign commercials, and then attacking them. A House rule prohibits use of the televised proceedings for political purposes but it is enforceable only against sitting members. Democrats had been considering a proposal to modify this rule, effective with the 104th Congress, to allow members to better defend themselves against opponents who might use excerpts of floor proceedings in potentially misleading ways, but the idea died with the 1994 election that turned over House control to Republicans.

Members of the House held a bipartisan retreat in March, 1997, in Hershey, Pennsylvania, as a reaction to the frequent vitriolic floor speeches and intense partisanship of the previous Congress. In a background report on *Civility in the House of Representatives,* political scientist Kathleen Hall Jamieson argued that traditional methods for striking inappropriate language from the *Congressional Record* and letting tempers cool had been rendered obsolete by television. "Not only is it impossible to strike words taken down from the C-SPAN record but the process, designed to enhance civility, may instead diminish it, as the offending Member plays to the cameras. C-SPAN footage also increases the likelihood that moments of incivility will be replayed on news."

Of course, some of these concerns reflect late twentieth-century sensibilities about the way a political process should be conducted. In earlier times, members of Congress sometimes fought each other in physical brawls on the floor and had duels with political opponents. So recent instances of incivility, while disturbing, pale in historical comparison.

Most observers of Congress agree that despite all the attention televised has generated, Congress survived the television revolution. It was a change the public would have forced eventually if the two houses had not acted. Television made the work of members of Congress more real and immediate to constituents, giving a sense of elected officials that voters often saw only in campaign commercials. In that sense, television strengthened Congress as an institution.

SOURCES: John Schachter, "Congress Begins Second Decade Under TV's Watchful Glare," *Congressional Quarterly Weekly Report,* March 11, 1989, 507–509; C-SPAN News Release, "New Survey: 22 Million Watch C-SPAN Weekly," January 6, 1997; Kathleen Hall Jamieson, *Civility in the House of Representatives,* (Philadelphia: University of Pennsylvania, Annenberg Public Policy Center, 1997), Report Series No. 10.

and reported. In addition to expediting floor action, the clean bill procedure also can eliminate problems of germaneness. House germaneness rules require only that amendments offered on the floor, including committee amendments, be pertinent to the bill; the rules do not apply to provisions of the bill itself as introduced. So any amendments made part of a clean committee bill are usually protected from points of order on the floor. (There are exceptions that can be used to delete provisions from bills that include tax or tariff matters not reported by the Ways and Means Committee, and provisions in appropriations bills that violate the jurisdictions of authorizing committees.)

In 1973 both chambers adopted new rules to encourage more committees to open their markup meetings to the public, and most committee meetings were opened. By 1990, however, there was a discernible trend toward closing some meetings, particularly on controversial bills. Advocates of closed sessions believed that members would make politically difficult decisions more easily in the absence of lobbyists and interested constituents. The minority, which often objected to the decisions made, pressed for greater openness and attacked closed sessions as a symbol of majority arrogance.

When the Republicans assumed control of the House in 1995, they amended rules for the conduct of meetings and hearings to make closed sessions more difficult. For example, the new rules

At a House Appropriations Committee meeting, Chairman Robert L. Livingston, R-La, right, and David R. Obey, D-Wis., conduct business at their lecterns.

allow a committee majority, by a roll-call vote, to close all or part of a meeting to consider legislation only by determining that an open meeting would endanger national security; compromise sensitive law enforcement information; tend to defame, degrade, or incriminate any person; or violate a law or rule of the House. Arguments to close as a matter of convenience or to satisfy members' desire for privacy no longer carried weight. All meetings and hearings open to the public were also open automatically to broadcast and photographic media, without the need for advance permission.

When a committee votes to approve a measure, it is said to "order the bill reported." Occasionally, a committee may order a bill reported unfavorably or without recommendation. The House Judiciary Committee, for example, voted 19–17 in June 1990 to report without recommendation a proposed constitutional amendment barring desecration of the American flag. In such cases, the committee may be acting only because of overwhelming political pressure to deal with legislation a majority of its members actually disapprove of but feel that they cannot avoid. This situation occurred after the Supreme Court threw out a statute barring the practice on constitutional grounds. The constitutional amendment later passed the House but failed in the Senate.

But because a committee can effectively kill a measure by not acting on it, committee reports almost invariably recommend passage. Those bills that are reported favorably have usually been amended to satisfy a majority of the committee's members.

Committee Reports. House rules and Senate custom require that a written report accompany each bill reported from a committee to the floor. The report, written by the committee staff, typically describes the purpose and scope of the bill, explains committee amendments, indicates proposed changes in existing law, estimates additional costs to the government of the recommended program changes, and often includes the texts of communications from department and agency officials whose views on the legislation have been solicited. Committee members opposed to the bill or specific sections of it often submit minority views in a separate section of the report. Bills discharged from a committee prior to formal committee action and brought up on the floor are not accompanied by a written report.

After enactment of the Legislative Reorganization Act of 1970, committees were required to publish in their reports all votes taken on amendments disposed of during markup as well as the vote to report the bill. Only vote totals were required, not the position of individual members on roll calls. Following rules changes in 1995, House committees were also required to publish in the report how members voted individually both on the bill and on any amendments considered and disposed of by roll-call vote, whether successful or not. Committees are required to keep a record of all roll calls and make it available to the public on request, which provides another source of information if a bill has never actually been reported. The Senate has similar, if somewhat looser, procedural requirements. It requires that the results of all votes, including the votes of individual senators, be included in the committee report unless previously announced by the committee.

Reports are numbered, by Congress and chamber, in the order in which they are filed (S Rept 105-1, S Rept 105-2, H Rept 105-1, H Rept 105-2, and onward, with the first number referring to the Congress in which the bill is reported) and immediately printed. The report number and the date the bill was reported formally are also shown on the bill. The reported bill is also printed with any committee amendments indicated by insertions in italics and deletions in stricken-through type.

Sometimes, a House committee will rework legislation well

after the time it is reported using the Rules Committee as a means to make final changes to its liking, or to accommodate other committees' interests, or to deal with concerns raised by the leadership. In these cases, the Rules Committee may make a new bill, often referred to as "an amendment in the nature of a substitute," the vehicle for formal debate and amendment on the floor, while retaining the shell of the bill's "HR" number. Adoption of the rule could substitute this new text for the original language, which would never be formally acted on and would disappear entirely once the bill is passed. Or the Rules Committee may allow consideration of a new bill with an entirely new number, making the legislative history of an issue into a tricky maze in which the original bill, along with its committee report, appear to die through lack of House consideration while actually forming the basis of eventual chamber action.

Legislative Intent. In some situations, the language of the report is as important as the bill itself. It has been common practice for committees, including House-Senate conference committees, to write in their reports instructions directing government agencies on interpretation and enforcement of the law. Moreover, courts have relied on these guidelines in establishing what is known as "legislative intent."

Some legal scholars, judges, and members of the Supreme Court have expressed skepticism about relying on these reports because they are not written into law, or relying on floor debate, complaining that Congress is often sloppy in its preparation for floor action. The most prominent and outspoken critic of "legislative intent" in the 1990s was Supreme Court Justice Antonin Scalia. Critics say they prefer to rely on the actual text of the measure as the basis for statutory interpretations. Others counter that divorcing a bill from the circumstances surrounding its passage can lead to misinterpretations.

Legal scholar Robert A. Katzmann of the Brookings Institution notes: "The more authoritative Congress is as to the appropriate use of such material, the more likely that legislative history will have the intended weight. Thus it is imperative that Congress develop means to clarify the use of such materials if courts are to better interpret legislative meaning." Katzmann suggests that Congress take care to use "more precise drafting, more authoritative legislative histories, and refinement of the process of revising statutes."[9]

Lobbyists are also vitally interested in the report language as one way to promote or protect their clients' interests. Many appropriations bills, for example, set out only the amount of money an agency or department might spend. But the accompanying committee report often contains directives on how Congress expects the money to be spent or warnings to bureaucrats not to take certain actions.

House Floor Action: Structured Efficiency

Because of the sheer number of representatives in the House—435—the chamber can appear disorderly, especially at the end of a session, with members milling about in small groups and streaming in and out of the chamber to answer to roll calls. But underlying this general hubbub is a structure for considering legislation that allows the House to act relatively efficiently and expeditiously. *(See box, Dilatory Tactics Are Limited in the House, p. 74.)*

SCHEDULING FLOOR ACTION

Bills can reach the House floor in a number of ways. Most are reported first by a committee. However, there is no requirement in the rules that a bill be reported by or even considered by a committee, or that any report be available for members prior to floor action, unless the bill was in fact actually reported. By unanimous consent, noncontroversial bills and resolutions can even be offered from the floor, considered, and passed without even being formally introduced and given a number first. Some bills receive committee consideration but may be called up for a vote without any final committee action or a report being filed. Major legislation, however, nearly always must survive the full stages of committee action culminating in a committee vote and report, and also receive a rule from the Rules Committee before being brought up for action. In practice, even noncontroversial bills brought up under an expedited procedure called suspension of the rules are accompanied by a committee report, or have received some committee action, in order to reassure members that the bill's presence on the floor has legitimacy and that interested members have been given sufficient notice to participate in the process.

After a bill is reported from a House committee and before it is scheduled for floor action, it is placed on one of three legislative calendars: Union, House, or Private. Bills already on the Union Calendar may also be placed on a "Corrections Calendar" at the Speaker's discretion. Another calendar, Discharge, is used only for motions to discharge committees from consideration of a measure, when such motions have received the signatures of a majority of members on a discharge petition. Each day the House is in session it publishes a Calendar of the House as a formal document that lists all matters on each of the calendars, and also provides a history of action on them by committees, the House and Senate, conferences, and the president.

All bills, including authorization bills, having any effect on the Treasury go on the Union Calendar, which is by far the most important. Technically it is the Calendar of the Committee of the Whole House on the State of the Union, so called because bills listed on it are first considered in the Committee of the Whole and reported back to the House for a final vote on passage. Other types of matters, such as investigative reports approved by committees, may also appear on the Union Calendar even though they will not be considered by the House. Legislation on the Union Calendar may be considered on the floor, debated, and amended in a wide variety of different ways under the rules of the House. *(See "Action in the Committee of the Whole," p. 83.)*

Matters that have no direct effect on the Treasury are placed

A TYPICAL SCHEDULE IN THE HOUSE

The House conducts different types of business on different days, so its daily routine will vary. However, from week to week, a pattern is usually followed.

• The House convenes early for "Morning Hour" debate for five-minute speeches on Mondays and Tuesdays sixty to ninety minutes prior to the formal opening of the day's session, even if that is in the afternoon. No votes or legislative business can occur. The House then recesses until the formal convening of the day's session.

• The chaplain delivers the opening prayer, and a House member leads the chamber in the Pledge of Allegiance.

• The Speaker approves the Journal, the record of the previous day's proceedings. Often a member demands a roll-call vote on the approval of the Journal, which can be used to determine who is present and to allow the leadership to "whip" them on other matters. The Journal vote can also be postponed by the Speaker until later in the day and clustered with other votes that may be occurring.

• After the House receives messages from the Senate and the president and privileged reports from committees, and conducts other similar procedural activities, members are recognized by unanimous consent for one-minute speeches on any topic.

• The House then turns to its legislative business. On Mondays and Tuesdays only, the House usually considers less controversial bills, sometimes dozens at a time, under the suspension of the rules process requiring a two-thirds majority for passage, and recorded votes are postponed until late in the day, or until the next day. Measures that are even less controversial are frequently passed by unanimous consent. A "Corrections Calendar" for the consideration of bills that the Speaker determines would change erroneous actions or regulations by the federal government may be called on the second and fourth Tuesdays of each month. A sixty percent majority of members present and voting is required for passage. The House must call the Private Calendar on the first Tuesday of each month and the Speaker may direct it to be called on the third Tuesday.

• Virtually every bill of any significance is considered under a special rule, reported from the Rules Committee, that sets guidelines for floor action. The rule may be approved with little opposition but the vote can also be a first test of a bill's popularity. If the rule restricts the amendments that may be offered those barred from offering amendments may work with opponents of the bill itself to defeat the rule or to defeat the previous question so that amendments to the rule can be offered.

• After the rule is adopted, the House resolves into the Committee of the Whole to consider the bill. The Speaker relinquishes the gavel to another member, who serves as chairman of this "committee" and presides over the activities. Debate time is controlled by the managers of the bill, usually the chairman and ranking minority member of the standing committee with jurisdiction over the measure. *(See "Action in the Committee of the Whole," p. 83.)*

After time for general debate has expired, amendments that are permitted under the rule may be offered and debated. Debate on an amendment may be for a fixed time. If none is specified in the rule it is conducted under the "five-minute rule," which limits each side to five minutes. However, members may obtain additional speaking time by offering amendments to "strike the last word," a pro forma action that allows additional time for discussion and debate.

Voting may be conducted in three different ways plus variations depending on whether the House or the Committee of the Whole is sitting: by voice, the usual procedure; by division (members stand to be counted but no record of names is kept); or by electronic device (referred to as "the yeas and nays" or a "recorded vote" depending on the parliamentary circumstances). Certain matters in the House require a roll-call vote under the Constitution (for example, to reconsider a vetoed bill) or the rules of the House (for example, passing a general appropriations bill or closing a conference committee meeting to the public). Most electronic votes last fifteen minutes. If several votes in sequence are conducted, the second and any subsequent votes are usually reduced to a minimum of five minutes. *(See box, Methods of Voting, p. 78.)*

• After the amending process is complete, the Committee of the Whole "rises," and the chairman reports to the Speaker on the actions taken. The House votes on whether to accept the amendments adopted in the Committee, usually a pro forma action. The House then votes on final passage of the bill, sometimes after voting on a motion by opponents to recommit the bill to its committee of origin, which would kill it, or to recommit the bill with instructions to report it back "forthwith" with additional amendments that would be adopted prior to final passage. After final passage, a motion to reconsider is in order but is usually announced as "laid on the table" by the Speaker to save time.

• After the House completes its legislative business, members may speak for up to sixty minutes each under "special orders," with hour speeches limited to four hours evenly divided between the parties (except on Tuesdays). Members must reserve the time in advance but can speak on any topic—often to an almost deserted chamber. Members seeking recognition for short periods of time, such as five or ten minutes, are recognized first, alternating between the parties. In 1994, the House limited the total time available for special orders to prevent sessions from extending too long but special orders cannot extend beyond midnight.

on the House Calendar. These bills or, far more commonly, resolutions, generally deal with administrative and procedural matters and are usually not considered by the Committee of the Whole but taken up directly by the House. However, some legislation of great significance, such as constitutional amendments and approval of compacts among states, appear on the House Calendar. Simple and concurrent resolutions also go on the House Calendar, including the concurrent resolution that starts off yearly action on the budget process and special rules reported from the Rules Committee allowing consideration of other legislation. On the floor, matters from this calendar may also be considered in several different ways.

Noncontroversial bills in the past had been placed on the Consent Calendar, but it was not used during the final years of Democratic control of the House that preceded the GOP majority starting in 1995. The leadership and committees preferred to use the "suspension of the rules" process, which is itself often mistakenly referred to as a calendar. The Consent Calendar was abolished in 1995 and replaced by the new Corrections Calendar.

The Corrections Calendar is completely under the control of the Speaker and was created by the new Republican majority as a vehicle to promote its political agenda. Bills may be placed there by the Speaker if they are considered noncontroversial and deal with correcting "mistakes" in previously enacted legislation or in government actions or regulations. The Republican Conference considered these types of measures to be a class of legislation that deserved special recognition and easy access to the floor. After putting this new device in place, Speaker Gingrich sought advice from a bipartisan task force he established to advise him on use of the calendar.

The Corrections Calendar may be called on the second and fourth Tuesdays of each month, if desired by the Speaker. The procedure for consideration of these bills is specified in House rules. Debate is limited to one hour, evenly divided between the majority and the minority, and only committee amendments or those offered by the chairman are in order. The minority is allowed to offer one motion to recommit, which may contain instructions providing for consideration of other amendments. Passage of all measures on the Corrections Calendar requires a 60 percent supermajority vote, which effectively prevents the Speaker from using it for consideration of controversial matters. After an initial flurry of partisan strife in 1995, the Corrections Calendar has not been employed frequently, and no measure called up on it had been defeated as of early 1998. If a measure were to fail, it would retain its place on its original calendar and could still be called up later under other procedures in House rules.

Private immigration bills and bills for the relief of individuals with claims against the United States are placed on the Private Calendar. This calendar must be called on the first Tuesday of each month, unless dispensed with by a two-thirds vote or by unanimous consent, which is what usually occurs unless there are a number of bills on the calendar ready for passage. The Private Calendar may also be called on the third Tuesday of each month at the Speaker's discretion. If two or more members object to the consideration of a bill it will be recommitted to the committee that reported it, but if there is some concern or uncertainty about a bill it may be passed over "without prejudice" by unanimous consent and still remain eligible for action on a future call of the Private calendar. Both major political parties appoint several members as "official objectors" to monitor such bills and ensure that only those that have overwhelming support pass using the Private Calendar. Most private bills are called up from the calendar and simply passed by unanimous consent without debate and without a recorded vote, but debate may occur under a procedure that allows any member to speak for five minutes. Amendments may be offered and debated for a maximum of five minutes in support, and five minutes opposed.

The Judiciary Committee handles most private relief bills, which typically deal with various claims against the government, and immigration status. Once enacted, private laws receive separate private law numbers, as opposed to the numeration given to public laws that Congress enacts. The quantity of private bills enacted into law, however, has dropped precipitously since the 96th Congress (1979–1981) when 123 private laws were enacted. In the 102nd (1991–1993), 103rd (1993–1995), and 104th (1995–1997) Congresses, there were twenty, eight, and four respectively. In the first session of the 105th Congress, only four became law. Congressional scholar Walter Oleszek has suggested that the transfer of jurisdiction over some of these issues to federal agencies, fears of scandals over favoritism to individuals, and reluctance to disburse federal funds for private concerns in an era of deficit spending led to a decline in popularity of the private law mechanism. As a result, the House does not call the Private Calendar very frequently anymore.

The House also has a Discharge Calendar. It is used to list motions to discharge committees from further consideration of bills or resolutions, when a majority of the total membership of the House—218—signs a discharge petition at the desk in the House chamber. Discharge motions are taken up on the second and fourth Mondays of each month and may be debated for twenty minutes, divided between a proponent and an opponent. If the motion is adopted, the measure discharged will then be considered in a number of possible ways. Since the discharge procedure is rarely attempted, and few discharge petitions obtain the 218 signatures, the Discharge Calendar usually consists of a restatement of the discharge rule followed by a blank page.

Discharge motions that have been filed but have not obtained the requisite signatures can be found in the *Congressional Record,* along with a current list of signers. *(See box, Prying Loose Legislation Stuck in Committee: Use of Discharge and Calendar Wednesday, p. 70.)*

The five calendars (Union, House, Private, Corrections, and Discharge) are printed in one document titled *Calendars of the United States House of Representatives and History of Legislation.* This calendar is printed daily when the House is in session. The first issue of the week lists in numerical order all House and most Senate measures that have been reported by committees, with a capsule history of congressional action on each. It also includes a general index and other valuable reference material.

Bills are placed on the calendars in the order in which they are reported. But they do not come to the floor in chronological order; in fact, some never come to the floor at all. The Speaker of the House, working with the majority leader, committee chairmen, and the Rules Committee, determines which bills will come to the floor and when. How the bill will be handled on the floor depends on whether it is noncontroversial, privileged, or major legislation that requires a special rule from the Rules Committee.

PRYING LOOSE LEGISLATION STUCK IN COMMITTEE: USE OF DISCHARGE AND CALENDAR WEDNESDAY

The House has two special procedures—the discharge petition and Calendar Wednesday—designed to bring to a vote legislation that has been blocked from floor consideration. Both devices were instituted during the speakership of Joseph G. Cannon, R-Ill., (1903–1911) in an effort to circumvent the near-complete control the dictatorial Speaker held over the legislative agenda. These procedures have been used rarely and are even more rarely successful. However, the threat of using a discharge petition has sometimes been successful in prompting action through the normal legislative process. *(See "Cannonism," p. 14.)*

DISCHARGE PETITION

The House's modern discharge petition was first adopted in 1910, reached approximately its present form in 1931, and was then further modified in the 1990s as public attention to the procedure increased. The discharge petition enables a majority of the membership to bring before the House any public bill blocked in a standing committee. With respect to the Rules Committee, it allows discharge of resolutions proposing changes in House rules and of resolutions providing special rules for consideration of any bill that has been before a standing committee.

While the discharge rule is specifically directed against committees, its use also serves as a check on the majority leadership. This is true because in cases where discharge is attempted a committee is usually working in concert with or at the direction of the leadership. (If the leadership wanted a vote on a measure, it could simply use the Rules Committee to bring it out to the floor.)

The discharge procedure may be used if a bill has been referred to a standing committee for at least thirty legislative days without having been reported. Members also have the option, in such cases, of introducing a special rule providing for consideration of the bill which, if not reported in seven legislative days, becomes subject to discharge. Any member may then file a motion to discharge a committee from further consideration, popularly known as a discharge "petition," which members may sign at the clerk's desk in the chamber whenever the House is in session. Members may withdraw their names until 218—a majority—have signed, at which point the motion to discharge is placed on the Discharge Calendar and the complete list of the names of the signers and the order of their signatures are published in the Calendar and in the *Congressional Record.*

The identity of the members signing a discharge petition was kept secret until 1993. Up to that point, the petition had been considered an internal matter in the House; secrecy was intended to ensure that the process was considered a last resort and to permit quiet efforts to persuade members to withdraw their names and to preserve opportunities to reach a compromise on an issue through the normal legislative process. From time to time, some members would threaten to reveal the names of their colleagues who had or had not signed a petition, in order to subject them to pressure from outside interest groups. There had been stories of members asking to view a petition, with each memorizing several names and then leaving to write them down until a comprehensive list was obtained.

The sponsors of the 1993 rules change, principally from the Republican minority, intended that it would pressure more members to sign such petitions. They viewed a discharge petition as a legislative mechanism that should be subjected to public scrutiny, much like a member's cosponsorship of a bill. The handful of members publicly opposed to opening the process worried that it might result in the more frequent consideration of irresponsible legislation and undermine the committee system.

Ironically, the resolution to open up the process to public view was only passed after itself being discharged from the Rules Committee. However, no significant changes in the normal legislative process were immediately evident. The names of members signing a discharge petition were published in the *Congressional Record* on a weekly basis and made public by the clerk of the House daily.

A motion to discharge must remain on the Discharge Calendar for seven legislative days before it can be called up for floor action. On the second and fourth Mondays of each month, except during the last six days of the session, any member who has signed the discharge petition may be recognized to move that the committee be discharged. Debate on the motion is limited to twenty minutes, divided equally between proponents and opponents. If the motion carries, any member who signed the petition can move for immediate consideration of the discharged measure, which then becomes the business of the House until it is resolved. Depending on the nature of the measure discharged, it may be considered either in the House or in the Committee of the Whole. If the House postpones action on the discharged measure, it is placed on the appropriate calendar, to be available for potential floor action just as other measures are.

Partly because the process is so cumbersome and time-consuming, and partly because members were, usually reluctant to challenge committees so directly, the discharge petition has seldom been successful. Between 1931 and 1996, 531 discharge petitions were filed, but only twenty-six measures were actually discharged. Of these, nineteen passed the House, but only two laws were ultimately enacted into law along with two resolutions changing House rules. The failure to enact more laws suggests that the resistance to such legislation in the normal House legislative process was not purely obstructionist. It often foreshadowed a level of controversy that reappeared again at other stages such as in the Senate or with the president. This made final success very difficult.[1]

Discharge petitions nonetheless can serve a purpose by focusing attention on a particular issue and sometimes forcing the recalcitrant committee to take action. In 1985, after 200 members signed a petition filed by Harold L. Volkmer, D-Mo., to discharge from the Judiciary Committee a Senate-passed bill weakening federal gun controls, that committee hastily reported out gun control legislation. Ultimately Volkmer's version of the measure passed the House, in part because his discharge petition, which was eventually signed by 218 members, forced the Rules Committee to make his version in order on the floor.

In modern practice, rather than discharge actual legislation, discharge supporters will instead usually target the Rules Committee, especially if they intend to make a serious effort to obtain 218 signatures. They introduce and attempt to discharge a special rule that not only brings up the legislation but does so employing procedures of the sponsors' choosing that provide maximum prospects for passage. (Discharging legislation directly to the floor without a rule can subject it to potentially cumbersome floor procedures that might inhibit passage.)

Constitutional amendments are frequently the subjects of discharge petitions. For example, in 1990, 1992, and 1994 special rules were discharged from the Rules Committee providing for consideration of constitutional amendments requiring a balanced budget. The Judiciary Committee, which had jurisdiction over the amendments, the Rules Committee and the majority leadership opposed floor action through normal procedures. In each case, the House ultimately fell short of the two-thirds majority required for passage. In 1995, the constitutional amendment was part of the Republicans' "Contract with America" and was reported out of committee and passed by the House using the normal legislative process. It failed by one vote in the Senate, however. The same thing happened again in 1997.

Longtime advocates of discharge quite understandably lost interest in it following the shift in party control and no measures were discharged during the first three years of Republican majorities starting in 1995. But, in another example of partisan turnabout, minority Democrats attempted to discharge campaign finance reform legislation in 1997 over the opposition of the Republican leadership. The effort stalled when Speaker Gingrich promised a vote on the issue in the spring of 1998.

However, Republican supporters of campaign reform who had shunned the discharge strategy later cried betrayal when Gingrich would only allow the issue on the floor using the two-thirds majority suspension process, which would prevent passage of any major legislation. Gingrich also barred action on the most important bipartisan proposal. Denouncing the Speaker for a cynical ploy, they quickly got behind the discharge petition sponsored by Rep. Scotty Baesler, D-Ky., which would have discharged an essentially open rule allowing consideration of the bill with substitute amendments made in order that embodied several major proposals. The rule used a "queen-of-the-hill" process in which, if any substitutes passed, the one receiving the most votes would become the basis for further action. As the petition moved above 200 signatures in April 1998, Gingrich capitulated and promised consideration under an open rule reported by the Rules Committee using a normal legislative process.

CALENDAR WEDNESDAY

Calendar Wednesday is a little-used method for bringing to the House floor a bill that has been blocked by the Rules Committee. Under the procedure, each Wednesday standing committees may be called in alphabetical order for the purpose of bringing up any of their bills that have been reported, except those that are privileged, on the House or Union Calendar. General debate is limited to two hours and action must be completed in the same legislative day. Bills called up from the Union Calendar are debated in the Committee of the Whole with amendments considered under the five-minute rule.

The procedure may be dispensed with at other times by a two-thirds vote and also during the last two weeks of the session if such a time frame is known in advance. In practice Calendar Wednesday is usually set aside prospectively, by unanimous consent, when the House adjourns at the end of the previous week's session.

Several limitations make the process cumbersome to use. Because committees are called alphabetically, those near the end of the list may have to wait several weeks before they are reached, and once a committee has brought up one bill under the procedure it may not bring up another until all other committees have been called. Because the bill must be disposed of in a single day, opponents need only delay to kill the bill.

During the 98th Congress (1983–1985) Republicans regularly objected to dispensing with Calendar Wednesday and forced a call of the Calendar to protest the Democratic leadership's failure to schedule action on legislation they supported, such as school prayer measures and a constitutional amendment calling for a balanced budget. The protests were purely symbolic because the committees to which these measures had been referred had never reported them and the reading clerk simply read the name of each committee in alphabetical order before the House moved on to other business. On January 25, 1984, the Democratic leadership allowed a minor agricultural bill to be considered under the Calendar Wednesday procedure—the first such passage since May 1960. Finding the process as cumbersome and ineffective as its earlier users had, the Republicans eventually stopped objecting to dispensing with Calendar Wednesday.

1. Richard S. Beth, "The Discharge Rule in the House of Representatives: Procedure, History, and Statistics," March 2, 1990, and "The Discharge Rule in the House: Recent Use in Historical Context," Congressional Research Service, Library of Congress, September 15, 1997.

Noncontroversial Legislation

The House has two time-saving procedures for passing noncontroversial bills or bills of minor interest—unanimous consent and suspension of the rules.

Unanimous Consent. The House may accomplish almost any action by unanimous consent, but the procedure is most commonly used to act quickly. Sometimes the actions desired can only be accomplished by unanimous consent because there is no readily available motion that can be used to force the matter before the House for debate and vote. In other instances, available motions might waste the time of the House with debate or votes since the matter is noncontroversial.

If the Speaker recognizes a member to make a unanimous consent request it will be granted unless another member objects. The Speaker can prevent a unanimous consent request from being placed before the House simply by withholding recognition, after inquiring "for what purpose does the gentleman rise?"—in effect signifying his own opposition to the request. Unanimous consent requests relating to action on legislation normally must be cleared in advance by the majority and minority or the Speaker will not entertain them. No debate is in order and no vote is held on unanimous consent requests, saving substantial time for the House. However, in order for the House to understand the purpose of a unanimous consent request, in many cases, when the Speaker asks "is there objection?" another member who supports the request will often "reserve the right to object" and yield to the maker of the request for an explanation. Several members may participate in an informal discussion in this manner until a legislative record has been made.

Unanimous consent requests are used dozens of times each day, most commonly to insert material into the *Congressional Record;* to address the House when no legislation is pending, such are during one-minute speeches at the beginning of the day and "special order" speeches at the end; to extend the time a member may speak on an amendment; to obtain a leave of absence from a House session; to discharge committees from consideration of noncontroversial matters and bring them directly to the floor; and to dispose of various motions that could normally be voted on if demanded by any member.

Suspension of the Rules. The suspension procedure is most often used to bring to the floor noncontroversial measures on the Union or House Calendars that have been reported from committee. Additionally, measures never considered by a committee or even those just introduced also may be taken up. The Speaker has total control over bringing legislation to the floor under this procedure, and he or she invariably recognizes only members of the majority party to offer motions to suspend the rules. However, bipartisan cooperation is required for passage of suspension motion because a two-thirds majority is needed for passage.

Any member may move to suspend the rules and pass a measure although it is generally a committee or subcommittee chairman, with the concurrence of the ranking minority member, who will be recognized for the purpose. The motion suspends all rules of the House that normally affect consideration of the bill, including referral to a committee and requirements for committee action such as preparation of a committee report. This precludes points of order against the legislation. A suspension motion may be debated for forty minutes and may not be amended from the floor, although amendments are permitted if initially stipulated in the motion. Time is normally evenly divided between the floor manager and a minority member, but any member who opposes a bill under suspension has preference to claim half the time.

Two-thirds of the members present must vote to suspend the rules and pass the measure involved. If a suspension motion is not approved, the bill may be considered later under regular House procedures. In 1979 the House amended its rules to give the Speaker discretion to delay final votes until all the suspension bills scheduled for the day have been debated. The bills then may be called up at some time within the next two days and voted on in succession. The Speaker also was given discretion to shorten the time for each recorded vote to five from fifteen minutes after the first vote in a sequence. These procedures have since become the normal means of considering suspensions.

Motions to suspend the rules are in order on Mondays and Tuesdays of every week, and also during the last six days of the session (but only if such a period has been formally designated by Congress, or in the days preceding the constitutional close of a session on January 3.)

The availability of the suspension motion has changed repeatedly over time. Originally in order on any day, in 1847 it was restricted to Mondays only and, in 1880, to the first and third Mondays of each month; in the 93rd Congress (1973–1975) it was made available also on the Tuesdays following those Mondays and, in the 95th Congress (1977–1979) it was amended to its current form. From time to time, especially toward the end of a session, or if Congress is returning to work at midweek, the Rules Committee reports and the House passes resolutions making the motion available at other times as well.

As adjournment nears there usually is a considerable backlog of legislation awaiting action. Members who might have voted against a measure under the suspension procedure earlier in the session because of the bar to floor amendments might in the final days support a suspension motion on the grounds that the unamended measure is better than no measure at all. Conversely, members opposed to a bill under suspension have maximum leverage to force the bill's manager to incorporate amendments in the motion, or risk losing it altogether.

Because they require a two-thirds vote to pass, most bills brought up under suspension of the rules are relatively noncontroversial, although there have been notable exceptions. The House declared war on the Axis powers in World War II through passage of joint resolutions under suspension of the rules. Ironically, when the House convened on Monday, December 8, 1941, following the attack on Pearl Harbor the day before, it was neither the first nor the third Monday, and the House needed unanimous consent to use the procedure to consider a declaration of war on Japan. Rep. Jeanette Rankin, R-Mont., the only member ultimately to oppose the joint resolution (she had also voted against American participation in World War I), failed to make a timely objection when she had the chance, and was then denied an opportunity to speak. Later in the week, the House followed a similar procedure to deal with Germany and Italy. (Rankin voted "present").

The Twenty-Fourth Amendment to the Constitution, abolishing the poll tax, was passed by the House using the suspension procedure on August 27, 1962, by a vote of 295–86. On November 15, 1983, an attempt to again pass the so-called "Equal Rights Amendment," which had expired without being ratified by a sufficient number of states, failed to receive the requisite supermajority under suspension of the rules by a vote of 278–147.

In the late 1970s, the Republicans accused the Democrats of using the shortcut procedure to push through some complex or controversial legislation without adequate debate or the opportunity to offer amendments. By 1978 the procedure had become as much of an issue as the bills themselves. The Democrats were highly embarrassed that year when a controversial education aid bill supported by President Carter failed under suspension on a vote of 156–218, in part because members were angry about the large numbers of suspension bills.

In 1979 the Democratic Caucus formalized guidelines that prohibited any bill with an estimated cost of more than $100 million in a single year from being taken up under suspension unless the Democratic Steering and Policy Committee granted a waiver to the Speaker. When the Republicans assumed control of the House in 1995, they continued to use the suspension procedure much as the Democrats had done. The Republican Conference rules largely mimicked the Democratic rules. Major legislation, however, is still sometimes passed under suspension, either because there is substantial bipartisan support for it or because an emergency situation warrants.

The Republican leadership in 1995 used the Rules Committee on several occasions to bring noncontroversial bills to the floor under open rules—bills that might ordinarily have been considered under suspension. Ironically, the Democrats complained that the new majority was avoiding the suspension process to inflate artificially the Rules Committee's claims that it was reporting a greater percentage of open rules than had been the case previously. The majority used these statistics to bolster its claims to have brought greater openness and fairness to House procedures.

The Democrats staged a series of dilatory tactics in 1997 to protest what they regarded as the Republicans' refusal to schedule a sufficient number of suspension bills offered by Democratic sponsors. They claimed that the Republicans, when in the minority, had been allowed far more access to the process. To retaliate, Democrats opposed a number of suspensions, ensuring their defeat, and forced a series of delays in voting on many others. After tempers had cooled, in an unusual procedure, the bills were finally approved en bloc by unanimous consent on the last day of the session.

Sometimes the suspension process has been used as a safe way to test sentiment on an issue or to allow members to go on the record while avoiding actually passing legislation. For example, in February, 1998, following more than a year of bitter partisan strife, the House dismissed an election challenge against Rep. Loretta Sanchez, D-Calif., after failing to find proof of sufficient voting irregularities to question the result. The Republican majority, however, still wanted to make a statement expressing concern about allegations that noncitizens had voted in the election. Their method of doing so was to immediately call up for consideration under suspension controversial legislation that would have required proof of U.S. citizenship for voting. The unsuccessful 210–200 vote for passage demonstrated some House interest in the concept, but the close margin also served as a warning that a full-fledged airing of the issues in the normal legislative process was called for before the bill made a reappearance on the floor.

At other times, however, the majority leadership's absolute control of the suspension process can lead to abuse and possibly even a revolt by the full House. In March 1998 Speaker Gingrich learned an embarrassing lesson about the limits of his ability to manipulate the process for political advantage. Gingrich used motions for suspension of the rules to create a series of "mock" votes to prevent passage of serious campaign finance reform legislation. The Republican leadership had promised to allow consideration of the issue but later balked when it seemed likely that a bipartisan bill they opposed, sponsored by Christopher Shays, R-Conn., and Martin Meehan, D-Mass., which commanded the broadest support, would pass by a simple majority if allowed to reach the floor. The leadership did not command the votes on the floor to bring out an alternative measure reported by the House Oversight Committee, because it lacked the votes to pass a rule for its consideration without also allowing a vote on Shays-Meehan.

Instead, the Speaker abandoned the idea of an open process with a rule, extensive debate, and amendments and chose four bills to take up but only under suspension, which ensured that no controversial matters could pass. Despite the protection of a two-thirds vote, he refused even to allow a vote on Shays-Meehan. Two minor bills did pass easily under suspension but two others were overwhelmingly defeated, including the Republican-sponsored omnibus measure that received a humiliating seventy-four votes. With the four votes concluded, the Speaker claimed that he had carried out his commitment for a vote on campaign finance reform.

Instead of burying the issue, however, the plan backfired explosively, energizing a Democratic-sponsored discharge petition on campaign reform legislation that had been languishing for months without significant Republican support. In addition, as outraged Republicans began to sign the petition in the aftermath of the suspension fiasco, the number crept above 200 and

DILATORY TACTICS ARE LIMITED IN THE HOUSE

The House does not permit the range of dilatory tactics common in the Senate. This is due to its much larger size, which does not permit the same degree of recognition for the interests of individuals; its rules, which limit the ability of members to obtain the floor except for specified purposes and which provide several mechanisms for cutting off debate; and its traditions of bringing business to some conclusion.

The House has a number of rules and practices not used in the Senate that operate to restrict debate:

- The motion for ordering the previous question in the House, which, if adopted, ends all debate and forces an immediate vote.
- The "one-hour rule," which prevents any member from being recognized for more than one hour at a time for debate, or to call up legislation. Business directly before the House, such as a conference report or a special rule from the Rules Committee, can only be considered for one hour unless additional time is granted by unanimous consent, the "previous question" motion ending debate is defeated, or special rule is passed.
- The Rules Committee, which can bring before the House a resolution providing a special rule for a debate and amending process that limits opportunities for delay and can force the House to consider such a resolution.
- An 1890 rule that "no dilatory motion shall be entertained by the Speaker."[1] On January 31, 1890, Speaker Thomas B. Reed ruled: "The object of a parliamentary body is action, and not stoppage of action," in refusing to allow the House to consider a motion to adjourn, one of the few procedural matters directly mentioned in the Constitution. The prohibition also may be applied to other motions including appeals from the ruling of the chair as well as to amendments. Its application is extremely rare.

Despite its rules, the House does not always operate like clockwork. It is possible to delay proceedings by forcing electronic votes on matters that might not otherwise merit one, such as on the Speaker's approval of the *Journal*, or by offering and then forcing electronic votes on motions to adjourn, motions to table, ordering the previous question, moving to rise (end proceedings) in the Committee of the Whole, reconsidering actions taken by the House and offering resolutions raising questions of the privileges of the House. Sometimes motions long forgotten or almost never seen on the floor, such as Texas Rep. Lloyd Doggett's 1997 motion to "reconsider the vote by which the yeas and nays were ordered" on a pending motion to adjourn, are resurrected to provide additional delaying tactics. Eventually, all of these options will be exhausted after some hours have elapsed and the House can conclude its legislative business.

In an extraordinary example of measures to ensure that the House can conduct its business, on October 8, 1968, the Speaker used his authority in the standing rules to order the doors of the chamber locked so that members could not leave while a quorum call was in progress. The House was attempting to complete the reading of the *Journal*, which had been demanded, so that it could move on to other business. During these proceedings, which lasted into the next day, thirty-three quorum calls delayed action. The House ultimately adopted a motion providing that the doors would be locked until the conclusion of the reading. Once a quorum had been established and with members locked in the chamber, the *Journal* was disposed of and the House got down to business.

Underlying the obscure parliamentary pyrotechnics were questions of the rawest politics. First, the minority Republicans wished to preserve their lead in the 1968 presidential election. Richard Nixon, the GOP nominee, was refusing televised debates with the Democratic candidate, Vice President Hubert Humphrey, and Democrats sought to embarrass Nixon.

The unsuccessful delaying tactics were intended to prevent consideration of a special rule, and, following that, a bill suspending the equal time requirements of the Communications Act of 1934, the enactment of which would have allowed Nixon and Humphrey to debate in the absence of other candidates. While the House went on to pass the bill it did not clear the Senate and was not enacted.

Second, the minority wanted to make a major issue of the Democrats refusal to consider reform proposals recommended by a 1965–1966 joint committee on the reorganization of Congress prior to final adjournment. Their delaying tactics were a means to draw attention to that issue. (The legislation was not considered until the next Congress when the Legislative Reorganization Act of 1970 was passed).

The potential for seemingly endless delay through repeated quorum calls was later eliminated by House rules changes in the 1970s.

When unanticipated delays arise, the majority can always employ the Rules Committee to remedy the situation. In 1997, the Democratic minority used delaying tactics on several occasions to signal its displeasure over what it considered the majority's failure to resolve the election challenge filed by former Rep. Robert K. Dornan, R-Calif., against Democrat Loretta Sanchez, who had defeated him in a close race in 1996. In November 1997, Democratic members announced their intention to present nearly two dozen consecutive privileged resolutions—each offered by a different member—in an effort to pressure the majority to dismiss the challenge. Pushing all of these resolutions out of the way, by moving to table each after it had been read but before any debate, would have disrupted the schedule of the House for a considerable period of time.

In a preemptive strike, the majority adopted a resolution from the Rules Committee barring such resolutions for the rest of the session unless offered by either the majority or minority leader. As expected, after its adoption the minority leader chose not to offer all of these resolutions himself. (The Democrats ultimately achieved their objective the following February when the election challenge was dismissed.)

1. Asher C. Hinds, ed. *Hinds' Precedents of the House of Representatives*, vol. 5 (Washington, D.C.: Government Printing Office, 1907.), sec. 5713, 358.

it seemed possible that 218 names might quickly be obtained, repudiating the GOP leadership and handing a bipartisan coalition control of the issue on the floor. Gingrich quickly capitulated, promising a new vote on campaign reform under an open process if Republicans would abandon the discharge strategy.

District Day. Another special procedure allowing consideration of certain noncontroversial legislation is "District Day," which was once used to bring up bills under the jurisdiction of the District of Columbia Committee on the second and fourth Mondays of each month. That committee was abolished in 1995 and its legislative jurisdiction and special floor privileges were transferred to the Committee on Government Reform and Oversight. However, "District Day" had already effectively become an anachronism because the District of Columbia Committee reported few bills and the House often dispensed with consideration of legislative business or votes on Mondays, making any use of the special day potentially inconvenient. No bills were called up using District Day in the 104th Congress. The "suspension of the rules" process has become by far the more likely choice for bringing minor legislation affecting the nation's capital to the floor.

Privileged Matters

House Rule XXIV provides a detailed order of business for the House each day, which has changed little since 1890. The rule (in slightly shortened form) reads as follows:

> First. Prayer by the chaplain.
> Second. Reading and approval of the Journal.
> Third. The Pledge of Allegiance to the Flag.
> Fourth. Correction of reference of public bills.
> Fifth. Disposal of business on the Speaker's table.
> Sixth. Unfinished business.
> Seventh. The morning hour for the consideration of bills called up by committees.
> Eighth. Motions to go into Committee of the Whole House on the State of the Union.
> Ninth. Orders of the day.

The House routinely ignores this order of business because over time many elements of the rule have become obsolete or different practices more efficiently accomplish the objectives. For example, the morning hour has not been used for decades, and the House, while it often resolves into the Committee of the Whole to debate and amend legislation, arrives there in a manner different from that contemplated by the rule.

The only elements of the order of business that always occur in the House are the first, second, and third. After that, other rules procedures, such as motions to suspend the rules, or special orders of business from the Rules Committee, are used to determine the House's actual agenda. In addition, other informal practices, such as the period at the beginning of the day when the Speaker, at his discretion, recognizes members to speak for one minute, occur routinely but are not mentioned in Rule XXIV.

The House operates by putting aside formal rules and making in order other matters in their place. Some observers have described this as the use of "privileged interruptions" in the order of business. This new business derives from the use of other rules of the House, or through the use of resolutions from the Rules Committee, to make legislation "privileged" for consideration, which means it cannot be stopped simply by the objection of a single member. The House must then decide whether it wants to conduct this privileged business. But assuming it does, legislation comes up for debate and votes.

In the House, the term "privilege" may have several meanings. The House's standing rules create privilege for certain measures or motions to come up on the floor, which might depend on the subject matter of the legislation, the committee reporting the measure, or both. For example, general appropriations bills that are reported from the Appropriations Committee may simply be placed before the House, requiring some action be taken as a result. The class of such privileged matters is relatively small compared to the total number of measures that the House considers each year. A bill revising criminal laws, on the other hand, is not privileged because neither the subject matter itself nor the committee that reported it—in this case, Judiciary—have been given any special recognition in the rules for such a purpose. Such a bill may not be brought up unless the rules are suspended to allow it to interrupt the order of business, or unless the House adopts a resolution reported from the Rules Committee to make it privileged. Such a resolution is called a "special rule" or a "rule providing a special order of business." (Not to be confused with "special orders," the speeches members give at the end of a day's session.)

In some cases, not only can committees call up bills they have reported without going first to the Rules Committee, but they can create and report out a measure without even introducing it first. Under House rules, these committees have "leave to report at any time."

Among the most significant types of legislation in this category are:

- General appropriations bills, as well as continuing appropriations resolutions reported after September 15.
- Concurrent budget resolutions reported by the Budget Committee in accordance with the Congressional Budget and Impoundment Control Act of 1974.
- Resolutions providing biennial committee funding and disposing of House election contests reported by the House Oversight Committee.
- Measures amending the rules of the House, or providing a "special order" for future consideration of a bill on the floor, reported by the Rules Committee.
- Resolutions dealing with ethics complaints against members reported by the Committee on Standards of Official Conduct.

Most privileged measures must lie over for some short period of time after they have been reported. This includes, for example, one day in the case of special rules from the Rules Committee and committee funding resolutions, and three days for general appropriations bills and the concurrent budget resolution, to give members an awareness of the contents and an opportunity to read the committee report on the legislation.

While "privilege" may convey status to a committee, it does not necessarily automatically convey additional power or political advantage on the floor. Indeed, the Ways and Means Committee lost its power to report legislation as privileged in 1975, but the committee has not suffered a loss in power as a result.

Certain other legislative matters in the House also are considered privileged and may be called up quickly. In this category, for example, are conference reports (after a three-day layover) and any bill vetoed by the president and returned to the House, which may be called up immediately for disposition.

Although a rule is not required to bring privileged legislation to the floor, the managers will often seek a rule anyway to waive the time layover requirements, eliminate points of order that might be lodged against the bill, and restrict or prevent the offering of floor amendments. Appropriations bills, for example, frequently contain authorizing language, which violates House rules. A waiver protects such language from a point of order, which, if upheld, would have allowed any single member to strike the provision.

To prevent floor amendments from unraveling compromises on complex legislation, committees routinely seek rules that permit only specified amendments to be offered on the floor. The Budget Committee, for example, effectively abandoned use of its power to call up budget resolutions as privileged in 1980 because the resolutions would be subjected to perfecting amendments in the Committee of the Whole on virtually any subject large or small without effective restrictions and could remain on the floor for weeks at a time. Instead, using the Rules Committee the leadership can usually pass the measure in only a day or two. Invariably it obtains a rule barring all amendments except a handful of complete substitute budgets offered by the minority party, the Congressional Black Caucus, a coalition of conservative members, supporters of a return to the "Gold Standard," and other identifiable groups. A common tactic used in the 1990s by both parties to embarrass the administration in power was to prepare a substitute labeled as the "president's budget," offer it as an amendment, and then watch it suffer overwhelming defeat.

The increasing use of the Rules Committee to protect even privileged legislation from points of order and a potentially lengthy amendment process is one of the most significant developments of the last two decades. It represents an increase in the ability of House leaders to exert control over virtually every committee and a corresponding loss of power by the House membership at large to alter legislation once it reaches the floor.

Gone are the days when the chairmen of the thirteen appropriations subcommittees, the so-called "College of Cardinals," would pride themselves on drafting their own bills, bringing them to the floor without a rule or consultation with the Speaker, and managing them as they saw fit. Floor time is too limited, and the potential for embarrassing surprises too great, for the kind of uncertainty this style of committee independence might generate, and the majority party has increasingly sought to structure floor action around its agenda rather than the long-standing traditions of committees or the egos of chairmen. In 1997, at a leadership meeting, Speaker Gingrich was reported to have upbraided Appropriations Committee Chairman Bob Livingston, R-La., for allowing a subcommittee chairman, Rep. Sonny Callahan, R-Ala., to make policy decisions on the bill he managed without approval of the leadership. Just a few years earlier, such criticism by a Speaker, along with the concept that the full committee chairman should control a subcommittee chairman, would have been considered an unprecedented assault on the integrity of the Appropriations Committee.

Major Legislation and the Rules Committee

Virtually all major legislation, including privileged bills and any measure considered controversial, is routed through the Rules Committee before going to the floor. The purpose is twofold. First, a special rule makes a bill in order for floor consideration even though it is not at the top of whichever calendar it is on. It might not ordinarily be considered at all without a rule. If bills were called in the order in which they appeared on the House calendars, much significant legislation would never reach the House floor. Second, the special rule sets out the guidelines for floor debate and amendment on the legislation.

Because it controls the flow of legislation from the committees to the full House, the power of the Rules Committee is considerable and its role in the legislative process crucial. The Rules Committee chairman, who is the Speaker's personal choice for the post, has wide discretion in arranging the panel's agenda. The chairman may call an "emergency meeting" of the committee whenever he or she wishes. Scheduling—or not scheduling—a Rules hearing on a bill usually determines whether it ever comes before the House for debate.

In the past the committee has used that power to kill bills it opposed even though they were supported by the majority leadership and a majority of the House. Since the House reforms of the 1970s, however, the Rules Committee has become an arm of the majority leadership and usually works with the Speaker and majority leader to expedite action on measures the leadership favors and to delay or modify measures that might not have sufficient support to pass or have other political problems. The Rules Committee and the leadership also consult often on the terms of debate and amendment that will be allowed for each bill.

Rules Committee Hearings. Usually the chairman of the committee or subcommittee that reported a bill requests a rule, technically a House resolution specifying a "special order of business." At Rules Committee hearings the chairman of the legislative committee, supported by the bill's sponsors and other committee members, proposes a rule to the Rules Committee. Members who oppose the bill or who want to offer floor amendments to it also may testify.

Rules Committee hearings also serve as a dress rehearsal for

The House Rules Committee meets in 1997. The Rules Committee has considerable power in controlling the flow of legislation from the committees to the full House.

the bill's floor managers. As political scientist Bruce I. Oppenheimer has pointed out, "The Rules Committee dress rehearsal gives them a chance to make errors and recover before going to the floor."[10]

Drafting the Rule. All rules limit the time for general debate on the House floor. The time permitted varies (it is often one hour equally divided between the two parties), depending largely on extent of controversy surrounding a bill. Many rules also waive points of order against certain provisions of the bill or against specified amendments that are expected to be offered on the floor. This waiver permits the House to violate its own rules by barring any objections to such matters.

During the 1980s the committee granted an increasing number of "blanket waivers," barring all points of order that might be raised against a particular bill. Most blanket waivers were granted for conference reports and for omnibus bills. The committee justified the increase by pointing to the growing number and complexity of procedural requirements, such as those added by the Gramm-Rudman-Hollings deficit reduction law, which made it difficult to specify exactly which rules needed to be waived. Failure to waive a specific rule would give opponents of the bill an opening to challenge it.

Republicans, when in the minority in the House, expressed their displeasure with the trend toward blanket waivers. They "are indicative of the [majority] leadership's willingness to permit committees to circumvent and violate House rules in order to advance their legislative agenda," Rep. Trent Lott, R-Miss., himself a member of the Rules Committee, said in December 1977.[11] Nonetheless, Republicans often did support such waivers when passage of an essential bill, such as a continuing appropriations resolution, was at issue. When Republicans assumed control of the House in 1995, they quickly discovered the wisdom of the approach they previously had so roundly criticized.

Rules also govern amending activity on the floor. The committee traditionally grants three kinds of rules affecting amendments: open, closed, or modified. These terms are not defined in the rules of the House or of the committee, are often used colloquially, and can have different meanings depending on the circumstances and the opinion of the person using the term. An "open" rule usually permits any germane amendment to be offered on the floor at the appropriate time. A rule that bars all amendments, or all but committee amendments is referred to as "closed," or often pejoratively by its opponents, as a "gag" rule. A "modified" rule generally permits amendments only to certain provisions or sections of the bill, or to specific subjects dealt with in the bill, or only allows certain specific amendments. Sometimes the terms "modified open" and "modified closed" are used as well, and the difference is usually in the eye of the beholder.

Shift toward Restrictive Rules

Until the 1980s the vast majority of rules were open. Closed rules were generally reserved for tax bills and other measures too complicated or technical to be tampered with on the House floor. But in the 1970s a number of developments led the Rules Committee to begin to draft more modified rules that specified which amendments could be offered and often stipulated in what order they would be considered.

For one thing, the decision to allow recorded votes on floor amendments significantly increased the number of amendments offered. Before 1971 only vote totals, not individual votes by members, were recorded on floor amendments in the Committee of the Whole, which made members much more accountable to their colleagues than to their constituents. Once their votes were routinely made public, however, members found it to their advantage to offer and vote for amendments their constituents supported even if those amendments were opposed by the reporting committee. Activist junior Republi-

METHODS OF VOTING IN THE HOUSE AND SENATE: PUTTING MEMBERS' POSITIONS ON THE RECORD

The House and Senate have each developed their own procedures for voting. Guiding them are voting rules spelled out in the Constitution. Most specific are requirements for roll-call votes: "The yeas and nays of the members of either house on any question shall, at the desire of one fifth of those present, be entered on the Journal." This constitutional provision also is aimed at preventing secret ballots. It is in the Constitution at Article I, Section 5, Clause 3.

HOUSE

The House has also developed a complex set of rules governing how members make demands on the House floor to have their votes recorded. The House regularly uses three types of votes: Voice, division, and votes recorded by the name of the member ("yeas and nays" or "recorded vote"). Often, the House takes several votes on the same proposition, using the most simple method first and then increasingly more complex voting methods, before a decision is reached. *(See "Action in the Committee of the Whole," p. 83.)*

A voice vote is the quickest method of voting and the type nearly always used first when a proposition is first put to the membership. The presiding officer calls for the "ayes" and then the "noes," members shout in chorus on one side or the other, and the chair decides the result.

If the result of a voice vote is in doubt or a single member requests a further test, a division, or standing vote, may be demanded. In this case those in favor of the proposal and then those against it stand up while the chair takes a head count. Only vote totals are announced; there is no record of how individual members voted. Few issues are decided by division vote. After a voice vote, members will usually skip it and ask for a vote in which members are recorded by name. This kind of vote, which is nearly always taken using the electronic voting system, draws many more members to the chamber. It is called "the yeas and nays" or a "recorded vote" depending on the circumstances in which it is taken, but the result is identical.

Since 1973 the House has used an electronic voting system for recording members' votes. Members insert white plastic cards into one of forty-four voting stations mounted on the backs of chairs along the aisles of the House chamber. When a member punches a button to indicate his position, a giant electronic board behind the Speaker's desk immediately flashes green for "yes" and red for "no" next to the legislator's name. Members may also vote "present," which shows up as a yellow light on the board. Members may change their votes at any time until the result is announced. The Speaker may vote on any matter but, by tradition, rarely does.

The "yeas and nays," provided for by the Constitution, is used only when the House itself is sitting, and never in the Committee of the Whole. This method of voting may be ordered by one-fifth of those present regardless of how few members are actually on the floor. House rules also provide that it may occur automatically whenever a quorum is not present on the floor when the question is put and any member objects to the vote on those grounds. The resulting vote both establishes a quorum and settles the question at issue.

A "recorded vote," provided for by House rules, may be demanded both in the House and in the Committee of the Whole, but it works differently in each case. In the House, it may be ordered upon demand of one-fifth of a quorum of 218, which is forty-four. For example, as a matter of strategy, a member would demand a recorded vote, rather than the yeas and nays, whenever a majority of the members was present on the floor because the requisite number (forty-four) would always be less than one-fifth of those present. In the Committee of the Whole a "recorded vote" is always ordered by twenty-five members.

Once any vote by electronic device begins members have fifteen minutes to record their votes, although an additional two minutes is usually allowed to accommodate latecomers. The voting time is often shortened to five minutes, if a number of votes have been clustered, for each vote beyond the first one; again, an additional two minutes may be allowed. Regardless of the time limit, any member who is in the chamber at the time the result is to be announced has the right to record a vote, or to change one already cast. Once the result has been announced, however, the vote is closed and members may not subsequently vote or change their votes, even by unanimous consent. Often members who miss a vote will insert statements in the *Congressional Record* immediately following the missed vote indicating what their position would have been, though there is no requirement that they do so.

Until 1971, the "yeas and nays" were the only votes on which House members were individually recorded. Votes in the Committee of the Whole were taken by methods that did not record the stands of individual members. Many questions were decided by "teller votes" under which the chair appointed tellers representing opposite sides on a vote and directed members to pass between them up the center aisle to be counted—first the "ayes" and then the "noes." Only vote totals were announced on teller votes.

In the 1960s, members and outside interest groups began to object to unrecorded votes in the Committee of the Whole. They believed that members could not be held accountable for saying one thing to their constituents but voting the opposite way by tellers. Members could effectively hide their votes on key amendments, which were sometimes closely contested and usually determined the final form of the bill, while going on the record on the less controversial matter of final passage in the House. Liberals also believed that their views might have a better chance to prevail against established institutional power centers, which were more conservative, if members were forced to go on record.

"A member can vote for any number of amendments which may cripple a water pollution bill or render ineffective a civil rights bill or fail to provide adequate funding for hospital construction or programs for the elderly, and then he can turn around on final passage and vote for the bill he has just voted to emasculate by amendment," Wisconsin Democrat David R. Obey said of the voting system.

A provision of the Legislative Reorganization Act of 1970 opened the way for "tellers with clerks," more commonly called "recorded teller votes." This procedure, used in 1971 and 1972, made it possible to record the votes of individual members in the Committee of the Whole. When the change first went into effect, members were required to write their names on red or green cards, which they handed to tellers. The consequence of the rules change was very swift; many more members appeared for these votes because absentees could now be noted by name in the *Congressional Record.* After the electronic voting system was installed in 1973, the recorded teller vote process became known simply as a recorded vote. The advent of recorded teller votes, and then the electronic voting system, rendered the old unrecorded teller votes essentially obsolete. However, unrecorded teller voting still remained as a potential fallback option in the rules until its formal abolition in 1993.

When members' votes first began to be recorded in the Committee of the Whole on amendments and other motions, only twenty members were required to stand and demand a recorded vote. This number was later raised to twenty-five in 1979 after some members complained that it was too easy to force votes. But there has been no evidence that the change to twenty-five made any significant difference.

In the Committee of the Whole, unlike the House, there is no means to force a vote automatically by claiming that a quorum (100) is not present; in such cases, a member usually will demand a recorded vote and, pending that, make the point of order that a quorum is not present. By doing so the member gains time to ensure the presence of at least twenty-five supporters when the chair announces whether sufficient support exits for a recorded vote. If a quorum is not present, the chairman will order a quorum call to establish one before determining whether twenty-five members will support the demand for a recorded vote. The chairman has two choices: to order a regular quorum call, which summons all 435 members, whose names are recorded in the *Congressional Record* after the vote; or a "notice quorum call," in which the chair simply stops the proceedings after 100 members have responded and no permanent record of those responding is kept.

In many cases, to save time, enough members will rise informally to indicate their support for a recorded vote while the chair is still counting for a quorum; the point of no quorum will then be withdrawn and a recorded vote will occur. If both the quorum call and then the recorded vote are used the quorum call will be fifteen minutes long, followed, if ordered, by a recorded vote, which the chairman may reduce to five minutes.

Before the electronic voting system was installed, yeas and nays were taken by calling the roll, a time-consuming process in the 435-member House. Each roll call took about half an hour. The Speaker still retains the right to call the roll rather than use the electronic voting system. The old-fashioned method is used when the electronic system breaks down, as it does from time to time. An archaic provision still exists in the rules that allows the Speaker to direct the clerk to "tell" the members by name in the House. In addition, on the opening day of each Congress the clerk calls each member by name to elect a Speaker, since members shout out the name of the person they support. Usually there are only two candidates, one Republican and one Democrat, but the 1997 election was unusual as four Republican members voted for persons other than Speaker Newt Gingrich for reelection because of ethics controversies surrounding him at the time. They voted either for another sitting Republican member or for former House members.

Use of the electronic voting system opened the possibility of "ghost voting" in which an absent member gave his voting card to a colleague. Such instances are exceedingly rare but the House has banned it by rule and has disciplined members suspected of violations.

No member may be deprived of his or her right to vote. House rules direct members to refrain from voting on an issue on the House floor if they have a conflict of interest, and also admonishes members in a "Code of Official Conduct" (House rule XLIII of the 105th Congress) not to vote on the floor or in committees if they have been convicted of crimes for which a sentence of two or more years imprisonment may be imposed. Compliance with these rules is strictly at the discretion of the member affected; however, convicted members who have continued to vote in such circumstances have been threatened with expulsion.

SENATE

Only two types of votes are in everyday use in the Senate—voice votes and roll-call votes ("yeas and nays"). Standing votes are seldom employed. The Senate does not use the teller vote and has no electronic voting system.

As in the House, the most common method of deciding issues is by voice vote. The presiding officer determines the outcome. Under the Constitution, one-fifth of the senators present must support a demand for a roll call. (Unlike the House, the Senate assumes that an actual quorum—fifty-one—is present when this demand is being made, so a minimum of eleven senators must rise in support. The number of senators who responded on the previous roll call will be used as a base, and one-fifth of that number—up to a maximum of twenty—could be required. However, informal practices have evolved in which a vote may be ordered by the chair if only a few senators are present and the two parties' floor managers agree.)

Unlike the House, where a demand for a roll-call vote comes only when debate has been concluded and the chair has put the question, senators may demand the yeas and nays on pending business at a time long in advance of the vote, assuming there is sufficient second. The Senate usually allows fifteen minutes for a roll-call vote, although unanimous consent requests may shorten the voting time in specific situations. The fifteen-minute period also may be extended to accommodate late-arriving senators. Senators who miss a vote cannot be recorded after the result has been announced. However, unlike the House, a senator who voted but was not recorded or was incorrectly recorded may, by unanimous consent, have the proper vote recorded if it would not change the result.

cans also took advantage of recorded votes to force the Democrats to vote repeatedly on politically sensitive issues such as abortion.

The erosion of seniority and the rise of subcommittees also had its effects. When most bills were managed by the chairman of the committee reporting the bill, or his or her designee, rank-and-file members tended to accept committee bills on the floor, in part because the chairman, and often others on the committee, had developed expertise in the subject area and in part because members might need cooperation from the chairman in the future. With the increase in the importance of subcommittees in the late 1970s, many bills came to be managed on the House floor by junior members often inexperienced in House procedure and without acknowledged expertise in the subject matter. In these situations, rank-and-file members were less inclined to defer to the subcommittee's judgment and more likely to offer amendments of their own on the House floor.

Consequently, the number of amendments offered on the floor increased substantially. According to political scientists Stanley Bach and Steven S. Smith, the number of floor amendments more than doubled, from 792 in the 92nd Congress (1971–1973) to 1,695 in the 95th Congress (1977–1979) before beginning to decline again.[12] And with this explosion of amendments the Democratic leadership and bill managers found it more and more difficult to know what was likely to be offered on the floor, whether it would win, and how long the whole process might take.

This pressure to regain control over the amending process was reinforced by several other developments.

First, the decision to allow a bill to be referred to more than one committee created a need for mechanisms by which conflicting recommendations could be resolved on the House floor in an orderly fashion. Bills that have been referred to more than one legislative committee can present special problems to the Rules Committee, particularly if the legislative committees report conflicting provisions. To prevent divisiveness, embarrassment, and perhaps defeat on the House floor, Rules will often ask the committees to try to negotiate their differences before a rule is granted. The resulting compromise, rather than the original reported legislation, is then made the basic legislation to be debated and amended on the House floor. This is called "an amendment in the nature of a substitute considered as original text." If negotiations are unsuccessful, the Rules Committee may write a rule that allows members to vote on the alternatives.

Second, many members were eager to open Ways and Means Committee bills, which had traditionally been considered under closed rules, to at least some adjustment on the floor. In 1973 the Democratic Caucus began to require committee chairmen to give advance notice in the *Congressional Record* whenever they intended to seek a closed rule. The caucus also adopted a rule allowing it to instruct Democrats on Rules to vote to make certain specific amendments in order during floor consideration. But after a brief flurry of activity in the 1970s, the power fell into disuse as the Rules Committee became a reliable arm of the party leadership and, as such, more representative of the views of the majority of the caucus.

Third, the increased partisanship in the House beginning in the 1970s erased earlier norms that had inhibited members of the minority from offering controversial proposals purely to embarrass the opposition. These votes created a record that could be attacked by interest groups in their "voting scorecards" and related materials disseminated to their membership. The majority, while it could not prevent all such votes, sometimes moved to restrict amendments to limit the damage.

Fourth, the increased political independence of members from their political parties, and the need to maintain a fund-raising apparatus, encouraged more members to freelance on the floor by offering amendments that might give them greater visibility. In many cases, while such amendments might have accomplished the objectives these members desired, they also might not contribute much of substance to the bill and could delay and distract the House, and the Rules Committee moved to limit them.

As a result of all these factors, the Rules Committee began to draft more rules controlling the amendment process. In the 95th Congress (1977–1979) only 15 percent of the rules reported to the House were closed or restrictive; by the end of the 101st Congress (1989–1991), that number had risen to 55 percent. As part of their broader critique of Democratic dominance of the chamber, Republicans attacked the majority constantly for using restrictive rules to stifle debate and block amendments. Rules that were defined as not being "open" became objects of opprobrium in a battle of dueling statistics, even though use of modified or closed rules might have been appropriate given the complexity and politics surrounding a particular bill.

In the 104th Congress, with a Republican-controlled Rules Committee, the new majority trumpeted important victories for openness in House procedures during consideration of its critical "Contract with America" bills, claiming to have issued open rules 72 percent of the time. The Democratic minority, however, responded that the correct figure was 26 percent. Predictably, each side differed on the definition of "openness" and which legislation should be included in the statistics.

The kinds of restrictive rules vary considerably. The Rules Committee may simply require that amendments will be in order only if they have been printed in the *Congressional Record* in advance of the debate. This practice may actually increase the number of amendments rather than reduce them. "When you see you are fixin' to be cut off and not be able to have an opportunity to offer an amendment you start conjuring up all possible amendments and you put them in the *Record*," Lott said.[13] But advance notice does help the leadership anticipate floor action and develop strategy to deal with it.

Structured Rules. A structured rule is a rule that can have many different forms. It usually can be anything other than a simple open rule but its principal purpose is to supply a sense of order on the floor as amendments are offered and debated in the Committee of the Whole. Such rules may specify the

PAIRS—ABSENT MEMBERS MAKE THEIR "PRESENCE" FELT

Pairs are names of members of Congress printed in the *Congressional Record* who did not vote, but had they been present would have been on opposing sides of an issue. In the past pairs were often considered "gentlemen's agreements" that House and Senate members used to cancel out the effect of absences on recorded votes. *Cannon's Procedure in the House of Representatives* notes that pairs are voluntary agreements between members: "The rules do not specifically authorize them and the House does not interpret or construe them or consider complaints arising out of their violation. Such questions must be determined by the interested members themselves individually."

There are two types of pairs in current use. A live pair involves a member who is present for a vote and another who is absent. The member in attendance votes and then withdraws the vote, announcing that he or she has a live pair with an absent colleague and stating how the two members would have voted, one in favor, the other opposed. In modern practice, live pairs have appeared from time to time in the Senate but are extremely rare in the House. A senator will withdraw his vote, vote "present," and announce he is granting a live pair to accommodate an absent colleague, who is identified by name. Senators will sometimes be approached in advance by colleagues who expect to be absent and will personally sign off on the arrangements. In other instances, the leadership will look for someone willing to grant this favor to an absentee.

In a specific pair, members in the House and Senate who anticipate being absent notify their cloakrooms and ask to be paired with another absent member on the opposite side of the issue. The staffs develop the pairings, and then the opposing stands of the two members are identified and printed in the *Record.*

Pairs are not counted in vote totals. If the vote is one that requires a two-thirds majority, creation of a live or specific pair requires two members favoring the pending matter and one opposed to it.

Because they are printed in the *Congressional Record* and have a long tradition, specific pairs remain in use even though they have no more weight than any other method of announcing a member's position. A member can ask unanimous consent to insert a statement in the *Record* directly after a vote indicating how he or she would have voted, which is a common practice. In the House, following the 1995 change in party control from Democrats to Republicans, there was some discussion of eliminating the use of pairs but ultimately the practice was not changed.

WHEN PAIRS MATTER

A live pair in the Senate may affect the outcome of a closely contested vote because it subtracts one "yea" or one "nay" from the final tally. In 1986, the "gentleman's agreement" of pairing crashed into hardball politics in a wild combination of circumstances that resulted in the confirmation of Daniel A. Manion as a federal appellate judge.

Manion's nomination reached the floor only after the Judiciary Committee reported it "without recommendation." Senators filibustering against the nomination thought they had a majority and unexpectedly offered to allow an immediate vote to occur. Majority Leader Bob Dole, R-Kan., agreed after three senators opposed to the nomination—Joseph Biden, D-Del., ranking minority member of the committee; Daniel Inouye, D-Hawaii; and Nancy Landon Kassebaum, R-Kan., were persuaded to grant live pairs to absent Republicans Bob Packwood, Ore., Paula Hawkins, Fla., and Barry Goldwater, Ariz., who, they were told, favored the nomination.

Unexpectedly, Slade Gorton, R-Wash., an expected opponent, voted to confirm Manion after he received a phone call from the White House during the vote promising to nominate a candidate he wanted for a federal district judgeship. Shocked opponents realized too late that their earlier firm majority had been picked apart as the nominee appeared headed for confirmation in a tie vote. Vice President George Bush was available to cast the potential tie-breaking vote in Manion's favor. However, none backed out of their pairs. Minority Leader Robert C. Byrd, D-W.Va., an opponent, switched to vote for Manion to make the final tally 48–46. Byrd, by voting on the prevailing side, was then eligible to move to reconsider the vote, hoping that once the situation had sorted itself out and absentees had returned confirmation could be undone on a later date. Under Senate rules, the confirmation vote was not considered final until that motion was disposed of.

The pairs became controversial because two of the Republican absentees later claimed to have been undecided, even though Manion opponents had been paired with them. Democrats claimed the "gentlemen's agreement" had been abused by the GOP leadership to mislead senators.

When the motion to reconsider was taken up the senators who had granted live pairs to Manion supporters were now free to vote as they wished but the same factors came into play to thwart them yet again. Packwood announced that he opposed Manion and supported reconsideration, Hawkins supported Manion and opposed reconsideration, while Goldwater was again absent but announced his opposition to reconsideration. However, he persuaded his home state colleague, Democrat Dennis DeConcini, who favored reconsideration, to grant him a live pair. Daniel J. Evans, R-Wash., who had voted against confirmation, voted not to reconsider, effectively reversing his position. The result was another tie which, with the final but unneeded addition of Bush's negative vote, produced a 49–50 vote against reconsideration.

Thus, due to incredible luck, skillful manipulation of the pairing process, and senators' reliance on personal relationships with colleagues, Manion was confirmed to a lifetime judicial appointment even though a majority of senators was actually opposed to his nomination.

amendments that can be offered, by whom, and, sometimes, in what order they will be considered. Structured rules may also set time limits on debate for the amendments. Most such rules are restrictive in that they prevent members from offering some amendments. However, structured rules may also be expansive, by making it in order for the House to consider amendments that are not germane to the bill. They may attempt to focus debate around entire substitutes for a bill, rather than numerous minor perfecting amendments; this invariably happens during consideration of the congressional budget resolution, since debate there deals with broad issues of policy and philosophy rather than the nuts and bolts of programs.

While some structured rules are clearly written to give an edge to the legislative proposal preferred by the majority leadership, many of these rules are intended primarily as a way to organize debate on the House floor and to ensure that members are given an opportunity to debate the major amendments and alternatives to a particular bill. In these cases, Bach and Smith have written, "the intent of special rules is to minimize uncertainty about process, not about policy—to control in advance what alternatives will be presented, not what the final shape of the legislation will be."[14]

In 1973 the House began using an electronic voting system. Members insert plastic cards in the voting boxes at forty-four stations throughout the chamber and vote "aye," "no," or "present." Their votes are displayed on the wall above the House gallery (top).

"King-of-the-Hill" Rules. One of the newer and more creative of the restrictive rules is known as the "king-of-the-hill" or "king-of-the-mountain" rule. It makes in order a series of alternatives to the bill under consideration and provides that even if a majority votes for two or more of the alternatives, only the last one voted on wins.

This procedure circumvents House rules that prohibit amending any portion of a bill that has already been amended. Under the normal rules, if a substitute for a bill is offered and adopted as an amendment, further substitutes or other amendments are precluded and the House moves to final passage. But king-of-the-hill rules allow amendments to continue to be offered.

In cases where the alternative favored by the majority leadership is sure of winning, this procedure provides a means to satisfy various factions within the House by letting them present, and the members vote on, their alternatives. In cases where the outcome is uncertain, positioning the preferred alternative last can give it an edge over its competitors.

"Queen-of-the-Hill" Rules. A king-of-the-hill variation first used in the 104th Congress is sometimes referred to as the "queen-of-the-hill" or "top-vote-getter" rule. As in king-of-the-hill, several substitutes for a bill can be voted on in succession, and a majority vote for any one of them does not result in the termination of the amending process. However, instead of endorsing the last such amendment considered that received a majority, under queen-of-the-hill rules, the amendment that passed with the largest number of affirmative votes, after voting on all substitutes, would prevail. If two amendments received an equal number of affirmative votes, the last one voted on would be reported.

Rules Committee Chairman Gerald Solomon, R-N.Y., argued that king-of-the-hill was flawed because it "allowed lawmakers to be on both sides of an issue and violated the democratic principle that the position with the strongest support should prevail."[15] However, it also could be argued that the new procedure represented less of an innovation than a reaction by the Republican majority against previous Democratic use of king-of-the-hill rules.

Queen-of-the-hill rules, similar to its sibling, allow the leadership to appease various factions and allow members to vote on various sides of a question. For example, during consideration in 1997 of a constitutional amendment limiting the number of years a member could serve in Congress, eleven substitute amendments were made in order under the queen-of-the-hill process precisely so that members from particular states could vote for the congressional term limit scheme adopted by those states. (Attempts by states to limit the terms of members of Congress by statute were later thrown out by the U. S. Supreme Court, thus necessitating a change in the U.S. Constitution to accomplish the purpose). All of the substitutes were rejected, as was the constitutional amendment itself.

Self-Executing Rules. Another innovative mechanism that Rules began to use in the 1980s was the self-executing rule, under which adoption of the rule also resulted in adoption of an amendment or amendments. Self-executing rules were devised originally to expedite consideration of Senate-passed amendments to House bills and to make technical corrections but they have also been used to enact more substantive and controversial measures.

In 1987, for example, a vote for a rule on a continuing appropriations resolution also had the effect of exempting members of Congress from a controversial pay raise. A vote for a rule on another continuing resolution earlier in the year was also a vote to provide $3.5 billion in humanitarian assistance to Nicaraguan contras fighting the Sandinista government there. The move, which was supported by the leadership of both parties, avoided a direct vote on the controversial issue of continued aid to the contras. The rule was adopted by voice vote.

In 1990, passage of a conference report on a major immigration bill was unexpectedly threatened when opposition developed to one of its provisions, leading to defeat of the rule. A second rule was then prepared and passed that self-executed adoption of a concurrent resolution changing the offending section of the conference report. Once the Senate sent a message that it had adopted the concurrent resolution, the conference report, as newly modified, was immediately available under the terms of the rule for consideration in the House. It then passed.

HOUSE FLOOR PROCEDURES

Procedural differences between the House and Senate are most visible on the chamber floors. Because of its size the House adheres strictly to detailed procedures for considering legislation. These procedures, which limit debate on bills and amendments, are designed to ensure majority rule and to expedite action. Although the opposition can slow legislation from time to time in the House, it usually cannot impede it altogether. In contrast, the much smaller Senate emphasizes minority rights and virtually unlimited debate.

The House tends to operate on a Monday-to-Thursday schedule, with Mondays reserved primarily for noncontroversial legislation considered under shortcut procedures such as suspension of the rules. Sessions occasionally are scheduled for Friday, but that day is often left free so that legislators can return to their districts for the weekend.

Daily sessions normally begin at noon, although earlier meetings are common as a session progresses. The day opens with a prayer and the pledge of allegiance, followed by approval of the Journal. Often a member demands a roll-call vote on approval of the Journal. This request may be dilatory in nature, or it may serve to determine which members are present. Once the Journal has been approved, the Speaker recognizes members for one-minute speeches and submission of material to be inserted in the *Congressional Record.* Messages from the president and the Senate are received.

Once this preliminary business is concluded, the House turns to the legislative business of the day. If the House is to take up legislation under its shortcut procedures, it remains sitting as the House, with the Speaker presiding. The rules for considering and passing legislation under these expediting procedures have been described above. Most major legislation, however, comes to the House floor under a special rule and is subject to a much more elaborate procedure. The process involves four steps: adoption of the rule governing debate on the bill; general debate on the bill itself; consideration of any amendments by the Committee of the Whole; and final passage of the bill by the full House.

Adoption of the Rule

Floor action on a major House bill ordinarily begins when the Speaker recognizes the member of the Rules Committee who has been designated to call up the rule for the bill. The rule may be debated for up to one hour, with, by custom, half the time allotted to the minority party. A simple majority is sufficient to adopt a rule.

Rules are seldom rejected. In 1987 the House voted 203–217 to reject the rule for consideration of budget reconciliation legislation because it included the text of a major welfare reform bill. The Democratic leadership realized that it had made a political error by overloading the process with too many divisive issues at once. The Rules Committee immediately revised the rule by dropping the welfare provisions. However, under normal circumstances a rule may not be taken up the same day it is reported unless permitted by a two-thirds vote of the House, and in this case it was unlikely that a two-thirds vote could be mustered. In a rare parliamentary maneuver, Speaker Wright arranged a successful motion to adjourn the House, reconvening it one minute—and one legislative day—later. Although Republicans bitterly complained about Wright's tactics, the House adopted the revised rule.

Opponents may also seek to amend a rule by defeating the "previous question." The previous question, a parliamentary device used only in the full House, is a motion that, if adopted, cuts off all further debate and amendments and requires an immediate vote on the matter at hand. Routinely, the Rules Committee member handling the rule will move the previous question to bring the rule to a vote. If that motion is defeated, the rule is then open to amendment. However, the tactic is very rarely successful, since defeat of the previous question has the effect of turning control of the floor over to opponents of the rule, who are likely to be members from the minority. Even majority members opposed to a rule are loath to do that, preferring instead to vote against the rule itself and have the Rules Committee report out another, while retaining control of the process.

In the most controversial recent instance of defeat of the previous question on a rule, in 1981, a coalition of Republicans and conservative Democrats blocked a deficit reduction package pushed by the Democratic leadership and substituted instead an alternative containing many elements of President Reagan's legislative program, embodied in the so-called "Gramm-Latta" bill. This conservative coalition defeated the previous question, adopted an amendment to the rule, adopted the revised rule, and went on to successful passage of their version of the legislation. In some instances the leadership may not realize that a rule faces defeat until it actually is being debated on the floor. In 1998, for example, a rule for consideration of major financial services legislation was withdrawn in the middle of debate when it became clear that defeat was possible.

Action in the Committee of the Whole

Once the rule has been adopted, the House resolves itself into the Committee of the Whole House on the State of the

Union to debate and amend the legislation. Not a committee as the word is usually understood, the Committee of the Whole is rather a parliamentary framework to expedite House action. Although all 435 House members are members of the Committee of the Whole, business may be conducted with a quorum of 100 members rather than the 218 members required in the full House.

The Committee of the Whole has no counterpart in the Senate, although for many years the Senate had a "Committee of the Whole" to deal with treaties. The concept developed in the British House of Commons when the Speaker was once considered to be an agent of the king. During periods of strained relations between the king and the lower house of Parliament, the procedure allowed members of Commons to elect a chairman of their own and to discuss matters, particularly matters pertaining to the king's household expenses, without observing the normal restrictions that applied to a formal session of the House of Commons.

Amendments are debated in the Committee of the Whole under the five-minute rule, which in theory but not in practice limits debate to five minutes for and against the amendment. They may then be voted on by voice vote or by division (standing) vote. There is only one way to obtain a recorded vote on an amendment or any other matter in the Committee of the Whole, unlike the situation in the House, where there are several possibilities. Twenty-five members must stand in support of a demand for a "recorded vote" in the Committee of the Whole. If a quorum is not present a quorum call may be demanded to bring additional members to the floor. To avoid using this time members will often routinely grant a colleague a recorded vote even on matters that have little substantive support. *(See box, Methods of Voting in the House and Senate, p. 78.)*

The Speaker does not preside over the Committee of the Whole but selects another member of the majority party to take the chair. The Mace is lowered from its position behind the Speaker's chair when the Committee of the Whole sits.

The Committee of the Whole cannot pass a bill. Instead it reports the measure back to the full House with whatever changes it has made. The House then may adopt or reject the Committee of the Whole's proposed amendments, amend a bill further through a motion to recommit with instructions, recommit it to the legislative committee where it originated, and finally, if the bill is still on the floor, pass or reject it.

Amendments adopted in the Committee of the Whole are always put to a second vote in the full House, which is usually a pro forma voice vote with all amendments considered en bloc. However, if the initial vote on an amendment in the Committee of the Whole was very close, the second vote in the House also may be a recorded vote as the losing side seeks to change the outcome. Sometimes proponents of an adopted amendment will attempt to discourage such reconsideration in the House, or express their displeasure, by threatening to demand recorded votes on all amendments reported back to the House, even of the most minor nature.

In 1993, Republicans led by Rules Committee ranking member Gerald Solomon of New York instituted a practice of demanding a separate recorded vote in the House on every amendment passed by a recorded vote in the Committee of the Whole. They objected to a new House rule passed at the beginning of that Congress granting the four delegates and the resident commissioner from Puerto Rico, all of whom sat with the Democratic Caucus, the right to vote in the Committee of the Whole even though the rule prevented their votes from affecting the outcome. However, these five could not vote in the full House. The minority demanded that more than sixty such votes be rerun without them after the Committee of the Whole rose to report its actions to the House. It desisted only after a federal appeals court ruled that the delegates' participation was constitutional. (A Republican-controlled House revoked these special voting rights in 1995.)

The Committee of the Whole itself may not recommit a bill, although it may recommend to the full House that the enacting clause be stricken—a parliamentary motion that, if adopted, kills the measure. However, the motion to strike the enacting clause is almost never successful, since members desiring to kill the underlying legislation can express themselves more clearly by defeating the rule prior to its consideration, or the bill itself on final passage. The motion to strike the enacting clause is sometimes made anyway because it guarantees five minutes of debate to the maker even under circumstances when debate may not be in order. After the member finishes, he or she withdraws the motion by unanimous consent without a vote. Recommittal must be voted on in the House rather than in the Committee of the Whole.

General Debate

After resolving into the Committee of the Whole, the first order of business is general debate on the bill. General debate, as Oleszek noted, serves both practical and symbolic purposes: complicated or controversial provisions of the legislation may be explained, a legislative record developed for the administrative agencies that administer the bill and the courts that interpret it, a public record built for legislators to campaign on. In the process, Oleszek wrote, general debate "assures both legislators and the public that the House makes its decisions in a democratic fashion with due respect for majority and minority opinion."[16]

But he and other congressional observers have questioned whether general debate actually influences members' views and policy outcomes in an era when there is little time to sit on the House floor or watch the proceedings on television. A 1992 examination of floor procedures by a group of scholars led by Thomas Mann and Norman Ornstein concluded that "General debate . . . has become a time of reading prepared statements by the floor managers and is widely considered a filler time between adoption of the rule and voting on amendments, during which members can leave the floor for other activities."[17]

The rules on most bills allot an hour of general debate, al-

FORCING A HOUSE VOTE CAN BE CONFUSING

In the House, members who desire a vote in which members are recorded by electronic device on a pending matter can usually get it in one of three ways: by objecting to a vote on the grounds that a quorum is not present; by asking for a recorded vote; or by asking for the "yeas and nays." However, sometimes this may not be as easy as it seems. There are circumstances in which it actually does matter which request is made. (Voting procedures in the Committee of the Whole are different.) *(See box, "Methods of Voting," p. 78.)*

On November 4, 1983, Democrat Henry B. Gonzalez of Texas waited for his turn to be recognized during special order speeches on the floor following the conclusion of legislative business for the day. A few Republicans members were finishing up their speaking time as another Democrat presided over the House as Speaker pro tempore. The Democratic leadership wanted the House to remain in session awhile longer so that the Rules Committee could file a report on the floor. The Republicans wanted to prevent that, so Rep. Dan Lungren (R-Calif.) initiated the following proceedings:

LUNGREN: "Mr. Speaker, I move that the House do now adjourn." (The motion to adjourn is highly privileged and must be voted on when made. With the House adjourned, the Rules Committee could not file until the following legislative day, which would delay consideration of any legislation requiring a rule for at least another day beyond that. And adjournment would also prevent Gonzalez from speaking, though Lungren assured him that was not his purpose.)

SPEAKER PRO TEMPORE: "The question is on the motion offered by the gentleman from California . . . The question was taken, and on a division (demanded by Mr. Lungren) there were—ayes 3; noes 1."

GONZALEZ: "I object to a vote on the ground that a quorum is not present."

SPEAKER PRO TEMPORE: "The chair would advise the gentleman from Texas that he cannot do that on an affirmative vote to adjourn, only on a negative vote." (Gonzalez had run into a rare exception to the normal operation of House rules. The Constitution provides that ". . . a Majority of each (House) shall constitute a Quorum to do Business; but a smaller Number may adjourn from day to day. . . ." So a simple majority of the handful of members present could decide that the House would adjourn; had the division resulted in a negative vote, any member could have obtained an electronic vote, calling all members to the House floor, by objecting that a quorum was not present. Since Gonzalez was momentarily outnumbered by the Republicans, the House would adjourn under the constitutional provision unless a vote could be held and bring majority Democrats to the floor. The Speaker pro tempore would ordinarily choose not to participate in a division vote but could do so if his vote changed the outcome.)

GONZALEZ: "Mr. Speaker, I demand a recorded vote."

SPEAKER PRO TEMPORE: "The gentleman cannot get a recorded vote in the House based on the number now present (since there were not forty-four members present to support the demand). Does the gentleman ask for the yeas and nays?"

GONZALEZ: "Mr. Speaker, on that I demand the yeas and nays."

SPEAKER PRO TEMPORE: "Those in favor of taking this vote by the yeas and nays will stand. . . . The yeas and nays were ordered." (Gonzalez, the Speaker pro tempore, and any other Democrats who may have appeared in the chamber during the preceding exchanges constituted one-fifth of those present).

The Democrats had succeeded in ordering a roll-call vote. The fifteen minutes for such a vote allowed enough time for other Democrats to return to the chamber. The final vote on whether to adjourn was: 99 yeas, 120 nays, 1 voting "present," and 213 not voting. So the House did not adjourn, the Republicans were foiled, the Rules Committee filed its report, and Gonzalez got to give his speech after all.

though more time may be granted for particularly controversial measures. The allotted time is divided equally between and controlled by the floor managers for the bill. Ordinarily the chairman of the committee or subcommittee that reported the measure acts as the floor manager for the bill's supporters, while the ranking minority member or his designee leads the opposition. If the ranking minority member supports the legislation, which often happens, that ranking member may allot some of his or her time to members opposing the bill. A bill that has been referred to more than one committee might have multiple floor managers, each of whom is responsible for the part of the bill that was before his or her committee and each controlling a small chunk of time. The importance of the managers is evident in their physical location on the House floor; they occupy designated seats at tables on either side of the center aisle, and they are permitted to bring several committee staff members onto the floor to assist them.

Floor managers are exactly what their name implies: managers of legislation while it is on the floor of the House, marshaling speakers and support for the majority or minority position. Regardless of his or her personal view on the measure or amendments, the majority floor manager is responsible for presenting the committee's bill in the most favorable light and for fending off undesirable amendments. The mark of a successful majority floor manager is the ability to get a bill passed without substantial change. The minority manager, if opposed to the bill, is expected to line up convincing arguments against the legislation and for amendments, if the rule permits, that would make the measure more acceptable to the opposition.

The Amending Process

Amendments, which provide a way to shape bills into a form acceptable to a majority, may change the intent, conditions, or requirements of a bill; modify, delete, or introduce provisions; or replace a section or the entire text of a bill with a different version. Amendments that seek to revise or modify parts of bills or of other amendments are called perfecting amendments.

Amendments that seek to add extraneous matter to the bill

under debate are sometimes referred to as "riders." They are far more common in the Senate than in the House, where a rule of germaneness protects the members from unexpected proposals. Riders do appear sometimes on appropriations bills where they may restrict the use of funds for a controversial program under the jurisdiction of an authorizing committee that may not have addressed the issue.

House rules require amendments to be germane, or relevant, to the bill itself. Any member may raise a point of order on the floor that an amendment is not germane but if there is general agreement on the need or desirability of a nongermane amendment it may be protected from a point of order by the Rules Committee.

Riders are often controversial for two reasons: the substantive provisions they contain and the potential that disagreements about them between the House and Senate, or between Congress and the president, will cause a deadlock delaying or preventing enactment of the main bill. Riders are especially visible on so-called "must pass" legislation such as appropriations bills. In 1997, a supplemental appropriations bill providing disaster relief to several states after heavy flooding was delayed because several controversial riders opposed by President Clinton were attached. One of these sought to alter the manner in which the 2000 census was scheduled to be conducted. The president vetoed the bill, and Congress succumbed to public pressure and passed it without the extraneous matters.

Substitute amendments aim at replacing pending amendments with alternatives. A variation of the substitute, known as an amendment in the nature of a substitute, seeks to replace the pending bill with an entirely new measure. The bill reported by the committee frequently is an amendment in the nature of a substitute for the original bill; the rule for its debate typically stipulates that it shall be considered the original bill for purposes of amendment.

Debate on Amendments. Once general debate is completed the measure is read for amendment, which constitutes the second reading of the bill. The special rule usually specifies that each part of a bill must be considered in sequential order. The bill may be read paragraph by paragraph, section by section, or title by title, and amendments are offered to the appropriate part as it is read. Once the reading of that part is completed, amendments to it are no longer in order except by unanimous consent. On occasion the Rules Committee may allow the bill to be considered as read and open to amendment at any point. Alternatively, the floor manager may make a unanimous consent request that the bill be open to amendment. Committee amendments are always considered before amendments offered from the floor.

Debate on any amendment is theoretically limited to five minutes for supporters and five minutes for opponents. Members regularly obtain more time, however, by offering pro forma amendments to "strike the last word" or "strike the requisite number of words." Under the Legislative Reorganization Act of 1970, ten minutes of debate, five minutes on each side, are guaranteed on any amendment that has been published in the *Congressional Record* at least one day before it is offered on the floor (assuming that the amendment is otherwise in order) even if debate has been closed on the portion of the bill to which the amendment is proposed. The change thus ensured that opponents could not block even an explanation of an important pending amendment, but it has also been used on a few occasions as a delaying device by members who have had dozens of amendments to a bill printed in the *Record,* all of which may be called up and debated for up to ten minutes. Committee floor managers encourage members to print their amendments in the *Record,* in order to obtain as complete a picture as possible of the political problems a bill may face. When the Republicans took power in the House in 1995 they began reporting rules that allowed the chairman of the Committee of the Whole to give preference in recognition to members who had preprinted their amendments.

Degrees of Amendments. Provided the special rule on the bill has not imposed specific restrictions, four types of amendments may be pending at any one time: a perfecting amendment to the text of the bill, also called a "first degree" amendment; an amendment to that amendment, which is called a "second degree" amendment; a substitute amendment for the original amendment; and an amendment to the substitute. An amendment to an amendment to an amendment, known as an amendment in the third degree, is barred under House rules.

Amendments to the original amendment are voted on first. Only one first degree amendment is in order at a time, but once it has been disposed of another may be offered immediately. When all amendments to the original amendment have been disposed of perfecting amendments to the substitute amendment are voted on one at a time. The perfected substitute is voted on next, followed by a vote on the original amendment as amended. If the substitute has been adopted, this last vote will be on the perfected original amendment as amended by the perfected substitute. Once an amendment has been offered in the Committee of the Whole its author may only modify it or withdraw it by unanimous consent but may not offer an amendment to it directly. A diagram of a so-called amendment tree and the order in which amendments must be voted on are shown below.

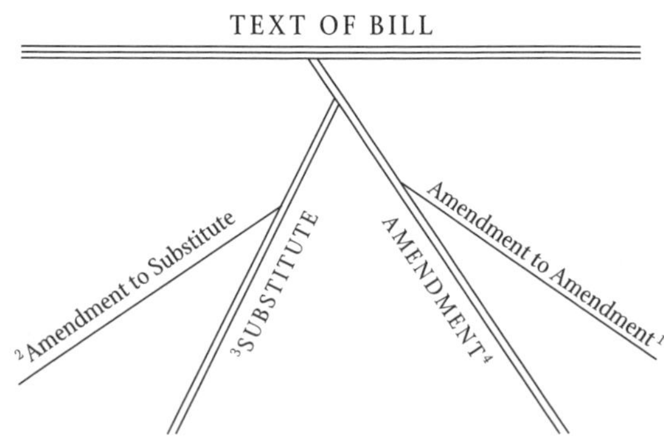

House members and staff enter and exit the Capitol during a 1998 vote on telecommunications.

This description may seem complex, but it gives only a hint of the total universe of amending possibilities. It can be mind-boggling when a substitute for the entire bill may be pending along with the base legislation, and such substitute may attract yet another substitute to itself as well as a panoply of perfecting amendments.

More than one vote may be taken on any given amendment. The Committee of the Whole may first take a voice vote and then, if members request, move on to division or recorded votes before finally deciding the questions. First-degree amendments (original amendments as amended) and amendments in the nature of substitutes, as amended, adopted in the Committee of the Whole are subject to roll-call votes after the committee rises and the chamber resumes sitting as the full House. Few roll-call votes actually are taken, and the full House rarely rejects amendments adopted in the Committee of the Whole. Amendments defeated in the Committee of the Whole cannot be offered again at this stage because the previous question has usually been ordered on the bill when the House adopted the rule for its consideration, barring additional amendments or debate once the Committee of the Whole has risen back to the House with its recommendation that the bill as amended be passed.

Action by the Full House

When the Committee of the Whole has completed its work on the bill, it "rises," according to the House's parliamentary terminology. The Speaker returns to the chair and the erstwhile chairman of the Committee of the Whole formally reports the bill to the House, with any amendments that have been adopted, and a recommendation that the bill pass.

If the previous question has been ordered by the special rule governing the bill—the usual procedure—the full House then votes immediately on amendments approved by the Committee of the Whole. As already noted, members may demand a roll call on any amendment adopted in the Committee of the Whole. Amendments not considered separately are approved en bloc by a pro forma voice vote.

Once the amendments have been disposed of the question is on engrossment (the preparation of an accurate version of the bill including all amendments) and third reading, by title only, of the bill. This too is nearly always pro forma. Prior to 1965, any House member could demand that the bill actually be "engrossed," that is, printed on special paper, prior to further proceedings. This was sometimes used as a dilatory tactic.

After engrossment and third reading, a member opposed to the bill may offer a motion to recommit the measure to the committee that reported it. The Speaker will inquire of a member attempting to make the motion whether he or she so qualifies. The Speaker typically asks "Is the (member) opposed to the bill?" and if the response is yes then that member is recognized. In practice, the motion to recommit belongs to the minority party and the Speaker looks first to the floor manager of the minority, then to other minority members of the committee, and then to any other minority member.

There are two kinds of recommittal motions: a nondebatable simple motion to recommit, sometimes called a "straight motion," which kills the bill if it is adopted by sending it back to committee; and a motion to recommit with instructions. The minority often moves to recommit with instructions directing the committee to report the bill back with amendments "forthwith." This tactic offers the minority members one last chance to amend the bill to their satisfaction. The minority may offer any germane amendment as part of its instructions, even one which had previously been offered and rejected in the Committee of the Whole. If the motion to recommit is adopted, the floor manager announces that the committee has reported the bill back to the House with the amendments contained in the instructions. The bill in this case is not literally recommitted to the committee that reported it. The amendment is then voted on again directly; this is usually a pro forma voice vote.

Instructions also can have the effect of removing a bill from the floor, however, if they contain nonamendatory provisions, such as directing the committee in question to hold hearings before bringing the bill back before the House.

The motion to recommit is privileged and the right to offer it is guaranteed by House rules but its use has been regulated by the Rules Committee. From 1934 to 1995 the majority reserved the right to restrict the motion in certain circumstances. The Rules Committee is forbidden by a House rule to report a rule for consideration of a bill or joint resolution that denies the right to offer a motion to recommit. However, a series of precedents was established that construed the rule so that members were guaranteed the right to offer only the "straight motion" to recommit without instructions.

A motion to recommit with instructions was, on occasion, barred by a special rule governing consideration of a bill. This might occur if the majority feared that last-minute amendments could pull apart the support built up for the pending legislation during the original amendment process, or if a minority proposal was considered potentially popular enough to pass. The Republicans, while in the minority for most of the four decades prior to 1995, often used a recommittal motion with instructions to present its alternative to the Democratic-crafted legislation being considered. They roundly criticized the constraints under rules governing recommittals that they considered a denial of basic rights, and frequently appealed rulings of the Speaker on this issue but always lost.

When Republicans gained control of the House in 1995, the new majority effectively wiped out the earlier precedents that had allowed the Rules Committee to prevent a motion to recommit with instructions from being offered to bills and joint resolutions, and amended House rules to guarantee that right to the minority leader or the minority leader's designee. In this respect, the Republicans increased the rights of the Democratic minority beyond what they themselves had enjoyed. However, other parliamentary restrictions may still apply to such a motion, such as the requirement that amendatory instructions be germane to the underlying bill.

A straight motion to recommit is not debatable. A motion to recommit a bill or joint resolution with instructions may be debated for ten minutes, evenly divided, although, since 1985, the majority floor manager—but not the minority floor manager—may ask for up to an hour of debate, which is then divided evenly between the two sides. That change was a direct result of a motion by Rep. Dan Lungren, R-Calif., in September 1984 to recommit the fiscal 1985 continuing appropriations resolution with instructions to add to it a Senate-passed crime bill, which, among other things, overhauled federal sentencing procedures. The House version of the crime bill had been bottled up in the Judiciary Committee. The motion was debated for ten minutes, and the House, to the majority leadership's embarrassment, adopted it on a vote of 243–166. The continuing resolution was then passed, and the crime package was eventually enacted.

Another example of amending strategy and clever use of the motion to recommit occurred in 1995 when Massachusetts Democrat Edward J. Markey offered a motion to recommit a telecommunications bill with instructions to include a provision mandating use of V-chip circuitry in televisions to allow parents to control more effectively their children's viewing habits. Markey had earlier offered a perfecting amendment to the bill in the Committee of the Whole to accomplish this, but he had been prevented from getting a direct vote when his proposal was altered by adoption of a second-degree Republican-sponsored amendment. The Republican proposal encouraged, but did not require, the new technology.

However, use of the motion to recommit in the House offered Markey, in effect, a "second bite of the apple" under parliamentary circumstances when a counterproposal could not be offered. Now forced to go on the record in an up-or-down vote on Markey's popular plan, the House effectively reversed its earlier vote and adopted the mandatory requirement.

These victories were unusual because few controversial recommittal motions are ever adopted. A competent majority strategy can usually anticipate and head off such dangers before a bill is reported, or through the amendment process on the floor as they attempted to do, ultimately unsuccessfully, in the Markey case cited above. In recent years, the motion has also become perceived more as a partisan vote in an increasingly partisan House, greatly reducing the minority's chances of success.

In 1981, there was an unusual instance of the majority attempting to seize control of the motion to recommit from the minority. This happened on the Gramm-Latta amendments to a budget reconciliation bill, in which a conservative group of Democrats combined with minority Republicans to seize control of the rule and control the floor debate and amendment process to promote the Reagan administration's legislative agenda. The majority party was effectively cut out of the process, but, once put in the position of being the opponents of the amended bill that was then overwhelmingly supported by Republicans, the Democrats could make a potential claim to the motion to recommit.

Anticipating a last-minute counterattack through a motion to recommit with instructions that might unravel the bill, the

Republicans needed to find someone qualified to offer the motion in order to keep it away from the Democrats. Since Republicans were the minority party, the Speaker would still look first to their side to offer the motion. They recruited one of their most liberal members, freshman Claudine Schneider, R-R.I. (1981–1991), to state her opposition to the bill. Schneider then offered a motion to recommit with instructions to amend the bill to reinstate a law guaranteeing semiannual cost-of-living adjustments to federal retirees' pensions. Her action had the effect of using up the single motion permitted under the rules, and on subject matter less controversial and far narrower than many other issues dealt with in the bill. Schneider made her status as a front for her party obvious when she yielded most of her time to the Republican leadership to explain her proposal.

The Democrats attempted to defeat the previous question on Schneider's motion. Ordering the previous question cuts off debate and further amendments to a proposal and forces it to a final vote. Defeating it would have allowed them to gain control of the floor and offer a new instruction with amendments aimed at the heart of the bill's provisions. However, Democratic defections that had allowed the Republicans to control the process throughout continued, and the previous question was ordered on Schneider's motion. With the vote over and the bill safe from further attack, the substance of Schneider's motion became irrelevant, and her motion was rejected by voice vote. Schneider then voted against the bill on final passage, as is customary for a member offering a motion to recommit.

If the motion to recommit is rejected, which it almost always is, the next step is the vote on final passage. If the bill is passed, a pro forma motion to reconsider the final vote is usually offered. A supporter of the bill then offers a counter motion to "lay the motion on the table," or kill reconsideration, thus safeguarding final passage. Or the Speaker will simply say "Without objection the motion to reconsider is laid upon the table." With that, the bill is considered to be formally passed by the House. At this point, the bill officially becomes an "act," although it generally still is referred to as a bill.

An engrossed copy of the bill, including changes made during floor action, is certified in its final form by the clerk of the House and transmitted to the Senate for its consideration. (An engrossed bill in the Senate must be certified by the secretary of the Senate.)

If a similar Senate bill has already reached the House, the rule providing for floor action on the House version might also have included a provision permitting the House to take it up, strike out the text, insert the text of the House-passed legislation, pass the "S" numbered bill and send it back to the Senate to await further amendments or a Senate request for a conference. Or the House itself could ask for the conference first. In these legislative scenarios, the House bill passed earlier would be laid on the table (killed) since it is no longer needed as a vehicle for further proceedings.

Senate Floor Action: Flexibility, Informality

House members elected to the Senate are inevitably struck by the difference in the way the two chambers operate. Although the Senate has an elaborate framework of parliamentary machinery to guide its deliberations, in practice its procedures are far more flexible than those of the House. Almost anything can be done by unanimous consent. That very flexibility also means that a single member can delay or threaten to delay action on a bill until his or her wishes are accommodated or a compromise is struck. The Senate also effects changes in its procedures from time to time, without formally changing its rules, by overruling decisions made by the presiding officer. The result of such a vote can establish a new precedent that would govern future proceedings.

From time to time the Senate reviews its procedures in an attempt to pick up the pace and predictability of action in the chamber. But the Senate is rarely receptive to the proposals for change that come forth from these reviews, largely because they almost always entail curbs on the rights of the individual member.

In 1982 Howard H. Baker Jr., R-Tenn., then the majority leader, expressed the prevailing attitude: "The Senate is a great institution. It is the balance wheel which keeps democracy on track. It is the framework on which the Republic is constructed. It is the essence of compromise. It is the only place where there is unfettered expression of individual views. It is the last fortress that can be used to defend against the tyranny of a temporary majority. I would not change a thing about that."[18]

SCHEDULING IN THE SENATE

In a chamber devoted to preserving individual rights, the challenge of scheduling floor action can sometimes be formidable. Senators can—and do—insist that the legislation in which they are interested be scheduled for floor action at a time convenient to them. At the same time senators faced with ever-increasing political, constituent, and legislative demands on their time have sought greater predictability in the Senate schedule.

Scheduling in the Senate is primarily the responsibility of the majority leader, who works closely with the majority party's policy committee, committee chairmen, and other partisan colleagues to develop a legislative program acceptable to a majority of the party. Because of the need to secure unanimous consent to bring up a bill, the majority leader also works closely with the minority leader and his staff in working out the schedule. This bipartisan cooperation is in sharp contrast to the House, where scheduling is solely a responsibility of a majority party that has the ability to enforce its decisions by majority vote.

A system based largely on unanimous consent also necessitates that the membership be kept informed about the status of pending legislation. The majority leader regularly begins each session with an announcement of the day's anticipated schedule and concludes it with the likely program for the next session.

THE PRESIDING OFFICER

Members of the House and Senate take turns presiding over floor debate, a job some view as drudgery and others see as an honor requiring finesse and skill. Members may speak on the floor and offer legislation, amendments, or motions for consideration only if the presiding officer permits, or "recognizes," them.

The presiding officer also rules on points of order and delivers other pronouncements that regulate floor debate. Members may appeal, or challenge, the presiding officer's decisions, and, in the House, these rulings can always be overturned by majority vote. Some rulings by the chair in the Senate, related to the budget process, require sixty votes to overturn. In the House, while rulings are occasionally appealed, none has been overturned since February 1, 1938. In the Senate, on the other hand, where procedure is more fluid and often yields to the political needs of senators, rulings of the chair have been appealed and overturned on various occasions in recent decades.

SPEAKER OF THE HOUSE

The presiding officer in the House is called "the Speaker," a position designated by the Constitution. When the House convenes to begin a new Congress, it is first presided over by the clerk from the previous Congress. After a quorum is established, the first order of business is to elect the Speaker. The election is nearly always pro forma because the actual decision is made earlier by the majority party's caucus or conference.

The Speaker need not be a member of the House but always has been. In the speakership election in January 1997 in the 105th Congress, two Republican members cast votes for former members of the House to protest the candidacy of Rep. Newt Gingrich, R-Ga., who was seeking reelection as Speaker but was also about to be disciplined for ethics violations.

The Speaker effectively serves as political leader of the majority power and also has rights as an elected representative to participate fully in all activities of the chamber. The Speaker may vote at any time but rarely does, except to break a tie.

By statute, the Speaker is next in line, behind the vice president, to become president of the United States in the event of a vacancy, although this has never occurred. The president pro tempore of the Senate follows the Speaker in order of succession.

The Speaker cannot preside over the House all of the time. When the Speaker is not present, a member of the majority party is designated as Speaker pro tempore, although any member may preside if called to the chair.

Unlike the Senate, in the House the presiding officer has broad authority to choose which member to recognize, and will inquire "for what purpose does the gentleman rise" to ascertain whether he wishes to recognize the member. Members seeking to conduct business made privileged under House rules will have priority in recognition.

When the House is considering bills for amendment in the Committee of the Whole, the Speaker steps down and appoints another member, who is called "The Chairman," to preside. When sensitive bills are under consideration, the Speaker's choice for the chair usually turns to senior members who are skilled parliamentarians or who are close to the leadership. Sometimes a tradition develops that the same member always presides over a certain bill whenever it comes to the floor. For example, Rep. Dan Rostenkowski, D-Ill. (1959–1995), best known as the longtime chairman of the powerful

Whip notices, televised floor proceedings, and an automatic telephone connection to each member's office help the leadership keep the membership informed.

To the extent possible the modern leadership tries to accommodate the schedules of individual senators. Most leaders have acknowledged the frustration inherent in the job. "It is extremely difficult to deal with the wishes of 99 other senators, attempting to schedule legislation," Majority Leader Robert C. Byrd, D-W.Va., said in 1987, "because in almost every case, at any time it is scheduled, it inconveniences some senator. . . ."[19]

All legislation reported from Senate committees is placed on the Calendar of General Orders, while all treaties and nominations that require the Senate's "advice and consent" are placed on the Executive Calendar. To consider treaties or nominations, the Senate resolves into "executive session" either by motion or unanimous consent. There are no restrictions on when the Senate may enter executive session. Despite its connotations, the term "executive session" is an open session of the Senate just like any other.

Senate rules require bills and reports on nonprivileged matters to lie over on the calendar for one legislative day before they are brought to the floor. This rule is usually waived by unanimous consent, and the Senate often stays in the same legislative day for a considerable period of time. Another rule requires that printed committee reports be available to members for two calendar days before a measure is debated. It too may be waived by unanimous consent.

The leadership evolved several ways to handle the various scheduling problems it regularly confronts. Different majority leaders have had their own ideas of how best to conduct business while giving their colleagues adequate "down time." In 1988, for example, the Senate worked for three weeks and then took a week off, giving members a set time to return to their states without running the risk of missing votes in the Senate or other legislative work of importance to them. However, this practice did not become institutionalized.

In the early 1970s Majority Leader Mike Mansfield, D-Mont., devised a system that allowed several pieces of legislation to be considered simultaneously by designating specific periods each day when the measures would be considered. The track system, still in use in the 1990s, affected all aspects of Senate procedure. When a filibuster was under way, the filibustered bill occupied one track while the Senate could proceed by unanimous consent to other legislation on the second track. But the ability of the

Ways and Means Committee, was usually named to preside over consideration of the annual defense authorization bill.

VICE PRESIDENT AND PRESIDENT PRO TEMPORE

The Speaker is far more powerful than his counterpart in the Senate, the vice president, who is not a member of the Senate and cannot speak except to recognize senators or make parliamentary rulings.

In the Senate, the presiding officer is always referred to as "Mr. (or Madam) President." The vice president of the United States serves formally as president of the Senate under the Constitution. It once was common for the vice president to preside over floor debates. In the modern Senate the vice president seldom is called in unless his or her vote might be needed if the Senate is evenly divided in order to vote to break a tie. In this case, only an "aye" vote can affect the result because a tie is considered defeat of a pending proposition. The vice president may not vote to create a tie. In theory, the vice president can vote when the Senate is evenly divided on matters requiring a supermajority vote for approval but since the proposition would thereby have been defeated anyway, the vice president could not affect the result. The vice president is rarely called on to vote. Between 1945 and 1998 only thirty-four such votes were cast.

The "president pro tempore" is a position created by the Constitution and is usually held by the senior member of the majority party in the Senate. This senator has the right to preside in the absence of the vice president but generally the Senate puts a freshman member in the chair. That relieves more senior members of a time-consuming task and gives newcomers firsthand lessons in Senate rules and procedures. Not surprisingly, new senators are heavily dependent on the parliamentarian for advice. In the Senate, the rules require the presiding officer to recognize "the Senator who shall first address him" if several senators are seeking to speak. However, by custom, the majority and minority leaders are always recognized first if they seek recognition when no one else holds the floor.

Many senators tend to view presiding as drudge work to be avoided, because the job frequently involves presiding over quorum calls that interrupt business while agreements are being worked out privately or senators are coming to the floor. However, some have embraced it and a custom has developed of giving a "Golden Gavel" to those who have presided for 100 hours.

Some House members also actively seek to preside. In an institution as large as the House it is one way for members to increase their visibility. The House puts no premium on giving new members experience in the chair; however, during routine business, it is not uncommon to see them there, visible to their constituents on C-SPAN, the cable network that broadcasts congressional events around the clock.

In both the House and Senate in 1998 only members of the majority party preside. Until 1977 members of each party took turns presiding in the Senate. The bipartisan practice was ended abruptly following an incident the previous year. The presiding officer, Sen. Jesse Helms, R-N.C., a member of the minority, broke with Senate custom by denying recognition to the majority leader, Sen. Mike Mansfield, D-Mont., in favor of conservative Sen. James B. Allen, D-Ala. The Democratic leadership then decided that the majority should retain control of the chair at all times, unless the vice president, who might be a member of the opposite party, decided to occupy it. Republicans continued this practice when they controlled the Senate.

Senate to continue its more routine work also encouraged senators to threaten to filibuster more frequently, since the incentives were much less for the leadership and other senators to try to stop them, and there were few negative consequences for those who filibustered.

The Senate normally recesses from day to day, rather than adjourns. The effect is the same—an end to the day's session—but a recess avoids creating a new legislative day that can, in some circumstances, create unwarranted procedural complications when the Senate next convenes. It is not uncommon for the Senate to remain in the same legislative day for weeks or even months at a time.

Unanimous Consent Agreements

The leadership has been most innovative with its use of unanimous consent requests, traditionally the mechanism the Senate uses to expedite business by circumventing its rules. As its name implies, a unanimous consent request may be blocked by a single objection. Once the request is agreed to, however, its terms are binding and can be changed only by another unanimous consent request.

There are two kinds of unanimous consent requests. Simple requests, which can be made by any senator, usually deal with routine business—asking that staff members be allowed on the floor, that committees be allowed to meet while the Senate is in session, that material be inserted in the *Congressional Record*, and the like. Noncontroversial matters, including minor legislation, private bills, and presidential nominations may be considered by unanimous consent; generally these matters are cleared with the leadership beforehand.

Complex unanimous consent requests set out the guidelines under which a piece of major legislation will be considered on the floor. In some respects like a special rule for guiding debate in the House, these unanimous consent requests usually state when the bill will come to the floor and set time limits on debate, including debate on motions, amendments, and final passage. For that reason they are often referred to as time agreements. Frequently the agreements stipulate that any amendments offered must be germane but, unlike House rules, they cannot prevent a senator from offering a particular amendment because the senator would have to be accommodated somehow to ensure there would be no objection to the request.

Lyndon B. Johnson, D-Texas, began to develop complex unanimous consent agreements during his tenure as majority leader from 1955 to 1960. Such agreements steadily grew more complex and were applied to more legislation. Negotiating a complex unanimous consent agreement can be complicated and time-consuming, involving the majority and minority leaders, the chairman and ranking minority member of the committee and/or subcommittee with jurisdiction for the bill, and any senator who has placed a "hold" *(discussed below)* on or otherwise expressed strong interest in the measure. The leadership tries to negotiate a unanimous consent agreement before the measure comes to the floor, but additional agreements—to limit time spent on a specific amendment, for example—may be fashioned on the floor.

The fundamental objective of a unanimous consent agreement, as Oleszek has observed, "is to limit the time it takes to dispose of controversial issues in an institution noted for unlimited debate."[20] The agreements are also valuable because they bring some predictability to Senate business.

But complex unanimous consent agreements "must not be viewed as rigid restrictions comparable to those found in House special rules," Steven Smith cautions. The need to obtain unanimous consent to ward off a potential filibuster "forces leaders to make concessions before and during floor debate on a scale that would seem quite foreign in the House. As a result, the new use of complex agreements on the floor does not alter the basic principles of Senate floor politics, which remain rampant individualism and the protection of minority rights."[21]

Holds

One scheduling complication the leadership has been unable to do away with is the practice of "holds." A hold is a request by a senator to the party leadership asking that a certain measure not be taken up. The leadership usually respects holds; to do otherwise would likely be self-defeating since the senator could easily block any unanimous consent request to consider the measure.

Most holds are kept confidential and are requested simply so that the senator will be told when the bill is likely to come up. But some senators have used them extensively as bargaining tools, to ensure that they will be able to offer their amendments or to force the leadership to call up some unrelated piece of legislation that otherwise might not have been scheduled for the floor. There have been instances of "rolling holds," in which one

A TYPICAL DAY IN THE SENATE

A typical day in the Senate might go like this:

- The Senate is called to order by the presiding officer. The constitutional presiding officer, the vice president, is seldom in attendance. Sometimes the president pro tempore presides over the opening minutes of the Senate session. During the course of the day, other members of the majority party take turns presiding.
- The Senate chaplain delivers the opening prayer.
- The majority and minority leaders are recognized for opening remarks. The majority leader usually announces plans for the day's business, which are developed in consultation with the minority leadership.
- The Senate usually conducts morning business (which need not be in the morning and should not be confused with the "morning hour," so if morning business is put off other business will necessarily precede it). During morning business senators may introduce bills and the Senate will receive reports from committees and messages from the president, and conduct other routine chores. Senators who have requested time in advance are recognized for speeches on any subject.
- The Senate may turn to consider legislative or executive matters. To begin work on a piece of legislation the majority leader normally asks for unanimous consent to call up the measure. If any member objects, the leader may make a debatable motion that the Senate take up the bill. The motion gives opponents the opportunity to launch a filibuster, or extended debate, even before the Senate officially begins to consider the bill. Certain types of measures, such as budget resolutions, omnibus budget reconciliation bills and reports from House-Senate conference committees, are privileged, and a motion to consider them is not debatable.

Floor debate on a bill is generally handled by managers, usually the chairman and ranking minority member of the committee with jurisdiction over the measure. Most measures are considered under a unanimous consent, or time, agreement in which the Senate unanimously agrees to limit debate and to divide the time in some prearranged fashion. In the absence of a time agreement any senator may seek recognition from the chair and, once recognized, may talk for as long as he or she wishes. Unless the Senate has unanimously agreed to limit amendments, senators may offer as many as they wish. In most cases, amendments need not be germane, or directly related, to the bill.

Most bills are passed by voice vote with only a handful of senators present. Any member can request a roll-call vote on an amendment or motion or on final passage of a measure. Senate roll calls are casual affairs. Senators stroll in from the cloakrooms or their offices and congregate in the well (the area at the front of the chamber). When they are ready to vote, senators catch the eye of the clerk and vote, sometimes by indicating thumbs up or thumbs down. Roll-call votes are supposed to last fifteen minutes but some have dragged on for more than an hour.

- Often, near the end of the day, the majority leader and the minority leader quickly move through a "wrap-up" period, during which minor bills that have been cleared by all members are passed by unanimous consent.
- Just before the Senate finishes its work for the day, the majority leader seeks unanimous consent for his agenda for the next session—when the Senate will convene, which senators will be recognized for early speeches, and specific time agreements for consideration of legislation.

senator withdraws a hold when it is discovered but another then steps in to retain the block in place, and even cases where a Senate staffer has applied a hold in a senator's name.

In the Clinton administration the president and even the chief justice of the Supreme Court objected to the practice by conservative senators of placing holds on large numbers of judicial nominations. The practice was not new, just more visible and seemingly more organized. Senators have also placed holds on legislation in behalf of the administration or an interest group. Sen. Jesse Helms, R-N.C., frequently placed holds on ambassadorial nominations to pressure the State Department into adopting policies more to his liking. Sen. Howard Metzenbaum (D-Ohio 1974; 1977–995) placed holds on all types of legislation, especially during the end of each session as the Senate rushed toward adjournment, to ensure that he was not unpleasantly surprised by unexpected developments.

In 1997, the Senate passed a proposal by Sen. Ron Wyden, D-Ore., and Sen. Charles Grassley, R-Iowa, to require senators to identify themselves when using holds, which would make it easier for opponents of a hold to apply pressure to allow consideration of a measure or a nomination. But the proposal was not adopted in the form of a simple resolution, which would have given it immediate effect, but rather as an amendment to an appropriations bill. This enabled the reform's opponents to drop the measure in conference, even though the House had no objection to it.

Other Scheduling Methods

Because the Senate allows nongermane amendments on most legislation, it has little need for procedures to wrest bills out of reluctant committees. A member may simply offer the legislation blocked by a committee as an amendment to another measure being considered on the floor. There are, however, three other ways that a senator may bring a bill to the floor, although none of them is used with any frequency.

First, all measures introduced in the Senate, including House-passed bills, must be read twice on successive legislative days before they are referred to committee. If any senator objects to the second reading of a bill, it is placed immediately on the calendar. This tactic was used to avoid sending the House version of the 1964 civil rights legislation to the Senate Judiciary Committee, which opposed it.

The Senate may also vote to suspend the rules by a two-thirds vote, but the procedure bears little relation to the similarly named House practice and has little practical use. While approval of the motion requires a two-thirds vote, it only suspends a rule but does not simultaneously pass a measure. The motion, and the measure, also remain subject to potential filibusters.

Finally, the Senate may discharge a bill from committee. The motion to discharge, which is debatable, must be made during morning hour. However, morning hour is rarely used in the Senate, and, even if it were, opponents would have ample opportunities to delay and render the discharge procedure inoperative. If debate is not completed by the time morning hour ends, the motion is placed on the calendar, where it can be subjected to another series of delays.

SENATE FLOOR PROCEDURES

While the Senate's rules establish elaborate procedures to conduct certain types of business, in practice many of these rules are either ignored or altered by unanimous consent. This is because efforts to invoke the formal rules may prove too cumbersome, provoking retaliation from opponents. The purported cure for a parliamentary stalemate or obstacle may prove to be worse than the disease. And some of the rules simply do not work.

The Senate may set a standard daily meeting time for noon but it frequently alters its meeting times by unanimous consent each day to accommodate the demands of the daily workload and the scheduling needs of individual senators who wish to be present for particular items of business. The Senate chaplain gives an opening prayer, and the previous day's Journal is approved. A rules change in 1986 made approval nondebatable, although amendments to correct the Journal may still be offered and filibustered. The majority leader and then the minority leader are recognized for brief periods. Usually they discuss the Senate's schedule for the day.

What happens next depends on whether the Senate is beginning a new legislative day. If the Senate recessed at the end of its previous session, it may proceed immediately to any unfinished business. If it adjourned, it must begin a new legislative day, which, after the opening preliminaries, requires the Senate to enter a two-hour period called "morning hour" (though this is almost always waived by unanimous consent). During that period members conduct what is known as "morning business"—introducing bills, filing committee reports, and receiving messages from the House and the president.

In the second hour, or at the conclusion of morning business, members may move to consider any measure on the calendar. This motion is not debatable, in theory, but in practice efforts to employ it to avoid a filibuster have been thwarted by the use of other provisions of the rules, making this "shortcut" effectively obsolete. After morning hour, because a motion to consider a nonprivileged measure is debatable, opponents of a measure have found ways to tie up the morning hour with other business and votes to prevent the leadership from forcing it up.

In an attempt to avoid a certain filibuster on the fiscal 1988 defense authorization bill on May 13, 1987, Majority Leader Byrd sought to call up the bill during morning hour. But before he could do that, the Journal of the previous day's proceedings had to be approved. Republicans requested a roll call on approval of the Journal and then used more arcane procedural tactics, demanding time to explain their individual votes and calling for votes on excusing them from voting, to further slow the proceedings. By the time the ensuing wrangle over the rules between Byrd and the Republicans had been untangled, seven roll-call votes had occurred, the period for morning hour had long since expired, and the motion to call up the defense bill was

SENATE PROCEDURES USED TO THWART SUBSTANTIVE ACTIONS

In a notable example in 1997 of the impact of Senate rules on debate and amendment strategy on controversial legislation, Senate Majority Leader Trent Lott, R-Miss., agreed to call up major campaign finance reform legislation, the so-called "McCain-Feingold bill" for proponents John McCain, R-Ariz., and Russell Feingold, D-Wis. As the most heavily promoted campaign reform vehicle in the Senate that bill would have banned "soft money" contributions to political campaigns—a method of support for candidates that fell outside the legal restrictions on contributions—and curbed "issue ads," often presented on television and radio by special interest advocacy groups that in many election contests were aimed more at electing or defeating candidates than at promoting debate on issues.

The legislation was certain to be filibustered, with Lott and Sen. Mitch McConnell, R-Ky., among its principal opponents. But supporters, consisting of the Democratic minority and a handful of Republicans, hoped that by getting the bill to the floor they could attract enough media attention and popular support, and work out compromises through the amendment process, to gain legislative momentum and overcome this obstacle.

Action stalled when the Republican leadership insisted on offering an amendment that would have required labor organizations, banks, or corporations to secure voluntary authorization from their members before using any membership dues, initiation fees, or other payments to fund political activities. They called the proposal the "paycheck protection act." Democrats, allied with labor and the primary beneficiaries of financial support from union leaders, filibustered against this amendment, knowing its adoption would prevent them from supporting the bill on final passage. Indeed, that was exactly the outcome Republicans were seeking as each side tried to blame the other for the failure to reform the nation's widely criticized and ineffective campaign finance laws. In the meantime most Republicans continued to filibuster the bill itself.

These stark partisan and ideological cleavages, exacerbated by the Senate's loose amendment rules and reliance on a sixty-vote supermajority needed to stop a filibuster, prevented compromise and smothered direct consideration of the legislation even as campaign finance scandals implicating both parties were being played out daily in highly publicized committee hearings in both chambers and on the front pages of major newspapers.

However, in the amending process of the Senate, which allows unrelated amendments to be offered to virtually any piece of legislation, hope springs eternal and often prevents the permanent demise of an issue. McCain-Feingold was resuscitated when its proponents threatened to attach it to other legislation as an amendment, and to filibuster if the majority leadership used its prerogatives to prevent this course of action. They blocked a major transportation reauthorization bill, which contained billions of dollars for highway construction and mass transit operations throughout the country, until an agreement was reached to allow a more direct vote on campaign finance reform in 1998.

But when the issue returned to the floor for a week in February 1998 the political and procedural dynamics remained essentially unchanged. In this case, Lott presented "paycheck protection" as the base bill; McCain-Feingold was a substitute.

While supporters of McCain-Feingold demonstrated a majority for their proposal and in opposition to "paycheck protection," they got nowhere near the sixty votes required to end debate. Nor were there actual votes on adoption of the various proposals. Instead, as is often the case in the Senate, procedural votes were employed as a safe test of strength; each side retained its full rights to filibuster if it did not get its way.

McConnell failed to table McCain-Feingold, 48–51. Sen. Olympia Snowe, R-Maine, proposed an amendment to the McCain-Feingold substitute to prohibit use of labor or corporate money to broadcast campaign ads shortly before a primary or general election. This was intended to weaken the appeal of "paycheck protection" and win over additional moderate Republicans to support cloture. It failed to do that, but a tabling motion to kill it failed 47–50. Snowe's amendment was then adopted by voice vote. Another effort to table McCain-Feingold, as amended, failed 48–50. A cloture vote on the McCain-Feingold substitute failed, 51–48. Lott could not obtain cloture on his paycheck protection base bill, 45–54, failing even to secure a simple majority.

All of the key votes, except for Snowe's amendment, were on either tabling motions or cloture. No direct votes were permitted on McCain-Feingold or the Lott bill. Lott then used his leadership prerogative to be recognized to offer multiple amendments and motions to recommit—to "fill the amendment tree"—with his proposals, which effectively precluded other senators from offering anything else and prevented further action on the bill.

once again debatable. Future majority leaders were thus put on notice that a similar parliamentary maelstrom could erupt if the use of the morning hour to circumvent a filibuster were ever attempted again.

Morning Business

The Senate rarely conducts morning business and the morning hour as stated in its rules because the formal procedures are too cumbersome and, as discussed above, do not really work to help the leadership avoid filibusters. However, it can conduct morning business at any time by unanimous consent.

The decision to adjourn or recess at the end of the day is made by unanimous consent or by motion, usually by the majority leader. The leadership generally prefers to recess from day to day because it can maintain greater control over the daily schedule. Senators seeking to delay action on a measure, however, may push for adjournment because the convening of a new legislative day offers them more opportunities to slow Senate deliberations.

If the Senate has recessed and there is no morning hour when it next reconvenes, it may still conduct morning business by unanimous consent. Within morning hour, morning business may be followed by the call of the Calendar of General Orders. During this procedure, which is almost always set aside by unanimous consent, the chair calls each bill in the order in which it appears on the calendar. If objection is raised to considering the bill, the chair moves on to the next measure. No senator may speak for more than five minutes on any one bill during the call of the calendar.

Morning hour may be followed by a period when members are given permission to speak for brief periods on virtually any topic. The Senate next turns to any unfinished business. If there is none, or if it is set aside by unanimous consent, the Senate may then take up new business.

Most major bills are brought up under unanimous consent agreements worked out in advance by the leadership. If a member objects to a unanimous consent request, the leadership may decide to try to renegotiate the consent agreement or it may move that the Senate take up the bill. Because most such motions are debatable, a filibuster could be launched against the bill before it is even technically on the floor. Motions to proceed to consider some measures, such as House-Senate conference reports, are not debatable, though the conference reports themselves may be filibustered once they become the pending business.

Floor Debate

Once a bill is brought to the floor for consideration, floor managers take over the task of guiding the legislation through the amendment process and final passage. As in the House, the chairman and ranking minority member of the committee or subcommittee with jurisdiction for the bill act as the majority and minority floor managers. Floor managers play much the same role in the Senate as they do in the House, mapping strategy for passing the bill, deflecting debilitating or undesirable amendments, offering amendments to attract additional support, and seeing that members in favor of the bill turn out to vote for it.

On measures brought to the floor under a unanimous consent agreement, the time allotted for debate is usually divided evenly between the two opposing sides. The chair gives preferential recognition first to the majority manager and then to the minority manager, who, if they control time, yield it to other senators. If there is no time agreement, any senator may seek recognition from the chair. Once recognized, in the absence of a time agreement, a senator may speak as long as he or she likes and on any subject, unless he or she violates the rules of the Senate. A senator may yield temporarily for the consideration of other business, after asking unanimous consent to do so without losing the floor, or to another senator who wants to ask a question, but he or she may not parcel out time to other members as floor managers in the House typically do and as Senate managers may when time is controlled. Typically, senators yielded to find ways to make broader statements within the guise of asking their questions.

The Senate does not consider bills in a Committee of the Whole or set aside a period for general debate before the amending process begins. Amendments are in order as soon as the bill is made the pending order of business.

Debate in the modern Senate is a far cry from debate during the Senate's "Golden Age," when great orators like Daniel Webster, John C. Calhoun, and Henry Clay fought an eloquent war of words over slavery and states' rights. While a few issues still engender lively debate on the floor, Senate speeches are seldom spontaneous; most are prepared by staff and read to an often nearly empty chamber or inserted, unread, in the *Congressional Record.* "Floor debate has deteriorated into a never-ending series of points of order, procedural motions, appeals and waiver votes, punctuated by endless hours of time-killing quorum calls," Sen. Nancy Landon Kassebaum, R-Kan., wrote in the *Washington Post.* "Serious policy deliberations are a rarity. 'Great debate' is only a memory, replaced by a preoccupation with procedure that makes it exceedingly difficult to transact even routine business."[22]

"There is dialogue and debate, but most of it does not take place on the floor under public scrutiny," Sen. Paul Simon, D-Ill., said in 1985.[23]

Comparatively few limits are placed on the debate that does occur on the Senate floor. Most unanimous consent agreements limit the time to be spent debating amendments and on debatable motions, points of order, and appeals of rulings. Some agreements also limit the overall time that the entire bill, including amendments, may be debated. A few statutes, such as the 1974 budget act, also effectively prohibit unlimited debate on such matters as budget resolutions and budget reconciliation bills. A motion to table, if adopted, also serves to cut off debate on an amendment or motion, but does not affect the right to offer additional amendments. And under Rule XXII, the filibuster rule, sixty senators may vote to invoke cloture, limit debate to a potential maximum of thirty hours, require amendments to be germane, and shut off a filibuster. The "previous question" motion, which brings debate to a close in the House, is not used in the Senate.

Senate rules bar members from speaking more than twice on the same subject in the same legislative day. This has not been an effective limit on debate, however, because each amendment is considered a different subject, and the "two speech rule" was effectively gutted by a Senate vote in 1986 overturning a ruling of the presiding officer after the issue of enforcing the rule was raised. The so-called "Pastore Rule" adopted in 1964, named after Sen. John O. Pastore, D-R.I., requires debate to be germane for the first three hours following the morning hour on a new legislative day, or after pending business has been laid before the Senate on any calendar day. However, the morning hour is almost never used; on other days, while the three-hour time is still tracked, the rule has not been enforced and has little practical impact today.

As in the House, the Senate presumes that a quorum is present until a member suggests otherwise. During floor debate a senator will often suggest the absence of a quorum. This is a tac-

At a Senate Budget Committee hearing, Chairman Pete Domenici, R-N.M., discusses the White House's 1997 proposed federal budget with Olympia Snowe, R-Maine.

tical maneuver designed to occupy time while the leadership negotiates a procedural agreement or to give a senator time to reach the floor to speak or to offer an amendment. Except in limited circumstances, the presiding officer is not permitted to count the senators on the floor to see whether a quorum really exists, as the House does, but must proceed to a call of the roll. When the reason for requesting the quorum call is resolved—that is, when the negotiation is completed or the senator is in the chamber and ready to proceed—the call may be suspended by unanimous consent.

This sort of quorum call differs from a "live" quorum, where a member insists upon a majority of the members actually appearing on the Senate floor. By refusing to answer the roll call, opponents of a bill or an amendment can delay action or even try to deny the Senate a quorum—in the absence of a quorum no business or debate may take place and the Senate must wait for one to appear, direct the sergeant at arms to obtain the presence of absentees, or adjourn.

A dramatic example of an attempt to force a quorum to appear occurred in 1988 during debate on a controversial campaign finance bill. To break a Republican filibuster, Majority Leader Byrd sought to keep the Senate in session all night. Republicans countered by calling for repeated live quorums and then refusing to come to the floor. That forced Democrats to keep enough members present to maintain the quorum needed for the Senate to remain in session. When the Democrats came up short around midnight, Byrd resorted to a motion directing the sergeant at arms to arrest absent senators and bring them to the floor. The sergeant at arms arrested Sen. Bob Packwood, R-Ore., after forcing his way into the senator's office, and escorted him to the entrance of the Senate chamber. When Packwood refused to go in under his own steam, two Capitol police lifted the senator and carried him feet first into the Senate chamber. Byrd had established his quorum, but he was ultimately unable to break the filibuster and the bill died.

The Amending Process

The flexibility that marks the Senate's rules of procedure also characterizes its amending process. When a bill is taken up for consideration on the Senate floor, it is not read for amendment by section, or title, as in the House, where amendments to the beginning of the bill are offered first, and so on. Any part of the measure is open immediately to amendment in the Senate, so the subject matter of debate may shift repeatedly while the bill is on the floor. Unlike the House, the Senate is not bound by a five-minute rule governing debate on amendments. Unless limited by a unanimous consent agreement or cloture, debate on amendments may continue until no senator seeks recognition to offer further amendments. The majority leader can obtain priority of recognition at any time no other senator has the floor, to try to advantage his party's positions on a pending bill.

Tax legislation is particularly susceptible to nongermane amendments for a special reason. The Constitution requires revenue measures to originate in the House, a stipulation that restricts the Senate to amending House-passed bills that contain tax provisions. The Senate cannot simply add a tax provision to a House-originated measure that does not contain any. If the Senate attempts to circumvent the constitutional restriction and send a tax provision to the House on its own, the House will "blue slip" the legislation—adopt a resolution as a question of the privileges of the House sending the offending matter back to the Senate without action. Despite this constitutional stricture, the Senate, nonetheless, takes the initiative on tax issues from time to time under its constitutional power to amend all tax bills as it may all other House-passed measures. It even may act first on its own tax bill, and add the provisions later as an amendment to a House-passed tax bill.

A noteworthy example occurred in 1982, when Congress approved a $98 billion tax increase that the House considered for the first time when it took up the conference report on the bill. The tax increase was required by the fiscal 1983 budget resolution. The House Ways and Means Committee took no action, in part because its members were unable to agree on what should go into a revenue-raising package and in part because Democrats wanted to force Republican President Reagan to share some of the blame for raising taxes in an election year. The Republican-led Senate Finance Committee wrote a bill raising revenue and then attached it to a minor tax bill the House had passed in 1981. After the Senate passed its version, the full House agreed with the Ways and Means Committee's recommendation to go straight to conference on the House-passed bill as amended by the Senate.

Moreover, amendments need not be germane, except in the case of general appropriations bills (though this restriction has been effectively gutted by Senate votes overturning rulings of the chair), bills on which cloture has been invoked, concurrent budget resolutions, budget reconciliation bills, and measures regulated by unanimous consent agreement. And the number of amendments that may be offered is rarely limited. Unanimous consent requests may disallow nongermane amendments but they seldom limit the number of germane amendments that may be offered. Once cloture is invoked, the Senate may consider only germane amendments. When a cloture petition is filed, senators anticipating that cloture may be invoked on a measure and wishing to protect their rights must submit first-degree amendments by one o'clock in the afternoon on the day following the submission of the petition and second-degree amendments by one hour prior to the beginning of the cloture vote.

The right of senators to offer nongermane amendments is a primary means of ensuring that legislation does not get bottled up in an unsympathetic committee. In 1983, for example, Senate Finance Committee Chairman Bob Dole, R-Kan., vehemently opposed a proposal to repeal a provision of the 1982 tax bill that required tax withholding on interest and dividends. But when proponents of repeal threatened to attach it to important jobs and Social Security legislation, the Senate leadership agreed to allow it to be offered as an amendment to an unrelated trade bill.

When the Senate requires that amendments be germane the test is stricter than that in the House. An amendment in the Senate is considered germane only if it deletes something from the bill, adjusts a figure up or down, or restricts the scope of the bill. An amendment is considered nongermane if it in some way expands the scope of the bill, no matter how relevant the subject matter of the amendment may be to the underlying legislation. An amendment adding a fourth country to a bill granting most-favored-nation trade status to three countries would be just as nongermane as an amendment revising the criminal code.

A sponsor may modify or withdraw an amendment at any time before a roll-call vote is ordered on it or it becomes the subject of a unanimous consent agreement. The amendment may then be modified or withdrawn only by unanimous consent. (In the House, members may modify or withdraw their amendments only by unanimous consent during consideration in the Committee of the Whole.) A sponsor may agree to modify an amendment to make it more acceptable to a greater number of senators. If a senator has offered an amendment simply to make a point, he or she may choose to withdraw it before it comes to a vote. Amended language cannot be changed again unless the change is part of an amendment that also changes other unamended parts of the legislation.

Amendments offered by the reporting committee are taken up before other amendments. Often, the Senate by unanimous consent agrees to the committee amendments en bloc, particularly if the amendments are extensive, and then provides that the bill as amended is to be "considered as an original text for the purpose of further amendment." Or, as is frequently the case with appropriations bills, the Senate might agree en bloc to all but one or two of the committee amendments, which are then considered separately. Such amendments are themselves open to amendment and must be disposed of before other unrelated amendments are proposed.

As in the House, the principles governing consideration of amendments in the Senate are similar: legislation may be amended in the first and second degree, which means that a proposed amendment to a bill may itself be amended; and again, substitutes may also be proposed for pending amendments as well as for the bill itself.

The Senate process, however, is more complex in its treatment of the precedence of different types of first- and second-degree perfecting amendments and substitutes. It differs somewhat from the House process in the order in which they may be offered. Another difference is the ability of senators to modify their amendments virtually at will, and, in some cases, to offer second-degree amendments to their own amendments. The majority leader, who always has priority of recognition, has sometimes used these tactics to offer several proposals himself and close off the "amendment tree" to opponents.

In voting on amendments, the Senate makes frequent use of a procedural device known as tabling to block or kill amendments. When approved, a motion to "lay on the table" is considered the final disposition of that issue. The motion is not debatable, and adoption requires a simple majority vote. In the Senate, a motion to table is usually offered after an amendment has been debated, rather than as a means to prevent debate. By voting to table, a senator can appear to avoid being recorded directly on a controversial amendment to a politically sensitive issue, though the substantive result is the same. (Although the House also has a motion to table, it is not in order in the Committee of the Whole and thus cannot be used to prevent consideration of amendments offered there. In the House, the motion is most commonly used to block any debate on "hostile" motions or resolutions—that is, those not supported by the majority leadership—that might otherwise be debatable and whose consideration would, unless tabled, give the minority party control of the floor.)

Like the House, the Senate has available motions to recommit a bill under consideration on the floor to a committee, which would terminate action on it. The Senate may also choose to recommit a bill to a committee with instructions to take certain actions, such as to report back "forthwith" with amendments, and such a motion if adopted would immediately bring the bill back to the floor in an altered form. The Senate motion to recommit is more flexible than its House equivalent, since it can be offered at any point during consideration of a measure, not just at the end of the amendment process, can be offered more than once, may be amended by proposing instructions or by offering amendments to instructions offered in the initial motion, and may be proposed by any senator, without preference to those in the minority. The motion also has precedence over the offering of amendments.

Filibusters and Cloture

In its most extreme form, the Senate's tradition of unlimited debate can turn into a filibuster—the deliberate use of extended debate or procedural delays to block action on a measure supported by a majority of members. Filibusters once provided the Senate's best theater. Practitioners had to be ready for days or weeks of freewheeling debate, and all other business was blocked until one side conceded. In the modern era, drama is rare. Disappointment awaits visitors to the Senate gallery who expect a real-life version of Jimmy Stewart's climactic oration in the 1939 movie, *Mr. Smith Goes to Washington.* They are likely to look down on an empty floor and hear only the drone of a clerk reading absent senators' names in a mind-numbing succession of quorum calls. Often today's filibusterers do not even have to be on the floor, nor do the bills they are opposing. *(See box, Dilatory Tactics: As Old as the Senate, below.)*

Despite the lack of drama, filibusters are still effective weapons. Any controversial legislation that comes to the floor without a prearranged time agreement is vulnerable to fili-

DILATORY TACTICS: AS OLD AS THE SENATE

The Senate was just six months old in 1789 when delaying tactics were first used, by opponents of a bill to locate the nation's capital on the Susquehanna River. By 1840 dilatory debate was so common that Henry Clay of Kentucky was demanding "a rule which would place the business of the Senate under the control of a majority."

The first full-fledged filibusters occurred the next year, when Democrats and Whigs squared off first over the appointment of official Senate printers and then over the establishment of a national bank. Slavery, the Civil War, Reconstruction, and blacks' voting rights in turn sparked the increasingly frequent and contentious filibusters of the nineteenth century. Because the Senate repeatedly rejected efforts to restrict debate, the majority's only recourse was to win unanimous consent for a time limit on considering a bill, on a case-by-case basis.

Minor curbs on debate were adopted early in the twentieth century. But they did not hinder Republican filibusterers from killing two of President Woodrow Wilson's proposals to put the nation on a war footing—bills in 1915 concerning ship purchases and in 1917 to arm merchant ships.

As a political scientist in 1882, Wilson had celebrated "the Senate's opportunities for open and unrestricted discussion." After the 1917 defeat, he railed, "The Senate of the United States is the only legislative body in the world which cannot act when the majority is ready for action. A little group of willful men . . . have rendered the great government of the United States helpless and contemptible."

On March 8, 1917, the Senate yielded to public outcry and adopted a cloture rule (Rule XXII), which required a vote of two-thirds of those present to end debate. The rule's framers predicted it would be little used, and for years that was the case.

The first successful cloture motion came in 1919, ending debate on the Treaty of Versailles, which nonetheless failed to be ratified. Nine more motions were voted on through 1927 of which three succeeded. Over the next thirty-five years, until 1962, only sixteen were voted on and not one was adopted.

In large part that reflected the politics of civil rights. Southern Democrats successfully filibustered legislation against the poll tax, literacy tests, lynching, and employment discrimination by building an anticloture coalition that included westerners and some Republicans. In 1949 proponents of the right to filibuster gained a further advantage when they were able to amend Rule XXII to require a two-thirds vote of the total Senate membership to invoke cloture. That change occurred after a coalition of northern Democrats and moderate Republicans sought to make it easier for the majority to invoke cloture.

Undaunted by its failure, a liberal-moderate coalition sought to ease Rule XXII nearly every time a new Congress convened. A key strategy was to assert the right of a majority to amend Senate rules at the beginning of a Congress. They received support from sympathetic vice presidents Richard Nixon, Hubert Humphrey, and Nelson Rockefeller. Filibuster supporters maintained that the Senate was a "continuing body" not subject to wholesale revision with each new class of senators who, after all, constituted only one-third of the chamber.

In 1959 Rule XXII was amended back to provide for limitation of debate by a vote of two-thirds of the senators present and voting, with the vote to occur two days after a cloture petition was submitted by sixteen senators. If cloture was adopted, further debate was limited to one hour for each senator on the bill itself and on all amendments affecting it. Amendments that were not germane to the pending business and dilatory motions were out of order. The rule applied both to regular legislation and to motions to change the Standing Rules of the Senate.

buster; success is most likely near the end of the session, when a filibuster on one bill may imperil action on other, more urgent legislation. Filibusters may be intended to kill a measure outright, by forcing the leadership to pull the measure off the floor so that it can move on to other business, but they are often mounted to force a compromise on the measure. Time is such a precious commodity in today's Senate that individual members who even threaten to hold a bill hostage to lengthy debate can usually force compromises on the measure, either in committee or on the floor.

Filibusters have always generated intense debate. Supporters view filibusters as a defense against hasty or ill-advised legislation and as a guarantee that minority views will be heard. Detractors contend that filibusters allow a minority to thwart the will of a majority and impede orderly consideration of issues before the Senate.

Silencing a Filibuster. A filibuster can be ended by negotiating a compromise on the disputed matter or by mustering a determined supermajority of senators to shut it off. Since 1917 the Senate has also been able to vote to invoke cloture to cut off a filibuster, though the supermajority required to do so has changed over the years.

The procedure to end a filibuster is contained in Senate Rule XXII. This cumbersome procedure requires sixteen senators to sign a cloture petition and file it with the presiding officer of the Senate. Two days later, and one hour after the Senate convenes, the presiding officer establishes the presence of a quorum and then poses the question: "Is it the sense of the Senate that the debate shall be brought to a close?" If three-fifths of the Senate (sixty senators) votes in favor of the motion, cloture is invoked. (A two-thirds majority of those present and voting, which would be sixty-seven senators if all were present, is needed to invoke cloture on proposals to amend the Senate's standing rules, including Rule XXII. This means that an even larger majority would be needed to change the rule. In practice, it puts an almost impossible task in front of advocates of ending the cloture rule entirely and creating a situation of simple majority rule in the Senate.)

Slowly, the anticloture coalition began to dissolve. In 1964 the Senate for the first time invoked cloture on a civil rights bill, cutting off the longest filibuster in Senate history. A year later cloture was approved for another civil rights measure, the Voting Rights Act, and in 1968 a filibuster on an open housing bill was cut off.

In 1969, the Senate came close to eviscerating the cloture rule, as Vice President Humphrey ruled that the Senate could end debate on a rules change by a majority vote at the beginning of a new Congress. However, the Senate promptly overruled Humphrey

By the early 1970s the liberals' victories on civil rights had cooled their ardor for cloture reform. Moreover, they had become the ones doing much of the filibustering—against President Nixon's Vietnam policies, weapons systems, and antibusing proposals.

In 1973, for the first time in years, the new Senate did not fight over the cloture rule. But in 1975 the liberals tried again—and won. After the Senate seemed ready on a series of procedural votes to adopt the principle that a simple majority could change the rules at the beginning of a Congress without having to invoke cloture, senators opposed to cloture reform agreed to relax the supermajority requirements if this precedent were overturned. Under Rule XXII as amended, three-fifths of the total membership of the Senate, or sixty votes, could shut off a filibuster—seven votes less than was needed under the old rule if every senator voted. (A two-thirds vote of those present and voting was still required to cut off debate on proposed rules changes.)

The 1975 revision made it easier for a majority to invoke cloture. But much of the revision's success relied on the willingness of the senators to abide by the spirit as well as the letter of the chamber's rules. When cloture was invoked on a particular measure, senators had generally conceded defeat and proceeded to a vote without further delay.

But in 1976 conservative James B. Allen, D-Ala., began violating this unwritten rule of conduct and finding ways around the existing restrictions. By capitalizing on a loophole that permitted unlimited postcloture quorum calls, parliamentary motions, and roll-call votes on amendments introduced before cloture was invoked, Allen was able to delay a vote on the issue itself for far longer than the hour allotted to him under the 1959 rules revision. In 1977, with Vice President Mondale presiding, Majority Leader Robert C. Byrd took the floor to have ruled out of order dozens of amendments filed by liberal Senators Howard Metzenbaum, D-Ohio, and James Abourezk, D-S.D., who were staging a postcloture filibuster on energy legislation, a major legislative priority of the Carter administration. The vice president refused to entertain appeals of his rulings or to recognize anyone other than the majority leader. Mondale and Byrd were subsequently criticized for heavy-handed and arbitrary tactics, but their actions stood amid indications that the Senate's tolerance for delaying tactics pushed to a potentially infinite degree was waning.

The Senate closed the postcloture loophole in 1979, when it agreed to an absolute limit on such delaying tactics. The rule provided that once cloture was invoked, a final vote had to be taken after no more than 100 hours of debate. All time spent on quorum calls, roll calls, and other parliamentary procedures was counted against the 100-hour limit. In 1986 the Senate reduced that limitation to thirty hours. The change, enacted as part of the Senate's decision to allow live television coverage of its floor action, was intended to quicken the pace of the proceedings.

Republican control of the Senate in 1981–1987, and since 1995, pretty much eliminated interest by liberals in further changes in the cloture rule. Indeed, the filibuster became an important tool used by Democrats to restrain Republican presidents and, later, to block key parts of the political agenda of House Republicans.

There is no limit on how long a filibuster must go on before a cloture petition can be filed. "Years ago, even Lyndon Johnson wouldn't try to get cloture until after a week," Sen. Strom Thurmond, R-S.C., said in 1987. "But now, after one day, if the leaders see you are really going to fight, they'll apply cloture immediately."[24] Thurmond's record for the longest filibuster by a single individual—twenty-four hours and eighteen minutes on a 1957 civil rights bill (which became law despite his efforts)—is likely to stand in the modern era.

Nor are there any limitations on the number of times the Senate can try to invoke cloture on the same filibuster. "There used to be an unwritten rule that three [cloture votes] was enough," said Robert B. Dove, who was Senate parliamentarian during periods of Republican control in the 1980s and 1990s.[25] But in 1975 the Senate took six cloture votes in a futile effort to cut off debate on a dispute over a contested Senate seat in New Hampshire. And in 1987–1988, the Senate took eight cloture votes to shut off a Republican filibuster of a campaign spending bill before conceding defeat and shelving the measure.

Increased Use of Filibusters. For most of the Senate's history, the filibuster was used sparingly and for the most part only on legislative battles of historical importance, such as peace treaties and civil rights matters. Since the mid-1970s, the Senate has seen a significant increase in its use. Members, Sen. Thomas F. Eagleton, D-Mo., said in 1985, "are prepared to practice the art of gridlock at the drop of a speech or the drop of an amendment."[26] Indeed, in some cases the majority leader, aware of potential controversy surrounding a bill, may offer a motion to proceed to its consideration and then immediately file for cloture on that motion to get a more accurate sense of the intensity of the opposition; if sixty votes are not available, he or she may not attempt to advance the legislation further.

Ironically, a change in Senate rules that made it easier to invoke cloture to cut off a filibuster coincided with their increased use. In 1975, after years of trying, Senate liberals succeeded in pushing through a change in the Senate's cloture rule. Instead of two-thirds of those voting (sixty-seven if all senators are present), three-fifths of the membership, or sixty senators, could invoke cloture on a filibuster.

Several factors account for the increase. More issues come

CONGRESSIONAL RECORD

The *Congressional Record* is the primary source of information about what happens on the floors of the Senate and House of Representatives. Published daily when Congress is in session, the *Record* provides an officially sanctioned account of each chamber's debate and shows how individual members voted on all recorded votes.

The *Record* is not the official account of congressional proceedings. That is provided in each chamber's Journal, which reports actions taken but not the accompanying debate. But the *Record* is often used by the courts to determine legislative history—what Congress intended when it passed a law. The status of tapes of televised broadcasts of House and Senate proceedings in such situations is undetermined.

By law the *Record* is supposed to provide "substantially a verbatim report of the proceedings." Exchanges among legislators can be quite lively and revealing, though watching Congress on television conveys far more of the flavor and atmospherics governing debate than reading the *Record.* Until recent years, there was broad discretion to edit remarks for the *Record,* fixing grammatical errors or even deleting words spoken in the heat of floor debate. Speeches not given on the floor were often included, although both the House and Senate have tightened rules about "inserting remarks," as the process is known. There have been complaints from time to time that this practice had been abused. The full texts of bills, conference reports and other documents, rarely read in full on the floor, are often printed in the *Record.*

When Republicans took control of the House in 1995, the rules were changed to limit alterations that members might make "only to technical, grammatical and typographical corrections . . . ," which prohibited removal of remarks actually made. Written statements can still be inserted in the *Record,* even within the text of actual remarks made by a member, as long as they appear in a distinctive typeface. The new stringency was ruled to apply even to the Speaker, who had customarily refined rulings made from the chair after the fact to ensure clarity. Now the Speaker's actual comments appear verbatim.

The Speaker often inserts written material into the *Record,* especially at the beginning of a Congress, to elaborate certain practices that he will follow in recognizing members, referring bills, and on other subjects.

HISTORY

Before 1825 reports of congressional debates were sporadic. In 1789–1790 Thomas Lloyd of New York took down congressional debates in shorthand. Four volumes exist of his *Congressional Register.* Between 1790 and 1825 debate in the House was reported haphazardly by some of the better newspapers. Senate debates scarcely were reported at all. In 1834 Gales and Seaton published the first of forty-two volumes of *Annals of Congress,* which brought together material from newspapers, magazines, and other sources on congressional proceedings from the First through the Twelfth Congress (March 3, 1789, to May 27, 1824).

From 1824 through 1837 Gales and Seaton published a *Register of Debate,* which directly reported congressional proceedings. In 1833 Blair and Rives began to publish *The Congressional Globe,* but debates were still not reported systematically until 1865, when the *Globe* took on a form and style that later became standard. When the government contract for publication of the *Globe* expired in 1873, Congress provided that the *Congressional Record* would be produced by the Government Printing Office.

PROCEEDINGS

The *Record* contains four sections. Two of them, the proceedings of the Senate and of the House, are edited accounts of floor debate before the Senate, making time an even scarcer commodity than in the past. More issues are controversial, and in a period of divided party rule between Congress and the White House, which has prevailed much of the time since the 1970s, more partisan. In addition, constituents and special interest groups put more pressure on members, and members are more apt to pursue their political goals even if it means inconveniencing their colleagues. In the 1990s, filibusters and threats of filibuster were common weapons of senators hoping merely to spotlight or change as well as delay, or kill legislation.

The track system, which allows the Senate to set aside a filibustered measure temporarily while it considers other legislation, also may have contributed to the heightened use of filibusters. "For senators peripheral to the fight on a filibustered measure, separate tracking made filibusters more tolerable, made them less resentful of the filibustering senators, and even may have reduced the incentive to vote for cloture," Steven Smith wrote. "And for the filibustering senators, tracking may have improved the chances of success and reduced the costs of filibustering."[27]

The Rise and Fall of the Postcloture Filibuster. Traditionally, filibusterers bowed to the inevitable in the face of a successful motion to invoke cloture, abandoning any further attempts to delay action on the disputed measure. After the Senate made it easier to invoke cloture in 1975, however, a postcloture filibuster quickly appeared. The tactic took advantage of the fact that the hour allotted each senator did not count time spent on procedural motions and that all germane amendments filed before cloture was invoked were in order. By filing dozens of amendments, demanding roll calls and quorum calls, and engaging in other parliamentary procedures, senators could delay final action for days or weeks.

The postcloture filibuster was developed largely by James B. Allen, a conservative Democrat from Alabama. But two northern liberals, James G. Abourezk, D-S.D., and Howard M. Metzenbaum, D-Ohio, exploited the tactic fully in 1977, tying up the Senate for two weeks after cloture had been invoked on a bill to deregulate natural gas. The postcloture debate was ended only after the presiding officer, Vice President Walter Mondale, in close consultation with Majority Leader Byrd, took the then-

and other action taken in each chamber. A member may request "unanimous consent to extend my remarks at this point in the *Record*," or to include extraneous matter, at any time he or she is able to gain recognition on the floor. When the request is granted, and it almost always is, a member may include a statement, newspaper article, or speech, which will appear in the body of the *Record* where the member requested.

Until March 1978 there was no way to tell whether a lawmaker had actually delivered his or her remarks or had them inserted. Since then, inserted remarks are indicated in the House proceedings by a different typeface; in the Senate they are denoted by black dots, or bullets. If a member read only a few words from a speech or article, it would appear in the *Record* as if the member had delivered it in its entirety. As noted, the House in 1995 restricted this practice to require all undelivered remarks to appear in a separate typeface.

Since 1979 time cues have marked House floor debate to show roughly when a particular discussion occurred. Senate proceedings have no indication of time.

EXTENSIONS OF REMARKS

In addition to inserting material, senators and representatives are given further space to extend their remarks. By unanimous consent, they may add such extraneous material as speeches given outside Congress, selected editorials, or letters. Such material may also be included in the body of the *Record* by unanimous consent if a representative or senator prefers.

DAILY DIGEST

The fourth section of the *Record* is the Daily Digest, which summarizes House and Senate floor action for the day as well as Senate and House committee meetings and conferences. It also notes committee reports filed and the time and date of the next House and Senate sessions and all committee meetings. The last issue of the Digest in the week lists the program for the coming week, including legislation scheduled for floor action if it has been announced, and all committee meetings. At the beginning of each month the Digest publishes a statistical summation of congressional activity in the previous month. An index to the *Record* is published semimonthly.

COSTS

About 9,000 copies of each day's issue of the *Record* are printed. In fiscal 1997 the total cost came to $18.9 million. An annual subscription cost $295 in 1998; an individual copy cost $2.50. Until 1970 a subscription cost only $1.50 a month. The *Record* is also available on microfiche.

Rules require that any insert of more than two pages include an estimate of printing costs by the Government Printing Office. One of the most expensive inserts appeared in the issue of June 15, 1987, when Rep. Bill Alexander, D-Ark., inserted 403 pages covering three and a half years of congressional debate on an amendment barring military aid to the antigovernment contra guerrillas in Nicaragua. Estimated cost of the insertion: $197,000.

COMPUTER ACCESS

The public can gain free access to the daily *Congressional Record* through Internet web sites run by the U.S. Government Printing Office (http://www.access.gpo.gov) and the "Thomas" service provided by the Library of Congress (http://thomas.loc.gov). *(See "Congressional Information on the Internet," p. 174, in Reference Materials.)*

extraordinary step of recognizing only Byrd, ruling amendments offered by the two senators out of order and refusing recognition to appeal his rulings. While these actions stood, effectively killed the filibuster, and ensured passage of the president's energy legislation, their arbitrary nature disturbed some senators since they placed "ends" (passage of a bill) ahead of "means" (each senator's right to use the rules).

In 1979 the Senate moved formally to eviscerate the postcloture filibuster by including all time spent on procedural activities as well as on substantive debate against each senator's allotted hour. That put a 100-hour cap on postcloture debate. Senators were also barred from calling up more than two amendments until every other senator had an opportunity to call up two amendments. And the presiding officer was authorized to rule clearly dilatory motions out of order. In 1986 the Senate agreed to cap postcloture debate at thirty hours. Senators could still be recognized for an hour, but the time was allocated on a first-come, first-served basis. Any senators who had not yet been recognized at the end of thirty hours were each entitled to receive ten minutes.

Final Senate Action

Once debate and voting on all amendments has ended and no senator wishes to speak, a final vote on the pending legislation is taken. Senate observers are often surprised to discover that most bills pass by voice votes with only a handful of senators present. Any member, however, can request a roll call on final passage and the Senate nearly always grants such a request.

After the final vote is announced, the Senate must dispose of the routine motion to reconsider before a bill is considered finally passed. A senator who voted for the bill (or who did not vote) moves to reconsider the vote; a second senator who voted for the bill moves to table the motion to reconsider, and the tabling motion is almost always adopted, usually by voice vote. In the House, the Speaker in order to save time usually says, "Without objection, the motion to reconsider is laid upon the table."

Final Action: Resolving Differences

Before a bill can be sent to the White House for the president's signature, it must be approved in identical form by both chambers of Congress.

There are three ways of resolving differences between the two Houses: one chamber may yield to the other and simply accept its amendments; amendments move back and forth between the two houses until both agree; or a conference committee may be convened. The strategy that is used can be determined by many factors—the nature of the legislation, the time of year it is being considered, and the desire to avoid procedural entanglements.

On many noncontroversial measures the second chamber may simply agree to the version approved by the first chamber. When that occurs, no further legislative action is required, and the bill can be submitted to the president.

On virtually all major legislation, however, the second chamber approves a version that differs, sometimes radically, from the measure adopted by the first chamber. (Often the second chamber already has a similar measure under consideration.) When that happens, the second chamber has two options. It may return the bill to the chamber of origin, which then has the choice of accepting the second chamber's amendments, accepting them with further amendments, or disagreeing to the other version and requesting a House-Senate conference. Or, less frequently, the second house itself may request a conference.

Sometimes one chamber accepts major amendments made by the other to avoid further floor action that might jeopardize the bill. That occurred on a bill involving Alaskan lands in the postelection session of 1980. Democratic sponsors of the House version bill knew that they would face a Republican-controlled Senate in 1981 as a result of the election, and that any conference agreement would face a successful filibuster from the newly energized Senate minority in the lame-duck session. As a result, the House grudgingly accepted the Senate version, which did not contain as many environmental protections, rather than risk ending up with no bill at all.

Often, after both chambers have passed different versions of the same measure, members and staff of the House and Senate committees with jurisdiction for the bill informally work out a compromise that one house adopts as an amendment to the other chamber's version. The latter chamber then agrees to the version as amended, avoiding a conference and clearing it for the president.

Just as neither chamber may offer amendments beyond the second degree, neither chamber may amend the other's amendments more than twice. Like other rules, however, this one can be waived and sometimes is. The budget reconciliation act of 1985 was shuffled between the two chambers nine times before agreement was finally reached the following year.

It should be noted that many bills pass one chamber of Congress never to be considered in the other. Those measures, as well as any on which the House and Senate are unable to reconcile their differences, die at the end of the Congress.

CONFERENCE ACTION

Sen. Joel Bennett Clark, D-Mo., once introduced a resolution providing that "all bills and resolutions shall be read twice and, without debate, referred to conference." He was joking, of course, but his proposal highlights the crucial role of conference committees in drafting the final form of complex and controversial legislation. Everything the bill's sponsors worked for and all the efforts exerted by the executive branch and private interests to help pass or defeat it can be won or lost during these negotiations. Some of the hardest bargaining in the entire legislative process takes place in conference committees, and frequently the conference goes on for days, weeks, even months, before the two sides reconcile their differences.

During floor consideration of a bill members may adopt certain tactics solely to better position themselves for the bargaining and compromise that is the hallmark of all conference nego-

House and Senate negotiators meet in conference to work out the final shape of a major transportation funding bill in 1998.

tiations. A senator, for example, may demand a roll call on a particular amendment to demonstrate to the House the Senate's solid support for the amendment—or its solid opposition. A committee may add some provisions to its version that can be traded away in conference. Or it may deliberately keep out a provision it knows the other chamber favors, again to have something to trade in conference. A floor manager may agree to an amendment, especially if he or she can persuade the sponsor not to ask for a recorded vote, knowing that it can be dumped in the conference.

Once in conference, conferees generally try to grant concessions only insofar as they remain confident the chamber they represent will accept the compromises. That is not always possible, however. The threat of a Senate filibuster on a conference report, for example, may influence House conferees to drop a provision that they believe too many senators might find distasteful. Time also may be a factor, especially at the end of a Congress when delay might cause a bill to die in conference.

Calling a Conference

Either chamber can request a conference once both have considered the same legislation. Generally, the chamber that approved the legislation first will disagree to the amendments made by the second body and request that a conference be convened. Sometimes, however, the second body will ask for a conference immediately after it has passed the legislation, assuming that the other chamber will not accept its amendments. The distinction can be important, since the chamber that requests the conference nearly always, by custom, acts last on the conference report. Depending on the political situation, this may have strategic importance affecting the legislation's chances for final passage.

Both chambers technically must go to conference on a single bill. Thus one chamber often takes up the other's version of the measure, strikes everything after the enacting clause, and substitutes its version for everything but the other chamber's bill number. Both versions can then be considered by the conference committee. Measures raising revenue and making appropriations that are sent to conference always have an "HR" designation. A conference cannot change the number of the bill committed to it or create a different-numbered bill.

A conference cannot take place until both chambers formally agree that it be held. The Senate usually requests or agrees to a conference by unanimous consent. However, a motion to do so is debatable and may be filibustered. In the House this action generally is taken by unanimous consent or, since 1965, by motion, if authorized by the committee managing the legislation and if the floor manager is recognized at the discretion of the Speaker for that purpose. Before 1965, if there was objection to unanimous consent, the House could go to conference only if it suspended the rules with a two-thirds majority or if the Rules Committee granted a rule that the House could adopt by majority vote. On some occasions, the Rules Committee refused to report a rule allowing a conference, which gave the conservative coalition that often controlled that committee prior to its expansion in 1961 another means of blocking legislative action.

Selection of Conferees

The two chambers have different rules for selecting conferees, or "managers," as they are formally called, but in practice both follow similar procedures. House rules grant the Speaker of the House the right to appoint conferees, but the Speaker usually does so only after consultation with the chairman and ranking minority member of the committee having jurisdiction over the legislation. As in the selection of members of standing committees, the minority selects its choices for conferees, which, by custom, are appointed by the Speaker without change. Once appointed, conferees normally serve throughout the con-

LEGISLATIVE ANOMALIES

Peculiar situations have arisen occasionally as Congress searches for an appropriate manner to achieve a new or unique result. And even if Congress cannot find one, it may do what it wants to anyway. Here are several examples.

In 1978 Congress attempted a new form of legislative enactment to extend the time permitted for ratification of a constitutional amendment. The so called Equal Rights Amendment (ERA), passed by Congress in 1972 and intended to enhance women's rights, carried within it a seven-year time limit for ratification by the requisite three-fourths of the states. It would die on March 22, 1979, unless ratified by thirty-eight states. Congress had first set time limits on amendment ratifications beginning in 1917 to ensure that the initial proposal of an amendment and its ultimate ratification were roughly contemporaneous.

With the deadline nearing Congress wanted to keep the amendment alive to see if several additional states might ratify the amendment. A joint resolution was passed extending the life of the amendment by thirty-nine additional months, until June 30, 1982. Congress first had determined, by simple majority, that a two-thirds vote was not required for passage of the time-extension. (It also would have been more difficult to obtain a two-thirds vote in 1978 than in 1972 because the amendment had become far more controversial after its passage.)

Once passed by both houses, the joint resolution was sent to President Jimmy Carter, who proceeded to sign it even while raising doubt that he had any role in the process and questioning whether the joint resolution was really a law. The Archivist of the United States, who received the joint resolution next, did not give it a public law number but instead notified the states of its existence. A federal judge ruled in 1981 that Congress had acted improperly but the question became moot when additional states failed to ratify the amendment even under the extended timetable. The Supreme Court dismissed the case as moot in 1982 and vacated the lower court's decision, leaving the ultimate validity of the congressional action in constitutional limbo.

Other examples of unusual legislative actions have involved constitutional amendments. Congress does not need to take any formal action once an amendment has been ratified. In 1868, however, Congress passed a concurrent resolution to declare that the Fourteenth Amendment to the Constitution had been ratified by the requisite number of states. In 1992, reeling from scandals and low public approval ratings, members rushed to identify themselves with the so-called Madison Amendment to the Constitution, which required that an election intervene before any congressional pay raise could take effect. The amendment, originally proposed by Congress in 1789, suddenly reemerged in 1978 after more than a century in limbo since the last time a state legislature had approved it, to begin a flurry of new ratifications. Previous historical concerns by Congress about contemporaneous enactment of constitutional amendments were thrown to the winds as members rushed to embrace what was still one of the most popular forms of Congress-bashing—denying themselves pay raises.

Each house passed a concurrent resolution stating that the new Twenty-Seventh Amendment was properly ratified, but neither house passed the concurrent resolution adopted by the other. Not satisfied with that, the Senate also adopted a simple resolution declaring ratification of the amendment. Adding to the confusion, the Archivist of the United States had already declared the amendment ratified on May 18, 1992, before Congress acted.

In 1998, as Congress awaited the results of an investigation by special prosecutor Kenneth Starr into scandals involving the Clinton administration, rumors of possible impeachment proceedings

ference process, but often, particularly on complex legislation that has conferees from several committees, the Speaker routinely announces changes in the composition of the conference. These actions usually reflected an error in the initial appointment that might not properly have reflected committee jurisdictions on a particular issue.

However, in 1993, the House amended its rules to give the Speaker formal authority to replace any conferee whenever he or she wished, obviating the need for a unanimous consent request required in earlier practice. While the new power has rarely been used for any substantive purpose, it does give the leadership substantial power in any conference negotiation and restrains conferees from bringing back a conference report likely to face defeat. Conferees technically may be named or replaced only by the Speaker, not by a Speaker pro tempore, except by unanimous consent.

Senate rules allow the chamber as a whole to elect conferees, but that rarely happens. The common practice is for the presiding officer, by unanimous consent, to appoint conferees on the recommendation of the appropriate committee chairman and ranking minority member. The process of going to conference and appointing conferees is debatable, however, and provides another potential choke point for opponents of a measure.

Those members who are usually selected as conferees are the chairmen of the committee(s) that handled the legislation, the ranking minority member(s), and other members of the committee(s) most actively involved. If a subcommittee has exercised major responsibility for a bill, some of its members may be chosen. Seniority once governed the selection of conferees, but it is quite common today for junior members in each chamber to be chosen, especially if they are particularly knowledgeable about or interested in the bill. Occasionally a member from another committee with expertise in the subject matter of the bill may be named to the conference, or one who sponsored a major amendment adopted on the floor.

Sometimes there have been questions about whether conferees are likely to uphold the chamber's position on key points in conference deliberations. There have also been charges that a waxed and waned on Capitol Hill with each passing news cycle. Under the Constitution, the House by majority vote can initiate articles of impeachment that would result in a trial by the Senate, where a two-thirds majority is required for conviction and removal from office. Only one president, Andrew Johnson (1865–1869) has ever been impeached, but he was acquitted by a single vote in the Senate. Richard M. Nixon (1969–1974) was believed to have faced certain impeachment, conviction, and removal from office had he not resigned first.

In March 1998 Senate Majority Leader Trent Lott, R-Miss., suggested an unusual alternative to impeachment—a "censure" of the president by Congress—if Starr's investigation did not warrant impeachment. The Senate had done this once before, to President Andrew Jackson in 1834, in a political dispute over the Bank of the United States. Jackson successfully vetoed a reauthorization of the Bank during his first term. He then easily won reelection in 1832, and subsequently directed that U.S. funds be removed from it and deposited in various state banks. Senate opponents of Jackson, such as Daniel Webster and Henry Clay, considered him a dictator whose actions threatened the Constitution. In 1834 the Senate passed two resolutions censuring Jackson and the secretary of the Treasury. Since the Constitution does not recognize any punishment of a sitting president other than impeachment and removal from office, the censure carried no legal weight and was never repeated by any future Congress. Jackson's allies gained seats in the Senate following the 1834 election, and in January 1837 less than two months before Jackson's retirement the Senate voted 24–19 to expunge the censure from the Senate Journal of the previous Congress.

Presumably, if Lott's suggestion were to be followed either House could initiate a concurrent resolution to censure the president or act separately by simple resolution but such measures would not be privileged for consideration in either chamber and would be subject to a filibuster in the Senate.

The Senate reached back to rewrite history again in 1997. In 1996 the House had passed a conference report containing continuing appropriations funding government agencies. However, to deal with possible Senate opposition the House also passed the funding as a separate bill that the Senate might amend if it chose to do so. Ultimately, the Senate passed both bills; the conference report was sent to the president and signed into law. However, instead of simply killing the unnecessary separate bill, it was passed without amendment by a roll-call vote and the Daily Digest of the *Congressional Record* noted that it was cleared for the president. However, this did not happen. The Senate never sent a message to the House formally notifying it of the bill's passage, which prevented the House from enrolling it for presentation to the president, as required by law. Presumably, had this been done, the president could simply have disposed of the bill with a quiet pocket veto. With the bill in limbo, the 104th Congress expired, preventing any enrollment.

Nevertheless, Rep. David Skaggs, D-Colo., concerned with setting a precedent that a bill passed in identical form by both houses of Congress could be kept from the president by direction of the majority leadership of one chamber, called Majority Leader Lott demanding an explanation. He also inserted a letter to Lott and a history of the incident into the *Record.*[1]

In response, in February, 1997, Majority Whip Don Nickles, R-Okla., rose on the floor to ask unanimous consent to amend the Senate Journal of the preceding Congress to state that the bill had been indefinitely postponed.

1. "Concerning a Congressional Failure to Comply with the Constitution During the 104th Congress," *Congressional Record,* January 7, 1997, E2.

chairman might have stacked a conference with members favoring his or her position rather than the position of the chamber majority. A member may have voted for final passage but still have opposed key amendments during committee or floor action. Each chamber has remedies in such situations that restrain conferees—motions to instruct conferees, motions to recommit a conference report, the filibuster in the Senate, and the Speaker's power to change conferees in the House.

The increase in the size of conference committees led to ways to limit the role of some conferees, particularly those who are not members of the principal committee of jurisdiction. General conferees have overall responsibility for the whole bill. "Additional" conferees consider and vote only on specific subjects or sections of the legislation. "Exclusive" conferees are the sole negotiators for their chambers on specified subjects or sections. Members who are general conferees may vote on the same issues as additional conferees but may not participate in the areas reserved for exclusive conferees unless they are also so named.

The number of conferees each chamber selects does not have to be the same. A majority in each delegation will be from the majority party in the chamber, however. That requirement means that each chamber must name at least three conferees on each bill, but there is no upper limit. Bills that have been referred to more than one committee usually entail large conferences because conferees are selected from each of the committees of jurisdiction.

Twenty-three committees, for example, sent conferees to the conference committee on the omnibus trade bill enacted in 1988. Budget reconciliation resolutions generally engender some of the largest conferences because they may affect the jurisdictions of almost every House and Senate committee. More than 250 conferees from both houses were appointed as conferees on the 1981 budget reconciliation bill, for example. Such large conferences usually divide up into smaller working groups, or subconferences, that deal only with specific parts of the bill. In more recent years, Congress has moved in the opposite direction, sometimes limiting conferences to only three members—the chairman, another majority member, and the ranking minority member—to expedite the process and ensure leadership control.

Conferees in both the House and Senate are expected to support the legislative positions of the chamber they represent. In an effort to ensure that its conferees would uphold its position, the House in 1974 modified its rules on conferees selection. The revised rule said that "the Speaker shall appoint [as conferees] no less than a majority of members who generally supported the House position as determined by the Speaker." A further revision, in 1977, said that "the Speaker shall name members who are primarily responsible for the legislation and shall, to the fullest extent feasible, include the principal proponents of the major provisions of the bill as it passed the House." Some of these changes were intended to further strengthen the Speaker and to give him authority to resist demands by committee chairmen that might not be in the majority's interest. The Speaker's conference appointments may not be challenged in the House. The 1993 rules change giving the Speaker power to name and replace conferees at will has effectively limited the independent power of conferees, individually or collectively, to actively defy the majority party's agenda.

In 1995, Speaker Gingrich used his appointment power in a new way to highlight divisions in the minority over legislation headed to conference. For example, on one occasion he appointed a conservative Democrat, Rep. Gary A. Condit of California, to a conference on legislation relating to curbing unfunded federal mandates to the states and localities. In another, conservative Rep. Mike Parker, D-Miss., was appointed a conferee on the concurrent budget resolution. (Parker later switched parties). These members had been passed over by Minority Leader Richard Gephardt when the Democrats announced their choices from among more senior members. But Gingrich did not violate the custom of allowing the minority exclusive power over its choices; the slots he gave to these Democrats were taken from the Republicans' own allotment.

Political scientist Barbara Sinclair described the process in choosing conferees for the 1995 budget reconciliation bill, which was later vetoed by President Clinton. The Republican Party leadership in both houses sought to ensure close control over the bill, both to achieve a satisfactory result and to conclude negotiations quickly. The conference consisted of forty-three senators in twelve subgroups and seventy-one House members in fourteen subgroups. "Had Gingrich not assertively exercised the Speaker's discretion . . . the House delegation could easily have been much larger. . . . Gingrich chose whenever possible members who could do double duty because they served on the Budget Committee and another concerned committee. A subgroup of eight House members had authority over the entire bill and included . . . a number of party leaders—Majority Leader Dick Armey of Texas, Majority Whip Tom DeLay of Texas, and Conference Chairman John A. Boehner of Ohio on the Republican side and Minority Whip David Bonior on the Democratic side. In the Senate, the group of three that had authority over the entire bill was confined to the Budget Committee leaders. The other subgroups consisted of members from committees with provisions in the bill and had authority over those provisions only."[28]

Instructing Conferees

Either chamber may try to enforce its will by instructing its conferees how to vote in conference but the rules do not obligate the conferees to follow the instructions. The Senate rarely instructs its conferees but the practice may be becoming more common. In both chambers, conferees may be instructed just prior to their appointment by the chair. In the House, they may be instructed again, day after day, if they have failed to report after twenty calendar days have elapsed. (One day's advance warning must be given in the House of the intention to offer such motions, along with the exact wording.)

Efforts to instruct conferees may reflect the degree of support in the chamber for certain provisions in either the House or Senate versions of a bill. Depending on the circumstances, votes to instruct may serve as warnings that conferees had better not stray too far from the language the chamber originally approved or they may have just the opposite intent and signal receptivity to a provision originated in the other chamber. In the House motions to instruct are often used to react to Senate provisions that the House, under its germaneness rules, would never have had the opportunity to consider.

The potential political advantages of forcing a vote on a motion to instruct have led to its frequent use in the House. In a 1997 example of the tactics involved as the House prepared to go to conference, Rep. Steny Hoyer, D-Md., offered a motion to instruct conferees on the Treasury-Post Office appropriations bill that directed conferees to increase funding for the Exploited Child Unit of the National Center for Missing and Exploited Children. As ranking minority member of that subcommittee, Hoyer had the right to priority of recognition to offer the motion, and under the rules only a single such motion was permitted. Hoyer's motion was not in dispute but was intended to prevent a vote on the far more controversial issue of a cost-of-living pay adjustment for members of Congress, which was scheduled to take effect automatically the following year. The pay raise was authorized by existing law and the subject matter of the appropriations bill was unrelated to it. The Senate version of the bill, however, contained an amendment prohibiting the raise.

If the House voted to instruct its conferees to agree to the Senate pay ban, it would become nearly impossible for the House conferees to oppose the Senate language. This was exactly what pay-raise opponent Rep. Linda Smith, R-Wash., hoped to achieve but she had no right to be recognized to offer the motion. Instead, she sought to seize control of it from Hoyer by defeating the previous question, the motion in the House that ends debate and forces a vote on the pending matter. Had that motion lost, Smith could then have been recognized to amend Hoyer's motion without violating the rule that only a single motion could be offered. In the end, Hoyer won as the House ordered the previous question by a vote of 229–199, then easily passed his original language. Members who had supported the previous question could shield themselves from attack by critics of congressional pay raises by claiming to have supported a procedural motion, or that they wanted to help exploited children. In conference, the Senate receded from its pay-ban amendment and the raise was allowed to take effect. When the conference report passed, press coverage at the time made much of the idea that Congress had "voted itself a pay raise" when in fact the raise did not require any vote. Congress had simply refused to take action to change existing law.

As noted, the minority party has preference to offer motions to instruct conferees in the House when the House first votes to go to conference. When such motions again become available to any member if the conferees have not reported after twenty days have elapsed, again it is the minority that is most likely to take the initiative in attempting to influence the conference. The minority has used the right to offer motions to instruct to embarrass the majority, or to force repeated votes on controversial issues. For example, during the 103rd Congress, the Republican minority offered numerous motions to instruct as a conference on major crime legislation dragged on for months. The tactic was so effective, and annoying, that the then-Democratic majority considered changing House rules for the next Congress to restrict such motions, but the subsequent shift in party control prevented any action.

Authority of Conferees

Theoretically House and Senate conferees are limited to resolving matters in disagreement between the two chambers. They are not authorized to delete provisions or language that both chambers have agreed to or to draft entirely new provisions. This is called staying "within the scope" of disagreements between the two chambers. When the disagreement involves numbers, such as the level of funding in appropriations bills, conferees are supposed to stay within the amounts proposed by the two houses. (Generally, they split the difference.)

In practice the conferees have wide latitude, except where the matters in disagreement are very specific. If one chamber has substituted an entirely new version of the bill for that approved by the other chamber—which is nearly always the case on major bills, except for appropriations—the entire subject is technically in disagreement and the conferees may draft an entirely new bill if they so choose. In such a case, the Legislative Reorganization Act of 1946 stipulates that they may not include in the conference version of the bill "matter not committed to them by either house." But they may include "matter which is a germane modification of subjects in disagreement." For appropriations bills, the Senate had long used specific amendments to a House-passed bill rather than sending a complete substitute back, but this practice may now be changing for the sake of convenience.

In the Senate, scope requirements were often ignored or difficult to enforce and may be a dead letter as a result of a 1996 vote overruling a decision of the chair that matter contained within a conference report was beyond the scope of the conference (which it obviously was). The result may further enhance the bargaining power of conferees at the expense of individual members of their respective chambers if future conferences are conducted in a parliamentary environment where the Senate conferees can agree to virtually anything and the House conferees can as well as long as they have leadership support and a friendly Rules Committee on their side.

The House has long objected to the inclusion in conference reports of Senate-passed amendments that are not germane. Because conference agreements may not be amended on the floor of either chamber, the House was often put in a "take-it-or-leave-it" situation, forced either to accept a nongermane amendment it may never have debated or to recommit or vote down the entire conference report, including provisions it favored. A series of rules changes in the 1970s, including one in 1972 that allows the House to take separate votes on nongermane amendments in conference reports, has given the House some leverage both in conference and on the Senate floor. Senate floor managers sometimes tried to turn away nongermane floor amendments by arguing that they might prevent the entire bill from winning approval in the House.

However, in more recent practice, the pendulum has swung back toward allowing conferees, with the concurrence of the leadership, greater flexibility to negotiate and present conference reports that produce the desired policy results, irrespective of procedural inadequacies. The House leadership has worked with the committees to protect conference reports from points of order and possible dismemberment on the floor by having the Rules Committee waive points of order, such as the germaneness of Senate provisions or the inclusion of legislation on appropriations bills. Indeed, by the end of the 1990s it had become more common to waive all points of order, including scope.

Appropriations bills used to return from conference with hundreds of "amendments in disagreement" at the insistence of the House. Disposition of compromise language on these amendments was considered separately after the House had adopted the conference report. Most of these amendments were reported in "technical disagreement," which meant there were technical violations of House rules involved and an agreement was not placed in the body of the conference report to avoid potential points of order against the entire report. The conferees actually had reached agreement on these issues but each such item was theoretically subject to separate debate and votes to ratify the decisions and even potentially to additional amendment. Of course, sometimes there were substantial issues in "true disagreement" that the two chambers sent back and forth until an agreement was reached. Both Houses had to reach final agreement on all of these amendments to conclude action on a bill and send it to the president.

After the Republicans took control of Congress in 1995 they stopped this practice, insisting that conferees reach agreement on all issues whenever possible before returning to the floor. Every provision was placed within the body of the conference report and, in the House, was protected by a rule waiving points of order. The result was a considerable simplification of the conference procedure and represented another step back from the rules changes of the 1970s, which had sought to preserve opportunities for individual members to modify conference reports that might contain some violation of House rules.

After the mid-1970s, the growing power of the House leadership of both parties at the expense of committees, as well as the creation of committee memberships more representative of their respective parties, decreased the importance on procedural protections for the membership as a whole because the ability of committees and conferees to defy the majority was drastically curtailed.

During the reform period of the 1970s, many members of the House felt the Senate's loose amendment procedures gave it a distinct advantage over the House in conferences. Since the Senate's adoption in 1985 of the "Byrd Rule" barring extraneous matters in budget reconciliation bills, however, many in the Senate feel the pendulum has swung back the other way. The Byrd Rule allows points of order against any matter in a reconciliation bill that violates the rule, including major provisions in a conference report that might have survived from the House version, unless sixty votes waive the point of order.

The House has complained bitterly that its ability to legislate on reconciliation bills and to negotiate in conference has been restricted because conferees on the bill risk rejection of their entire product if it includes a provision that violates the Senate rule and cannot command sixty votes. The Senate argues that the Byrd Rule is vital to protect the Senate' tradition of unlimited debate because reconciliation bills, by statute, are immune from filibusters. In the absence of the Byrd Rule, the House could use conference reports on such bills to force the Senate to act on matters that might be filibustered if considered separately outside the budget process.

If conferees find they are unable to reach agreement they may report their failure to reach agreement to the parent chamber and allow the full House or Senate to act as it wishes; if neither chamber is willing to yield the legislation will die.

House rules allow conferees to be discharged and replaced by new conferees if they fail to reach agreement within twenty calendar days (or within thirty-six hours of their appointment during the last six days of a session), but this authority is rarely invoked.

Adoption of the Conference Report

When a majority of the conferees from each chamber have reached agreement on a bill, conference committee staff—generally the staff of the committees with jurisdiction over the measure—writes a conference report indicating changes made in the bill and explaining each side's action. If the two sides have been unable to reach a compromise on particular House or Senate amendments, those amendments are reported "in disagreement" and are acted on separately after the conference report itself has been agreed to.

The conference report must be signed by a majority of conferees from each chamber and submitted in document form to each house for approval. Minority reports or statements of minority views are not permitted, though sometimes a member will note next to his signature "except section ___" or a similar notation indicating partial disapproval. Until the 1970 Legislative Reorganization Act required House and Senate managers to prepare a joint explanatory statement discussing the specific changes made by the conferees, the conference report was printed only in the House, together with an explanation by the House conferees. The joint statement ensures that both houses have the same interpretation of the actions taken by the conferees, in addition to having an identical bill text. Although the conference report is supposed to be printed in the Senate, that requirement is frequently waived by unanimous consent. The report is always published in the *Congressional Record.* House rules also require that conference reports lie over three days before the House takes them up. The Senate requires only that copies be available on each senator's desk.

Each chamber must vote on a conference report as a whole. No new amendments may be considered. The Senate can still filibuster a conference report. In the House, conference reports may be called up at any time after the three days have expired. This requirement has been increasingly waived in the 1990s, either by unanimous consent or through adoption of a rule. Often members are forced to consider huge bills with little notice or even access to the written text of the legislation. In 1997, for example, members complained that copies of huge budget reconciliation/tax reduction legislation, which was supposed to lead to a balanced federal budget, were not available except for a few copies in the hands of the floor managers. In perhaps a portent of things to come in the use of technology by Congress, the Republican leadership responded by advising members to check for the legislation on the Speaker's Web site.

For complex legislation, the House Rules Committee is usually asked to report a rule waiving points of order. Protection from points of order may be critical because a point of order against the conference report—for example, that it contains matter beyond the scope of the disagreements committed to conference—would, if sustained, kill the conference report immediately without any vote and return the bill to its parliamentary status prior to the conference. There may be no time for a new conference, and the result would be the death of the legislation.

The house that agreed to the other chamber's request to go to conference on a bill acts first on the conference version. This procedure, followed by custom rather than by rule, is sometimes ignored; the Senate, for example, asked for the conference on the 1981 tax cut, and it acted first on the conference report.

Which chamber acts first or last can occasionally influence the outcome. The chamber to act first has three options: it can agree to the conference report, reject it, or recommit it to the conference committee for further deliberation. Once the first chamber has acted, however, the conference committee is dissolved, and recommittal is no longer an option. The second chamber must vote the conference report up or down.

The pressure on reluctant members to support a report that the other chamber has already approved can be intense. Rep. Jack Brooks, D-Texas, counted on that intense lobbying when he maneuvered in 1979 to have the House take up the conference report creating the Department of Education after the Senate had already agreed to it. Brooks's strategy worked; the House, which had originally approved creation of the department by a four-vote margin, agreed to the conference report with fourteen votes to spare.

While the conference version of the bill must be approved or rejected in its entirety by both bodies, in the House exceptions are made for nongermane Senate amendments. Unless a special rule has waived all points of order, any member of the House may make the point of order that a particular section of a conference report contains nongermane material and move to reject the offending language. Forty minutes of debate, equally divided between opposing sides, is allotted for such motions. If the motion carries, the nongermane material is deleted, the conference report is considered as rejected, and the House may go on to approve the remaining text of the conference report, minus the deletion, as a further amendment to the bill. The bill as amended must then go back to the Senate, which can either accept the amendment by the House, reject it, amend it further, or ask for a new conference.

If conferees have been unable to agree on any of the amendments in disagreement, separate votes are taken in both houses to resolve the differences. One chamber may insist on its amendment, or it may move to "recede and concur" in the other chamber's position. Occasionally the amendment in disagreement will be returned to conference for further compromise efforts.

Conference reports are seldom rejected, in part because legislators have little desire to begin the entire legislative process all over again and in part because members tend to defer to the expertise of the conferees, just as they tend to defer to the recommendations of the legislative committees. If a bill dies once it has reached conference, it is more likely that conferees have been unable to reach a compromise before the end of the Congress. That is what happened to the 1990 campaign finance bill.

Sometimes the House Rules Committee has been asked to make changes in a pending conference report through the device of allowing passage of a concurrent resolution "changing the enrollment of a conference report." These changes, for example, might be altering the text to enhance chances for passage. If the Senate also passes such a concurrent resolution, the conference report is modified by the enrolling clerk and sent to the president in its new, "improved" form.

FINAL LEGISLATIVE ACTION

After both houses have given final approval to a bill, a final copy of the bill, known as the enrolled bill, is prepared by the enrolling clerk of the chamber in which the bill originated, printed on parchment-type paper, and certified as correct by the secretary of the Senate or the clerk of the House, depending on which chamber originated the measure. No matter where the bill originated, it is signed first by the Speaker of the House and then by the vice president or president pro tempore of the Senate, and sent to the White House.

The president has ten days (not counting Sundays) from the day he receives the bill to act on it. In modern practice, an enrolled bill may be sent to the president even as the Congress that passed it is expiring, and the president still may act on it even though a new Congress has convened. If he approves the measure he signs it, dates it, and usually writes the word "approved" on the document. The Constitution requires only the president's signature.

A bill may become law without the president's signature in one of two ways. If the president does not sign a bill within ten days (Sundays excepted) from the time he receives it, the bill becomes law provided the Congress that passed it is in session. A bill may also become law without the president's signature if Congress overrides a veto.

When the president signs some bills, especially major legislation, he may stage a signing ceremony at the White House or some other appropriate location to draw attention to the new law and to honor its congressional sponsors and other supporters. The president, in such circumstances, uses numerous pens to affix his signature to the document and passes them out to his audience.

Another variation of the method of presidential signing might be called the "yes, but . . ." approach. During the 1980s, Presidents Ronald Reagan and George Bush occasionally issued "signing statements" when they approved some bills, objecting to certain provisions as unconstitutional and stating that they would ignore them. Members of Congress have sometimes voiced objection to such actions as inappropriate, but executive officials in recent years have argued that the president had a right to state an executive branch interpretation for the courts to consider in a potential legal action, just as Congress did when it made "legislative history." However, there is no evidence that courts have given such presidential statements any weight.

The idea was not new, and had appeared occasionally in more radical forms. In 1842, President John Tyler sent Congress a message noting that he had signed a bill and that it had been filed with the Secretary of State with "an exposition of my reasons for giving it my sanction." Tyler was promptly criticized for this action by Rep. John Quincy Adams of Massachusetts, a former president (1825–1829), who successfully moved to have a select committee examine the matter. Adams later filed a critical report from the select committee, which also submitted a resolution warning " . . . of evil example for the future." The resolution was not, however, adopted by the House. The select committee noted in its report that it

> can find . . . no authority given to the President for depositing in the Department of State an exposition of his reason for signing an act . . . and most especially none for making the deposit in company with the law . . . unless disavowed and discountenanced . . . its consequences may contribute to prostrate in the dust the authority of the very law which the President has approved with the accompaniment of this

most extraordinary appendage, and to introduce a practice which would transfer the legislative power of Congress itself to the arbitrary will of the executive.

A House committee also criticized President Andrew Jackson for an 1830 action when he had signed a bill and then written on the bill itself his views as to its meaning, views not shared by many in Congress.[29]

The Veto Power

If the president does not want a bill to become law he may veto it by returning it to the chamber in which it originated without his signature and with a message stating his objections. If no further action is taken the bill dies.

The Constitution provides that Congress may attempt to enact the bill into law "the objections of the president to the con-

LINE-ITEM VETO EXPERIMENT ENDED BY SUPREME COURT

Congress's historic enactment in 1996 of a law giving the president a "line-item veto" began a short-lived experiment with a power that Republicans had long sought for the executive branch. The line-item veto lasted only until June 1998, when the Supreme Court declared it unconstitutional.

The Line-Item Veto Act, which took effect on January 1, 1997, gave the president the power to strike out, or "cancel" dollar amounts of discretionary spending, new "direct spending," and certain forms of new tax benefits in bills signed into law. Congress could vote to pass the item(s) again, but the president could then use his constitutional veto power to kill this legislation, forcing Congress to find a two-thirds majority to override the veto in the normal manner.

Proponents of the line-item veto, generally political conservatives opposed to government spending and programs, argued that the overwhelming majority of state governors possessed the line-item veto in some form and that it had proved to be a useful tool in controlling expenditures. They responded to constitutional concerns by arguing that there was a long history of presidential action declining to carrying out spending passed by Congress, and that Congress could properly delegate authority to the president to declare cancellations of spending authority.

Opponents argued that the Constitution clearly required that bills be approved or rejected by the president in their entirety, not in pieces. They said that the new procedure gave the president the power to change laws after their enactment—in effect, to make laws, a power reserved exclusively to Congress—and to leave on the statute books truncated laws in a form that Congress might never have chosen to enact. The most fundamental argument, however, went to the balance of power between Congress and the executive branch. Opponents warned that a line-item veto would upset this balance among the branches of government by ceding too much political power to the president while Congress considered legislation. Beyond the basic principle, they feared the executive branch would have enormous leverage to offer to withhold cancellations if members backed unrelated presidential priorities.

OPERATION OF THE LINE-ITEM VETO

The 1996 law allowed the president to look not only at the specific language of new spending and tax laws but to examine other elements of the legislative package that described these laws, including tables, charts, or explanatory text included in the statement of the managers accompanying a conference report. In other words, the president was allowed to locate spending wherever it tried to hide, subject to limitations of the act. If an item of spending could be clearly identified, the president could only cancel the entire amount (not simply reduce it in part).

It was anticipated that the president's use of the line-item veto would focus on appropriations bills, since there are thirteen of them that contain discretionary spending. But when President Bill Clinton first employed his new power in 1997, appropriations bills had not yet reached his desk. Consequently, he targeted other forms of spending defined by the law—new direct spending and limited tax benefits contained in the Balanced Budget Act and the Taxpayer Relief Act of 1997.

The president was allowed to use the line-item veto to cancel items of "new direct spending," which would encompass any new entitlement programs Congress passed. (He could not attack existing entitlements.) The president was also allowed to block "limited tax benefits," a provision that was put into the law to satisfy members who believed that tax benefits were just as much a form of spending as appropriations and deserved the same treatment.

The law allowed the president to target federal tax benefits that went to 100 or fewer beneficiaries and in certain other limited situations. The Joint Committee on Taxation of Congress also could have included a statement in legislation specifying which provisions qualified as limited tax benefits, and if it did so the president would have been able to examine only those provisions. If it did not, he could have examined the whole bill to make a determination based on definitions in the act.

The president had to use the line-item veto within five days (excluding Sundays) of his signature on a bill or forfeit the power. He could not use it on bills he allowed to become law without his signature. If he used it, he had to send a message to Congress enumerating the items he had chosen, and included other information, such as the impact on the federal budget and the specific states and congressional districts affected. The effect of sending the message was to immediately "cancel" the item in question.

THE PRESIDENT AS FISCAL GUARDIAN

Presidents dating back to Ulysses S. Grant (1869–1877) have advocated a line-item veto for themselves or their successors. President Clinton had long supported a line-item veto, a version of which he employed at the state level as Arkansas governor. It finally sprang to life as part of the Republican's "Contract with America" in the 104th Congress.

The intellectual concept behind the law was that Congress had demonstrated many times it could not restrain its urge to spend. In an era of huge and seemingly ever-expanding and intractable deficits, Congress needed to be held in check by the president, who was—in this concept—defined as an opponent of waste and "pork barrel" politics. The idea of the president as a fiscal disciplinarian and opponent of increased spending was without historical foundation but it fit especially well into the political rhetoric of the 1980s and early 1990s, when a Congress usually controlled by liberal Demtrary notwithstanding." A two-thirds vote of those present and voting in both chambers is required to override a veto. There must be a quorum present for the vote, which must be by roll call, and whether the two-thirds majority is achieved is determined only from the number of "yea" and "nay" votes. Those who vote "present" are not considered.

Despite the Constitution's provision that Congress "shall proceed to reconsider" veto messages, the language has been interpreted to give each chamber various procedural options under its rules that do not require an immediate vote to override or sustain the veto. In the House, a vetoed bill is usually handled in one of four ways:

• It may be called up and debated for one hour, after which a vote on an override is held.

ocrats faced conservative Republican presidents Ronald Reagan and George Bush. Historically, there were many presidents of both parties—including such unquestioned conservatives as Dwight D. Eisenhower and Richard Nixon—who backed huge spending programs.

Once the new law was passed, however, times had changed. The Republican Congress postponed the effective date until after the 1996 election to prevent President Clinton from using it during his first term. Clinton was reelected, and when the historic moment for the unveiling of the first line-item veto finally came in 1997, it was a Democratic president facing off with a Republican Congress that controlled the purse strings and had its own spending and tax reduction priorities. Instead of huge deficits, federal red ink was decreasing each year and a large and growing budget surplus was anticipated as early as fiscal 1998.

CLINTON V. CONGRESS

When President Clinton employed the new tool to cut spending he opposed, he was accused of playing politics by Republicans in Congress. Some said that the administration was using veto threats to bargain with members on unrelated issues, such as the renewal of "fast track" authority for trade agreements. In other words, the dreaded fears of line-item veto opponents that the law would give a president unprecedented political leverage might actually prove to be true. Some earlier veto proponents switched sides and suggested repeal of the law.

In reality, the line-item veto was used sparingly in its debut. Clinton employed it eighty-two times in 1997, for an estimated savings of $1.9 billion over five years. But this was only about two-tenths of a percent of the $9 trillion the federal government was estimated to spend during that time.

In addition to the entitlement and tax provisions that Clinton had initially targeted to unveil his new power, and which became the basis for Supreme Court review in 1998, he canceled items on nine of the appropriations bills enacted in 1997. The cancellations represented a tiny amount of total spending in each bill.

In another court case, Judge Thomas P. Hogan, who was to later declare the line-item veto unconstitutional, blocked on statutory grounds Clinton's use of a line-item veto to kill a provision allowing federal employees to change pension plans. The administration agreed that the veto had been improperly cast, since the provision did not fit the definition of spending items the president could cancel, and the provision was restored as law.

In 1997, following procedures in the act, Congress passed a bill to reinstate all of the president's cancellations of $238 million for items in a military construction appropriations bill. This had been Clinton's most controversial use of the new power, and was the only time he was seriously challenged within Congress. The president admitted that some cancellations he made in the bill had been in error, but he vetoed the restoration bill that would have undone all of them. Both houses easily overrode him, the Senate in 1977 and the House following the convening of the second session of the 105th Congress in 1998.

VETO DECLARED UNCONSTITUTIONAL BY COURT

Two federal district judges agreed that the law was unconstitutional in decisions in 1997 and 1998. The Supreme Court turned back the first challenge to the law, in *Byrd v. Raines,* in 1997. The Court did not rule on the line-item veto's constitutionality because it said that the members of Congress who brought the lawsuit lacked legal standing to do so. The president had not actually used the line-item veto yet at that point.

The second case combined *City of New York v. Clinton* and *Snake River Potato Growers Inc. v. Rubin,* which were responding to the president's actual use of the line-item veto, enabling the new plaintiffs to argue directly that they had been injured by it use.

In February 12, 1998, Federal District Judge Hogan ruled that the line-item veto was unconstitutional. The Clinton administration immediately appealed his decision to the Supreme Court. On June 25, 1998, in a 6–3 decision, the Court upheld the lower court ruling, affirming the unconstitutionality of the veto.

The majority of the Court ruled that Congress had gone beyond the Constitution in allowing the president the power to cut out individual elements within a single spending bill. In a sense, this veto gave the president an unconstitutional role in altering legislation. Justice John Paul Stevens wrote for the majority:

> There is no provision in the Constitution that authorizes the President to enact, to amend, or to repeal statutes. . . .
>
> If the Line-Item Veto Act were valid, it would authorize the President to create a different law—one whose text was not voted on by either House of Congress or presented to the President for signature. . . .
>
> If there is to be a new procedure in which the president will play a different role in determining the final text of what may 'become a law,' such change must not come by legislation but through . . . amendment."

After the decision was announced, congressional supporters of the line-item veto immediately vowed to press the search for a constitutional means of giving such power to the president. With the decline of the federal deficit, the main impetus for the line-item veto, and the unhappiness of many members of Congress over President Clinton's use of the veto, most analysts felt that Congress's experiment with sharing its legislative power would not be repeated any time soon.

Stymied often by vetoes by President George Bush, House Democratic leaders display their view of the president's veto pen at a 1991 press conference.

• It may be immediately referred back to its committee of origin by motion, with the expectation that it will remain there and no veto override vote will ever be held.

• It may be referred back to committee to be "parked" for awhile, awaiting a decision on scheduling a future override vote. The committee may not amend the bill but could theoretically hold further hearings on it to generate or increase public support for an override. (A motion on the floor to discharge a vetoed bill from a committee is privileged and may be made by any member each day.)

• It may remain at the Speaker's table but with further action postponed to a later date, either by motion or unanimous consent.

The last two options may be employed either to gain additional time to assemble the needed two-thirds majority, or to schedule a vote closer to the next election for maximum political visibility. A vetoed bill may not be amended in any manner, only repassed or rejected.

In the Senate, if a vetoed bill is not considered immediately on receipt, the majority leader is normally permitted to bring it up at any time. A vetoed bill may be subject to a filibuster, but this rarely occurs because if there is any realistic chance of overriding the veto the bill's supporters would almost certainly have at least the sixty votes needed to end the filibuster. If they did not, there would be little point in taking up the bill at all. Vetoed bills are normally considered subject to a time agreement arrived at by unanimous consent.

The Senate has used another procedural mechanism, the "motion to reconsider" (the meaning of which differs from the Constitution's use of the same word), to give itself two chances to override a veto. In 1987, following President Reagan's veto of a major highway and mass transit funding bill, the House overrode but the Senate appeared about to sustain the veto by a single vote, with all senators voting, as a previously undecided Sen. Terry Sanford (D-N.C.) voted "nay." Majority Leader Robert C. Byrd changed his vote to "nay" before the result was announced, making the final vote 65–35, to vote on the prevailing side and be eligible under Senate rules to make a motion to reconsider the vote. His action kept the vetoed bill on parliamentary life support until the following day, when Sanford changed his mind, the Senate adopted Byrd's motion to reconsider the earlier vote, and then finally overrode the veto by a 67–33 vote.

This is an excellent example of occasional disparity in the practices of the two houses even on such a supposedly fixed constitutional procedure as a veto override. House precedents would have barred a motion to reconsider the result of a veto override vote. Under Senate precedents, had the veto initially been overridden, no motion to reconsider would have been permitted as the bill would have effectively left the chamber and become law.

If the first house to act fails to override the veto, the bill is dead and the matter ends there. If the vote to override succeeds, the measure is sent to the second house. If the veto is overridden there, the bill becomes law without the president's signature; otherwise, the veto stands and the bill is dead. The attempt to override can occur at any time during the Congress that passed the legislation. For example, a vote in the House on overriding President Reagan's veto of a protectionist textile bill was delayed from December 1985 to August 1986, when it was finally sustained.

The Pocket Veto

The Constitution also provides that a bill shall not become law if "Congress by their adjournment prevent its return." The president can then "pocket veto" the bill since he does not have an opportunity to return it to Congress for further consideration. Unlike the veto specifically provided for in the Constitution, which is sometimes called a "return veto" because it is returned to Congress without the president's signature and with a statement of his objections, a pocket veto is accomplished wholly by inaction. However, it has become a common practice in recent years for the president, at his discretion, to issue a statement called a "memorandum of disapproval" with such pocket vetoes explaining the reason for his refusal to sign, and Congress has published these in the *Congressional Record.*

The president clearly may pocket veto any bills that are still awaiting his approval when Congress adjourns *sine die.* The Supreme Court ruled in the 1929 *Pocket Veto Case* that the president may pocket veto a bill when Congress has adjourned its first session *sine die* fewer than ten days after presenting it to him for its approval. But whether it is proper for the president to pocket veto bills during congressional recesses of more than three days or between sessions of the same Congress when the two houses have made arrangements to receive presidential messages is still unsettled in the law.

Federal courts have ruled such pocket vetoes to be unconstitutional, but the Supreme Court has not made a definitive ruling on the issue. President Gerald Ford, after losing a case in a federal appeals court, entered into a consent decree agreeing to use the "return veto" during intersession and intrasession adjournments where each house had provided for the receipt of such messages. The Supreme Court in 1987 threw out a federal appellate court ruling against an intersession Reagan pocket veto as moot *(Burke v. Barnes),* without reaching the merits of the issue. President Bush raised these issues again in two pocket vetoes during his term, but they were resolved congressionally before reaching the Court. President Clinton, through his first five years in office, did not use a pocket veto.

Sometimes Congress has refused to recognize a purported "pocket veto" and has treated it as a "return veto" and conducted a vote to override it, leading to further confusion. In the second session of the 93rd Congress (1974), for example, President Ford returned a bill to Congress without his signature while asserting that he had pocket vetoed it during an adjournment of the House to a day certain. However, each house treated it as a return veto and then proceeded to override. The bill was sent to the Archives to receive a public law number. The administrator of General Services, on advice from the Justice Department, refused to promulgate the bill as law. Without acquiescing in this interpretation, both houses then passed an identical bill that the president signed.

The House has authorized its clerk and the Senate its secretary, to receive veto messages when either body is in recess when a veto message arrives. Both houses have asserted that this procedure allows them to properly receive the vetoes, which awaiting the reconvening of the receiving chamber for formal action. But presidents have not accepted this mechanism as a means of restricting their broad claims of authority to issue pocket vetoes.

NOTES

1. Walter J. Oleszek, *Congressional Procedures and the Policy Process,* 4th ed. (Washington, D.C.: CQ Press, 1996), 20.

2. *National Review,* February 27, 1987, 24.

3. Janet Hook, "Speaker Jim Wright Takes Charge in the House," *Congressional Quarterly Weekly Report,* July 11, 1987, 1486.

4. Steven S. Smith, *Call to Order: Floor Politics in the House and Senate* (Washington, D.C.: Brookings Institution, 1989), 9.

5. *Congressional Quarterly Almanac 1986* (Washington, D.C.: Congressional Quarterly, 1987), 33.

6. *Washington Post,* June 26, 1983, A14.

7. Quoted in *Congress A to Z: A Ready Reference Encyclopedia,* 2nd ed. (Washington, D.C.: Congressional Quarterly, 1993), 180.

8. Oleszek, *Congressional Procedures,* 4th ed., 93.

9. Robert A. Katzmann, *Congress and Courts* (Washington, D.C.: Brookings Institution, 1997), 64–65.

10. Bruce I. Oppenheimer, "The Changing Relationship between House Leadership and the Committee on Rules," in *Understanding Congressional Leadership,* ed. Frank H. Mackaman (Washington, D.C.: CQ Press, 1981), 217.

11. Walter J. Oleszek, *Congressional Procedures and the Policy Process,* 3rd ed. (Washington, D.C.: CQ Press, 1987), 127.

12. Stanley Bach and Steven S. Smith, *Managing Uncertainty in the House of Representatives: Adaptation and Innovation in Special Rules* (Washington, D.C.: Brookings Institution, 1988), 28.

13. Janet Hook, "GOP Chafes Under Restrictive House Rules," *Congressional Quarterly Weekly Report,* October 10, 1987, 2452.

14. Bach and Smith, *Managing Uncertainty in the House of Representatives,* 73.

15. Oleszek, *Congressional Procedures,* 4th ed., 149.

16. Ibid., 169.

17. Thomas E. Mann and Norman J. Ornstein, *Renewing Congress: A First Report* (Washington, D.C.: Brookings Institution and American Enterprise Institute, 1992), 49.

18. Smith, *Call to Order,* 243.

19. Jacqueline Calmes, "Byrd Struggles to Lead Deeply Divided Senate," *Congressional Quarterly Weekly Report,* July 4, 1987, 14[illegible]

20. Oleszek, *Congressional Procedures,* 4th ed., 210.

21. Smith, *Call to Order,* 128.

22. Nancy Landon Kassebaum, "The Senate Is Not in Order," *Washington Post,* January 27, 1988, A19.

23. Oleszek, *Congressional Procedures,* 4th ed., 231.

24. Jacqueline Calmes, "'Trivialized' Filibuster Is Still a Potent Tool," *Congressional Quarterly Weekly Report,* September 5, 1987, 2120.

25. Ibid.

26. Smith, *Call to Order,* 97.

27. Ibid., 96.

28. Barbara Sinclair, *Unorthodox Lawmaking: New Legislative Process in the U.S. Congress* (Washington, D.C.: CQ Press, 1997), 202.

29. Asher C. Hinds, ed., *Hinds' Precedents of the House of Representatives,* vol. 4 (Washington, D.C.: Government Printing Office, 1907.), sec. 3492, 336–338.

SELECTED BIBLIOGRAPHY

Bacchus, William I. *Inside the Legislative Process.* Boulder, Colo.: Westview Press, 1983.

Bach, Stanley, and Steven S. Smith. *Managing Uncertainty in the House of Representatives: Adaptation and Innovation of Special Rules.* Washington, D.C.: Brookings Institution, 1988.

Berman, Daniel M. *How a Bill Becomes a Law: Congress Enacts Civil Rights Legislation.* New York: Macmillan, 1966.

Bibby, John F. *Congress Off the Record: The Candid Analysis of Seven Members.* Washington, D.C.: American Enterprise Institute, 1983.

Birnbaum, Jeffrey H., and Alan S. Murray. *Showdown at Gucci Gulch.* New York: Random House, 1987.

Brown, William H. *House Practice: A Guide to the Rules, Precedents and Procedures of the House.* Washington, D.C.: Government Printing Office, 1996.

Byrd, Robert C. *The Senate, 1789–1989.* 4 vols. Washington, D.C.: Government Printing Office, 1988.

Cannon, Clarence, ed. *Cannon's Precedents of the House of Representatives.* 6 vols. Washington, D.C.: Government Printing Office, 1936.

——. *Cannon's Procedure in the House of Representatives.* Washington, D.C.: Government Printing Office, 1963.

Congress A to Z: A Ready Reference Encyclopedia. 2nd ed. Washington, D.C.: Congressional Quarterly, 1993.

Connelly, William F. Jr., and John J. Pitney Jr. *Congress' Permanent Minority.* Lanham, Md.: Rowman, 1994.

Cooper, Joseph, and G. Calvin Mackenzie. *The House at Work.* Austin: University of Texas Press, 1981.

Davidson, Roger H., and Walter J. Oleszek. *Congress and Its Members.* 6th ed. Washington, D.C.: CQ Press, 1998.

——. *Governing: Readings and Cases in American Politics.* Washington, D.C.: CQ Press, 1987.

Deering, Christopher J., and Steven S. Smith. *Committees in Congress.* 3rd ed. Washington, D.C.: CQ Press, 1997.

Deschler, Lewis. *Precedents of the House of Representatives.* Vols. 1–9. Washington, D.C.: Government Printing Office, 1977.

Deschler, Lewis, and William H. Brown. *Precedents of the House of Representatives.* Vols. 10–13. Washington, D.C.: Government Printing Office, 1996.

Deschler, Lewis, and William H. Brown. *Procedure in the House of Representatives.* Washington, D.C.: Government Printing Office, 1982; 1987 supplement.

Democratic Study Group, House of Representatives. "A Look at the Senate Filibuster." DSG Special Report, June 13, 1994.

Dodd, Lawrence C., and Bruce I. Oppenheimer, eds. *Congress Reconsidered.* 6th ed. Washington, D.C.: CQ Press, 1997.

Eidenberg, Eugene, and Roy D. Morey. *An Act of Congress: The Legislative Process and the Making of Education Policy.* New York: Norton, 1969.

Evans, C. Lawrence, and Walter J. Oleszek. *Congress Under Fire: Reform Politics and the Republican Majority.* Boston: Houghton Mifflin, 1997.

Fenno, Richard. *Congressmen in Committees.* Boston: Little, Brown, 1973.

Fox, Harrison W. Jr. *Congressional Staffs: The Invisible Force in American Lawmaking.* New York: Free Press, 1979.

Froman, Lewis A. Jr. *The Congressional Process: Strategies, Rules, and Procedures.* Boston: Little, Brown, 1967.

Galloway, George B. *The Legislative Process in Congress.* New York: Crowell, 1953.

Goodwin, George. *The Little Legislatures.* Amherst: University of Massachusetts Press, 1970.

Hinds, Asher C., ed. *Hinds' Precedents of the House of Representatives.* 5 vols. Washington, D.C.: Government Printing Office, 1907.

Jewell, Malcolm E., and Samuel C. Patterson. *The Legislative Process in the United States.* 4th ed. New York: McGraw-Hill, 1985.

Johnson, Charles W. *Constitution, Jefferson's Manual, and Rules of the House of Representatives.* 104th Cong., 2nd sess., 1997. House Doc. 104-272.

Katzmann, Robert A. *Courts and Congress.* Washington, D.C.: Brookings Institution, 1997.

King, David C. *Turf Wars: How Congressional Committees Claim Jurisdiction.* Chicago: University of Chicago Press, 1997.

Kingdon, John W. *Congressmen's Voting Decisions.* 3rd ed. New York: Harper and Row, 1989.

Kornacki, John J., ed. *Leading Congress: New Styles, New Strategies.* Washington, D.C.: Congressional Quarterly, 1990.

Loomis, Burdett A. *Setting Course: A Congressional Management Guide.* Washington, D.C.: American University, 1984.

Luce, Robert. *Legislative Procedure.* Boston: Houghton Mifflin, 1922. Reprint. New York: Da Capo Press, 1972.

Malbin, Michael J. *Unelected Representatives.* New York: Basic Books, 1980.

Mann, Thomas E., and Norman J. Ornstein. *The New Congress.* Washington, D.C.: American Enterprise Institute, 1981.

——. *Renewing Congress: A First Report.* Washington, D.C.: Brookings Institution and American Enterprise Institute, 1992.

——. *Renewing Congress: A Second Report.* Washington, D.C.: Brookings Institution and American Enterprise Institute, 1993.

Manual on Legislative Procedure in the U.S. House of Representatives. 6th ed. Prepared under the auspices of the Minority Leader, U.S. House of Representatives, 1986.

Minority Rights, Prerogatives and Protections in the Committee on Government Reform and Oversight. Prepared by the Minority Staff, Committee on Government Reform and Oversight, U.S. House of Representatives, 1997.

Nickels, Ilona B. *Parliamentary Reference Sources: An Introductory Guide.* Washington, D.C.: Congressional Research Service, 1986.

Oleszek, Walter J. *Congressional Procedures and the Policy Process.* 4th ed. Washington, D.C.: CQ Press, 1996.

Ornstein, Norman J., ed. *Congress in Change: Evolution and Reform.* New York: Praeger, 1975.

Ornstein, Norman J., Thomas E. Mann, and Michael J. Malbin. *Vital Statistics on Congress, 1997–1998.* Washington, D.C.: Congressional Quarterly, 1997.

Parker, Glenn R., ed. *Studies of Congress.* Washington, D.C.: CQ Press, 1985.

Peabody, Robert L., et. al. *To Enact a Law: Congress and Campaign Financing.* New York: Praeger, 1972.

Price, David. *Who Makes the Laws?* Cambridge, Mass.: Schenkman, 1972.

Redman, Eric. *The Dance of Legislation.* New York: Simon and Schuster, 1973.

Reid, T. R. *Congressional Odyssey: The Saga of a Senate Bill.* New York: Freeman, 1980.

Riddick, Floyd M., and Alan S. Frumin. *Riddick's Senate Procedure: Precedents and Practices.* 101st Cong., 2nd sess., 1992. Senate Doc. 101-28.

Rieselbach, Leroy N. *Congressional Reform.* Washington, D.C.: CQ Press, 1994.

Ripley, Randall B. *Congress: Procedure and Policy.* 4th ed. New York: Norton, 1988.

Sheppard, Burton D. *Rethinking Congressional Reform: The Reform Roots of the Special Interest Congress.* Cambridge, Mass.: Schenkman, 1985.

Siff, Ted, and Alan Weil. *Ruling Congress: How House and Senate Rules Govern the Legislative Process.* New York: Grossman, 1975.

Sinclair, Barbara. *Unorthodox Lawmaking: New Legislative Processes in the U.S. Congress.* Washington, D.C.: CQ Press, 1997.

Smith, Steven S. *Call to Order: Floor Politics in the House and Senate.* Washington, D.C.: Brookings Institution, 1989.

Tiefer, Charles. *Congressional Practice and Procedure.* Westport, Conn.: Greenwood Press, 1989.

Unekis, Joseph K., and Leroy N. Rieselbach. *Congressional Committee Politics: Continuity and Change.* New York: Praeger, 1984.

U.S. Congress. Senate. Committee on Rules and Administration. *Senate Manual Containing the Standing Rules, Orders, Laws, and Resolutions Affecting the Business of the United States Senate.* 104th Cong., 1st sess., 1995. Senate Doc. 104-1.

Vogler, David J. *The Third House: Conference Committees in the United States Congress.* Evanston, Ill.: Northwestern University Press, 1971.

Whalen, Charles, and Barbara Whalen. *The Longest Debate: A Legislative History of the 1964 Civil Rights Act.* Washington, D.C.: Seven Locks Press, 1985.

CHAPTER 3

The Committee System

THE COMMITTEE SYSTEM in Congress has been under assault so frequently, and for so long, that it is important to remember that committees still matter:

• They continue to perform important work that cannot be duplicated elsewhere in Congress.

• They operate in open view under the microscope of extensive coverage by television and the press.

• They endure despite efforts to weaken their chairmen, rotate chairmen out of office, and transfer committee powers to political party bodies or ad hoc entities.

Members of Congress seem to agree. No reform proposals are more abundant than those that would reform or even eviscerate the existing committee structures and jurisdictions of the House and Senate. Nonetheless, despite periodic changes in the institution, the committee system at the end of the twentieth century had remained basically intact for the last fifty years. Although scholars and participants alike still see many deficiencies in the system, members clearly believe that it works and that experimentation with other means of processing legislation should be attempted only incrementally and with careful monitoring.

Committees are the infrastructure of Congress. They are where the bulk of legislative work is done—where expertise resides, where policies incubate, where most legislative proposals are written or refined, where many necessary compromises are made, where the public can make its views known, where members of Congress build influence and reputations.

Committees have enormous power, especially in the House of Representatives. They hold hearings, conduct investigations, and oversee government programs. They initiate bills, approve and report legislation to the floor, control most of the time for debate on the floor, have preference in offering amendments, and take the lead in representing their chamber in conferences with the other house. They can kill measures through inaction or defeat. In the Senate, where individual senators' prerogatives may hold sway over collective interests and where the ability to offer amendments is practically unlimited, committees can be more readily bypassed and do not perform the same "gatekeeper" role in determining access to the floor. Still, the ability of committees to influence the ultimate disposition of an issue remains substantial.

It is difficult—at times virtually impossible—to circumvent a committee that is determined not to act. A bill that has been approved by a committee may be amended when it reaches the House or Senate floor but extensive revisions generally are more difficult to achieve at that stage. The actions of the committees, or their failure to act, more often than not give Congress its record of legislative achievement or failure.

Congressional expert Walter J. Oleszek has observed that the rules and precedents of both chambers reinforce committee prerogatives. Because "committee members and their staffs have more expertise on matters within their jurisdiction than members of Congress as a whole, the fundamental outlines of committee decisions generally will be accepted."[1]

Committees in Transition

As Congress approaches the twenty-first century, it is readily apparent that committees lack the clout they once did. They are no longer the imperial "little legislatures" of political science literature that once so dominated the presentation of legislation to Congress and set the agenda from floor action through presidential action. Committees are affected by the same factors that transformed the broader operations of Congress and the relationships between politicians and the American public. Changes in membership, shifts in power in relation to the leadership, the evolution of new rules and procedures, demands of partisan political agendas, extensive media coverage, and the availability of new sources of information and technology have all served to alter the balance of power within Congress. Sometimes these changes have pulled the institution in opposite directions over relatively short periods of time.

During the 1970s, reforms initiated earlier by a new generation of younger, activist Democrats came to fruition with the election of the large 1974 class of "Watergate babies," as they were known after their election in the wake of the political scandal that drove President Richard Nixon from office. Their numbers provided the votes to complete an institutional revolution that weakened committee chairman, dispersed power to subcommittees, strengthened the leadership, increased accountability to the House Democratic Caucus, and fostered the growth of staff on both sides of the Capitol. Power was diffused and rival power centers emerged. Many lawmakers no longer deferred to committees on the details of legislation. Floor challenges to committees became more common once members had gained the expertise and staff needed to make independent judgments.

Unchallenged in previous Congresses, committee leaders be-

HOUSE GOP CONFERENCE, DEMOCRATIC CAUCUS CONTROL POWER STRUCTURE

The organizations of the House's two political party—the Republican Conference and Democratic Caucus—exercise complete control of committee assignments, committee chairmanships, and ranking minority member positions. Committee assignments and seniority rankings are ratified by the House through the adoption of privileged resolutions offered by direction of the parties and may be altered at any time.

The longtime Democratic majority from 1955–1995 created an increasingly complex system to resolve competing claims for committee chairmanships and assignments while giving members hope that they would be considered fairly for important posts at some point in their careers. Party leadership exercised considerable influence over the process but sometimes could be effectively pushed or challenged by the general membership depending on the salience of the issue involved. Many of the major committee-related reforms of the 1970s, for example, along with the principal efforts to unseat conservative committee chairmen, were driven by younger, more liberal members, sometimes over leadership opposition.

The Republican minority, without real power, quarreled with the Democrats over committee ratios, sued them unsuccessfully in court, offered its reform proposals on the House floor at the organization of each new Congress, and developed a critique of Democratic control that gradually became the "forty years of corruption" theme used successfully in the 1994 elections.

During the reform period of the 1970s, the Democratic Caucus had threatened to intrude on committee independence and to direct action on legislative matters by instructing committee members but this quickly sparked a counterreaction and the caucus initiatives did not last long. Changes in committee chairmanships and memberships accomplished the objective of ensuring greater responsiveness to the caucus using more traditional means.

However, the activist tradition reemerged in 1993 with a demand by junior members to discipline subcommittee chairmen who had voted against President Bill Clinton's budget reconciliation legislation, which had passed by only two votes over unified Republican opposition. But the effort faded rapidly after liberals had vented their anger.

The Republican Conference, once in the majority in 1995, assumed an immediate aggressive posture. The conference, new to power, had little tradition of deferring to committees that it had not controlled for forty years. The GOP conference had an activist agenda coming out of the 1994 election campaign and wanted action as quickly as possible.

Far more than the Democrats, the Republican leadership led by Speaker Newt Gingrich, R-Ga., who was credited with masterminding the campaign for majority status, was deferred to by a party containing many members with little political experience. The Speaker intervened freely in the legislative process, sometimes reaching down to the level of dictating subcommittee agendas and subcommittee chairmen. He exercised far greater influence over the committee system than Democratic leaders could have ever dreamed of. Demands were even made for individual dissenters to explain to the conference their votes against party's positions on the floor. For example, a handful of rebellious members who voted against, and helped defeat, the 105th Congress's committee funding resolution in 1997 were called upon to explain themselves. Later in the year senior members of the GOP leadership were forced to explain their knowledge of and roles in a celebrated and unsuccessful effort to replace Gingrich as Speaker.

COMMITTEE ASSIGNMENTS

The two parties developed rules dividing the various committees into different classifications, to ensure a fair distribution of desirable committee assignments, and mechanisms to distribute committee and subcommittee chairmanship and ranking minority member posts. Both parties consider the Appropriations, Commerce, Rules, and Ways and Means Committees as "exclusive," meaning that no member of one of them may serve on any other committee unless specifically permitted in the rules. There are also various "grandfather clauses" allowing certain members to escape these restrictions. In addition, exclusive committee members are allowed to serve on committees on House Oversight, Standards of Official Conduct, and the Budget, which is required by House rules to have some members from Appropriations and Ways and Means.

Members who are not awarded exclusive posts—meaning most members of the House—usually serve on two standing legislative committees. Exceptions are sometimes made when the majority party needs members on less desirable panels to ensure its numerical control. The Democrats grappled for years with the problem of "temporary" members serving on committees, who existed principally to fill vacancies that other members did not want and to provide proxy votes to the committee chairman. Temporary assignments were often denounced by reformers but in the absence of any rules governing committee sizes, the caucus realized it could not dispense with the practice entirely. Indeed, the Democratic leadership sometimes encouraged it by promising politically vulnerable members additional assignments.

The Republicans in 1995 passed new rules in the House itself purporting to regulate and rationalize the number of committee and subcommittee assignments, restricting members to two standing committees and four subcommittees. But they soon found themselves in the same bind as the Democrats, further complicated by the fact that the new majority had deprived itself of the convenience of proxy voting. Quickly, exceptions to the rules again began to be made. *(See box, Proxy Voting, p. 132.)*

ROLE OF MAJORITY AND MINORITY RULES

The voluminous House Democratic Caucus rules, when that party last controlled the House, illustrated the importance of process to regulate the many ways in which power was dispersed. Because committee and subcommittee chairmanships, assignments, and seniority represented raw power and could make or break members' careers, the application of the rules assumed tremendous importance. Indeed, the existence of increasingly complex rules became essential to maintain a balance between different factions, to let members feel they were being treated fairly, and to settle contests for important posts with highly structured competition. They provided checks and balances among the leadership, the committees, and the general caucus membership.

Committee chairs held great power but there were mechanisms developed that could remove them and allow others to run against them directly in the caucus. The Steering Committee dominated by the Democratic leadership could almost always get its way in selecting members of the most important committees but other candidates could run from the floor. Members could bid by order of seniority for subcommittee chairmanships on their committees but challengers could announce opposition, run elaborate campaigns to reject the senior members on secret ballots, and then, if successful, claim the posts themselves.

The caucus rules reflected decades of adjustments and accommodations made for different reasons at different times. Eventually, they became so filled with multiple classifications of committees and with service and chairmanship limitations, all further layered with exceptions geared to specific individuals, that the system became increasingly difficult to comprehend and administer. Issues such as the proper size of committees and their jurisdictional workloads, which might have been used to distinguish between "major" as opposed to "non-major" committees, were often ignored and took a back seat to the political needs of members or the leadership's desire to grant special favors.

After Democrats became a minority in 1995 and lost their power to control committee ratios and a legislative agenda, the need for such a complex rules structure diminished. Members had less interest in their share of a minority with little power, which opened the way for a further enhanced leadership role in the committee assignment process and even returned some power to the ex-committee chairmen, now the ranking minority members. The new decisions that had to be made reflected ways to limit the pain of minority status, rather than to distribute additional rewards, so members were more willing to leave such decisions to the leadership's discretion.

The most important rules change by the new Democratic minority weakened the so-called "subcommittee bill of rights" created during the reform period of the mid-1970s that had allowed each subcommittee chairman the right to hire one staffer. The Republican majority in 1995 dramatically cut back the number of committee staff, claiming that it was making a one-third cut. That change, along with minority status, so decimated available Democratic staff positions that it made less sense to guarantee staff to ranking subcommittee members and created an argument for recentralization so that the core committee staff had enough resources to function. A new rule allowed each committee's Democratic caucus to decide the staff allocations and some chose to return control over them all to the ranking minority member.

The Republican Conference rules remained far simpler because in the minority complex rules had not been needed. So when majority status finally came the leadership found itself with fewer existing constraints. Republicans had never undergone the relentless push for democratization reflected in Democratic rules fights over more than two decades, with their complex procedures guaranteeing bidding rights for subcommittee chairmanships and assignments, and battles over expanding ways to discipline committee chairmen. Republican Conference rules give the Steering Committee the right to nominate candidates for committee chairs, without regard to seniority, until a nominee is approved. They also give committee chairmen the right to take the initiative in selecting subcommittee chairmen and members, subject to modification by the full committee caucus, which allows the chairmen greater influence over assignments.

The first years of the House Republican majority starting in 1995 emphasized party discipline and the need to enact the party's political and legislative agenda. Strict adherence to party rules, seniority, and accommodations with individuals were of secondary importance and were dispensed with when they interfered with the primary objectives.

If the Republicans retain the majority for a substantial period, however, it seems inevitable that pressures for dispersion of power and "sharing the wealth" will eventually complicate their internal party processes just as they did with the Democrats.

Committees are where the bulk of legislative work is accomplished. Here the Senate Labor and Human Resources Committee meets in 1997.

came accountable for their actions and could be ousted by a vote of their party. This happened to Democratic committee chairmen six times in the House between 1975 and 1990, though not in the Senate. (No Democratic committee chairman was removed after 1990.) Indeed, House reformers struggled repeatedly over a period of more than twenty years to find better ways to control, restrict, discipline, or challenge chairmen, and to remind them that they were always under scrutiny. No ideal formula ever emerged, and committees and their leaders remained imperfect vehicles for fulfilling the aspirations of their fellow politicians. Some prominent leaders, such as former Ways and Means Committee Chairman Dan Rostenkowski, D-Ill., often maintained a tense relationship with substantial segments of their party membership.

Committees routinely shared their once exclusive domains with other committees, particularly in the House, through the use of bill referrals to more than one committee. Committees had to comply with timetables for action set by the House Speaker. The traditional authorizing committees found their power diluted, if not eclipsed, by the Appropriations and Budget committees as Congress had less time for floor action on committee initiatives. Summits, task forces, and other ad hoc groups were convened on occasion to handle controversial issues as traditional channels worked less well. Massive pieces of omnibus legislation often were used to conduct the most important business and on occasions were the only way to get work done. Congressional leaders tried to orchestrate a changing legislative process that sometimes seemed out of control.

As the decade of the 1970s closed, the committee structure was still firmly entrenched in Congress, but much of the power and prestige that had been held by the full committees had been transferred to the subcommittees and to a new, larger corps of chairmen, especially in the House. Subcommittees took on the institutional characteristics and vested interests of their parent committees. People began to talk about "subcommittee government" instead of "committee government" on Capitol Hill.

This empowerment of subcommittees led to a decentralization of power and to heavier legislative workloads for members of both houses. Critics noted a slowing down of the legislative process. "On balance, Congress has become more decentralized, more responsive to a multitude of forces inside and outside its halls, and, as a result, more hard pressed to formulate and enact coherent, responsible public policies," wrote Leroy N. Rieselbach.[2]

So great was the proliferation of subcommittees that limits on their number were set in both chambers. Other changes and accommodations were made as well.

By the mid-1990s, before a recentralization of power in the House further undermined their autonomy, subcommittees were widely blamed for the inability of Congress to act coherently on major issues. Of course, other factors—the increasing political independence of members from their parties, weak congressional leadership, multiple jurisdictional requirements, and increased partisanship in both houses—also created unpredictable obstacles in the traditional paths to legislative achievement.

The mix of historic precedents and contemporary reforms placed committees in a state of flux. "[L]ike other institution features, congressional committees are dynamic rather than static. Indeed, in a variety of small ways committees change almost constantly," political scientists Christopher J. Deering and Steven S. Smith observed.[3] On the one hand, committees were still the central players in the legislative process. Yet, committees were also much less autonomous than they were just a few decades earlier.

When Republicans gained control of both chambers of Congress in the 1994 elections, for the first time in four decades, many of the common patterns of congressional organization were disrupted. The new majority had a well-defined political and legislative agenda but inherited traditional legislative institutions to enact it. The role of committees and subcommittees, relationships between committees and the leadership, and seniority all became subordinate to the need to build a record that would allow continued GOP control of Congress; committees and their procedures had little claim to legitimacy based merely on past history.

After the Republican takeover, House committees initially were eclipsed by the leadership using the Republican Conference, the organization of all House GOP members, and ad hoc task forces as vehicles to drive a conservative policy agenda known as the "Contract with America" that Republican candidates had used with great success in the 1994 elections. When committees did consider contract legislation early in 1995, their actions were often pro forma while the Democratic minority's ability to offer amendments and debate the proposals in committee were sometimes curtailed to an unusual degree. "I am a transmission belt for the leadership," said Judiciary Committee Chairman Henry Hyde. "Either I don't live up to the Contract, or I move faster than both I and the Democrats want."[4]

In the 105th Congress, starting in 1997—following a series of legislative defeats at the hands of President Bill Clinton and his allies and the GOP's near loss of their House majority in the 1996 election—the value of the committee process became more apparent to Republican leaders and attempts to bypass it were less blatant. A less impatient GOP took more time to learn how to use the traditional tools of committee leadership.

Nevertheless, some changes in the relationship between Congress and its committees did occur. It is unquestioned that by 1998 committees were much less the independent power centers than they were thirty years earlier. Committees now served many political masters who were no longer reluctant to crack the whip to obtain the legislative performance desired. There also was no doubt that the party leadership would go around committees to attain important political goals.

After attaining the majority in 1995, Republicans were well positioned after four decades in a minority to reexamine practices to which they had never been wedded and that might not serve their particular needs. After assuming the speakership, Newt Gingrich, R-Ga., made and unmade committee leaders at will, even influencing subcommittee chairmanship selections. Nevertheless, it was not certain by 1998 whether the changes Republicans made in the conduct of House business would take hold for the long-term, or how quickly such institutionalization might occur. Some observers wondered if Congress—and the House in particular—had entered a period of instability in the late 1990s with the use of a more ad hoc "ends justify the means" style of legislating.

Evolution of the System: Growth and Reform

Congressional committees became a major factor in the legislative process by evolution, not by constitutional design. Committees are not mentioned in the Constitution. The committee concept was borrowed from the British Parliament and transmitted to the New World by way of the colonial legislatures, most notably those of Pennsylvania and Virginia. But the committee system as it developed in Congress was modified and influenced by characteristics peculiar to American life.

In the early days of the Republic, when the nation's population was small and the duties of the central government were carefully circumscribed, Congress had little need for the division of labor that today's committee system provides. A people who viewed with grave suspicion the need to delegate authority to elected representatives in Washington were served by a Congress that only grudgingly delegated any of its own powers to committees.

In the earliest Congresses, members were few in number and their legislative workload was light. Temporary committees served their needs. But as the nation grew and took on more complex responsibilities and problems, Congress had to develop expertise and the mechanisms to deal with the changing world. And so, from a somewhat haphazard arrangement of ad hoc committees evolved a highly specialized system of permanent committees.

Standing committees were institutionalized and multiplied in the nineteenth century. Efforts in the twentieth century to consolidate the burgeoning committee system—especially through the 1946 Legislative Reorganization Act—served to strengthen the streamlined committees and their leaders. So overriding did the influence of committees in the legislative process become that scholars over the years called them "little legislatures"[5] and their chairmen "petty barons."[6]

None of this could have been foreseen during the First Congress, when many of the "Founding Fathers" served and took major roles in every issue that came along. In the early Congresses, legislative proposals were considered first in the Senate or House chamber, after which a special or select committee was appointed to work out the details of the legislation. Once the committee submitted its report on the bill, it was dissolved. Approximately 350 such committees were created during the Third Congress alone.[7]

As legislation increased in volume and complexity, permanent ("standing") committees gradually replaced select committees, and legislation was referred directly to the committees without first being considered by the parent body. This proce-

DATES STANDING COMMITTEES WERE ESTABLISHED

Only committees in existence in 1998 are listed. Where major committees have been consolidated, the date cited is when the component committee was established first. Names in parentheses are those of current committees where they differ from the committees' original names.

HOUSE

1789—Rules (originally as select committee; became permanent in 1880)
1789—Enrolled Bills (House Oversight)
1795—Commerce and Manufactures (Commerce)
1802—Ways & Means
1805—Public Lands (Resources)
1808—Post Office and Post Roads (Government Reform and Oversight)
1808—District of Columbia (Government Reform and Oversight)
1813—Judiciary
1813—Pensions and Revolutionary Claims (Veterans' Affairs)
1816—Expenditures in Executive Departments (Government Reform and Oversight)
1820—Agriculture
1822—Foreign Affairs (International Relations)
1822—Military Affairs (National Security)
1822—Naval Affairs (National Security)
1837—Public Buildings and Grounds (Transportation and Infrastructure)
1865—Appropriations
1865—Banking & Currency (Banking and Financial Services)
1867—Education & Labor (Education and the Workforce)
1941—Select Small Business (Small Business)
1958—Science & Astronautics (Science)
1967—Standards of Official Conduct
1974—Budget
1977—Select Intelligence

SENATE

1789—Enrolled Bills (Rules & Administration)
1816—Commerce and Manufactures (Commerce, Science & Transportation)
1816—District of Columbia (Governmental Affairs)
1816—Finance
1816—Foreign Relations
1816—Judiciary
1816—Military Affairs (Armed Services)
1816—Naval Affairs (Armed Services)
1816—Post Office and Post Roads (Governmental Affairs)
1816—Public Lands (Energy & Natural Resources)
1825—Agriculture (Agriculture, Nutrition & Forestry)
1837—Public Buildings and Grounds (Environment & Public Works)
1842—Expenditures in Executive Departments (Governmental Affairs)
1867—Appropriations
1869—Education & Labor (Labor & Human Resources)
1913—Banking & Currency (Banking, Housing & Urban Affairs)
1950—Select Small Business (Small Business)
1958—Aeronautical & Space Sciences (Commerce, Science & Transportation)
1970—Veterans' Affairs
1975—Budget
1976—Select Intelligence

SOURCES: *Constitution, Jefferson's Manual and Rules of the House of Representatives* (105th Congress); House Practice; George Goodwin Jr., *The Little Legislatures: Committees of Congress* (Amherst: University of Massachusetts Press, 1970).

NOTE: Both the House and Senate Select Intelligence committees are permanent committees, but for reasons relating to congressional rules on committee organization they are listed as select committees.

dure gave the committees initial authority over legislation, each in its specialized jurisdiction, subject to subsequent review by the full chamber.

The House led the way in the creation of standing committees. The Committee on Elections, created in 1789, was followed by the Claims Committee in 1794 and by Commerce and Manufactures and Revision of the Laws committees in 1795. The number had risen to ten by 1810. The next substantial expansion of committees did not occur until the administration of President James Monroe (1817–1825). Between the War of 1812 and the Civil War the standing committee system became the standard vehicle for consideration of legislative business by the House but it was not yet fully exploited as a source of independent power. The dramatic growth of the House and its workload contributed to the institutionalization of committees. House Speaker Henry Clay of Kentucky also found a responsive committee system helpful to his policy goals and thus encouraged the creation of committees.[8]

The Senate was slower in establishing standing committees. In the first twenty-five years of its existence, only four standing committees were created, and all of them on the whole were more administrative than legislative. Most of the committee work fell to select committees, usually of three members, appointed as the occasion demanded and disbanded when their task was completed. These occasions were so frequent that during the session of 1815–1816 between ninety and one hundred select committees were appointed. Frequently, however, related legislation would be referred to special committees already in existence and the same senators often were appointed to committees dealing with similar subjects.

In 1816 the Senate, finding inconvenient the appointment of so many ad hoc committees during each session, added eleven standing committees to the existing four. By 1863 the number had grown to nineteen.[9] But prior to the Civil War committees still played a relatively small role in the Senate.

COMMITTEE MEMBERSHIP

Each chamber developed its own method of making appointments to the committees. The rule established by the House in 1789 reserved to the whole House the power to choose the membership of all committees composed of more than three members. That rule gave way in 1790 to a rule delegating this power to the Speaker, with the reservation that the House might direct otherwise in special cases. Eventually, however, the Speaker was given the right to appoint the members as well as the chairmen of all standing committees, a power he retained until 1911. The principle that the committees were to be bipartisan, but weighted in favor of the majority party and its policies, was established early.

In making committee appointments and promotions certain principles governed the Speaker's choices. The wishes of the minority leaders in filling vacancies going to members of their party usually were respected. Generally, seniority—length of service on the committee—and factors such as geographical distribution and party loyalty were considered. But the Speaker was not bound by such criteria, and there were cases where none of those factors outweighed the Speaker's wishes. Despite complaints and various attempts to change the rule the system remained in force until 1911, when the House again exercised the right to select the members of standing committees. *(See "Committee Assignments," p. 146.)*

In the Senate assignment to a committee was made by vote of the entire membership until 1823. Members wishing to serve on a particular committee were placed on a ballot, with the choicest committee assignments going to those receiving the most votes. The senator with the largest number of votes served as chairman.

By the 1820s, however, a number of difficulties with the ballot system had become evident. The arrangement proved tedious and time-consuming and provided no guarantee that the party in control of the chamber would hold a majority of seats on the committee or retain control of the committee chairmanships in the event of a vacancy. Several times in the ensuing years the Senate amended its rules to provide for appointment to committees by a designated official, usually the vice president or president pro tempore. However, abuse of the appointment power and a transfer of power between the two parties compelled the Senate to return to use of the ballot.

In 1823 senators rejected a proposal that the chairmen of the five most important committees be chosen by the full Senate, and that the chairmen then have the power to make all other committee assignments. The Senate instead amended the standing rules to give the "presiding officer" authority to make committee assignments, unless otherwise ordered by the Senate. Since Daniel D. Tompkins, vice president during the administration of James Monroe, scarcely ever entered the chamber, committee selection was left to the president pro tempore, who in effect had been chosen by and was responsible to the Senate majority leadership. But when the next vice president, John C. Calhoun, used the assignment power with obvious bias the Senate quickly and with little dissent returned to the election method to fill committee vacancies.

This time the chairmen were picked by majority vote of the entire Senate; then ballots were taken to select the other members of each committee, with members' rank on the committee determined by the size of their plurality. The Senate in 1828 changed the rules to provide for appointment to committees by the president pro tempore, but in 1833 it reverted to selection by ballot when control of the Senate changed hands. Since 1833 the Senate technically has made its committee assignments by ballot, although the last time a formal ballot appears to have actually been taken—on assigning new committees to Sen. Wayne Morse of Oregon, a Republican-turned independent—was in 1953.

To avoid the inconveniences inherent in the ballot system it became customary between 1833 and 1846 to suspend the rule by unanimous consent and designate an officer (the vice president, the president pro tempore, or the "presiding officer") to assign members to committees.

The method of selecting committee members in use today was—with some modification—developed in 1846. In that year a motion to entrust the vice president with the task was defeated, and the Senate proceeded under the regular rules to make committee assignments by ballot. But after six chairmen had been selected, a debate began on the method of choosing the other members of the committees. At first, several committees were filled by lists—arranged in order of a member's seniority—submitted by the majority leader. After a number of committees had been filled in this manner the ballot rule was suspended and the Senate approved a list for the remaining vacancies that had been agreed upon by both the majority and minority leadership.[10]

Since 1846 the choice of committees usually has amounted to routine acceptance by the Senate of lists drawn up by special committees of the two major parties (in 1998 the Committee on Committees for the Republicans and the Steering Committee for the Democrats).

INCREASE IN STANDING COMMITTEES

The standing committee system, firmly established in the first half of the nineteenth century, expanded rapidly in the second half. Several factors influenced the role of committees, Smith and Deering wrote.

> First, dramatic economic, geographic, and population growth placed new and greater demands on Congress, which responded with more legislation and new committees. Second, further development of American political parties and the increasing strength of congressional party leaders, especially in the late nineteenth century, led to an even greater integration of congressional parties and committee systems. Third, members of Congress, first in the Senate and then in the House, came to view service in Congress as a desirable long-term career, which in

HOUSE RULES COMMITTEE FUNCTIONS AS ARM OF MAJORITY LEADERSHIP

The Rules Committee is among the most powerful committees in the House. Often described as the gatekeeper to the floor, the committee works with the majority leadership to control the flow of legislation and set the terms of floor debate. The Speaker and minority leader nominate all of its members. Because the majority party in recent decades has always insisted on holding a "two-to-one-plus-one" ratio in the committee's membership, even if it controls only a small majority in the House, an occasional defection on a vote does not affect its control.

GRANTING A RULE

Controversies have occurred frequently throughout the House's history over the function of the Rules Committee in the legislative process: whether it should be a clearinghouse (or traffic cop) for legislative business, the agent of the majority leadership, or a superlegislative committee editing the work of the other committees.

For major bills, the committee writes a resolution, or "special rule" that, subject to the approval of the House, sets the time limit on general debate, and regulates how the bill may be amended.

Before granting a rule, the committee usually holds a hearing at which only members of the House are able to testify. The chairman of the committee reporting the bill usually requests the kind of rule desired. Members testify for and against the bill and to ask that their amendments be made eligible for consideration. The hearing procedure is usually informal, with members being added to or dropped off the witness list on a continuing basis. The committee usually will listen to any member who wishes to be heard. It may then either grant a rule immediately or meet again later after controversies and strategies have been considered privately.

When the committee orders a rule reported, the chairman and ranking minority member decide who will manage the one hour of House floor debate on it. Once the rule is filed on the House floor, it may be considered on the next legislative day, or even on the same day if a two-thirds majority of the House votes to do so.

In many cases, the committee will restrict amendments. It may forbid all amendments; allow only amendments proposed by the legislative committee that handled the bill; allow only certain specified amendments; allow only amendments that are printed in the *Congressional Record* prior to their consideration on the floor; or allow only amendments that can be called up within a fixed time limit.

On complex bills, the committee may create its own original text, called "an amendment in the nature of a substitute," that incorporates provisions desired by the various committees to which a bill might have been referred or represents a compromise. The committee may also propose perfecting amendments to a bill, which it "self-executes" within the proposed rule—that is, adoption of the rule automatically adopts the amendments, even before the bill is formally considered on the floor.

CHANGING ROLE OF THE COMMITTEE

Established in 1789, Rules originally was a select committee authorized at the beginning of each Congress. Because the rules of one Congress usually were readopted by the next, this function was not initially of great importance, and for many years the committee never issued a report.

In 1858 the Speaker was made a member of the committee, and in subsequent years Rules gradually increased its influence over legislation. The panel became a standing committee in 1880, and in 1883 began the practice of issuing rules—special orders of business—for floor debate on legislation. Other powers acquired by the committee over the years included the right to sit while the House was in session, to have its resolutions considered immediately, and to initiate legislation on its own.

Before 1910 the Rules Committee worked closely with the leadership in deciding which legislation to allow on the floor, and was often chaired by the Speaker himself. But in the Progressive revolt of 1910–1911 against the arbitrary reign of Speaker Joseph G. Cannon, R-Ill., a coalition of Democrats and insurgent Republicans succeeded in enlarging the committee and excluding the Speaker from it. Alternative methods of bringing legislation to the floor while avoiding the committee—the Discharge Calendar, Calendar Wednesday, and the Consent Calendar (repealed in 1995)—were created and added to standing rules. *(See box, Prying Loose Legislation, p. 70.)*

By the late 1930s the committee had come under the domination of a coalition of conservative Democrats and Republicans. From then until the 1970s it repeatedly blocked or delayed liberal legislation. Opposition to the obstructive tactics led, in 1949, to adoption of the "twenty-one-day rule." It allowed a committee chairman whose panel approved a bill to call it up on the House floor if the Rules Committee failed to act within twenty-one days of receiving a request to grant a rule. The Speaker was required to recognize the chairman for this purpose. Two years later, after the Democrats had lost twenty-nine seats in the midterm elections, the House repealed this procedure. Although used only eight times, the threat of its use was credited with prying other bills out of the Rules Committee.

HOUSE REVOLT

After the Rules Committee in the 86th Congress (1959–1961) blocked or delayed measures that were to later become key elements in the new Kennedy administration's legislative program, Democratic reformers pressured Speaker Sam Rayburn, D-Texas., to act against it. In 1961 the House by a 217–212 margin agreed to enlarge the committee from twelve to fifteen members. That gave Rayburn and the incoming administration a delicate eight to seven majority on most issues coming before the committee.

Nevertheless, dissatisfaction continued, and following a 1964 Democratic election sweep the twenty-one-day rule was revived. The new version adopted by the House in 1965 gave the Speaker discretion whether to recognize a committee chairman to call up legislation. The new rule, employed successfully only eight times, was abandoned in 1967 following Republican gains in the 1966 midterm elections.

The House adopted a rule in 1965 that curbed the committee's power to block conferences on legislation. Before 1965 most bills could be sent to a conference committee only through unanimous consent, suspension of the rules or adoption of a special rule from the Rules Committee. The change made it possible to send any bill to conference by majority vote of the House if the committee that reported the bill authorized such a motion and the Speaker recognized a member to make it.

Despite repeal of the twenty-one-day rule in 1967, the committee continued generally to pursue a stance more accommodating to the leadership. Several factors contributed to the committee's less conservative posture. First, it had lost its chairman of twelve years, Rep. Howard W. Smith, D-Va., who was defeated in a 1966 primary election. Smith was a skilled parliamentarian and the acknowledged leader of the House's conservative coalition, a voting alliance of Republicans and southern Democrats. He was replaced by Rep. William M. Colmer, D-Miss., who was unable to exert the high degree of control over legislation that Smith had exercised. In addition, new rules governing committee procedures reduced the arbitrary power of the chairman. The rules took from the chairman the right to set meeting dates, a power Smith frequently had used to postpone or thwart action on bills he opposed.

Another effort to revive a twenty-one day rule in 1971 failed when a conservative coalition blocked the Democrats' rules package on the House floor at the opening of the Congress and passed an amendment excising the provision.

Effective leadership control over the Rules Committee finally came when the Democratic Caucus voted in December 1974 to give the Speaker the power to nominate all of its Democratic members, subject to caucus approval. Using this power, Speaker Carl Albert of Oklahoma nominated liberals to fill two vacant positions. The Republican leader later acquired the same power over GOP members.

Although the committee's power remains immense, the loss of influence by its members as individuals has reduced the panel's attractiveness as an assignment. Ambitious members seeking power in the institution, or a base to aid their constituencies, will look to committees such as Appropriations, Commerce and Ways and Means. The era of recent Rules Committee members considered powerful in their own right, such as chairmen Howard Smith, D-Va., and Richard Bolling, D-Mo., is probably over.

RESTRICTIVE RULES

No matter who was Speaker, the panel was used increasingly to limit amendments and debate on the House floor, provoking an outcry from Republican members usually in the minority. Democratic leaders argued that the Rules panel was an essential tool of a well-managed House. Such limits, they argued, helped focus debate on central issues, weed out dilatory amendments, and still ensure that major alternatives were considered. The Republicans themselves, despite decades of complaints about the committee, adopted and even expanded some of these restrictive practices when they took control in 1995.

Use of more complex rules also reflected institutional changes that had little to do with a deliberate strategy of closing off amendments. After 1974, when House rules were changed to allow more than one committee to handle a bill, the Rules Committee had to set guidelines for resolving conflicts and eliminating overlap when several committees marked up a single bill. Moreover, faced with huge budget deficits and waning public enthusiasm for government programs in the 1980s, the House considered fewer authorizing bills, the sort of legislation that had usually received an open rule. Increasingly, authorizing legislation was folded into omnibus measures, which usually were not entirely open to amendment.

ERA OF RAPID CHANGE

The chairmanship of the Rules Committee turned over several times in the 1970s and 1980s, accommodating a variety of diverse personalities in an era of rapidly increasing partisanship in the House. Leadership influence, cemented by the Speaker's power to select all Democratic members, ensured that the committee would operate as a loyal instrument of the Democratic Caucus. *(See box, Rules Committee Seniority, p. 126.)* When party control shifted in 1995, ranking Republican member Gerald B. H. Solomon of New York, an aggressive partisan, assumed the chairmanship. Former Democratic chairman Joe Moakley of Massachusetts stayed on as the leader of a four-member Democratic minority.

The Republican-controlled Rules Committee became a more visible forum for advocates of changes in House rules, though the majority had already implemented its most controversial proposals directly on the floor during the first two days of the 104th Congress. The committee held hearings on issues such as how changing technologies would affect the operations of the House in the twenty-first century. Under the Democrats, the committee had largely shunned institutional oversight. It left nearly all such activities to be handled privately in the Democratic Caucus, out of concern by the leadership that hearings or other formal action on controversial matters in a public setting might prove divisive or provide Republicans with a forum to launch attacks. This posture effectively marginalized the Rules Committee as a vehicle for dealing with institutional problems in the years preceding the loss of Democratic control of the House.

Solomon acted quickly in response to leadership directives to modify, or repeal, long-standing institutional practices when they inhibited achieving the majority's political agenda. For example, in 1995, the Rules Committee abolished the moribund Consent Calendar and substituted the more politically promotable Corrections Calendar as a vehicle to attack government regulations. In 1995 and 1997 it gave the staff of the Government Reform and Oversight Committee, which was investigating scandals in the Clinton administration, the power to take depositions from witnesses under oath. In 1997 it overrode GOP rules changes passed just two years earlier limiting the number of subcommittees in order to give Government Reform an extra one to deal with controversy surrounding conduct of the year 2000 census. And in 1997 it repealed a long-standing rule, inspired by the excesses of the McCarthy era, that had given witnesses appearing at House committee hearings under subpoena the right to bar photographs and television and radio broadcasts of the proceedings.

turn gave more personal significance to congressional organization, particularly the committee systems.[11]

The number of standing committees reached a peak in 1913, when there were sixty-one in the House and seventy-four in the Senate. The House Appropriations, Rules, and Ways and Means and the Senate Finance committees, in particular, exercised great influence; some others were created and perpetuated chiefly to provide members with offices and clerical staff.

Initial efforts to consolidate the House committee system occurred in 1909, when six minor committees were dropped. Two years later, when the Democrats took control, six superfluous committees were abolished.

In 1921 the Senate reduced the number of its committees from seventy-four to thirty-four. In many respects this rationalization of the committee structure was simply the formal abandonment of long-defunct bodies such as the Committee on Revolutionary Claims. The House in 1927 reduced the number of its committees by merging eleven expenditures committees, those dealing primarily with oversight, into a single Committee on Expenditures in the Executive Departments.

The next major overhaul of the committee structure took place in 1946 with enactment of the Legislative Reorganization Act. By dropping minor committees and merging those with related functions, the act achieved a net reduction of eighteen in the number of Senate committees (from thirty-three at that time to fifteen) and of twenty-nine in the number of House committees (from forty-eight at that time to nineteen). The act also defined in detail the jurisdictions of each committee and attempted to set ground rules for their operations.

For the next three decades, until a partial reorganization of Senate committees in 1977, only minor changes were made in the committee structure in Congress. During that period many of the achievements of the 1946 act were weakened by the creation of additional committees as well as the proliferation of subcommittees.

In 1993, the House began a modest cycle of reexamination of its committee system. It abolished four constituent-dominated select committees, temporary entities that had acquired seemingly permanent status.

In 1995, following a shift in party control from Democrats to Republicans, the House abolished three minor standing committees: District of Columbia, Post Office and Civil Service, and Merchant Marine and Fisheries.

In the 105th Congress, 1997–1998, the House had nineteen standing committees and one permanent select committee; the Senate had seventeen standing committees, two permanent select committees, and one permanent "special committee." There were also four joint committees.

The Legislative Reorganization Act of 1946, in fact, had led to an explosion at the subcommittee level. The number of subcommittees grew gradually after its passage, reaching more than one hundred in the House and more than eighty in the Senate by 1964. Smith and Deering found that: "The growth in the number of subcommittees had roots in the practical problems involved in managing larger and more complex workloads, in the desire of larger numbers of senior members for a 'piece of the action,' and in isolated efforts on individual committees to loosen the grip of chairs on committee activity."[12] In 1998 there were eighty-seven subcommittees in the House, and sixty-eight in the Senate.

But the creation of a larger network of subcommittees in the years following the 1946 act did not mean that power automatically gravitated there. Until the early 1970s, most House committees were run by chairmen who were able to retain much of the authority for themselves and a few trusted senior members, while giving little power to junior members or subcommittees.

THE SENIORITY SYSTEM

As the committee system grew so too did a system that awarded power on committees to the member with longest service on the committee. Seniority—status based on length of service, to which are attached certain rights and privileges—pervades nearly all social institutions. But in no other political group has its sway been stronger than in the United States Congress.

Despite frequent references to a "seniority rule" and a "seniority system," observance of seniority in Congress was never dictated by law or formal ruling. It developed as a tradition. The formal rules simply stated that the House or Senate should determine committee memberships and chairmen. *(See box, Seniority Under Fire, p. 134.)*

Seniority on Capitol Hill is based on the length of service in Congress, referred to as congressional seniority, or on the length of consecutive service on a committee, called committee seniority. As the system developed in both houses, it affected the assignment of office space, access to congressional patronage, and deference shown members on the floor. But seniority was most apparent—and important—in the selection of committee chairmen and in filling vacancies on committees, although state and regional considerations, party loyalty, legislative experience, and a member's influence with his or her colleagues always were important factors in making committee assignments.

Seniority had been relatively unimportant in the early years of Congress when political parties were weak, turnover of congressional membership was frequent, and congressional careers were brief.

By 1846, however, party control had become so firm that committee assignment lists supplied by the parties were approved routinely. With party domination of assignments, the principle of seniority also appeared. Seniority came to be applied both to committee assignments and to advancement within a committee.

The seniority principle caught hold earlier in the Senate than in the House. As the Civil War neared, southern Democrats, who dominated Senate committee chairmanships, "supported the hardening of seniority to protect their position so that they could defend slavery," Randall B. Ripley wrote.[13] During the Civil War and Reconstruction period, between 1861 and

Many southern Democrats who opposed the national party programs held committee chairmenships, thanks to seniority in the decades following World War II. Sen. James. O. Eastland, D-Miss., who chaired the Senate Judiciary Committee from 1956 to 1979, was notorious for bottling up civil rights bills sought by party leaders.

1875, Democrats virtually disappeared from Congress, and Republican senators disregarded seniority in committee assignments. But when Democrats began to reappear in the Senate, the Republican majority returned to the seniority system to keep peace among party members. Republican leaders found they had to rely on the support of all their party colleagues, Ripley wrote. And one way to gain this support was to agree to an "automatic and impartial rule for committee advancement. The leaders of the party thus helped institute this limit on their own power."[14]

As committees developed into powerful, autonomous institutions, committee chairmen assumed ever greater powers over legislation. So great was their influence that Woodrow Wilson in 1885 could write: "I know not how better to describe our form of government in a single phrase than by calling it a government by the chairmen of the standing committees of Congress."[15]

In the House committee chairmen and the evolving seniority system suffered a temporary setback during the speakership of Joseph G. Cannon, R-Ill., in the early 1900s. The period from the Civil War to 1910 had seen the gradual development of an all-powerful Speaker. Through his power to name committee members and chairmen, the Speaker was able to control legislation, grant favors or impose political punishments, and ride roughshod over the minority party. "Czar" became a title the press frequently bestowed on the Speaker.

Finally, in 1910–1911, insurgent Republicans in the House, led by Nebraska's George Norris, combined with Democrats to strip Speaker Cannon of much of his power. The Speaker could no longer name committee members, chair or even serve on the Rules Committee, or hold unchallenged control over recognizing representatives who wished to bring legislation to the floor. *(See "Cannonism," p. 14, in Chapter 1.)*

The successful revolt against Cannon returned the right to appoint committee members and chairmen to the political party structures, but it was several decades before the seniority system was strictly followed.

The gradual lengthening of congressional careers had much to do with the dominance of seniority, which was solidified by the Legislative Reorganization Act of 1946. The consolidated committees produced by the act had wider jurisdictions than before and their chairmen gained greater power.

The Democrats' almost unbroken dominance in Congress during the fifty years after World War II meant relatively little turnover in their membership and long tenure for chairmen elected from the Democrats' safest seats—those in the South and in predominantly urban areas often dominated by party machines. These men grew increasingly unrepresentative of the party as younger members were elected in the political landslides of 1958 and 1964, many of whom came to be identified with advocacy of new social programs, civil rights and, later, opposition to the Vietnam War.

Members who were out of step with their party's program or with the mood of the country, because of advanced age, ideology, or both, chaired important committees thanks to seniority. James O. Eastland, D-Miss., chairman of the Judiciary Committee from 1956 to 1979, routinely tried to bottle up civil rights bills and initially opposed the appointment of Thurgood Marshall to the federal judiciary. A party loyalist, Sen. Carl Hayden, D-Ariz., became chairman of the Appropriations Committee at age seventy-eight and served until he was ninety-one, setting a record for longest service in Congress, fifty-six years (counting both House and Senate service). Emanuel Celler, D-N.Y., longtime House Judiciary Committee chairman and liberal stalwart, ended his career as an opponent of the proposed constitutional amendment providing equal rights for women and lost a primary to a liberal feminist in 1972. F. Edward Hebert of Louisiana, a strident supporter of military programs and the Vietnam War who chaired the Armed Services Committee, opposed the appointment of African Americans and women to his committee. When antiwar liberals Ronald V. Dellums of California, a black, and Patricia Schroeder of Colorado forced their way onto the committee in 1973, Hebert provided only one chair for them in the committee hearing room, until the leadership intervened. He saw his career ended by the 1974 Democratic freshmen after he referred to them condescendingly as "boys and girls."

Sen. Strom Thurmond, R-S.C., the oldest person ever to serve in Congress, holds the record for Senate service (1955–1956, 1956–); he chaired both the Judiciary and Armed Services

RULES COMMITTEE SENIORITY

For decades, few committees illustrated the importance of seniority more vividly than did the House Rules Committee. Rep. Thomas P. "Tip" O'Neill Jr., D-Mass., a longtime committee member before giving up his seat in 1973 to become majority leader, joked that he had served for eighteen years on the panel (1955–1973) and had moved from eighth to fifth in seniority; in the party leadership, on the other hand, O'Neill was appointed to the post of majority whip in 1971 and moved up to become Speaker after only six years.

The Rules Committee had once been a strong arm of the majority party leadership, chaired by the Speaker himself, until the revolt against Speaker Joseph G. Cannon, R-Ill., resulted in his removal from the committee in 1910. *(See "Cannonism," p. 14, in Chapter 1.)*

For most of the decades after that until the early 1960s, Rules served as a power center for conservatives opposed to the Democratic congressional leadership and presidential administrations. Its independence began to be curbed beginning in 1961, when its size was expanded, and continued in the 1970s with party rules changes giving the Speaker control of Democratic appointments.

From 1949 until 1979, except for a two-year interval when Republicans ran the House, the Rules Committee was chaired by two elderly Democrats from the rural South and three others who came out of big-city machine politics. They were: Reps. Adolph Sabath of Chicago (chairman in 1949–1953), who died at age eighty-six while still chairman; Howard W. Smith of Virginia (chairman in 1955–1967), leader of the southern bloc in the House, who at age eighty-three was upset in his party's 1966 primary; William M. Colmer of Mississippi (chairman in 1967–1973), who retired from Congress upon reaching age eighty-two; Ray J. Madden of Gary, Ind. (chairman in 1973–1977), who became chairman at age eighty and was defeated in the Democratic primary four years later; and James J. Delaney of New York City (chairman in 1977–1979), who succeeded Madden for one Congress.

"Judge" Smith, as he was known, was so antagonistic to liberal Democratic programs and worked so well with Republicans that Speaker Sam Rayburn, D-Texas, reluctantly agreed in 1961 to increase the committee's size to fifteen, from twelve. The new 10–5 party ratio (instead of 8–4) diminished the prospect of tie votes, when Smith and Colmer had voted with Republicans to create a deadlock. Rayburn agreed to "pack" the Rules Committee with two additional Democrats willing to vote for programs of the newly elected administration of John F. Kennedy. The passage in 1974 of a Democratic Caucus rule giving the Speaker the power to nominate the chairman and all other Democratic members of the Rules Committee finally secured full control of the committee for the party leadership. *(See box, House Rules Committee Functions as Arm of Majority Leadership, p. 122.)*

Richard Bolling, D-Mo., chairman from 1979–1983 and the most significant figure to head the committee since Smith, was recognized as one of the ablest legislators in the House and was one of only a handful of recent Rules Committee members who had significant expertise and interest in the rules and structure of the institution. He had chaired the Select Committee on Committees in the 93rd Congress (1973–1974), which proposed a number of significant reforms but is perhaps best remembered for its radical, and unsuccessful, scheme to reorganize the House committee system and limit members' committee assignments. A power broker in his own right who had run unsuccessfully for majority leader, and the author of several books on Congress, Bolling served as a link between the committee's jurisdictional responsibilities for the structure of the House and its

Committees at different times and served as president pro tempore, third in line for the presidency. Rep. Jamie Whitten, D-Miss. (1941–1995), holds the record for House service; Whitten chaired the Appropriations Committee from 1979–1993.

The lengthy terms of these men were testaments to the growing careerism in Congress that gradually spread also to members who could rely on mastery of the media, campaign skills, and a strong fund-raising base to compensate for the lack of a safe seat. But tenure and age made it increasingly difficult for elderly members to adjust to changing political climates and younger, more demanding and less deferential colleagues.

With the long tenure of senior members, a generation gap developed. Roger H. Davidson observed:

> In 1973 the average House committee chairman was 66 years old and had almost 30 years of congressional service behind him; the average Senate chairman was 64 years old and had 21 years' experience. Not only did such a situation squander talent in the mid-seniority ranks, but it eventually generated frustration and resentment.[16]

The gap between leaders and backbenchers, covering not only age but also region, type of district, and ideology, "lay at the heart of the Democrats' seniority struggles in the 1970s," Davidson wrote.

The regional imbalance in top committee posts was especially irksome to Democratic liberals. In 1973 the six chairmen of the most powerful committees in Congress—those dealing with taxes, appropriations, and the armed services—came from just four states in the south central part of the country: Louisiana, Arkansas, Mississippi, and Texas. Congress was ready for change.

1970S REFORM MOVEMENT

Frustration with the existing system led by the late 1960s to concerted demands for reforms. As Smith and Deering noted:

> These demands were especially strong among junior members and some long-standing liberal Democrats, who found their efforts to shape public policy stymied by their more conservative senior colleagues. . . . These members, and the outsiders whose causes they supported, were concerned about issues that were not receiving active committee consideration and did not fall easily into existing committee jurisdictions. A nascent environmental movement, opposition to the Vietnam conflict, and a continuing interest in civil rights legislation placed new challenges before congressional committees.[17]

other role as a loyal processor of special rules to promote the majority's agenda.

After Bolling retired for health reasons, the committee entered a period of drift. With its perceived loss of influence came reduced desirability as a committee assignment. Would-be power brokers now had little room to operate. Relatively junior members were recruited to fill vacancies because there was less need for the leadership to require members to serve an apprenticeship elsewhere to see if they had the temperament for the job. Committee size varied from the fifteen established by Rayburn in 1961, to sixteen from 1975–1985, then back to thirteen.

There was an effort in 1983 to persuade octogenarian Rep. Claude Pepper, D-Fla., not to assume the chairmanship, but Pepper quickly dismissed that suggestion. The Speaker named him and he held the post until his death in 1989, when he was the House's oldest member. Pepper was regarded as an ineffective chairman whose principal interest remained issues affecting elderly Americans, which he had long championed. Other Democratic members assumed more visible roles to fill the vacuum. Rep. Joe Moakley, D-Mass., an O'Neill protégé who served as chairman from 1989 to 1995, restored a sense of order to the committee's role in reporting special rules and coordinating business with the leadership. But the committee largely sat on the sidelines during controversies over whether, and how, to reform the House and to respond to the Republicans' increasingly effective institutional attacks on Congress and the Democratic Party in the 1980s and 1990s. When Democrats lost control of the House in 1994, Moakley stayed on as ranking minority member.

Despite—or possibly because of—the 1974 Democratic Caucus rule giving the Speaker the power to nominate all Democrats on the Rules Committee, the seniority system continued to be followed rigidly. Speakers always appointed the senior Democratic member as chairman and reappointed all serving members. Ironically, instead of opening the door for membership changes, the rule may have had the opposite effect; with leadership control of the committee secured, the threat of potential removal controlled committee votes without the need for violations of seniority, which might have seemed threatening to the rest of the caucus.

The pattern of the Republican minority's assignment process on the Rules Committee, by contrast, began to evolve to reflect its more aggressive, partisan role and the minority's increasing willingness to use its limited resources more effectively. The minority leader, like the Speaker, exercised the power to select his party's membership. For years, the most visible Republican member of the committee was Minority Whip Trent Lott of Mississippi, R-Miss., who served as the leadership spokesperson on the committee until his election to the Senate in 1988, even though he was not the senior member. The seniority tradition was formally breached during the 1990s and the weakening of the practice had important consequences when the party finally took over the House.

In 1991, Republicans moved aside their longtime ranking minority member, 75-year-old James H. "Jimmy" Quillen, R-Tenn., and replaced him with Gerald B. H. Solomon, R-N.Y., a younger and far more aggressive partisan who had served on the committee for only two years. Solomon was made chairman in 1995 by Speaker Newt Gingrich, R-Ga., and served as a vigorous advocate for the "Contract with America" and other elements of the party's conservative agenda. Solomon announced his retirement from Congress at the end of the 105th Congress.

The reformist trend in Congress on domestic policy was greatly accelerated by the election of President John F. Kennedy in 1960, which focused responsibility for the obstruction of liberal policy goals squarely on congressional impediments within the congressional majority party.

Rule by seniority reigned supreme until the early 1970s. At that time, Democrats had controlled both houses of Congress for all but four years since 1933. Then, changing circumstances caught up. The principal change was the election to Congress of dozens of new members—persons who had little patience with the admonition to newcomers, credited to Speaker Sam Rayburn, that "to get along, go along." New members, who did not have much influence in the Senate or House, joined forces with disgruntled incumbents, who had chafed under the often heavy-handed rule of arbitrary chairmen. Thus, in the late 1960s and early 1970s a revolt began that was to undermine the seniority system and lead to numerous other procedural changes that redefined the role and power of committees and their chairmen.

The 1970s revolt began in the House as membership turnover accelerated and the proportion of younger, first- and second-term members increased. These lawmakers demanded fundamental changes in the way Congress—and particularly the committees—operated. Major changes in Democratic Caucus rules and, to a lesser extent, in the standing rules of the House and the Senate, diluted the authority enjoyed by committee chairmen and other senior members and redistributed the power among the junior members.

The newcomers balked at the traditions of apprenticeship and deference to committee leaders, congressional scholar Leroy Rieselbach pointed out.

> Moreover, many of these new members found it electorally advantageous to run for Congress by running against Congress, . . . to criticize the legislative establishment and upon arriving in Washington to adopt a critical, reformist view of congressional structure and procedure. Finally, the new electoral circumstances that protected most incumbents from November surprises at the polls—effective personal campaign organizations and the ready availability of funds from the proliferating political action committees . . . —gave new members the independence they needed to pursue their own political agendas, agendas that included reform.[18]

On the House side, the newcomers breathed life into a dormant Democratic Caucus and gave would-be reformers the votes they needed to effect change. The reform movement took off in the 1970s. The single most important factor that undermined the chairmen's authority was the decision by Democrats in both chambers to allow chairmen to be elected by their party's caucus. The change came gradually, beginning in 1971. By 1975 Democrats had adopted rules providing for secret-ballot election of the top Democrats on committees. A secret vote was automatic in the House and held at the request of 20 percent of Senate Democrats. That year three House chairmen were ousted in caucus elections. (Others followed in 1984 and 1990).

The election requirement made chairmen accountable to their colleagues for their conduct. Caucus election of committee chairmen was only one of a number of changes that restricted the chairmen's power. Committees were required under the 1970 Legislative Reorganization Act to have written rules. In 1973 House Democrats adopted a "bill of rights" that reinforced subcommittee autonomy. And before the decade was over, the committee system had been radically restructured. The era of the autocratic committee chairman who answered to no one was over. Junior and minority party members of Congress now had positions, privileges, and resources earlier members had been denied. Committee operations and votes were opened to the public eye. *(See box, Congress Adapts to "Sushine" Reforms, below.)*

In later years House Democrats gave members of each committee the power to determine the number of subcommittees

CONGRESS ADAPTS TO "SUNSHINE" REFORMS

By the late 1990s, Congress continued the process of adapting to demands for greater public access to its proceedings that began with so-called "sunshine" rules in the 1970s requiring open committee and conference committee meetings. The media also gained virtually unfettered access to committee hearings and meetings.

The initial sunshine reforms were part of an effort to improve Congress's image, which had suffered dramatic reversals after a series of widely publicized scandals. They were further accelerated by the public's disgust for excessive government secrecy as revealed in the Watergate scandal in the 1970s that led to the resignation of President Richard Nixon. Proponents maintained that open meetings helped protect the public interest and made lawmakers more accountable to the electorate.

During the 1980s, there was some retreat from the reforms, including votes by a number of key panels to close their doors during consideration of major legislation. Votes to close committees had to be conducted in open session by roll-call vote with a quorum present. The House Ways and Means Committee, perhaps the most heavily lobbied committee in the House, chose to close its doors to write such landmark legislation as a historic tax-overhaul bill in 1985 and trade and catastrophic illness insurance bills in 1987. Ways and Means Chairman Dan Rostenkowski, D-Ill., argued: "It's just difficult to legislate. I'm not ashamed about closed doors. We want to get the product out." Other panels—notably House Appropriations subcommittees—also met privately to draft legislation. Sometimes committees' decisions were made by small groups of members behind the scenes, then ratified in open session. Defenders of closed sessions argued that committee members were more open, markups more expeditious, and better laws written away from lobbyists' glare.

However, efforts to institutionalize a pattern of exceptions to the rules failed in the face of continuing public suspicions about the operations of Congress and the ability of special interest groups to influence the legislative process. In 1995, after Republicans took control of the House, the rules were further amended to prevent committees from closing their sessions merely for the sake of convenience. Committees wishing to close had to determine by roll-call vote that disclosure of testimony or other matters to be considered would endanger national security, compromise sensitive law enforcement information, or would tend to defame, degrade, or incriminate any person. The House Committee on Standards of Official Conduct was exempted from these requirements in 1997.

SUNSHINE RULES

The Legislative Reorganization Act of 1970 took the first steps toward more open committee meetings and hearings and required that all House and Senate committee roll-call votes be made public. The House in 1973 voted to require that all committee sessions be open unless a majority of the committee voted in public to close them. The Senate adopted a similar rule in 1975. Both chambers in 1975 voted to open conference committee sessions, unless a majority of the conferees of either chamber voted in public to close a session. The House amended this rule in 1977 to require a recorded vote by the full House to close a conference committee meeting. Conferences have been closed for legislation dealing with sensitive intelligence and national security matters.

BROADCASTS

While the Senate had a long tradition of broadcasting hearings, the House did not sanction such broadcasts until passage of the 1970 reorganization act. In 1974 it decided to allow broadcasts of markup meetings as well. The Senate left decisions on broadcast coverage to its committees. The House for many years set more stringent standards for broadcast coverage of hearings or bill-drafting sessions, considering it a special privilege to be granted or denied, but the House was eventually forced to stop nit-picking requests for media access. House rules were amended in 1995 to require that all open committee sessions be opened to press coverage, including radio and television broadcasts, without the need for special permission. Televised broadcasts of floor debate began in the House in 1979 and in the Senate in 1986. *(See box, Televised Floor Debates Here to Stay, p. 64.)*

their committee would have. Most committees were required to have subcommittees. Because of concerns over their proliferation, even on minor committees the number of subcommittees was subsequently further limited by caucus rule, and, after the Republican takeover in 1995, by House rule.

Staffing prerogatives were extended to members other than the chairman. This change made members less subservient to the chairman by giving them professional staff help on legislative issues.

Both chambers also attempted to limit the influence of chairmen and other senior members by restricting the number of chairmanships and committee slots that any one member could hold.

REVIVAL OF THE DEMOCRATIC CAUCUS

In the late 1960s, the House Democratic Study Group (DSG), a legislative service organization within the House funded collectively by a group of liberal members, accelerated the drive to overhaul the seniority system and open House procedures. The outlook for the DSG agenda brightened with the revival of regular meetings of the House Democratic Caucus in 1969 following a challenge to the reelection of Speaker John W. McCormack, D-Mass. The retirement of McCormack at the end of the 1970 session deprived the dominant committee chairmen of a powerful ally at the top of the House leadership structure and opened the way for younger liberals to operate more freely under his successor, Carl Albert, D-Okla.

The caucus revival meant that moderate and liberal Democrats elected to the House in the 1960s, who were frustrated by the operation of a committee system that tended to freeze them out of power, at last had a vehicle to change House procedures. Their actions were directed at undercutting the power of committee chairmen and strengthening the role of the subcommittees, where the opportunity lay for them to gain a greater role and make an impact on the legislative process.

The drive had a sharp generational edge. Many middle-ranking Democrats elected in the late 1950s and 1960s were allied against the senior members and the leadership. Between 1958 and 1970, 293 Democrats entered the House. Between 1970 and 1974, another 150 Democrats were elected. From this group, many of whom tended to be more moderate or liberal than their predecessors, sprang pressure for reform. This influx of Democrats—especially the seventy-five comprising the "Class of 1974," otherwise known as the "Watergate babies"—provided the votes needed to effect change.

HARBINGERS OF REFORM

Though it preceded the period of sustained reform by more than a decade, the fight for expansion of the size of the Rules Committee in 1961 represented a sign of things to come. Speaker Sam Rayburn, D-Texas., allied himself with the incoming Kennedy administration to break the conservative coalition that frequently stymied the majority's ability to bring legislation to the floor or to go to conference with the Senate. By a vote of 217 to 212, with many conservative Democrats opposing Rayburn, the House increased the size of the committee from twelve (an 8–4 party ratio) to fifteen (a 10–5 party ratio). Chairman Howard W. Smith, D-Va., and William M. Colmer, D-Miss., had often joined the Republicans to create a tie, paralyzing legislative action. The new configuration, with two additional Democrats handpicked by Rayburn, prevented that and gave the Speaker greater assurance that Rules would not routinely stymie the party's more activist legislative agenda. But the leadership's control of the committee was still far from assured.

The push for further reforms in the early 1960s led to the creation in 1965 of a Joint Committee on the Organization of Congress, headed by Sen. A. S. Mike Monroney, D-Okla., and Representative Ray J. Madden, D-Ind. The following year the panel recommended a wide-ranging set of reforms including proposals to curtail the powers of committee chairmen, to limit committee assignments, and to increase committee staff resources. However, unlike the reforms of 1946, there was no immediate consensus about the joint committee's work, and it was not immediately enacted in the years that followed.

Some of the committee's procedural recommendations were enacted into law in the Legislative Reorganization Act of 1970. Its recommendations opened the processes of Congress to greater public view and fostered participation in key decisions by more members but it did not directly attack the power bases of senior members. The law encouraged open committee proceedings, required that committees have written rules, required that all committee roll-call votes be made public, allowed radio and television coverage of committee hearings, and safeguarded the rights of minority party members on a committee. The law made only minor revisions in the committee structure itself, and it left the seniority system intact, after the House rejected two proposals to modify the system. Perhaps its most significant change for the House of Representatives was a provision requiring recorded teller votes in the Committee of the Whole, which forced members to vote publicly on key amendments and undermined the control of proceedings by senior committee members who had once stage-managed legislation with sparse attendance on the floor.

Although the 1970 law had limited effects, it marked a turning point in the reform movement, signaling an end to an era when committee chairmen and senior members could block reforms and the beginning of nearly a decade of change. Because the reform goals of the two chambers were different and the pressure for change was greatest in the House, subsequent attempts at change took the form of intrachamber reform efforts rather than bicameral action. That was perhaps inevitable because, in the House, the next steps in reform became more intensely personal through political assault on committee chairmen and others deemed unresponsive to the caucus, the undermining of chairmen's power bases, and, in some cases, actual removal from leadership positions.

Loosening the grip of seniority was seen as a crucial step toward changing committee operations. The issue of committee seniority was treated as strictly a party matter. Democratic leaders feared that if seniority changes were proposed through legislation instead of through party rules, a coalition of members of both parties could upset the majority party's control of the legislative program. When changes in seniority were offered as amendments on the floor of the House and Senate, they consistently had been defeated.

The "go-it-alone" strategy for congressional reform has prevailed for each chamber ever since. The most recent attempt at bicameral coordination—the 1993 Joint Committee on the Organization of Congress—failed at least in part because in an atmosphere of increased tension between the houses the bicameral structure created another layer of obstacles to be overcome.

HOUSE COMMITTEE CHANGES

The first blow to seniority in the House came when both parties decided that the selection of committee leaders no longer had to be dictated by seniority. In January 1971 the House Democratic Caucus voted to adopt modest changes recommended by its Committee on Organization, Study, and Review, created in 1970 to examine the party's organization and the seniority system. The committee was headed by Julia Butler Hansen, D-Wash.

The principal changes agreed upon were:

• The Democratic Committee on Committees, composed of the Democratic members of the Ways and Means Committee, would recommend to the caucus nominees for the chairmanship and membership of each committee, and such recommendations did not have to follow seniority. (The committee's power was transferred in December 1974 to the Steering and Policy Committee, a leadership entity.)

• The Committee on Committees would make recommendations to the caucus, one committee at a time. Upon the demand of ten or more caucus members, nominations could be debated and voted on.

If a nomination were rejected, the Committee on Committees would submit another nomination.

• In an important breakthrough for midcareer Democrats, the caucus decided that no member could chair more than one legislative subcommittee. That change made it possible to break the hold of the more conservative senior Democrats on key subcommittees, and it gradually made middle-level and even some junior Democrats eligible for subcommittee chairmanships. The rule in its first year gave sixteen Democrats who came to the House after 1958 their first subcommittee chairmanships.

House Republicans also in 1971 agreed that the ranking Republican on each committee would be selected by vote of the Republican Conference, comprised of all House Republicans, and not automatically by seniority. They also bypassed Armed Services Committee member Alvin O'Konski, R-Wis., who was next in line to be ranking member, by allowing the more senior Minority Whip Les Arends, R-Ill., to take the post even though party rules would have prevented him from holding both jobs. In 1973, the Republican Conference confirmed moderate Frank Horton of New York as ranking member of the Government Operations Committee, deflecting a challenge from the junior but more conservative John Erlenborn of Illinois. (While Republicans have on rare occasions bypassed seniority, unlike the Democrats they have never formally ousted a committee leader in a vote of the full conference.)

House Democrats in January 1973 altered their chairmanship selection procedures by allowing a secret-ballot vote on any committee chairman when 20 percent of the caucus demanded it. The expectation was that votes would be taken on all candidates. (This cumbersome procedure was replaced in 1974 by an automatic secret vote.) In 1973 all the chairmen survived, as did the seven ranking Democrats marked for elevation by the retirement of their predecessors.

Subcommittee Rights

The House Democratic Caucus in January 1973 adopted a "subcommittee bill of rights." The new caucus rules created a party caucus for Democrats on each House committee and forced the chairmen to start sharing authority with other Democrats. Each committee caucus was granted the authority to select subcommittee chairmen (with members allowed to run for chairman based on their seniority ranking on the full committee), establish subcommittee jurisdictions, set party ratios on the subcommittees to reflect the party ratio of the full committee, write the committee's rules, provide a subcommittee budget, and guarantee all members a major subcommittee slot where vacancies made that possible. Each subcommittee was authorized to meet, hold hearings, and act on matters referred to it.

Under the bill of rights, committee chairmen were required to refer designated types of legislation to subcommittees within two weeks. They no longer could kill measures they opposed by pocketing them, at least not at the subcommittee stage.

Compromise Hansen Plan

Further procedural changes, along with minor committee jurisdictional shifts, were approved by the House in 1974 in a new package of recommendations put forward by Hansen's study committee. The Hansen plan was a substitute for a much broader bipartisan proposal, drafted by a select committee headed by Rep. Richard Bolling, D-Mo. The Bolling committee's call for wholesale restructuring of the committee system had triggered a flood of protests from chairmen and committee members who would have been adversely affected. It was decisively rejected in favor of the Hansen substitute, which made some jurisdictional shifts—such as giving the Public Works Committee control over more transportation matters—but mainly retained the existing committee structure dating from 1946.

Under the Hansen plan, each standing committee's permanent staff, beginning in 1975, was increased from six to eighteen professionals and from six to twelve clerks, with the minority party receiving one-third of each category. And in what would prove to be the most controversial provision, the plan gave the minority party control of one-third of a committee's investigative staff funding. As the 94th Congress convened to adopt its rules, the Democratic Caucus engineered repeal of the one-third provision before it could take effect. However, each side received more staffing and subcommittee chairmen and ranking members were allowed to hire one staff person each to work directly for them on their subcommittees.

In other changes, which also took effect in 1975, committees with more than fifteen members (increased to those with more than twenty members by the Democratic Caucus in 1975) were required to establish at least four subcommittees. This change was directed at the Ways and Means Committee, which had operated without subcommittees during most of the sixteen-year chairmanship of Wilbur D. Mills, D-Ark. It also created an important precedent in that it institutionalized subcommittees for the first time.

Committees with more than fifteen members (increased to those with more than twenty in 1975) were required to set up an oversight subcommittee or to require their legislative subcommittees to carry out oversight functions.

In addition, the Hansen plan gave the Speaker new powers to refer legislation to more than one committee and banned proxy voting in committee. (In 1975 proxy voting was effectively restored by the Democratic Caucus and remained in effect for twenty years until Republicans took control in 1995; House rules were amended to allow each committee to decide in its own rules whether to allow proxies, and most did; proxies were allowed on a specific issue or on procedural matters, and they had to be in writing and given to a member, among other requirements.) *(See box, Proxy Voting, p. 132.)*

More Blows to Seniority

Further changes in House committee operations unrelated to the Hansen plan were made in late 1974 and early 1975 by the Democratic Caucus after the party's overwhelming victory in post-Watergate elections resulted in a two-to-one majority. Meeting in December 1974 to organize for the next Congress (as had been required under the Hansen plan), Democrats decided to require a secret-ballot vote on the election of each committee chairman. The new procedure allowed competitive nominations for chairmen if the original Steering Committee nominee was rejected. Democrats immediately made use of their new rule by deposing three committee chairmen. *(See box, Seniority Under Fire, p. 134.)*

In other changes the Democratic members of the Ways and Means Committee were stripped of their power to select the party's members of House committees; this authority was transferred to a revamped Democratic Steering and Policy Committee, chaired by the Speaker. Many of the other members served in the leadership or were appointed by the Speaker, along with members elected from specific geographic regions. Over time, both the size of the Steering Committee and the number of leadership-influenced appointments increased. At the same time the caucus increased the size of the Ways and Means Committee from twenty-five to thirty-seven members, a change designed to give the committee a more liberal outlook and thus make it more likely to support party-backed proposals on tax revision, health insurance, and other issues.

In actions affecting the independence of subcommittees, the caucus directed that the entire Democratic membership of each committee, rather than the chairman alone, was to determine the number and jurisdiction of a committee's subcommittees. The Democratic caucus of each committee drafted and approved a committee's rules, which incorporated the number, size, and jurisdiction of its subcommittees. And the caucus specified that no Democratic member of a committee could become a member of a second subcommittee of that committee until every member of the full committee had chosen a subcommittee slot. (A grandfather clause allowed sitting members on subcommittees to protect two subcommittee slots, but this protection for the second subcommittee was eliminated in 1979.)

One group of subcommittees always had been semiautonomous—the powerful units of the House Appropriations Committee. The thirteen subcommittees were organized to parallel the executive departments and agencies, and most of the annual budget review was done at that level. The staggering size and complexity of the federal budget required each subcommittee to develop an expertise and an autonomy respected and rarely challenged by other subcommittees or by the full committee. Because of the panels' special role the caucus decided that, like full committee chairmen, all nominees for chairmen of these subcommittees would have to be approved by the Democratic Caucus. (Nominees for Appropriations subcommittee chairmen were selected by the membership of each subcommittee, with members bidding for a subcommittee chairmanship in the order of their seniority on the subcommittee.)

The Speaker's powers were further buttressed by allowing him to select the Democratic members of the Rules Committee, subject to caucus approval.

In a change adopted by the Democratic Caucus in December 1976, the chairmen of the Ways and Means and Appropriations committees were stripped of their power to nominate members from their committees to serve on the Budget Committee; that power was transferred to the Democratic Steering and Policy Committee.

In December 1978 the House Democratic Caucus voted to prohibit, as of the next Congress, a committee chairman from serving as chairman of any other standing, select, special, or joint committee; some chairmen were exempt because they were required by law to also chair joint committees.

PROXY VOTING

Proxy voting in House committees was abolished in 1995 as part of the Republican majority's new rules package. It continues to be used in Senate committees and in House-Senate conferences by members from both chambers. Proxy voting is not permitted on the floor of the Senate or House.

Proxies permit one committee member to authorize another to cast votes for that person in the member's absence. The device is a convenience for members of Congress caught between conflicting demands of busy schedules, which often include more than one committee or subcommittee meeting at the same time. A proxy is nearly always given to a committee or subcommittee chairman, or, if the member differs from the chairman on an issue, to another member who is on the same side of the issue as the absentee. Although proxy voting may seem an innocuous practice, it was the bane of the minority party in Congress and a target of reformers for years.

Controversy over proxy voting focused principally on the House, where one member could cast many proxies. The practice is viewed less harshly in the Senate because of the large number of committee and subcommittee assignments held by each senator and the tradition of accommodating the convenience of individuals. In addition committees do not have the same power or importance in the Senate.

HOUSE

Proxy voting was an important tool for the majority in operating committees because it allowed members to cope with multiple simultaneous scheduling commitments while ensuring that political control could not slip away to a well-organized minority that might concentrate its strength at a single location for a "sneak attack" on the majority. In this respect, proxy voting was simply a means of ensuring majority control over committees as subunits of the House and preventing such control from succumbing to whims of committee scheduling or flukes of member absences.

Proxy voting was denounced by the minority members and reform advocates outside the House for encouraging absenteeism and irresponsibility. Perhaps more significantly, it tended to discourage efforts to improve the coordination of the scheduling of committee and subcommittee meetings as well as to reduce the number of subcommittees and member assignments.

Before 1970 the use of proxies was regulated by custom or by guidelines established by individual committees and differed from committee to committee. Some committees never used them. Before the power of House chairmen was diminished by the Democratic Caucus in the 1970s, proxy voting reinforced their domination of committees. A chairman had little trouble procuring and using proxies, while opponents actually had to appear, and in significant numbers, to change the outcome on a key vote unless they were capable of organizing themselves around a proxy campaign as well.

The Legislative Reorganization Act of 1970 was the first measure to alter proxy voting. That act prohibited proxy voting unless a committee's written rules specifically allowed it, in which case it was limited to a specific bill, amendment, or other matter. Proxies also had to be in writing, designating the person on the committee authorized to use them.

In October 1974, as part of the Select Committee on Comittee's resolution making changes in the committee system, the House voted 196–166 to ban proxy voting entirely, effective at the beginning of the subsequent Congress. But the ban never took effect. The Democratic Caucus, voting this time without the Republicans, modified the ban before the 94th Congress convened in 1975 to adopt House rules on a party-line vote. The revision once again gave committees the authority to decide whether to permit proxy voting. If a committee allowed proxy voting, it was to be used only on a specific measure or matter and related amendments and motions. General proxies, covering all matters before a committee for either a specific time period or for an indefinite period, were prohibited, except for votes on procedural matters. As before, they had to be in writing, with a member designated to cast the proxies. The proxy vote also had to be dated and could not be used to make a quorum.

During its brief consideration of reform proposals recommended by the Joint Committee on the Organization of Congress as adjournment approached in 1994, the House Rules Committee considered amendments to the rules that would have further restricted or abolished the practice of proxy voting. With several Democrats reportedly considering support for such reforms the committee recessed and never resumed the markup, preventing any votes on the joint committee's proposals.

Each House Democrat was limited to five subcommittee seats on House standing committees. In 1987 waivers to the five-subcommittee rule—which had become routine—were barred in most cases, but the change proved ineffective. In order to maintain effective control of a subcommittee, it was sometimes necessary to add members who might violate the assignment limit. Attempts to restrict subcommittee assignments were frequently disregarded, especially when the leadership supported exceptions.

In addition, the caucus decided that the bidding for subcommittee chairmanships would be based on a member's seniority rank on the full committee, with the exception of Appropriations subcommittee chairmen.

Decline of Reform Zeal

Toward the end of the decade while there were occasional important struggles over who would occupy committee and subcommittee chairmanships, the broad agenda for House reform among Democrats abated. Liberals who dominated the Democratic Caucus had gotten virtually everything they wanted, the leadership had been strengthened in its relationships with chairmen, and junior members who served long enough

Ironically, following the abolition of proxy voting when House rules were adopted in January 1995, the Republicans endured immediate political pain for their decision. They were forced to conduct numerous simultaneous committee meetings and House floor votes to ensure prompt passage of the legislative agenda promised in the election campaign, while struggling to maintain voting control with the narrowest House majority in forty years. Although pleas by a few members for a return to proxy voting were not heeded, the Republicans eventually loosened some of the other restrictions they had passed on the number of committee and subcommittee assignments members might hold, so they would be able to place enough majority members in the right places to ensure control.

SENATE

For Senate committees the 1970 act provided little restraint on the use of proxies. The law said proxy votes could not be used to report legislation if committee rules barred their use. If proxies were not forbidden on a motion to report a bill, they nevertheless could be used only upon the formal request of a senator who planned to be absent during a session. To prevent the use of general proxies, Senate rules bar the use of a proxy if an absent member "has not been informed of the matter on which he is being recorded and has not affirmatively requested that he be so recorded." Proxies cannot be counted toward the quorum needed for reporting legislation.

In addition to proxy voting, some Senate committees permit polling—holding an informal vote of committee members instead of convening the committee. Such votes usually are taken by sending a voting sheet to committee members' offices or by taking members' votes by telephone.

Because Senate rules require a quorum to be present for a committee to report legislation, polling is supposed to be restricted to issues involving legislation that is still pending before the committee, to matters relating to investigations, and to internal committee business.

If polling is used to report a matter, any senator can challenge the action by raising a point of order. Such was the case in December 1980 when opponents of a Carter nominee for a federal judgeship charged that the nomination had not been properly reported because the Judiciary Committee had approved it by a written poll. The issue was dropped and the nominee was approved when Judiciary Chairman Edward M. Kennedy, D-Mass., gained Republican support by agreeing not to push other Carter lame duck judicial nominations pending in the committee.

FROM PROXY VOTING TO A CYBER-CONGRESS?

Neither House of Congress has ever allowed members to vote by proxy on the floor, and the House has disciplined members who used another's voting card to cast votes in his absence. But in recent years some members raised the issue of voting from other locations, as long as it was concurrent with voting on the floor and their votes could be verified through a secure system. Improving technology could, at some point, allow members of Congress working in their states or districts to participate in real time in congressional debates.

Members broached these ideas as a way of enhancing their personal convenience and allowing them to perform more of their congressional functions, but perhaps at the expense of Congress's broader purposes. The concept of representation and the role of members of Congress has changed in the latter part of the twentieth century as Congress stayed in session longer and members had less time to spend time in their districts. The demands of campaign fund-raising and the need for direct constituent contact at town meetings and other events increased pressure on congressional schedules. Members also had less time to spend with their families.

Congress traditionally fears change and has resisted even modest technological intrusions. Both chambers long resisted television. The House in 1995 banned the use on the floor of any personal electronic office equipment, including cellular telephones and computers. The Senate, similarly, banned the use of laptop computers on the grounds that they would disrupt floor proceedings and distract senators.

Critics of the use of technology to allow absent members to legislate say this development would contradict the very essence of Congress, which requires an interaction of legislators face to face. In addition, the Constitution requires that Congress "assemble" to exercise its power. It is doubtful that video-conferencing or a "Congress-Online" could qualify.

were assured of eventually acquiring the titles of subcommittee chairs along with increased staff resources. There were no important constituencies left to satisfy; with a sharply reduced House majority and policy divisions between the party's liberal and conservative factions during and after the presidency of Republican Ronald Reagan (1981–1989) other subjects dominated the caucus's attention.

The more self-satisfied attitude was reflected in a less than hospitable reception accorded to some of the limited reform efforts that emerged in this period. A House Commission on Administrative Review, headed by Rep. David Obey, D-Wis., concluded that members had too many committee assignments and that existing committee jurisdictions were too confused. But its recommendations for improving committee operations went down to defeat in October 1977. The House also declined to consider its proposals to change the administrative operations of the House.

The House in March 1979 once again set up a Select Committee on Committees to recommend how to improve the House's internal organization and operations. But the effort proved to be little more than lip service to the idea of reform, since substantive changes would have proved too threatening to

SENIORITY UNDER FIRE—HOUSE OUSTS CHAIRMEN, SENATE FOLLOWS TRADITION

Both political parties in the House and Senate in the 1970s decided that seniority—status based on length of service—should no longer be the sole determinant in selecting committee leaders. The House took substantive steps to implement this reform, while the Senate did not. But even the threatened use of this authority gave rank-and-file members a potent weapon.

The House Democratic Caucus shook the foundations of the committee structure by ousting three autocratic chairmen in 1975. It was a watershed that redirected the flow of institutional power in the House. The caucus rules required an automatic yes-or-no vote on a candidate for a chairmanship nominated by the Steering and Policy Committee if the nominee was either the incumbent chairman or the senior Democrat seeking the post if the chairmanship was vacant. Other candidates were only allowed to run if the chairman or senior member were rejected by the Steering Committee, or by the full caucus. In 1992, the rules were further liberalized to allow others to run directly if fourteen or more members opposed the nomination of the chairman or senior member in the Steering Committee, or if fifty members signed a petition.

The House Republican Conference took a somewhat different approach to seniority. There were few direct challenges to ranking minority committee members because those posts had little power relative to the chairmanships controlled by the majority. Moderate Rep. Frank Horton, R-N.Y., was challenged as ranking minority member of the Government Operations Committee in 1972 by conservatives supporting Rep. John N. Erlenborn, R-Ill. Horton easily won confirmation in an up-or-down vote. In 1992, an attempt by the Steering Committee to nominate Rep. Paul Gillmor, R-Ohio, as ranking member of the House Administration Committee over incumbent Rep. William M. Thomas, R-Calif., whose relations with the leadership were sometimes testy, was rejected by the conference.

Upon taking power of Congress in 1995, however, the GOP immediately demonstrated it was less concerned about seniority than the Democrats. Speaker Newt Gingrich, R-Ga., hand-picked chairmen of the Appropriations, Commerce, and Judiciary Committees, bypassing senior members. Rep. Carlos Moorhead, R-Calif., senior member of both the Commerce and Judiciary Committees, was denied either chairmanship. Moorhead retired in 1997. Rep. Joseph M. McDade, R-Pa., was denied the Appropriations chairmanship in 1995 because he was under a federal indictment for corruption. Gingrich then skipped over the next two senior members to select Rep. Robert Livingston, R-La., as chairman. After McDade was acquitted, however, Livingston remained chairman and McDade had to be satisfied with the title of vice chairman and a subcommittee chairmanship. He announced his retirement at the end of the 105th Congress.

HOUSE CHAIRMEN OUSTED

In 1971 House Democrats and Republicans decided that seniority need not be followed in the selection of committee leaders. In 1973 Democrats permitted one-fifth of their caucus to force a vote on a nominee for committee chairman, and in 1974 that vote became automatic for all nominees.

Rank-and-file Democrats in January 1975 asserted their new power by unseating three incumbent chairmen: Armed Services Committee Chairman F. Edward Hebert of Louisiana; Agriculture Committee Chairman W. R. Poage of Texas; and Banking, Currency, and Housing Committee Chairman Wright Patman of Texas. Hebert and Poage were both replaced by the next ranking Democrat on their committees, but, in yet another blow to the seniority system, the fourth-ranking Democrat on the Banking Committee, Henry S. Reuss of Wisconsin, was elected to succeed Patman. The autocratic manner in which the three chairmen had run their committees was primarily responsible for their downfall.

In 1984 the Democratic Caucus voted narrowly to remove elderly Melvin Price of Illinois from the chairmanship of the Armed Services Committee and replace him with Les Aspin of Wisconsin, the panel's seventh-ranking Democrat, despite an impassioned plea in behalf of Price from Speaker Thomas P. "Tip" O'Neill Jr., D-Mass. Many Democrats had complained that Price's infirmity allowed the Republican minority to exercise effective control of the conservative panel.

Aspin nearly suffered the same fate two years later. Many liberal Democrats were distressed at what they considered his betrayals on several controversial defense issues. Aspin lost his chair in early January 1987 in a yes-or-no vote in the Democratic Caucus on his reelection, with no other name on the ballot. But two weeks later, pitted against three other committee members, Aspin won it back on the third ballot over the more conservative Rep. James Marvin Leath of Texas.

Democrats ousted two committee chairmen in December 1990, as they organized for the 102nd Congress. Public Works Chairman Glenn M. Anderson, D-Calif., and House Administration Chairman Frank Annunzio, D-Ill., were regarded as weak, ineffective leaders. They were rejected and then replaced by younger Democrats: Rep. Robert A. Roe of New Jersey, the second-ranking Democrat on Public Works, defeated third-ranking Rep. Norman Y. Mineta of California (who would become chairman in the next Congress); and Rep. Charlie Rose of North Carolina, the third-ranking Democrat on House Administration.

Use of caucus rules to challenge committee chairmen usually was at the behest of the rank-and-file membership and was often unsuccessfully opposed by some in the party leadership, who feared disruptions from ongoing competition for committees and subcommittee posts. There were important exceptions, however.

In the most significant recent contest, Rep. David Obey, a senior member of the Appropriations Committee and one of the House's most aggressive and partisan liberals, benefited from the weakening of the seniority tradition in 1994 when Chairman William H. Natcher, D-Ky., became terminally ill. Obey, the fifth-ranking member, was supported by the leadership and easily won a vote of the Steering and Policy Committee to succeed Natcher as "acting chairman" over the third-ranking Democrat, Neal Smith of Iowa, who argued that he deserved the post as a veteran liberal who had served for thirty-five years. Obey automatically assumed the chairmanship upon Natcher's death.

SUBCOMMITTEE CONTESTS

In 1973 Democrats allowed their party members on each committee to select subcommittee chairmen. Previously, they had been picked by the committee chairman. In 1975 Democrats decided that all subcommittee chairmen on the Appropriations Committee should be subject to election by the full Democratic Caucus; on the highly decentralized Appropriations panel it was argued that those subcommittee chairmen were as powerful as most chairmen of legislative committees. In 1990, the rule was also applied to subcommittee chairmen on the Ways and Means Committee.

The seniority system suffered another reversal in January 1977 when the Democratic Caucus for the first time rejected a sitting subcommittee chairman of the Appropriations Committee. The target was Robert L. F. Sikes of Florida, the longtime chairman of the Military Construction Subcommittee who had been reprimanded by the House the year before for conflicts of interest.

Democratic caucuses on other committees have also ousted subcommittee chairmen or rejected senior members who had been heirs apparent. Several of these contests were significant in influencing party policies for years to come. In 1975, on the then–Interstate and Foreign Commerce Committee, Rep. John Moss, D-Calif., ousted Rep. Harley Staggers, D-W.Va., from the chairmanship of the Oversight subcommittee. Staggers's loss was an especially significant slap at the seniority system since he was also chairman of the full committee. In 1979, on the same committee, Rep. Henry Waxman, D-Calif., defeated the more senior and conservative Rep. L. Richardson Preyer, D-N.C., for the vacant chairmanship of the important Health subcommittee after a bitter contest focusing on allegations that Preyer's status as heir to a pharmaceutical fortune created a potential conflict of interest, and complaints about Waxman's campaign contributions to other committee Democrats.

Perhaps the strangest contest occurred in 1981 on the then–Foreign Affairs Committee. Rep. Michael Barnes, D-Md., a second-term liberal, challenged the conservative subcommittee chairman Rep. Gus Yatron, D-Pa., for his post on the Western Hemisphere subcommittee. With Yatron perceived as vulnerable, Rep. Dan Mica, D-Fla., a conservative, also decided to run. Mica had been elected to the House and the committee along with Barnes but had been ranked ahead of him in the committee's order of seniority determined by lot. When the voting began by secret ballot, caucus rules required a yes-no vote on each candidate, who bid for a chairmanship in order of full committee seniority until the post was filled. Yatron lost by one vote, which was known to be Mica's. Angered by Mica's opportunism, Yatron then voted against him, resulting in Mica's defeat by one vote. Barnes, who bid next, was then easily elected chairman and led Democratic opposition to the Reagan administration's policies in the region.

SENATE ADHERES TO SENIORITY

The Senate also decided in the 1970s that seniority should not dictate the choice of committee leaders. Senate Republicans adopted the policy in 1973 and the Democrats in 1975. Yet the Senate continued to adhere to the seniority tradition, and in the smaller body longtime personal relationships among senators also worked to smooth over arguments that ideology should be a more significant determinant of chairmanships.

In 1977, in the most visible attempt to undermine seniority, the liberal-dominated Democratic Conference took a secret ballot vote on all nominees for chairmen, with opposition centering on Finance Committee Chairman Russell Long of Louisiana. He won overwhelmingly, 42–6.

A battle in 1987 over the position of ranking minority member on the Foreign Relations Committee was settled primarily on the issue of seniority. The contest was between Republican Jesse Helms, R-N.C., and the more moderate Richard G. Lugar, R-Ind. The situation was somewhat unusual because Lugar had been chairman of the Foreign Relations panel for the previous two years while the Republicans controlled the Senate. Helms tended to North Carolina issues as chairman of the Agriculture Committee. But when the Senate reverted to the Democrats, Helms, who had joined the Foreign Relations panel the same day as Lugar, decided he wanted the position of ranking Republican on the committee and claimed seniority by virtue of his four years of longer service in the Senate.

Under the rules of the Senate Republican Conference, each committee chooses its top ranking member, subject to confirmation by the entire conference. Republicans on the Foreign Relations Committee nominated Lugar as ranking member, but the full Republican Conference rejected him, 24–17. Helms—and the seniority system—won out. Lugar then became ranking minority member of the Agriculture Committee, and both he and Helms became chairmen of these committees when Republican Senate control resumed in 1995.

The apparent personal animus between Helms and Lugar lingered, and the fallout from their contest had interesting repercussions for years to come. Lugar led the opposition to Helms' refusal in 1997 to hold a confirmation hearing for William Weld, a moderate Republican nominated as ambassador to Mexico. In an unprecedented action, a committee majority forced Helms to schedule a meeting at which they intended to discuss the Weld nomination, but Helms successfully used his chairmanship powers to deny most other senators, including Lugar, a chance to speak. Lugar, in turn, threatened to use his powers as Agriculture chairman against North Carolina tobacco interests.

Despite dramatic conservative gains in the Republican Conference, more moderate senators continue to rely on seniority to obtain and keep important positions on committees. Sen. Mark O. Hatfield, R-Ore., a veteran liberal, was not removed as Appropriations Committee chairman during the 104th Congress after he cast the lone—and decisive—vote to kill a balanced budget constitutional amendment, and Sen. John H. Chafee, R-R.I., assumed the chairmanship of the Environment and Public Works Committee. In the 105th Congress, a rumored challenge to Sen. James M. Jeffords, R-Vt., for the open chairmanship of the Labor and Human Resources Committee by conservative Sen. Dan Coats, R-Ind., never developed.

a wide variety of entrenched interests. When the panel, chaired by Jerry M. Patterson, D-Calif., closed its doors in April 1980, it left behind barely a trace of its thirteen-month-long effort to change the House committee system. Only one of its recommendations—a plan to create a separate standing committee on energy to untangle overlapping committee jurisdictions—went to the House floor, where the proposal was promptly gutted. In place of the select committee's plan, the House merely decided to rename its Commerce Committee as the Energy and Commerce Committee and to designate that panel as its lead committee on energy matters.

The Patterson committee's other recommendations had included proposals to limit subcommittee assignments as well as the number of subcommittees. The committee said the proliferation of subcommittees had decentralized and fragmented the policy process and had limited members' capacity to master their work. The Patterson committee report emphasized that on no other issue concerning committee reform had it found greater agreement than that there were too many subcommittees in the House and that members had too many subcommittee assignments.

There were few major rules proposals considered after the 1970s. Over a twenty-year period, Democrats continued to make a series of incremental adjustments in House floor rules that gave the Speaker power to postpone and cluster certain votes, to eliminate "ordering a second" (a potentially dilatory additional vote) on motions to suspend the rules, and to abolish the vestiges of nonrecorded teller voting. Giving the leadership the ability to coordinate a more rational floor schedule, it was argued, would enhance the ability of committees to conduct business with fewer interruptions.

House Democrats in January 1981, amended their caucus rules to limit the number of subcommittees and similar committee subunits that could be established by standing committees. Under the new rule, the Appropriations Committee was allowed to retain all of its thirteen panels but all other standing committees were restricted to a maximum of either eight (if the standing committee had at least thirty-five members) or six for smaller committees. In 1992, Democrats amended the caucus rules further to limit most committees to a maximum of five subcommittees, but, in a gesture to the importance of placating individuals and avoiding sacrifice, they also guaranteed that no subcommittee chairman would lose a post.

One subject—administrative reform of the House—never effectively addressed by the Democratic Caucus because it was not perceived to involve real power and most members had little awareness of it would eventually surface with a series of scandals in the 1990s that helped to undermine the Democratic House majority.

The Joint Committee on the Organization of Congress, created for the first session of the 103rd Congress, was structured similarly to previous joint committees whose work had achieved some success with the legislative reorganization laws in 1946 and 1970. But ultimately that was all it had in common with them.

For example, the joint committee discussed many ideas for reform of the committee system in the House but accomplished little except the compilation of diverse proposals. There was little appetite in the House for significant change among Democrats, and Republicans were anxious to take credit for the idea of reform and to use the theme of institutional corruption in the next campaign. The Democratic leadership wanted the issue to go away, while simultaneously claiming public credit for working on it. They continued to make commitments to consider the committee's recommendations on the House floor in 1994, scheduling a "reform week" late in the second session that never came to pass.

The joint committee foundered over bitter partisanship in the House and poisonous bicameral relations when Senate Republicans angered Democrats by employing filibusters against Clinton administration proposals. House Democrats refused to consider enhanced minority rights for Republicans, such as a guarantee that the minority could offer amendatory instructions in the motion to recommit bills to committees, unless the Senate agreed to reforms in the filibuster, anathema to key senators from both parties. These issues were difficult enough without the addition of changes in committee structure and jurisdiction.

After the 103rd Congress expired, party control of both chambers shifted and reforms again became a unicameral, partisan initiative, this time in GOP hands. In 1995, the House abolished the District of Columbia, Merchant Marine and Fisheries, and Post Office and Civil Service Committees, three minor panels whose absence had little effect on the operation of the chamber.

SENATE COMMITTEE CHANGES

While most of the attempts to reorganize the committee system in the 1970s were directed at the House, the Senate committee system was altered in 1977 by the first comprehensive committee consolidation in either house since passage of the 1946 reorganization act. Earlier in the decade the Senate had adopted important procedural changes involving committees. Later attempts to use another bicameral vehicle, the 1993 Joint Committee on the Organization of Congress, to implement new reforms ultimately failed.

Committees and committee assignments are much less important in the work of the chamber and in determining the course of a member's career than in the House. In the Senate, the parties also control the assignment process, but some assignment limitations that do exist are actually set out in the rules. Consequently proposed reforms might open the door to the delicate subject of amendments to Senate rules. The Senate often prefers instead to adjust committee structure and assignment issues by creating new exceptions, irrespective of the rules, that benefit individual senators while taking nothing away from anyone else. Each party also privately determines policies affecting its own members, which has the advantage of avoiding messy floor debate and keeps the parties out of each other's affairs.

Challenges to Seniority

The Senate had struck the first successful blow to the seniority system in the post–World War II period. As Senate minority leader in 1953 Lyndon Johnson proposed that all Democratic senators be given a seat on one major committee before any Democrat was assigned to a second major committee. The proposal, which became known as the "Johnson Rule," was a stunning blow to seniority. But it had the backing of Sen. Richard Russell of Georgia—the powerful leader of the southern Democratic bloc that dominated the Senate for years—and was approved by the Democratic Steering Committee that made Democratic committee assignments in the Senate. It was fitting that Johnson had successfully staged the breakthrough because he was a junior senator, chosen as his party's leader while still in his first Senate term. He had served six terms in the House, however, and had become a protégé of House Speaker Rayburn.

Later, Senate Republicans adopted the same party rule, first informally in 1959 and then through the Republican Conference in 1965.

In 1971, under renewed pressure to modify the seniority system, Senate Democrats and Republicans agreed to further changes. Majority Leader Mike Mansfield, D-Mont., announced that a meeting of the Democratic Conference would be held at the request of any senator and any senator would be free to challenge any nomination by the Steering Committee of a committee chairman. Republicans adopted a proposal that a senator could be the ranking minority member of only one standing committee. (After the GOP took control of the Senate in 1981, Republicans applied the same rule to the selection of committee chairmen.)

The Senate rejected a major challenge to the seniority system in 1971 when it blocked, on a 48–26 vote, a resolution that would have permitted the selection of committee chairmen on some basis other than seniority. The resolution had provided that in making committee assignments "neither [party] conference shall be bound by any tradition, custom, or principle of seniority."

But in 1973 Senate Republicans decided to choose their top-ranking committee members without regard to seniority. Republicans adopted a plan to limit the seniority system by having members of each standing committee elect the top-ranking Republican on that committee, subject to approval by a vote of all Senate Republicans.

And in 1975 Senate Democrats also voted to choose committee chairmen without regard to seniority. A secret ballot would be taken whenever one-fifth of their conference requested it. The provision was first used in 1977 when twelve senators made a request for a secret ballot, though several of them said they still intended to support the committee chairmen. Unlike the changes underway in the House, the new rule failed to reveal any significant dissatisfaction with the traditional seniority system even on a secret ballot, as only a handful of votes were cast against any chairmanship nominees. Sen. Russell Long, D-La., supposedly a long-time target of reformers, was easily renominated by a 42–6 vote. Appropriations Committee Chairman John McClellan, D-Ark., received an identical tally. Majority Leader Robert C. Byrd, D-W.Va., later forced a separate Senate vote on Long's election as chairman to demonstrate what he called the democratic nature of Senate rules. Long won 60–0.

Also in 1975, junior senators obtained committee staff assistance for the first time. A new rule authorized them to hire up to three committee staffers, depending on the number and type of committee assignments they had—to work directly for them on their committees. In the past, committee staff members had been controlled by the chairmen and other senior committee members.

1977 Committee Reorganization

The 1977 Senate reorganization consolidated a number of committees, revised jurisdictions of others, set a ceiling on the number of committees and subcommittees on which a senator could serve or chair, gave minority members a larger share of committee staff, and directed that schedules for committee hearings and other business be computerized to avoid conflicts. The organizational and procedural changes were the product of a special panel, chaired by Sen. Adlai E. Stevenson III, D-Ill.

One of the biggest organizational changes was the consolidation of most aspects of energy policy, except taxes, in one committee. Although the final result fell short of the Stevenson committee's goals for consolidating and merging committees, three committees were abolished: District of Columbia, Post Office, and Aeronautical and Space Sciences, as well as the joint committees on Atomic Energy, Congressional Operations, and Defense Production. (The decision to end the joint committees was a unilateral Senate action. The House continued the Congressional Operations panel as a select committee for another two years.) Special interest groups were able to preserve several other committees slated for extinction, such as Small Business.

Changes also were made in Senate committee procedures.

Senate reformers, like their House counterparts, were concerned with the proliferation of committees and subcommittees. In 1947 most senators served on two or three subcommittees. By the 94th Congress (1975–1977) they held an average of eleven assignments on subcommittees of standing committees.[19] Stevenson's Temporary Select Committee to Study the Senate Committee System stated in its report:

> Proliferation of committee panels means proliferation in assignments held by Senators. And the burdens and frustrations of too many assignments, whatever the benefits, produce inefficient division of labor, uneven distribution of responsibility, conflicts in the scheduling of meetings, waste of Senators' and staff time, unsystematic lawmaking and oversight, inadequate anticipation of major problems, and inadequate membership participation in committee decisions.[20]

As part of the 1977 reorganization, the Senate prohibited a senator from serving as chairman of more than one subcommittee on any committee on which he or she served. This, in effect, placed an indirect cap on subcommittee expansion by limiting the number of subcommittees of any committee to the number of majority party members on the full committee.

House and Senate negotiators meet in a budget reconciliation conference in 1997.

With certain exceptions, each senator was limited to membership on two major committees and one minor committee. Each senator was limited to membership on three subcommittees of each major committee on which he or she served (the Appropriations Committee was exempted from this restriction). And each senator was limited to membership on two subcommittees of the minor committee on which he or she served.

Though it was not made a requirement, the Senate adopted language, similar to that in the House, stating it to be the sense of the Senate that no member of a committee should receive a second subcommittee assignment until all members of the committee had received their first assignment.

The Senate also prohibited a senator from serving as chairman of more than one committee at the same time; prohibited the chairman of a major committee from serving as chairman of more than one subcommittee on the senator's major committees and as the chairman of more than one subcommittee on his or her minor committee; prohibited the chairman of a minor committee from chairing a subcommittee on that committee; and prohibited the senator from chairing more than one of each of his of her major committees' subcommittees.

The Senate in addition required the Rules Committee to establish a central computerized scheduling service to keep track of meetings of Senate committees and subcommittees and House-Senate conference committees.

Finally, the Senate required the staff of each committee to reflect the relative size of the majority and minority membership on the committee. On the request of the minority party members of a committee at least one-third of the staff of the committee was to be placed under the control of the minority party, except that staff deemed by the chairman and ranking minority member to be working for the whole committee would not be subject to the rule.

1980s Reform Attempts

Frustration with Senate procedures ran high in the 1980s, but despite several serious proposals for reform no major changes were achieved by the end of the decade.

A 1983 report by former Sens. James B. Pearson, R-Kan., and Abraham Ribicoff, D-Conn., urged major changes in the Senate structure and procedures, including restrictions on subcommittees and a reduction in the number of committees. Under their plan, subcommittees would not have been permitted to report legislation nor would the panels have been staffed, a move aimed at eliminating what they saw as time-consuming specialization at the subcommittee level.

The following year another Temporary Select Committee to Study the Senate Committee System, chaired by Dan Quayle, R-Ind., recommended, among other things, strictly limiting the number of committee and subcommittee assignments each senator could have. The panel called for the strict enforcement of the existing rule allowing senators to serve on two major committees and one minor committee.

The Senate Rules and Administration Committee in 1988 proposed changes in committee and floor procedures. To reduce the number of competing demands on senators' time, the panel proposed allowing subcommittees to hold only hearings, thus requiring all legislative drafting sessions to be held at the full committee level.

In 1993, the Joint Committee on the Organization of Congress proposed a variety of ideas to revise committee structure, assignments, and procedures, although it did not recommend abolition of any existing committee. Among its proposals: limiting senators to three committees; restricting major committees (called "super A" and "A") to three subcommittees (except Appropriations) and minor "B" committees to two subcommittees; limiting senators to service on two subcommittees per "A" com-

TERM LIMITS ON COMMITTEE CHAIRMANSHIPS AND SERVICE

Congress historically has resisted limiting the length of time members may serve on committees. To do so, it was argued, would detract from the expertise that committees possess in dealing with complex legislation. Limitations also would disrupt the concept of seniority that provides a stable mechanism for determining committee leaders over long periods of time and avoiding power struggles.

However, in 1995, the new Republican majorities in the House and Senate took important steps toward legitimizing term limitations for top committee posts. They not only amended House rules at the beginning of the 104th Congress to place a three-term service limit on all committee and subcommittee chairs but placed a four-term limit on the speakership. The House rules changes were effective immediately.

The Senate's term limitation was a Republican Conference rule, not an amendment to the chamber's rules. It was adopted prospectively to limit full committee chairmen to six years of service, and the clock began to run only in 1997.

The three-term/six-year chairmanship limits was a significant movement away from seniority and toward a broader sharing of power in Congress.

The "Contract with America," a GOP political agenda used in the 1994 elections, contained a proposal for a constitutional amendment requiring term limits on service in Congress itself. However the amendment was easily defeated in 1995 and 1997 when brought to a vote. *(See box, Contract with America, p. 26.)*

Whether the changes would hold up was uncertain. Many things could happen in the interim that would prevent the new rules from taking effect. Because they were created by Republican majorities, any shift in party control back to the Democrats would very likely result in numerous changes in the rules, including possible repeal or modification of term limits. At the very least the effective date would be postponed to accommodate a new generation of Democratic committee chairmen. The new House rule does not apply to ranking minority members of committees and subcommittees, and the Democratic Caucus in 1997 overwhelmingly rejected a proposal to implement a term limitation through the party's caucus rules. The Republicans themselves could have second thoughts as the deadline approaches. They would face wholesale replacements of committee leadership as a new presidential administration was taking office and possible retirements by departing chairmen, creating vacant seats that might endanger control of the House.

Reformers in the past have argued for even broader committee service limitations for the entire House membership to break up entrenched oligarchies on committee and encourage members to explore new interests across the jurisdictional spectrum. The idea never attracted significant support because by disrupting seniority it removed the most significant source of stability and predictability for members as they planned their congressional careers. There were also legitimate questions about how any wholesale rotation would work when hundreds of members might be affected at once.

The use of term limits in very limited circumstances is not new in Congress, however. Two House standing committees—Budget and Standards of Official Conduct—have employed term limits since their inception. The Budget Committee, which is supposed to have a broad range of membership, including mandatory representation from the Appropriations and Ways and Means Committee, began with a two-term limit and gradually expanded to three terms, then to four terms in the 104th Congress. Technically, the rule limits members to no more than four terms out of six successive Congresses, thus preventing them from leaving the committee and quickly being brought back. The chairman can serve for an additional term, if necessary, to allow him a minimum of two terms in that post.

The Democrats refused to adopt the new four-term limit, retaining the three-term limit in their caucus rules and making Budget the only committee in Congress in which each party uses a different term limit. The Democrats' decision did not represent a judgment of the appropriate length of service on the committee; instead, they sought to use the already scheduled three-term rotation to create some vacant seats to give to members because so few committee assignments were available under the ratios created by the new Republican majority.

In the case of the Standards Committee, term limits have varied. Effective in 1997 a service limitation of no more than two Congress in any period of three successive Congresses was imposed. However, there is no demand for service on the committee. The size of the committee was fixed at fourteen by the Ethics Reform Act of 1989, but the controversy associated with the committee's workload made that number unrealistic; only ten seats were occupied in each of the 104th and 105th Congresses. Rules changes in 1997 allowed twenty members who do not serve on the committee—ten from each party—to serve in a pool from which members could be drawn to join regular committee members in filling subcommittees to investigate ethics violations.

The lone House select committee, Permanent Intelligence, originally had a six-calendar-year service limitation, which was changed to four-terms-out-of-six successive Congresses in 1995, as had been recommended by the Joint Committee on the Organization of Congress. Proponents of term limits had argued at the committee's inception that a limitation would refresh the membership and prevent it from being coopted by the intelligence community. The rule was also amended to allow a member selected as chairman in his or her fourth Congress of service to be eligible to serve for a fifth term if reappointed as chairman, in order to ensure greater continuity of the committee's work; these provisions copied the rule from the Budget Committee. Due to defects in the operation of the original six-year rotation rule, there had been criticism that the committee had been weakened because nearly all of its chairman (except the first) had been effectively limited to only two years in that post and could not establish strong and stable working relationships with executive branch entities.

The Senate does not employ rotation on any of its standing committees, so the shifting members of the House Budget Committee face a Senate counterpart with long-term permanent membership. (The Senate chairman in 1998, Pete V. Domenici of New Mexico, also held the post during an earlier period of Republican Senate control in the 1980s.) The Senate Select Intelligence Committee, however, has an eight-year limit that the House has now essentially copied.

mittee (except Appropriations) and one per "B" committee; requiring bipartisan leadership approval and a Senate recorded vote for extra assignments; allowing majority and minority leaders to make committee assignments, subject to party rules; setting meeting days for the various classifications of committees to reduce scheduling conflicts; and barring use of proxies if they affected the result of a vote.

The Joint Committee's recommendations were reworked by a Republican task force appointed by incoming Majority Leader Bob Dole, R-Kan., in 1994, which called for Senate floor action on:

• Barring major committees (except Appropriations) from having more than five subcommittees in the 104th Congress and four in the 105th (as opposed to the limit of three proposed by the joint committee). Senate rules have no limits.

• Barring senators from serving on more than two major and one minor committee, a provision already in the Senate rules but often ignored.

• Abolishing joint committees.

• Abolishing committees deemed too trivial or unpopular with senators to continue to exist, but defining them only as any committee that dropped to less than 50 percent of the membership it had in the 102nd Congress.

• Allowing proxy voting only if it did not affect the outcome of a committee vote.

None of these proposals was adopted, but Republicans in the 104th Congress later considered several proposals in their party conference. Most significantly they approved a six-year term limit on committee chairmen, to begin in 1997, that would also apply if Republicans returned to minority status. Democrats

CONFERENCE COMMITTEES

The conference committee is an ad hoc joint committee appointed to reconcile differences between Senate and House versions of pending legislation. The conference device, used by Congress since 1789, had developed its modern practice by the middle of the nineteenth century. *(See "Conference Action," p. 102, in Chapter 2.)*

Before a bill can be sent to the president, it must be passed in identical form by both chambers. Whenever different versions of the same bill are passed, and neither chamber is willing to yield to the other or make modifications by sending a bill back-and-forth, a conference becomes necessary to determine the final shape of the legislation. It is unusual for the Senate or House to reject the work of a conference committee.

In the past, conference committees were composed of the senior members of the committees that handled the bill. This remains generally true today, but there are opportunities for junior members to be appointed and occasionally even members who were not on a committee that originally reported the measure. Conferees are appointed by the Speaker of the House and the presiding officer of the Senate upon the recommendations of the committee chairmen and ranking minority members. Although the chairmen, by tradition, have played the principal role in picking conferees, in the House the Speaker retains the substantive power to make the appointments, subject only to the restrictions in Rule XI, clause 6 that he "shall appoint no less than a majority of Members who generally supported the House position as determined by the Speaker . . ." and "shall name Members who are primarily responsible for the legislation and shall, to the fullest extent feasible, include the principal proponents of the major provisions of the bill as it passed the House." The Speaker's appointments may not be challenged on a point of order for alleged violations of these criteria.

Recent Speakers intervened more frequently to select members they want to serve as conferees and to bar those they do not. Speaker Newt Gingrich, R-Ga., even appointed members of the Democratic minority to serve in conference slots reserved for the majority in order to highlight differences within the minority.

In 1993, the House changed its rules to give the Speaker the power, after a conference has been appointed, to appoint additional conferees and to remove conferees as he wishes. Before then, any changes in the composition of a conference after its appointment had required unanimous consent. While the change by 1998 had no dramatic impact on the operation of conferences, it effectively prevented conferees from defying the will of the majority leadership. Largely because of complexities in the House created by multiple referrals of bills to different committees and the increasing use of massive omnibus bills to deal with budget and tax matters, the size of conference delegations increased during the 1980s and in subsequent years. Scholars Walter Oleszek and C. Lawrence Evans have noted that committee chairs in the 1980s often demanded positions on conferences from Democratic Speakers, who often found it politic to accommodate them. In 1981, for example, more than 250 members of Congress participated in a conference on a budget reconciliation bill, making it the largest conference in history. The conference split up into fifty-eight subgroups to consider various sections of the legislation.

It is possible that 1995 rules changes in the House requiring a primary committee be designated for each bill, rather than the previous practice of joint referrals, may swing the trend back toward less complex conference structures. Evans and Oleszek have observed that the new rule gave Speaker Gingrich "the procedural rationale for resisting chairs' demands for conference slots."[1] Data indicates that, for legislation in conference which received multiple referrals, the average size of the House delegation dropped from 42.7 members to 29.1 between the 103rd and 104th Congresses.

CONDUCTING A CONFERENCE

There need not be an equal number of conferees (or "managers," as they are called) from each house. Each house's delegation has a single vote, which is determined by a majority vote of its conferees. Therefore, a majority of both the Senate and House delegations must agree before a provision emerges from conference as part of the final bill. Both chambers permit proxy voting in conferences.

Both parties are represented on conference committees, with the majority party having a larger number, and a majority of conferees would not be affected. Unlike the House, which wrote term limits into the chamber's rules in 1995, the Senate rules were not amended to incorporate the proposal. The Republican Conference also mandated a secret-ballot vote by Republican members of a committee in nominating a candidate for chairman and required a chairman, if indicted for a felony, to step aside temporarily until the matter was resolved. *(See box, Term Limits on Committee Chairmenships and Service, p. 139.)*

The Committee Structure

There are three principal classes of committees in Congress:

• Standing committees, by far the most important and most numerous, with permanently authorized staff and broad legislative mandates.

• Select or special committees that have a limited jurisdiction, may be restricted to an investigative rather than a legislative role, and may be temporary in that they are authorized to operate for a specific period of time or until the project for which they are created has been completed.

• Joint committees that have a membership drawn from both houses of Congress and usually are investigative or housekeeping in nature.

Conference committees, a special variety of joint committee, serve only on an ad hoc basis to resolve differences in Senate and House versions of the same legislation. *(See box, Conference Committees, p. 140.)*

Below the committee level are a plethora of subcommittees that are functional subdivisions of the committees. Like the full committees they are composed of members of the majority and

from each house must sign the conference report. In the past conference committees met on the Senate side of the Capitol, with the most senior senator presiding, but this custom is no longer followed. Conferences now meet anywhere in the House, Senate, or Capitol complexes, with members of either House presiding, though the role is largely honorific. For certain legislation considered on an annual basis, such as appropriations bills and the congressional budget resolution, the chairmanship alternates between the chambers.

Most conference committees met in secret until late 1975 when both chambers amended their rules to require open meetings unless a majority of either chamber's conferees vote in open session to close the meeting for that day. In 1977 the House amended its rules further to require open conference meetings unless the full House voted by recorded vote to close them. That rule was never adopted by the Senate but in practice Senate conferees have always gone along with the representatives on those occasions—limited to defense and intelligence agency bills—when the House has voted to close a conference committee. Despite the "sunshine" rules, committees have found various ways to avoid negotiating in public, including the use of informal sessions, separate meetings of each delegation with staffers as go-between, and meeting rooms too small to accommodate all who wish to attend.

Conferees may be "instructed" by the House, just before they are appointed and while they are meeting, although the instructions are not binding and are sometimes ignored. When conferees are about to be appointed, the principal manager for the minority is usually recognized to offer a motion to instruct, and sometimes a motion may be offered pro forma in order to prevent another member from offering a less desirable proposition. The House also has a rule that allows any member, with preference for recognition again going to the minority party, to offer a motion to instruct its conferees or to dismiss them if a conference has not reported after twenty calendar days. This form of motion to instruct may be offered repeatedly by any member until the conferees finally report. This motion has sometimes proved a useful device for the minority to bring attention to a conference's failure to act or to force the House to vote for or against legislative provisions proposed in the Senate. The Senate rarely instructs its conferees, but there have been some indications the practice may be becoming more popular.

After conferees reach agreement, they sign a conference report and submit it and a statement of managers providing a detailed explanation of their actions to each chamber. Unlike a bill reported by a House or Senate legislative committee, conferees who disagree may not include any "minority views." Sometimes conferees who sign the report but object to certain provisions include a notation, such as "except section XXX," next to their names, but these caveats have no substantive effect. When conferees are unable to agree, the bill may die in conference if they take no formal action. Sometimes conferees file a report incorporating only matters on which they have agreed, leaving out others on which they disagree to await further negotiation or additional votes on the floor of each House to see if one chamber or the other will compromise. On rare occasions conferees formally report "in disagreement" and await further amendments by both houses.

Once their report is approved by the first of the two houses to consider it, the conference committee automatically is dissolved and the report goes to the remaining house for a vote. If either chamber rejects the conference report, the legislation remains before it in the form it existed prior to its commitment to conference, to await additional amendments or a new conference. The first chamber to consider the report also has the option to "recommit" it to conference, usually with instructions, to change an unacceptable provision. This action has the effect of rejecting the initial conference report but does not require the appointment of a new conference. The conferees may simply resume meeting. However, it may endanger chances for a new agreement if the other chamber refuses to accede on the issue in question. If an agreement is reached on the issue in dispute the filing process is repeated de novo. In the Senate, conference reports may be filibustered like other legislation.

1. C. Lawrence Evans and Walter J. Oleszek, "Procedural Features of House Republican Rule," paper presented at a conference at Florida International University, Miami, January 31, 1998, 16.

minority parties in roughly the same proportion as the party ratios on the full committees.

Beginning in the 1970s additional mechanisms were developed to consider legislation apart from the traditional committee structure. Appearing principally in the House, these include the creation of ad hoc committees by the chamber to deal with complex legislation within the normal jurisdiction of several committees. This mechanism requires formal approval by the House and should be considered a variation of a multiple referral.

On the other hand, the use of informal leadership task forces to develop or refine legislation occurs outside the committee process entirely, at least until the bill is ready to be considered more formally.

STANDING COMMITTEES

The standing committees are at the center of the legislative process. Legislation usually must be considered and approved in some form at the committee level before it can be sent to the House or Senate for further action. *(See Chapter 2, The Legislative Process, p. 51.)*

The 1946 reorganization act organized the Senate and House committees along roughly parallel lines, although eventually divergences emerged. One of the act's purposes was to eliminate confusing and overlapping jurisdictions by grouping together related areas. The legislative committees (as distinct from the Appropriations committees) generally were regrouped to follow the major organizational divisions of the executive branch.

SUBCOMMITTEES

Most standing committees have a number of subcommittees that provide the ultimate division of labor within the committee system. Although they enable members of Congress to develop expertise in specialized fields they often are criticized on grounds that they fragment responsibility, increase the difficulty of policy review, and slow down the authorization and appropriation process.

Subcommittees play a much larger role in the House than in the Senate. In the House subcommittees usually are responsible for hearings and the first markup of a bill before a measure is sent on to the full committee. In the Senate subcommittees may hold hearings but the full committee generally does the writing of legislation. And, Deering and Smith write, "on nearly all Senate committees the work of subcommittees on important legislation is shown little deference by the full committees."[21]

Subcommittees also vary in importance from committee to committee. Some, especially the Appropriations subcommittees in both chambers, have well-defined jurisdictions and function with great autonomy. Much of their work in both the House and Senate is often endorsed by the full committee without significant change, though, as noted, both the desire and the capacities of individual members to intervene in the legislative process have dramatically increased over time.

A few committees such as House Ways and Means and Senate Finance long resisted the creation of subcommittees even though there were logical subdivisions into which their work could be divided. Subcommittees were established by the Finance Committee in 1970, and by Ways and Means only in 1975

A House subcommittee meets to mark up a bill to improve regulation at the Food and Drug Administration.

after the House Democratic Caucus voted to require them. The subcommittee requirement was established in part because of dissatisfaction with the power and performance of Ways and Means Chairman Wilbur Mills. But these subcommittees, unlike those on the Appropriations Committee, never became autonomous legislative power centers because tax bills were put together as a unified package that required negotiations with all members of the full committee.

Ways and Means subcommittee chairmen became subject to caucus election in 1990 after two chairmen defied the leadership on tax legislation in 1989. However, none of the chairmen were ever seriously challenged for reelection to their positions.

After Republicans took over the House in 1995, committee chairmen exercised greater influence in the selection of subcommittee chairs than had been the case under the Democrats, subject to approval by GOP members of the committee.

The House and Senate Budget committees were among the few panels that had no subcommittees in the 105th Congress. Under Democratic control, the House panel had task forces that allowed a variety of members to chair oversight hearings on subjects of interest and to justify additional staffing but they were not integral to the committee's work.

SELECT AND SPECIAL COMMITTEES

Select and special committees are established from time to time in both chambers to study special problems or concerns, such as population, crime, hunger, or narcotics abuse. On other occasions, they deal with a specific event or investigation. Major investigations have been conducted by select committees such as the Senate panel that investigated the Watergate scandal in 1973–1974 and the House and Senate panels that jointly investigated the Iran-contra affair in 1987.

The size and life span of select and special panels usually are fixed by the resolutions that create them. In most cases, they have remained in existence for only a short time. Ordinarily they are not permitted to report legislation although there are exceptions such as the 1973–1974 Select Committee on Committees chaired by Rep. Richard Bolling, D-Mo. However, much of its work was rejected when the House, reexamining itself again with a new Select Committee on Committees in 1979– 1980, chaired by Rep. Jerry Patterson, D-Ca., withheld legislative authority from the panel. Some of these committees, however, such as the Special Aging Committee in the Senate, have gone on continuously and are, for all intents and purposes, permanent. *(See box, House Abolishes Select Committees, p. 144.)*

Unlike most select committees the Intelligence committees in both chambers have legislation referred to them and consider and report legislation to the chamber. But this is a special case, as the committees are effectively permanent entities. The Intelligence panels' subject matter is much narrower than that of most standing committees. In the House the panel is maintained as a select committee and appointed by the Speaker to insulate it from the normal political competition of the committee assignment process. Speakers have complained of being deluged by requests from members to serve. In 1995, House rules were amended to make the Speaker himself an ex officio member of the House panel, replacing the majority leader in this role. The new rule replaced an earlier one adopted in 1989 that had given the Speaker the right to attend the committee's meetings and to receive access to its information.

JOINT COMMITTEES

Joint committees are permanent panels created by statute or by concurrent resolution that also fixes their size. Of the four functioning in the 105th Congress (1997–1998), none had the authority to report legislation. The Joint Economic Committee is directed to examine national economic problems and review the execution of fiscal and budgetary programs. The Joint Committee on Taxation, made up of senior members of both parties from the House Ways and Means and Senate Finance committees, serves chiefly to provide a professional staff that long enjoyed a nonpartisan reputation on tax issues. When the Republicans assumed control of both houses in 1995, the new majority used it as a resource to develop its agenda for enacting major tax cuts. The other two joint committees deal with administrative matters: the Joint Committee on Printing oversees the Government Printing Office and the Joint Committee on the Library oversees the Library of Congress.

Chairmanships of joint committees generally rotate from one chamber to another at the beginning of each Congress. When a senator serves as chairman the vice chairman usually is a representative and vice versa.

The last joint committee to have legislative responsibilities was the Joint Committee on Atomic Energy, which was abolished in 1977.

The most recent temporary body, the Joint Committee on the Organization of Congress, which existed in 1993 to propose reforms in the operations of the House and Senate, adopted a report that was never formally acted upon in either house.

AD HOC COMMITTEES

The Speaker of the House has the authority to create ad hoc committees, if approved by a vote of the House, to consider legislation that might be within the jurisdiction of several committees. Membership of such ad hoc committees would come from committees that would otherwise have exercised legislative jurisdiction. This authority, created in 1977, has been used twice, most notably in the 95th Congress to handle consideration of major energy legislation proposed by the Carter administration.

In 1995 the new Republican majority extended this idea to oversight, giving the Speaker the power to propose, subject to a House vote, the creation of ad hoc oversight committees to review specific matters within the jurisdiction of two or more standing committees. While aggressive use of oversight to investigate the Clinton administration became one of the new majority's priorities, it was conducted through the standing committees with efforts at coordination by the leadership. Through the

HOUSE ABOLISHES SELECT COMMITTEES

The rise and sudden fall of the supposedly temporary House panels known as select committees was a small but significant illustration of the inability of House Democrats to conduct oversight of the committee system. In the 1980s and 1990s it became increasingly difficult for the majority party to get rid of these entities once they had come into existence. They acquired virtually permanent status.

The initial urgency that was often used to justify the creation of a select committee to study an issue and hold hearings was quickly transformed into an argument that the subject matter was important enough to require an ongoing panel. Once established, abolition would have constituted a slap at interest groups, such as the elderly or children's lobbies, which viewed the select committees as friendly forums tailor-made to promote their issues.

In fact, the subject matter may have been a secondary consideration. Select committees were regarded as a prestigious reward for the member chairing the committee, who controlled a staff and budget, and as patronage for the Speaker, who appointed the chairman and all other members of such committees. Moreover, members could chair subcommittees of the select committees, even if they already chaired other subcommittees on their permanent committee assignments, because the select subpanels were usually outside the multiple-chairmanship restrictions in Democratic Caucus rules.

Attempts to abolish select committees, or even to conduct oversight of their usefulness, were regarded as challenges to a comfortable status quo. Two of the five select committees in existence at the end of the 102nd Congress existed as part of the rules of the House. Three others were reestablished by resolutions reported from the Rules Committee at the beginning of each Congress and passed by the House, and their funding was folded into the annual resolution which provided money for most standing committees.

Following the 1992 election, however, the push for reform of Congress was gaining momentum as a result of scandals in the operation of the House. Members of the large new freshman class were looking for potential targets. The Republican minority proposed a raft of changes in the structure and operations of the House, many of them quite radical, but in the renewed climate of public scrutiny some Democrats were also looking for at least a symbolic way to support reform without causing major disruptions in the House.

Four select committees, each without legislative jurisdiction, proved to be vulnerable:

- Permanent Select Committee on Aging. Created in 1975, it was made a permanent part of the House rules and was recreated automatically on the opening day of each Congress, along with the Permanent Select Committee on Intelligence, which had legislative jurisdiction. The Aging panel had sixty-eight members, making it larger than any other House committee, a staff of thirty-seven, and a budget of $1,542,240 in 1992.
- Narcotics Abuse and Control. Created in 1976, it had thirty-five members, a staff of eighteen, and a budget of $729,502 in 1992.
- Children, Youth and Families. Created in 1983, it had thirty-six members, a staff of eighteen, and a budget of $764,593 in 1992.
- Hunger. Created in 1984, it had thirty-three members, a staff of sixteen, and a budget of $654,274 in 1992.

The Democratic Caucus, meeting in December 1992 to organize for the next Congress, eliminated the Select Committee on Aging from House rules as a permanent body, effectively abolishing it and requiring it to seek renewal and survive a House floor vote just like the other select committees. The proposal slipped through in part because the chairmanship was vacant, so there was no incumbent to be displaced, and no clearly designated successor. Reps. William J. Hughes, D-N.J., and Marilyn Lloyd, D-Tenn., were competing at the time to get Speaker Thomas S. Foley's nod for the position. And few believed the rules change seriously threatened the panel.

Once the 103rd Congress convened in 1993, the Rules Committee reported separate resolutions recreating the four select committees. However, the first to be considered by the House, the popular anticrime narcotics panel, went down to a surprising defeat by a vote of 180–237. An unusual coalition of opponents consisted of near-unanimous Republicans, a small number of Democratic reformers, and a group of committee chairmen and other senior members. Members of the latter group had always regarded the existence of the select committees as an implicit slap at the standing committees, which had the actual legislative jurisdiction, for inattention to these issues, and a source of competition for media coverage and financial resources. They had long waited for an opportunity to get rid of them.

Surprisingly, the large class of freshman Democrats, many of whom had been elected on pledges to reform Congress, strongly supported the narcotics panel chaired by senior Ways and Means Committee member Charles B. Rangel, D-N.Y., a member of the Congressional Black Caucus.

Defeat of the narcotics committee surprised the Democratic leadership. Despite an attempt by the Rules Committee to reverse the result by repackaging all of the select committees in a single resolution to try to maximize support from the combination of special interest constituent groups that wanted them, it quickly became apparent that their time had passed in the House and no new floor vote was ever held. Rep. Tony Hall, D-Ohio, went on a hunger strike to protest the abolition of that committee, which he had chaired.

Only the Permanent Select Committee on Intelligence, created by House Rule XLVIII, which reports the intelligence authorization bill and is really a legislative committee but with members appointed by the Speaker rather than elected by the House, survived. Some members had advocated abolishing the panel and creating a joint committee with the Senate to reduce the number of members involved in intelligence issues and the possibility of security leaks. When Republicans assumed control of the House in 1995, they retained the select committee, increased the term of service on the rotating panel, and even added the Speaker as an ex officio member.

end of 1997, no ad hoc oversight committees had been created by the House.

TASK FORCES

Task forces operating outside the committee system are not mentioned in the rules of the House and usually have no official status. (Some committees have created task forces within themselves that perform certain functions of subcommittees.) They are groups of members working collectively for a specific purpose, usually by appointment of party leadership. Both the majority and minority have used task forces, mostly to work within the respective party caucuses. In some cases the task forces produce a useful product that can be further developed, perhaps as a bill referred to a committee. In others, their creation is intended as little more than another title on a member's stationery. When the Democrats controlled the House there were some complaints from legislative committees that task forces were becoming too visible but this represented more of an institutional jealousy than reaction to substantive work by task forces.

On rare occasions task forces have played the principal role in creating legislation, most notably in enacting the Ethics Reform Act of 1989 that restricted honoraria and secured enactment of a long-delayed pay raise for members. In the House the bill was written by a bipartisan Leadership Task Force on Ethics and introduced by the Speaker himself. In 1995 Speaker Gingrich created a bipartisan task force on the Corrections Calendar to develop issues that might be considered using that new mechanism. In 1997 a bipartisan task force developed proposals to reform the ethics process in the House after the existing process had created tremendous partisan divisions in reprimanding and fining the Speaker for ethics violations at the beginning of the session. However, its recommendations were substantially changed by the House.

The Republican leadership from 1995 to 1998 dramatically increased the use of task forces of Republican members to prepare legislation and for other purposes. The practice had the advantage, from the point of view of the leadership, of maximizing its control over an issue and simplifying the legislative process by reducing controversy surrounding such issues as committee jurisdiction. On the other hand, the practice was attacked because much of the work was conducted outside the normal protections of public hearings and written committee reports that allow access by other members, the media and the public. Task forces in the 104th and 105th Congress, the two after the Republican Party gained full control of Congress in the 1994 elections, were criticized for meeting in secret, giving too much influence to lobbyists allied with the majority, and weakening the committee system.

COMMITTEE SIZES, RATIOS

The 1946 reorganization act set not only the jurisdiction of congressional standing committees but also their size. Fifty years later, however, the size of committees in both chambers was usually settled through negotiations between majority and minority party leaders. The House dropped nearly all size specifications from its rules in 1975; in the 105th Congress (1997–1998), only the Permanent Select Committee on Intelligence had one. Senate standing rules in 1997 still included committee sizes, necessitating some adjustments at the beginning of a Congress. Each chamber in effect endorses leadership decisions on committee sizes, as well as party ratios, when it adopts resolutions making committee assignments.

One potential disadvantage of the system in the House in 1998 is that committees consist of the number of members who happen to be assigned to them throughout the Congress, with little consideration given to a committee's optimal size. The largest committee in either house in the 105th Congress was the popular Committee on Transportation and Infrastructure with a huge and often unmanageable seventy-five members. One reason for its popularity was the expectation that the 105th Congress would pass well-funded multiyear highway and mass transit program reauthorizations. (Congress passed the reauthorization in June 1998.)

Congressional scholars Deering and Smith found that modern House Democratic leaders had expanded committee sizes to meet member demand and maintain party harmony. The authors found less pressure for committee expansion in the Senate due to the fact that most senators held two major committee assignments. They also found that senators generally were less concerned with their committee assignments than their House colleagues.[22]

The standing rules of each chamber are silent on the matter of party ratios on committees. The Senate traditionally has more or less followed the practice of filling standing committees according to the strength of each party in the chamber. The House, on the other hand, has been less inclined to allocate minority party representation on committees on the basis of the relative strength of the two parties. Under Democratic control that party's caucus rules stipulated that committee ratios be established to create firm working majorities on each committee and instructed the Speaker to provide for a minimum of three Democrats for every two Republicans, although this did not always occur. (The House and Senate committees dealing with ethics matters have equal party representation with the chairman from the majority party in the chamber.)

Democrats in the House felt little need to accommodate their political opposition, especially on exclusive House committee assignments such as Appropriations, Rules, and Ways and Means. House Republicans in the 1980s complained bitterly of mistreatment by Democrats and argued that the Democrats had been in the majority for so long that they had become arrogant in the use of power. Fourteen Republicans filed a lawsuit in 1981 after the defeat of their attempts on the floor to change the party ratios on four key committees—Appropriations, Budget, Rules, and Ways and Means—to reflect the gains made by their party in the November 1980 congressional elections. Republicans charged the Democrats with unconstitutionally discriminating against GOP members and their constituents when they set the party ratios. The case was dismissed by the U.S. District Court for the District of Columbia in October 1981, and the Supreme Court refused to review it in February 1983. In response to the angry Republican protests Democratic leaders in 1985 agreed to give Republicans more seats on most major committees.

When the Republicans took control in 1995, however, these earlier stands were quickly overlooked, given the necessity of controlling the tools of legislative power. The party copied the Democrats' practices of ensuring domination of important committees, even though its majority was far smaller than the ones the Democrats had enjoyed. Even on a housekeeping committee such as House Oversight, the leadership took more direct responsibility for sensitive issues involving internal management of the House and expanded their party's ratio of control in the 105th Congress to two-to-one (six to three), exceeding ratios previously employed by the Democrats.

THE CHAIRMAN'S ROLE

Each committee is headed by a chairman, who is a member of the majority party of a chamber. A chairman's power once resulted from the rigid operation of the seniority system under which a person rose to a chairmanship simply through longevity in Congress. The unwritten seniority rule conferred a committee chairmanship on the member of the majority party with the longest continuous service on the committee. As long as the chairman's party retained control of Congress he or she normally kept this position; if control passed to the other party he or she changed places with the ranking member of that party. The seniority system, intermittently observed from the mid-1800s, took firm hold in the Senate after the Civil War. It became entrenched in the House within a few decades of the 1910 revolt against the all-powerful speakership of Joseph Cannon, R-Ill.

In Congress at the end of the 1990s, most chairmen were still usually the most senior member of the committee in terms of consecutive service. However, because of the Democratic Caucus reforms of the 1970s and the new powers enjoyed by Speaker Gingrich under House Republicans, this was no longer an ironclad rule in that chamber. In the 104th Congress, the House adopted a new rule limiting committee and subcommittee chairs to a maximum service of three terms. The impact of the provision would be felt beginning in 2001 (provided the GOP held onto the majority). In 1995, Senate Republicans adopted a party rule, effective in 1997, to limit committee chairmen to three terms.

Even with the many changes committee chairmen remained powerful figures on Capitol Hill, especially in the Senate, although they still had to answer to fellow party members. At the full committee level, the chairman calls meetings and establishes agendas, schedules hearings, coordinates work by subcommittees, chairs markup sessions, files committee reports, acts as floor manager, recommends conferees, controls the committee budget, supervises the hiring and firing of staff, and serves as spokesperson for the committee and the chairman's party in the committee's area of expertise. The House allows committees to establish rules that permit the full committee chairmen to issue subpoenas on behalf of the committee in the conduct of an investigation. For example, use of the authority by the chairmen of the Government Reform and Oversight and Education and the Workforce committees in the 105th Congress sparked bitter partisan controversies.

Republican Chairman Bill Archer of Texas, left, confers with ranking Democrat Charles D. Rangel of New York during markup of trade legislation before the House Ways and Means Committee in 1997.

The committee's ranking minority member may also be an influential figure, depending to some degree on the person's relationship with the chairman. Where the two do not get along, or the committee has a partisan tradition, the minority can be marginalized. The ranking member assists in establishing the committee agenda and in managing legislation on the floor for the minority, nominating minority conferees, and controlling the minority staff. The ranking member serves as spokesperson for the committee's minority members. In the Senate, the ranking minority member benefits, as do all senators, from the powerful rules and traditions that require them to be consulted. Chairmen and ranking minority members often sit "ex officio" on all subcommittees of their committee of which they are not regular members.

Committee Assignments

The rules of the House and Senate state that the membership of each house shall elect its members to standing committees. In the House all rules, committees, and assignments from the previous Congress effectively expire on January 3 of each odd-numbered year, and committees cannot function until they are recreated in the rules on opening day and members are reappointed. That sometimes can create an extended hiatus if the next Congress convenes late in January, during which committees and subcommittees cannot meet because they do not yet exist. Sometimes the committees try to get around this by inviting witnesses for "forums" that allows the returning committee members to gather and discuss issues or informally question witnesses as "guests."

Senate committees remain in existence in that "continuing body" with members being carried over from the previous Congress while they await a full complement of new members. The committees retain full power to act.

The committee assignment procedure applies to all members and takes place at the beginning of every Congress and throughout the next two years as vacancies occur. There are numerous changes at the beginning of every Congress, as members switch committee assignments, seeking posts of either greater power or greater personal interest to them. Incumbent members are nearly always permitted to retain their existing assignments unless the party ratio changed substantially in the preceding election or partisan control of the chamber shifted. In the House in 1995 dramatic committee ratio changes were involuntary after Republicans gained control in the 1994 election. Republicans assumed control of all committees and reduced the number of Democratic seats. Both parties also faced the problem of reassigning members who had served on three committees that were abolished. The Democrats were forced to remove several members each from the Appropriations, Ways and Means, and Rules Committees. The caucus guaranteed these members their old seats back as soon as vacancies developed. By the beginning of the 105th Congress in 1997, all of the dislocated members who wanted to had been returned to their old assignments.

Representatives of the two parties agree on committee assignments and party ratios in advance and then submit the committee rosters to their party caucuses and finally the full chambers. The key decisions are made in each party's committee on committees with caucus and floor approval basically pro forma. There are always some adjustments in each new Congress in both chambers to take into account the recent election results, member preferences, and the shifting demands that the ebb and flow of issues place on committee workloads. With some exceptions the method currently in general use was adopted by the Senate in 1846 and by the House in 1911.

In the House nothing in the rules guarantees members any committee assignments. However in practice each member who wants to serve on a committee has at least one assignment. Since committee assignments originate from political parties, members who switch parties automatically lose their seats under House rules. The Republicans, who have benefited from most party switches since the 1970s, have made a point of allowing their new recruits to retain their old posts, usually with seniority, or have given them even more desirable assignments to help them win reelection. (This does not always work; Rep. Greg Laughlin, R-Texas, a 1995 party switcher who was placed on the prestigious Ways and Means Committee, lost the nomination in the subsequent Republican primary.)

Even Rep. Bernard Sanders of Vermont, a self-proclaimed socialist and the House's only independent member since 1991, received two assignments when there was a Democratic majority in the House. When the Republicans controlled the House in 1995, and thereafter, his seats came out of the Democrats' minority allotment. Sanders was even allowed to become the ranking minority member of House subcommittees in the 105th Congress, even though he was not a member of the Democratic Caucus, because no Democratic committee members sought to block him.

Until 1995 the number and types of committees and subcommittees on which any member might serve were left almost entirely to the discretion of the Republican Conference and the Democratic Caucus, which presented privileged resolutions to the House electing committee members. House rules were largely silent and the Rules Committee played no role in this process. As part of its rules changes in the 104th Congress, the Republican majority limited each member to a maximum of two committee and four subcommittee assignments. However almost immediately exceptions started to be made. The party realized that while rules and formulas for organizing committees sounded good when talking about reform, they were less important than the need to retain effective numerical control of committees and satisfy members' political needs.

Only rarely is a committee seat taken away to punish a member. The last attempt to do this involved a House committee at the start of the 98th Congress in 1983. The Democrats attempted to discipline Phil Gramm, D-Texas, for leaking details of their secret caucuses on the Budget Committee in the previous Congress to the Reagan administration. The Steering and Policy Committee did not renominate Gramm to the Budget Committee. He promptly resigned from the House and was reelected as a Republican, and was then returned to the committee. *(See box, Loss of Committee Positions as Punishment, p. 148.)*

In the 104th Congress Appropriations Chairman Bob Livingston, R-La., removed conservative freshman Mark Neumann, R-Wis., from the powerful Defense Appropriations subcommittee because Neumann opposed Republican spending priorities. The outcry from the huge freshman class, however, proved so intense that Speaker Gingrich had to mollify Neumann with an additional committee assignment on the Budget Committee, bumping a senior member off to make room.

THE SENIORITY FACTOR

Both parties in each chamber generally follow seniority in positioning members on committees and in filling vacancies, with new members being ranked at the bottom of their committees. However, starting in 1974 the House Democratic Caucus began the practice of occasionally bypassing seniority if a chairman had been nonresponsive to party policies. *(See box, Benefits of Seniority, p. 150.)*

More recently, some conservative Senate Republicans, once in the majority after the 1994 elections, argued that fealty to party policy should play a more significant role in determining

LOSS OF COMMITTEE POSITIONS AS PUNISHMENT

Stripping a member of his position on a committee as a punishment for political heresy has been resorted to occasionally on Capitol Hill. In 1866, for example, three Senate Republican committee chairmen were dropped to the bottom of their committees for failing to vote with the Radical Republicans on overriding a presidential veto of a civil rights bill.

In 1859 the Senate Democratic Caucus removed Stephen A. Douglas, D-Ill., from the chairmanship of the Committee on Territories because he refused to go along with President James Buchanan and the southern wing of the party on the question of slavery in the territories.

In 1923 Sen. Albert B. Cummins, R-Iowa, lost his chairmanship of the Interstate Commerce Committee in a fight with the Progressive wing of his party. But the next-ranking Republican, Sen. Robert M. La Follette, R-Wis., was then passed over because of his unpopularity with the regulars of the party, and the chairmanship was given to the ranking Democrat, Ellison D. Smith, D-S.C.

Members of the Progressive wing of the Republican Party in the House also were denied the fruits of seniority in this period after they put up their own candidate for Speaker in 1925. Two of their leaders were ousted from their committee chairmanships for having campaigned as La Follette Progressives and nine GOP members from the Wisconsin delegation who voted with the insurgents' candidate for Speaker were either dropped to the bottom rank on their committees or moved to less prestigious committees. La Follette had been the Progressive Party's candidate for president in 1924.

In 1965 and 1969 the House Democratic Caucus dropped three southern Democrats to the bottom of their committees because two of them had campaigned for presidential candidate Sen. Barry Goldwater, R-Ariz., in 1964 and the other for former Alabama governor George C. Wallace (American Independent) in 1968.

Another southern Democrat who had supported Goldwater in 1964, Sen. Strom Thurmond, S.C., avoided party discipline by switching to the Republican Party. Republicans rewarded him by allowing him to carry over his seniority rights to the GOP side of his committees.

In 1983 House Democrats stripped conservative Rep. Phil Gramm of Texas of his seat on the Budget Committee because of his two-year collaboration with the White House in supporting President Ronald Reagan's budget. Gramm's apostasy was especially aggravating to the Democratic leadership because he had been placed on the committee with the strong support of Majority Leader Jim Wright, D-Tex., after Gramm had given assurances that he would be a team player. Gramm resigned from Congress, switched to the Republican Party, and won his seat back in a special election. And then the Republicans put him right back on the Budget Committee.

In 1995, some conservative Senate Republicans advocated stripping Sen. Mark O. Hatfield, R-Ore., of his chairmanship of the Appropriations Committee because he had cast the lone Republican—and deciding—vote which defeated a balanced budget amendment to the Constitution. The amendment was a major element in the new Republican majority's legislative agenda and had earlier passed the House for the first time. After debate in the Republican Conference, no action was taken against Hatfield. He retained the chairmanship, but announced shortly thereafter that he would not seek reelection.

chairmanships. The criticism was aimed at Senate Appropriations Committee Chairman Mark Hatfield, R-Ore., in 1995 after he cast the deciding—and only—Republican vote against a balanced budget constitutional amendment on the Senate floor, a vote that resulted in defeat of the long-cherished GOP proposal. The Republican Conference declined to discipline Hatfield.

Sometimes arcane questions of congressional seniority can even play a role in presidential politics. In 1995, it was known that Sen. Phil Gramm, R-Texas., a candidate for the party's presidential nomination, wanted an open seat on the prestigious Finance Committee. However, the front-runner, Majority Leader Bob Dole, R-Kan., reportedly urged more senior senators to claim available seats to block Gramm. Since Republican senators can claim such posts in order of seniority, Gramm was, at least momentarily, stymied. He did finally gain a seat on the committee later in the Congress.

Members who stay on the same committee from one Congress to another are given the same seniority ranking they had in the previous Congress unless a death, resignation, or retirement on the committee allows them to move up a notch. But if members, even senior members, transfer from one committee to another they are ranked at the bottom in seniority on their new committees. There are exceptions to these rules in unusual circumstances. The five Democratic House members and the two Democratic senators who switched to the Republican Party in 1995 were given some seniority on their new committee assignments or carried their existing seniority with them on the same committee. This helped newly minted Republican Senators Ben Nighthorse Campbell of Colorado and Richard Shelby of Alabama move through the ranks so quickly that they found themselves committee chairmen as the 105th Congress began.

As a rule members of Congress remain on their major committees throughout their careers, gradually working their way up in seniority. Those who do wish to switch, usually to one of the exclusive committees in the House (Appropriations, Commerce, Rules, Ways and Means) or the "Super A" committees in the Senate (Armed Services, Appropriations, Finance, Foreign Relations) make the effort very early in their careers before they accumulate too much seniority on their original assignments and lose the incentive to leave. If a member continues to be reelected and does not have an equally successful, ambitious, and younger colleague ahead of him or her on the committee roster, that member usually can expect to become a chairman or ranking minority member.

Changes in Democratic Caucus rules in the House beginning during the 1970s were therefore extraordinarily controversial, not only because they allowed far greater ease in challenging the reelection of chairmen but because in certain circumstances a junior member who challenged a chairman successfully could jump over others less daring. In effect the defeat of a chairman by the right opponent at a particular time could end not only the career of the ousted chairman but the long-term futures of other members who might be bypassed. The most dramatic instance of this occurred when seventh-ranking Les Aspin, D-Wis., ousted Chairman Melvin Price, D-Ill., of the Armed Services Committee in 1984. Price lost, 118–121, on the first up-down vote, which then opened the process for other candidates to run against each other. Aspin then defeated second-ranking Charles E. Bennett, D-Fla., also effectively jumping over four other senior, and older, Democrats who either would not contest the chairmanship because they respected the seniority tradition and backed Bennett or could not because they did not have the political strength to compete. If Aspin had not run and won at that time, it is possible that some of these members would have achieved the chairmanship through seniority in later years.

A similar example occurred in 1994 when David Obey, D-Wis., ranked fifth on the Appropriations Committee, won a contest over Neal Smith of Iowa, the third-ranking Democrat. Chairman William H. Natcher, D-Ky., and the second-ranking Democrat, former Chairman Jamie L. Whitten, Miss., had been incapacitated by illness. Smith's defeat was used by his Republican opponent as a sign of his ineffectiveness and he lost his bid for reelection. In addition the elderly Sidney Yates of Illinois, ranked fourth, was effectively removed from any chance of succession.

Many factors are involved in the decisions of the party leadership in assigning new members to committees, but once the member has the seat seniority remains the most important single factor in determining his or her advancement on that committee.

In the Senate the Democratic committee roster is drawn up by the Democratic Steering Committee, whose chairman and members are appointed by the party leader. The Senate Republican committee roster is drawn up by the Republican Committee on Committees, which is appointed by the chairman of the Republican Conference. Republican Party leaders are ex officio members.

The committee assignment process in the House, with 435 members, four delegates, and a resident commissioner involved, can be quite complex in itself and is made more so by mechanisms to ensure that various factions are fairly represented. The Democrats have had basically the same system since 1974. The Republicans have used different methods but by the mid-1990s had a system that is similar in many respects.

The Democratic committee roster is drawn up by the party's Steering Committee, a far larger body than its Republican counterpart. The Steering Committee is chaired by the minority leader (or Speaker, if in the majority). It also consists of the whip, caucus chairman, caucus vice chairman, chairman of the Democratic Congressional Campaign Committee, a cochairman of the Steering Committee, two vice chairmen of the Steering Committee, four chief deputy whips, a freshman class representative, twelve members appointed from equal regions, ten members appointed by the leader (or Speaker), and the ranking members of the Appropriations, Budget, Commerce, Rules and Ways and Means committees. The number of leadership-appointed members has increased steadily. Each member has only one vote. (From 1911 until 1974 Democratic committee assignments were made by the Democratic members of the Ways and Means Committee.) An exception applies to the Democratic members of the Rules and House Oversight Committees. In 1974, the caucus rules gave the Speaker (or minority leader, after the 1994 elections) the power to nominate all party members of Rules. House Oversight was included under this provision in 1994. Nominations to all standing committees are subject to ratification by the caucus.

Republican committee nominations in the House are determined by the party's Steering Committee, which is chaired by the Speaker. In the 105th Congress it also consisted of the floor ("majority") leader, whip, conference chair, Policy Committee chair, National Republican Congressional Committee (campaign committee) chair in the 105th Congress and his predecessor in the 104th, the chairmen of the Appropriations, Budget, Rules, and Ways and Means committees, nine members elected from geographic regions, two members of the 104th freshman class, and one from the 105th.

The two parties' systems diverge as the Republicans allocate additional voting strength to the Speaker and floor leader and make allowances for the needs of small states. (The Democrats' approach was to allow the party leader to appoint additional members to the committee.) The Speaker receives five votes and the floor leader two. The Speaker can give away up to two of his votes to other members he may appoint to the committee; Gingrich gave these to the vice chair and secretary of the Republican conference. If members elected to represent the nine regions come from states that have four or more Republican members, a "small state" group will be triggered to elect a member to Steering. The "small state" group will be comprised of states that have three or fewer Republican members.

The Rules Committee and House Oversight are again exceptions. GOP members of those committees are nominated by the Speaker (or minority leader, as the case may be).

Once the committee rosters are approved by the two parties in each chamber, they are incorporated in resolutions and put to votes before the full chambers. With approval usually automatic the votes merely formalize recommendations by the two parties and the party ratios previously agreed upon by the leadership. Neither party interferes with the individual committee assignments made by the other; to attempt to do so would be a serious violation of comity. However, the minority may not attempt to exceed the allotment of seats on any committee

BENEFITS OF SENIORITY

There are three kinds of "seniority" in Congress:

- Seniority within the chamber among the entire House or Senate membership
- Seniority within a political party in the chamber
- Seniority on a committee

The second and third are linked because members are chosen for service on committees by the political parties and listed in order of seniority only with others from the same party. Members elected to a committee at the same time are then ranked in order of their full chamber seniority.

Seniority within the House and Senate as a whole is of limited importance but it helps determine who has access to the most desirable office space and a few other privileges. Representatives and senators choose their offices by order of chamber seniority. Senior members also have the right to claim a limited number of suites in the Capitol building itself as private "hideaways" for their personal use, which provides extra space and reduces the need to return to their regular offices after voting.

SENATE SENIORITY

The most senior member of the majority party in the Senate is elected automatically to the virtually powerless office of president pro tempore, a position mentioned in the Constitution. The president pro tempore has the right to preside in the absence of the president of the Senate (the vice president of the United States) and may often be from the opposite party as the vice president. However this senator may wield substantial influence in another role because his longevity would almost certainly also make him chairman of a committee. In the 105th Congress, president pro tempore Strom Thurmond, R-S.C., chaired the Armed Services Committee. His Democratic predecessor was Sen. Robert C. Byrd, D-W.Va., who was simultaneously Appropriations Committee chairman and before that a former majority and minority leader. By law the president pro tempore is next in the line of succession to the presidency after the Speaker of the House.

The most important leadership positions in Congress—Speaker and Majority Leader of the Senate—have never been filled on the basis of seniority. *(The Seniority System, p. 124.)*

The seniority system has its greatest impact within each political party for determining rank on committees.

Senators and representatives are given a seniority ranking vis-à-vis party colleagues in their chamber at the beginning of each two-year term of Congress.

Senate rank generally is determined according to the official date of the beginning of a member's service, which is January 3 except in the case of a new member sworn in after Congress is in session. For those elected or appointed to fill unexpired terms the date of appointment, certification, or swearing-in, determines the senator's rank.

When senators are sworn in on the same date custom decrees that those with prior political experience take precedence. Counted as political experience, in order of importance, are senatorial, House, and gubernatorial service. In the past a senator who was retiring or was defeated for reelection occasionally left office a few days before the end of his term, allowing his successor to be appointed and thereby gain a few days' seniority over other freshman senators. In 1980, however, Senate Republicans and Democrats, acting separately, eliminated the principal advantages of this practice. Members appointed to fill out the remaining days of their predecessors' terms no longer were given an edge in obtaining their choice of committee assignments.

If all other factors are equal, senators are ranked by the population of their state in determining seniority. Thus, the lowest ranking member in the 105th Congress was Mike Enzi, R-Wyo., who had no previous congressional or gubernatorial service when he took office in 1997, and who represented the nation's smallest state.

Within each state delegation in the Senate the member who as-

awarded to it by the majority or its assignment resolution would be rejected on the floor. On several occasions House Republicans, when in the minority, forced votes on Democratic committee assignments to protest what they regarded as excessively advantageous majority committee ratios on some committees. In 1995 the Democrats responded in kind by forcing a vote on the assignment of party-switcher Greg Laughlin, R-Texas, to the Ways and Means Committee, which further expanded the majority's ratio there from that set at the beginning of the 104th Congress. In 1997, the Republicans moved to table (kill) a Democratic committee assignment resolution when they believed the minority was attempting to increase its strength on a committee without permission, but after brief discussion the misunderstanding was cleared up and an embarrassing vote avoided.

PLUM ASSIGNMENTS

In both chambers committee assignments are extremely important to members. The Senate, with less political selection procedures and proportionately more plum seats than the House, tends to see less maneuvering, lobbying, and horse-trading for desired committee slots. There are fewer members competing for influence and looser floor rules than in the House. Each senator therefore has a greater chance to affect legislation of all stripes.

In the House influence often is closely related to the committee or committees on which a member serves. Moreover assignment to a powerful committee virtually guarantees large campaign contributions.

Just wanting to be on a committee is not enough. In most cases members have to fight for assignments to the best comsumed office first, regardless of party, is always referred to as "the senior senator from (state)" while the other is "the junior senator."

HOUSE SENIORITY

In the House being the most senior member carries no formal status although by custom the member with the longest period of consecutive service, irrespective of party, administers the oath of office to the Speaker when a new Congress convenes. In the 105th Congress that was Rep. John D. Dingell, D-Mich. Rep. Sidney Yates, D-Ill., had served longer than Dingell but his service was not consecutive. The most senior member from each state may sometimes be referred to as the "dean of the delegation," regardless of party, and in some state delegations may preside over delegation meetings if any are held.

Rank in the House generally is determined by the official date of the beginning of a member's service, January 3, except when a representative is elected to fill a vacancy. In such cases the date of election determines the rank. When members enter the House on the same date they are ranked in order of consecutive terms of House service. Any former members returning to the House are ranked above other freshmen, starting with those with the most previous terms of service. Experience as a senator or governor is disregarded.

These factors are taken into account when committee assignments are made by each party to decide the order of seniority in which members will rank along with others of their party on each committee.

Members chosen to fill an open seat on a committee always rank below those who served in the previous Congress and are being reappointed except in very unusual circumstances. For example, several Democratic members who switched to the Republican Party in the 104th Congress received seniority while remaining on the same committee or in moving to a new one. Often when several vacancies on a committee are being filled by each party's Steering Committee at the same time, a junior member may be chosen before a more senior member wins a seat. In the committee roster the member with more House seniority would nonetheless be ranked ahead of the other.

Other procedures have evolved to deal with members who have equal seniority in the House. If several members of equal seniority win seats on the same committee at the same time the order they are ranked could have significant consequences decades later. In 1993 Rep. Norman Y. Mineta, D-Calif., was nominated to fill the vacant chairmanship of the Public Works and Transportation Committee because he had been ranked first on the Democratic committee list by lot ahead of Rep. James L. Oberstar, D-Minn., in 1975 when both were freshmen. At that time Oberstar had actually been selected first by the Steering Committee. Twenty years later the Democratic Caucus changed the rule so that, in cases such as this, members of equal seniority would be ranked in the order they were selected in the Steering Committee.

Neither party gives formal recognition to prior service on a committee as a factor in seniority. In the 105th Congress, however, Republicans gave freshman Rep. Bob Smith, R-Ore., not only seniority but the chairmanship of the Agriculture Committee. Smith, who had retired from the House and the committee in 1995, was promised the chairmanship if he agreed to return and ensure continued GOP control of the House seat after his one-term successor became embroiled in scandal. With his mission accomplished Smith declined to run again in 1998. Democrats also rewarded a former member who was returning to the House, Rep. David Price, N.C., (1987–1995, 1997–), who wanted back the Appropriations Committee seat he had lost with his election defeat. While the Democratic Caucus in the 104th Congress had agreed to eventually restore seats to incumbents ousted from their committees by party ratio changes, Price did not qualify because he was not a member in that Congress. Nonetheless, on Appropriations he was ranked ahead of Rep. Chet Edwards, D-Texas, a sitting member who was switching committee assignments to join Appropriations.

mittees. In each chamber a few committees are considered most powerful and difficult to get on. But congressional leaders often have to go looking for "volunteers" to serve on less attractive panels.

Traditionally the premier House committees sought by representatives have been Appropriations, Rules, and Ways and Means, although the attraction of Rules under the Democrats was reduced after its members were nominated directly by the Speaker and lost much of their power to operate and vote independently. In the 1980s members also avidly sought seats on Budget and Energy and Commerce (now simply Commerce). In the 1990s Public Works and Transportation (now Transportation and Infrastructure), often either desired or reviled by members for its traditional "pork barrel" programs, regained popularity so quickly that there were jokes that the public seats in the committee room would have to be removed to accommodate all of the new members.

In the Senate the most popular committees traditionally have been Appropriations and Finance. Both the Budget Committee and Armed Services have also been in demand. Foreign Relations, once considered highly prestigious, fell steadily in influence and desirability after the defeat of Chairman J. William Fulbright, D-Ark., in 1974 because of a series of weak chairmen and its continuing inability to pass major authorization bills on the floor. After Republicans took control in 1995 activist conservative Chairman Jesse Helms, R-N.C., was credited with helping to revive the committee's importance.

While other panels wax and wane, Appropriations, Finance, and Ways and Means have never been wholly eclipsed because they control the flow of money into and out of federal coffers.

Seniority still plays a major role in the power structure of both houses of Congress. In 1998 by virtue of his seniority, Strom Thurmond, R-S.C., was president pro tempore of the Senate and chairman of the Armed Services Committee.

In the 1980s and 1990s these taxing and spending committees were thrust to the center of action more than ever before by Congress's increasing tendency to pile most of its legislative work onto a handful of fiscal measures.

Committee Procedures

Committee procedures are regulated by Senate and House rules that incorporate many of the provisions in the Legislative Reorganization Acts of 1946 and 1970 and other measures. In many cases these rules serve to protect minority rights and the rights of witnesses at committee hearings.

One of the basic goals of the 1946 act was to standardize committee procedures in regard to holding regular meeting days, keeping committee records and votes, reporting legislation, requiring a majority of committee members to be in attendance as a condition of transacting committee business, and following set procedures during hearings.

The 1946 rules were not uniformly observed by all committees. The continuing dissatisfaction with committee operations led in the 1970 reorganization act to further efforts to reform committee procedures, particularly to make them more democratic and accountable to the membership and the public. The House has more restrictive provisions than the Senate but the majority still has broad flexibility in running a committee's business.

Each Senate and House committee is required to establish and publish rules of procedure. These rules have stipulated that each chamber's standing committees must fix regular meeting days, although the rules authorize the chairman to call additional meetings.

The rules also must contain procedures under which a committee majority may call a meeting if the chairman fails to do so even though use of such a procedure would be a serious affront to a chairman. House rules also allow a committee majority using this process to place items of its choosing on the agenda.

An attempt to undercut a chairman's authority over committee meetings actually was made in the Senate Foreign Relations Committee in 1997 after Chairman Jesse Helms, R-N.C. declared his refusal to hold a hearing on the nomination by President Clinton of Gov. William Weld, R-Mass., to be ambassador to Mexico. Helms was adamantly opposed to the liberal Weld, even though he was a fellow Republican, for a variety of philosophical reasons. It appeared likely that a majority of both the committee and the Senate would confirm Weld if allowed to vote. A committee majority was able to force Helms to convene a meeting but was unable to take control of the agenda away from him. With the Senate parliamentarian sitting near him, Helms allowed no debate on the Weld nomination and spent most of the meeting denouncing his opponents. The episode illustrated how little Senate traditions have changed despite reforms of the rules and the unwillingness of senators to push powerful colleagues too far.

Committees were required by the 1970 act to keep transcripts of their meetings and to make public all roll-call votes. In the House the rules require that information about committee votes be made available to the public at the committees' offices. The committees are directed to provide a description of each amendment, motion, order, or "other proposition" voted on, the name of each committee member voting for or against the issue, whether the vote was by proxy or in person, and the names of those present but not voting. The rules also require that the results of all votes to report legislation be published in the committee reports. In 1995 the rules were further amended to require that on all votes conducted in a committee markup on a reported bill or other matter reported to the House the report contain the number of votes cast for or against and how individual members voted.

In the Senate the rules are less specific. They require that a committee's report on a bill include the results of roll-call votes on "any measure or any amendment thereto" unless the results have been announced previously by the committee. Senate rules require that in reporting roll-call votes the position of each voting member is to be disclosed.

The rules stipulate that it is the chairman's "duty" to see to it that legislation approved by his or her committee is reported. And there are procedures by which a committee majority may force a bill out of committee if the chairman refuses to bring it up for consideration or to report it after the committee has acted favorably. The rules prohibit a committee from reporting any measure unless a majority of its members are actually present. Members were allowed time to file supplemental and minority views for inclusion in committee reports but in the House Republicans restricted the minority's long-standing rights to have three full days following the vote on reporting a bill to submit them. In 1997 the rule was amended to reduce the time by counting the day in which the committee ordered a bill reported as the first day.

House rules require committees and subcommittees to announce hearings at least one week in advance unless the chairman and ranking minority member jointly or the committee itself by vote sets a shorter period. A Republican proposal to give this power to the chairman alone was successfully resisted by the minority in 1995. In most circumstances committees are required to conduct meetings and hearings in open session and to require witnesses to file written statements in advance. The rules allow minority party members to call witnesses during at least one day of hearings on a subject.

Jurisdictional Conflicts

Most bill referrals to committees are routine matters handled by the parliamentarians of each chamber. Committee jurisdictions outlined in each chamber's rules as well as precedents and public laws normally dictate where a bill is sent. But sometimes things are not quite so clear-cut.

Jurisdictional disputes between and among committees have been evident since the inception of the standing committee system. The Legislative Reorganization Act of 1946 attempted to eliminate the problem by defining each committee's jurisdiction in detail. But the 1946 act was not able to eliminate the problem.

As early as 1947 a fight broke out in the Senate over referral of the controversial armed forces unification bill. In the House the measure had been handled by the Committee on Executive Expenditures (now the Government Reform and Oversight Committee), which had jurisdiction over all proposals for government reorganization. But in a Senate floor vote that chamber's Armed Services Committee successfully challenged the claim of the Expenditures Committee (now the Governmental Affairs Committee) to jurisdiction over the bill.

Such problems have continued to arise because the complexities of modern legislative proposals sometimes make it impossible to define jurisdictional boundaries precisely.

In the House the problem has been aggravated by a failure to restructure the committee system to meet new developments and national problems. The problem of conflicting and overlapping jurisdictions became acutely obvious in the 1970s as Congress attempted to formulate a coherent energy policy. When President Jimmy Carter in 1977 submitted his comprehensive national energy program the impending jurisdictional tangle forced Speaker Thomas P. "Tip" O'Neill Jr., D-Mass., to establish an ad hoc energy committee to review the work of five House committees and to guide energy legislation through the House. (An attempt to consolidate energy responsibilities in one committee as the Senate had done in 1977 was soundly defeated in the House in 1980.)

Occasionally when the opportunity arises a bill is drafted in such a way that it will be referred to a committee favorable to it. The 1963 civil rights bill for example was worded somewhat differently in each chamber so that it would be referred to the Judiciary Committee in the House and the Commerce Committee in the Senate. Both panels were chaired by strong proponents of the legislation while the chairmen of the House Interstate and Foreign Commerce Committee (now the Commerce Committee) and the Senate Judiciary Committee were opposed to the legislation. Congressional expert Oleszek noted that "careful drafting therefore coupled with favorable referral decisions in the House and Senate prevented the bill from being bogged down in hostile committees."[23]

Most bills, however, are subject to strict jurisdictional interpretation and rarely open to the legerdemain given the 1963 civil rights bill or the special handling the Speaker was able to give the 1977 energy bill. Oleszek observes:

> Committees guard their jurisdictional turfs closely and the parliamentarians know and follow precedents. Only instances of genuine jurisdictional ambiguity provide opportunities for the legislative draftsman and referral options for the Speaker and the presiding officer of the Senate to bypass one committee in favor of another.[24]

MULTIPLE REFERRAL

The practice of multiple referral has been permitted in the Senate by unanimous consent although it is used less frequently there than in the House, which did not permit the practice until the rules were amended in 1975. In that year the Speaker was permitted to refer a bill to more than one committee.

There were three types of multiple referrals: joint, when several committees consider a bill at the same time; sequential, when a bill is referred first to one committee, then to another, and so on; and split, when parts of a bill are referred to different committees. The most common method was joint referral; split referral was the least used. The Speaker was also given the authority subject to House approval to create an ad hoc committee to consider legislation when there were overlapping jurisdictions.

In 1977 the Speaker was permitted to impose reporting deadlines on the first committee or committees to which a bill was referred. In 1981 Speaker O'Neill announced that in making multiple referrals he would consider not only the content of the original bill but also amendments proposed by the reporting committee. And in 1983 the Speaker announced that he had the authority to designate a primary committee on jointly referred bills and impose time limits on other committees after the primary committee issued its report.

Since 1975 the number of multiple referrals grew significantly in the House and so did the importance of multiply referred bills. "In one form or another multiple referral is now employed on a multitude of significant legislation and exists as a prominent feature of congressional operations," wrote Melissa P. Collie and Joseph Cooper.[25]

Collie and Cooper interpreted the arrival of multiple referral in the House "as a signal that committee turf is no longer what it has been cracked up to be." They contend that legislators have

HOUSE, SENATE RULES GOVERNING COMPOSITION OF COMMITTEE MEMBERSHIP

Because Republicans were in the majority in both houses in the 105th Congress (1997–1999), they chose all committee and subcommittee chairmen, while the Democrats selected ranking minority members. House practices are determined by the rules of the Republican Conference and Democratic Caucus, although the rules of the House stipulate certain requirements. The Senate guidelines are governed by the chamber's standing rules, with some party regulations. The guidelines below covers the principal assignment practices, but not every possible rule, contingency, or exception.

HOUSE REPUBLICANS

The Republicans, through their conference, divide the House committees into two categories: exclusive and nonexclusive. Exclusive committees are Appropriations; Commerce; Rules; and Ways and Means. Nonexclusive committees are almost everything else: Agriculture; National Security; Banking and Financial Services; Education and the Workforce; International Relations; Judiciary; Transportation and Infrastructure; Budget; Government Reform and Oversight; House Oversight; Resources; Science; Small Business; and Veterans' Affairs.

The Committee on Standards of Official Conduct is not classified and members may serve on it, as well as House Oversight, irrespective of their other committee assignments. This practice technically violates a House rule sponsored by Republicans in the 104th Congress that limited all members to service on no more than two standing committees. In order to ensure that members serve on these less desirable, internal housekeeping panels, the Republicans got around the House rule by simply having the House vote to approve the additional committee assignments.

Republicans serving on an exclusive committee may not serve on any other standing committee, with the exception of the Budget Committee (which is required by House rules to have members from the Appropriations Committee and Ways and Means Committee), House Oversight, and Standards. GOP membership of the Budget Committee includes three members each from the Appropriations Committee and the Ways and Means Committee as well as one leadership member appointed by the minority leader. (Other GOP Budget members include one member appointed by the Republican leadership.)

Chairmen of full committees are recommended by the Steering Committee without regard to seniority and are voted on by secret ballot of the conference. However, the Speaker nominates the chairman and other Republican members of the Rules and House Oversight Committees, subject to conference approval. If any nominee is rejected by the conference, the Steering Committee, or Speaker, as the case may be, must make a new nomination until one is approved. Development of procedures for the selection of Republican subcommittee chairmen and members is at the discretion of the chairman of a committee, unless a majority of the GOP members of the full committee disapproves.

No Republican may serve as the chairman of more than one standing committee or subcommittee of a standing committee, although chairmen of the Standards and House Oversight Committees are exempt from the restriction. The chairman of the Appropriations Committee is not permitted to head a subcommittee of that committee, and a subcommittee chairman of a standing committee may also chair a subcommittee of the Permanent Select Committee on Intelligence. A 1995 House rules change limits committee and subcommittee chairmen to three terms in these positions.

HOUSE DEMOCRATS

The rules of the Democratic Caucus have many similarities to the House Republican Conference procedures but are more complex. The same committees are classified as exclusive or nonexclusive. Members assigned to an exclusive committee may be on no other standing committee, but Budget, House Oversight, and Standards are again the exceptions. Two Democrats each from Appropriations Committee and Ways and Means Committee serve on the Budget Committee, as well as one leadership member appointed by the minority leader. (When the Democrats controlled the House, the majority leader always occupied this slot.)

Minority members of the Permanent Select Committee on Intelligence and joint committees are selected by the minority leader and then appointed by the Speaker.

No Democrat may serve on more than two nonexclusive committees, with exceptions allowed for House Oversight and also for Standards, which, as noted, is outside the classifications.

Democrats are nominated to serve on most committees by the Steering Committee, subject to caucus approval. Members of the Rules and House Oversight Committees are nominated by the minority leader subject to Democratic Caucus approval.

The rules of the caucus are more restrictive than those of the House regarding service on the Budget Committee. Democratic Budget Committee members may serve for only three terms out of every five consecutive terms, instead of the four-of-six terms permitted in House rules and used by Republicans. Exceptions to this limitation include the Democratic leadership–designated member of the Budget Committee, who may stay indefinitely, as well as the ranking minority member, who may stay on for an additional two years, if required, in order to serve a second term in that position.

Democrats are limited to one full committee ranking minority member position. They may not simultaneously rank on another full, select, permanent select, special, ad hoc, or joint committee. Ranking minority members of a standing committee may not rank on any subcommittee, but the ranking members of the House Oversight and Standards Committee are exempted. The ranking member of the Appropriations Committee may rank on a subcommittee of that committee. No Democrat may rank on more than one subcommittee of a committee or select committee with legislative jurisdiction. Ranking minority members of the following nonexclusive committees, which were previously classified as "major committees" prior to a 1995 rules change, may not serve on any other committee: Agriculture, Banking and Financial Services, Education and the Workforce, International Relations, Judiciary, National Security, and Transportation and Infrastructure.

Most nominations for ranking minority members are made by the Steering Committee and without regard to seniority, though it is extremely rare for Steering to take the initiative to reject an incumbent. (It most recently did so in the 105th Congress, nominating John LaFalce of New York as ranking minority member of the Banking Committee instead of incumbent Henry B. Gonzalez of Texas. Gonzalez then challenged him before the caucus. With a third candidate also in the race, Gonzalez finished first on the initial ballot, but lacked a majority. LaFalce then withdrew and Gonzalez was confirmed for another term. The caucus votes on all nominations individually by secret ballot.)

Exceptions to the practice of Steering Committee nominations are the Rules Committee and House Oversight ranking members, who are nominated by the minority leader, and the ranking member of the Budget Committee, who is selected from among members choosing to run for the position on the floor of the caucus.

Subcommittee ranking members of the Appropriations Committee also are voted on by secret ballot in the party caucus. If an Appropriations subcommittee ranking member is deposed, his or her replacement must come from among the members of that subcommittee. The committee caucus may use subcommittee seniority as the criterion in nominating candidates for subcommittee chairmen. Beginning with the 102nd Congress (1991–1993), subcommittee ranking members of the Ways and Means Committee also were elected by the Democratic Caucus.

On other committees, ranking subcommittee members are elected by the Democrats on their committee. (Special rules allow such choices to be brought before the full caucus for a vote if they are especially controversial, but this has never been done.) Committee members are entitled to bid for subcommittee ranking memberships in the order of their seniority on the full committee, with members choosing which subcommittee they would bid for, and an up-or-down vote is then held on that member's candidacy. If a candidacy is rejected, under a 1995 rules change the next member in order of committee seniority can bid for any open subcommittee ranking post; before the change, the committee had to fill the post selected by the rejected candidate before moving on.

SENATE REPUBLICANS AND DEMOCRATS

The Senate divides its committees into "major" and "minor" committees in its Rule XXV—although those words are not actually used in the rule. Major committees are Agriculture, Nutrition, and Forestry; Appropriations; Armed Services; Banking, Housing, and Urban Affairs; Commerce, Science, and Transportation; Energy and Natural Resources; Environment and Public Works; Finance; Foreign Relations; Governmental Affairs; Judiciary; and Labor and Human Resources. Minor committees are Budget; Rules and Administration; Veterans' Affairs; Small Business; Aging; Intelligence; and Joint Economic. Committees on Ethics, Indian Affairs, and the Joint Committee on Taxation are also considered minor committees but do not count toward the service limits outlined in the paragraph below, nor does membership on any joint committee that a senator is required by law to serve on.

Senate rules also regulate both service and chairmanships, but chamber rules may be supplemented or superseded by party rules, sometimes resulting in variations in practice from one Congress to the next. Exceptions are also granted to individual senators from various rules.

Senators sit on two major committees and may serve on one minor committee. Party practices limit senators to service on only one of the so-called elite or "Super A" committee—Appropriations, Armed Services, Finance, and Foreign Relations, although there have been exceptions. Senators are limited to membership on three subcommittees of each major committee on which they serve (the Appropriations Committee is exempt from the limit) and on two subcommittees of each of their minor committees. The chairman or ranking minority member of a committee may serve as an ex officio member without a vote on any subcommittee of that committee. There are numerous exceptions to these rules that protect senators who would have been in violation at the time they took effect. By agreement of the majority and minority leaders, the membership of a committee may be temporarily increased above the size limits set by the rules—but by no more than two members—in order to maintain majority party control, and any senator serving on a committee for this purpose would be allowed to serve on three major committees.

Both parties guarantee their members one seat on a major committee before any member receives a second top assignment.

The Senate requires that membership on the Select Intelligence Committee be rotated. No senator may serve on the committee for more than eight successive years.

A senator generally may serve as chairman or ranking minority member of only one standing, select, special, or joint committee, though again there may be exceptions, especially with regard to service on joint committees. A Republican Conference rule effective in 1997 limits GOP senators to no more than three Congresses of service as a committee chairman.

Under Senate rules, the chairman of a major committee may serve as chairman of only one subcommittee among all of his or her major committees and one subcommittee of his or her minor committee. The chairman of a minor committee may not serve as chairman of any subcommittee on that committee; he or she may chair one subcommittee of each of his or her major committees. A senator who does not otherwise chair a committee may chair only one subcommittee of each committee on which he or she serves.

The Senate Republican Conference's Committee on Committees makes committee assignments on major committees and the Rules and Administration Committee. Other assignments are made by the majority leader. Members of each Senate committee elect the chairmen of their committee, subject to the approval of the Republican Conference. Votes in the Committee on Committees and in the conference are by secret ballot.

Senate Democratic committee assignments and nominations for ranking minority members are made by the Steering Committee and circulated to all Senate Democrats. A party rule adopted in 1975 provides for a secret ballot vote on an individual nominee for chairman (or ranking member) if requested by 20 percent of the Senate's Democrats.

surrendered their exclusive autonomy over legislation for access to all legislation to which they have claims.[26]

The growth of multiple referrals in the House affected key aspects of the legislative process including the Speaker's prerogatives, the work of the Rules Committee, floor proceedings, and relations with the executive branch and interest groups. It encouraged members, committees, and staff aides to negotiate with one another rather than acting separately as traditionally done, according to scholars Roger Davidson, Oleszek, and Thomas Kephart. "More importantly, the procedure at the same time has greatly augmented the powers of the Speaker and the Rules Committee, by strengthening their role in centralizing and coordinating the House's workload. That may well be the most profound effect of the multiple-referral procedure."[27] However these changes came with a price of greater complexity in the legislative process as bills had to be tracked through multiple locations and battles among committees over jurisdiction and the type of referrals they would receive, creating controversies that the Speaker was often called upon to mediate.

When Republicans assumed control of the House they instituted changes intended to streamline the process and reduce such distractions.

Joint referrals were replaced in 1995 in the House by a procedure that required the Speaker in cases in which more than one committee had a jurisdictional claim to designate a committee as the "primary" committee for consideration. Other committees could be granted secondary or sequential referrals with time limits at the Speaker's discretion. This is sometimes called "additional initial referral," perhaps to ease the loss of status by the other committees involved. The change was not radical inasmuch as the Speaker already had the power to designate a committee as the primary panel in cases of multiple referrals even though he rarely did so. The change did have the effect of simplifying the referral process and placing greater responsibility in the primary committees. It also reduced the intense competition among committees for referrals that sometimes had produced distracting jurisdictional wars among chairmen and staff during the period of Democratic rule, with the Speaker in the middle.

SPENDING RIVALS

The relationships between the Appropriations and legislative committees traditionally have provided striking illustrations of intercommittee rivalries. Legislative committees handle bills authorizing funds but usually only the Appropriations committees are permitted to consider the actual spending permitted for federal agencies and programs. There are exceptions for certain instances of "direct spending" approved by legislative committees such as entitlement programs authorized by permanent law.

The Appropriations committees are theoretically barred by the standing rules from inserting legislative provisions in their appropriations bills but they habitually do so, often out of necessity. Indeed, while the legislative committees often grumble about the usurpation of their authority by the appropriators, the committees also often cooperate because legislative committees must rely on the appropriations process to include provisions regulating the programs they administer if the normal authorization bills cannot be enacted.

The creation of the House and Senate Budget committees in 1974 added yet another dimension to committee rivalries. The new committees were charged with the task of preparing two congressional budget resolutions (later reduced to only one when the original procedure proved impractical) setting out goals for spending and revenues in the next fiscal year. They also were to monitor the revenue and spending actions of the House and Senate.

With the country's increasing preoccupation with budget deficits in the 1980s the power relationships among these various committees started to shift. The authorizing committees went from proposing various new programs to a fallback position of defending existing ones. "Squeezed between the budget resolution and appropriations stages there is little time left for debating the recommendations of the authorization committees," Oleszek observes. "As a result these panels have lost influence to the Appropriations and Budget committees."[28]

The Appropriations committees also benefited in the 1980s from Congress's increasing reliance on omnibus continuing appropriations resolutions that were used when legislators almost routinely failed to pass some or all of the individual appropriations bills. These bills in the 1980s and 1990s became vehicles for authorizing legislation. As a result, Deering and Smith note:

> ... appropriators gained a voice in shaping legislation that they otherwise would not have had, particularly in conference. And the continuing resolutions gave appropriators—as well as other members through appeals to appropriators and through floor amendments—an opportunity to pursue legislative matters without the consent and cooperation of the affected authorizing committee.[29]

Yet the Appropriations committees also lost influence. They had to share power with party and budget leaders in negotiating budget resolutions and then had to operate within the rigid constraints of those resolutions.

The Budget committees also had ups and downs. Originally considered power centers with seats carefully balanced, especially in the House, among various other committees and factions, they lost attraction as a committee assignment for members as available funds for discretionary government programs were squeezed out in the face of growing deficits. Members preferred the power of awarding funds for programs to other colleagues and to constituents but balked at the pain of searching for cuts year after year. Adoption of a budget resolution each year was often delayed by broad disagreements among the parties or between Congress and the president. Rep. Martin Russo, D-Ill., who rotated off the House Budget Committee in 1991 found service there so painful that he rejoiced, he said, that "my sentence is over."

Smith and Deering summed up the power shifts:

> As partisan conflict over budget priorities intensified and produced policy stalemates among the House, Senate, and White House, both ap-

The Senate Foreign Relations Committee holds a public hearing in the Hart Office Building. Behind the senators are staff aides and between the senators and the witness table are the press photographers.

propriations and authorizing committees lost autonomy. Party and Budget Committee leaders became central to resolving the conflict. Normal legislative procedures were ignored, set aside temporarily, and in some cases directly altered. All committees learned new legislative tricks to minimize the damage to programs they wanted to protect, but most could not avoid deep encroachments on their traditional autonomy. . . . Thus, in the quite unsettled power structure of Congress, leaders and budget committees fared well, appropriations committees survived but were injured, and authorizing committees took strong blows to their autonomy.[30]

After party control switched in the House in 1995 the Budget Committee regained visibility under the chairmanship of Rep. John Kasich, R-Ohio, a close ally of Speaker Gingrich, and also benefited from rules changes that expanded the committee's jurisdiction over the structure of the budget process itself. But once again factors beyond the control of Congress were bringing matters full circle. By 1998 a soaring economy was pouring such huge amounts of tax revenue into the government's treasury that a budget surplus was anticipated for fiscal 1998, and quite possibly some years into the future. Debate shifted to a subject members enjoyed and better understood: how to deal with spending rather than cutting.

BUDGET SUMMITRY

The frequent use in the 1980s of executive-legislative budget conferences to work out fiscal issues added yet another twist to the power relationships. Authorizing and appropriations committees—already wary of a budget process that had shifted some of their control over tax and spending issues to the Budget committees—viewed the high-level talks, where budget decisions were further centralized, with even greater suspicion.

A 1989 budget-summit deal collapsed in part because chairmen of key committees required to enact the plan were not involved in crucial negotiations. The tax-writing committees were given a revenue-raising target without any agreement on how the figure would be attained.

Attempting to avoid a replay congressional and White House leaders involved key committee chairmen in a 1990 budget summit from the start. Although the authorizing committee chairmen were still excluded, the congressional negotiating team included the chairmen and ranking members of the tax-writing and Appropriations committees in both the House and Senate, along with the Budget committees and other congressional leaders.

After intermittent talks beginning in May 1990 two dozen congressional and White House negotiators in September went into seclusion at Andrews Air Force Base outside Washington, D.C., for what they hoped would be a final round of budget talks. A budget agreement ultimately was reached by eight congressional and administration officials.

But many members of Congress were not pleased with an agreement reached by a handful of leaders in secrecy away from Capitol Hill, a process that seemed to some observers to cast aside the committee system and political accountability. Many committee chairmen in the House were up in arms about provisions of the agreement that trod on their turf. More than half of the committee chairmen voted against the budget along with seven of the thirteen Appropriations subcommittee chairmen. The summit agreement went down to humiliating defeat in the House, leading to a three-day shutdown of the government.

The budget crisis finally was resolved and the resulting budget reconciliation package boded further power shifts in the budget process. The new law gave the executive branch closer scrutiny of legislation as it was being crafted. But whatever the near-term outcome the rivalries among the spending committees were certain to continue.

Oversight Mandate

In addition to their lawmaking function committees bear important responsibilities for overseeing implementation of the laws already on the books. Congress has given the executive branch broad authority over the vast array of agencies and programs it has created. As the range of activities of the federal government has grown so too has the need for Congress to oversee how the executive branch administers the laws it has passed. Oleszek explains:

> A thoughtful, well-drafted law offers no guarantee that the policy intentions of legislators will be carried out. . . . The laws passed by Congress are often general guidelines, and sometimes their wording is deliberately vague. The implementation of legislation involves the drafting of administrative regulations by the executive agencies and day-to-day program management by agency officials. Agency regulations and rules are the subject of "legislative oversight"—the continuing review by Congress of how effectively the executive branch is carrying out congressional mandates.[31]

Congress did not officially recognize its responsibility for oversight until enactment of the 1946 Legislative Reorganization Act. That law mandated that the House and Senate standing committees exercise "continuous watchfulness of the execution by the administrative agencies" of any laws under their jurisdiction. The 1946 law divided oversight responsibilities into three areas: the legislative or authorizing committees were to review government programs and agencies, the Appropriations committees were to review government spending, and the committees currently named House Government Reform and Oversight and Senate Governmental Affairs were to probe for inefficiency, waste, and corruption in the federal government. But, as Oleszek points out, "to some degree all committees perform each type of oversight."[32]

Since enactment of the 1946 law Congress has passed several measures affecting oversight activities. In the 1970 Legislative Reorganization Act Congress increased staff assistance to all House and Senate committees, recommended that committees ascertain whether programs within their jurisdiction should be funded annually, and required most committees to issue oversight reports every two years.

Congress acted in 1974 to improve its oversight procedures when it passed the Congressional Budget and Impoundment Control Act. That act strengthened the role of the General Accounting Office (GAO) in acquiring fiscal, budgetary, and program-related information from federal agencies, authorized the GAO to establish an office to develop and recommend methods by which Congress could review and evaluate federal programs and activities, and authorized committees to assess the effectiveness of such programs and to require government agencies to carry out their own evaluations.

Congressional committees have a variety of ways of exercising their oversight responsibilities. The traditional and most obvious way is through normal legislative procedures. Congress can examine agency performances through committee hearings and investigations ranging from routine reviews to such highly publicized probes as the 104th Congress's investigations of personnel firings at the White House travel office, access by Clinton administration officials to FBI files on former Republican White House staffers, and the Whitewater real estate deal involving President and Mrs. Clinton, and the 105th Congress's hearings on campaign finance law violations in the 1996 election and IRS abuses of taxpayers' rights.

It is often difficult to interest members in conducting routine oversight over government agencies unless there are visible political rewards for those participating. Oversight does not involve obtaining funds for projects or trading favors with colleagues. When the House mandated that most committees create subcommittees specifically devoted to oversight, the panels often became the last chosen in the internal subcommittee assignment bidding process and were often chaired by junior members.

There were some powerful members who vigorously pursued oversight agendas and employed the full range of Congress's investigative powers, in recent years most notably Rep. John D. Dingell, D-Mich., who chaired both the House Energy and Commerce Committee (1981–1995) and its oversight subcommittee. He conducted highly publicized investigations ranging across his committee's vast legislative domain, which he frequently fought to expand. After Democrats lost control of the House in 1995, in order to make more key subcommittee posts available for other members Dingell and most other committee ranking minority members were barred from also ranking on any subcommittee. Even though he no longer could control a committee or subcommittee agenda, Dingell vigorously but unsuccessfully fought the change, arguing that it needlessly downgraded the conduct of committee oversight and left it to junior members who either did not care or lacked the expertise to investigate effectively.

Committees can use their subpoena powers broadly to demand information from government agencies and even hold executive officials in contempt for failure to comply, subject to approval by the parent chamber. The House voted several times during the 1980s to hold executive branch officials in contempt, most notably Anne Gorsuch, the administrator of the Environmental Protection Agency during the Reagan administration.

In 1996 the House Government Reform and Oversight Committee voted to hold White House counsel Jack Quinn in contempt for refusing to respond to a committee subpoena for documents, generating controversy over whether a committee had the authority to vote contempt without first giving the person cited a chance to appear and offer some defense. The majority determined that it had the power to proceed; after the vote, White House compliance was obtained and no House vote on contempt was held.

The use of the contempt power may become a first resort, rather than a last, in highly charged, partisan confrontations between the branches over information. Late in 1997 Attorney General Janet Reno was threatened with contempt by the committee, even before she testified, when it was learned that the Department of Justice would not supply a copy of a memorandum from the director of the FBI to Reno reportedly outlining why he disagreed with her decision not to appoint an independent counsel to investigate allegations of improper fund-raising by the president, vice president, and others during the 1996 election campaign.

Alleged scandals in the Clinton administration provided many opportunities for congressional oversight and substantial media coverage. Republicans seemed to have concluded that by weakening the Democratic president, political prospects might improve for enactment of their legislative agenda.

The GOP leadership, especially in the House, took on a major new role in selecting topics for committees to examine. Leadership intervention extended so far as selecting subcommittee chairmen and obtaining additional funds for investigations and expenses in the biennial committee funding resolution passed by the House and even afterwards

For example in the 105th Congress Speaker Gingrich recommended that additional funds be allocated for the Education and the Workforce Committee to use to investigate organized labor. The money was subsequently provided on a party-line vote of the House Oversight Committee, with no House vote required, using new House rules that allowed a "set-aside" of extra money in the committee funding resolution that the Speaker could direct to special projects. Democrats called this a "slush fund," claiming that it undermined the requirements of fiscal discipline and advance planning that the committee funding resolution was supposed to place on committee activities. They also argued that the investigation was a sham intended as retribution to organized labor for its massive spending to overturn the Republican majority in the 1996 election. The Democrats demanded unsuccessfully that the full House vote on all such reallocations of funds. Republicans countered that flexibility was essential in the conduct of congressional oversight to deal both with new issues and expansions of previously planned investigations and that Congress should not be straight-jacketed by funding priorities made very early in a two-year cycle.

Special reports required from agencies, investigations by agencies' inspectors general, audits by the GAO, and studies by congressional support agencies are other oversight tools. The substantial growth in reports required by Congress has triggered some complaints within both the executive branch and Congress that legislative committees are attempting to "micromanage" administrative details. The 104th Congress passed a "Reports Elimination Act" in response to these complaints to reduce the number of reports required but the traditional tension between the legislative and executive branches concerning oversight is unlikely to be relieved simply by paperwork reduction.

The legislative veto had been a popular oversight mechanism since 1932 when Congress began attaching to various statutes provisions giving one or both chambers or individual committees authority to veto government actions, regulations, and orders. The Supreme Court threw out the legislative veto in the 1983 *INS vs. Chadha* decision on the grounds that Congress could only exercise such power through the enactment of legislation presented to the president for signature or veto. Some of these provisions continue to exist in statutes, however, and can occasionally still be used under the rules of each chamber to make a political point, even though they no longer have legal effect. For example in 1998 Rep. Tom Campbell, R-Ca., used a provision of the War Powers Act to force a House vote on a concurrent resolution purporting to force withdrawal of U.S. troops from a peacekeeping mission in Bosnia. (The resolution was reported adversely from committee and defeated on the floor). Since *Chadha*, Congress has either rewritten many of these laws to pass constitutional muster or has found other informal ways to continue to exercise its influence.

Congress also has at its disposal nonstatutory controls, such as informal contacts between executive officials and committee members and staff, and statements made in committee and conference reports as well as statements during hearings and floor debates. Davidson and Oleszek observe: "Although there is no measure of their usage, nonstatutory controls may be the most common form of congressional oversight."[33]

NOTES

1. Walter J. Oleszek, *Congressional Procedures and the Policy Process*, 4th ed. (Washington, D.C.: CQ Press, 1996), 121.
2. Leroy N. Rieselbach, *Congressional Reform* (Washington, D.C.: CQ Press, 1986), 110.
3. Christopher J. Deering and Steven S. Smith, *Committees in Congress*, 3rd ed. (Washington, D.C.: CQ Press, 1997), 2.
4. Oleszek, *Congressional Procedures and the Policy Process*, 4th ed., 112.
5. George Goodwin Jr., *The Little Legislatures: Committees of Congress* (Amherst: University of Massachusetts Press, 1970).
6. Woodrow Wilson, *Congressional Government: A Study in American Politics* (Boston: Houghton Mifflin, 1885; Cleveland: Meridian Books, 1956), 59.
7. George B. Galloway, *Congress at the Crossroads* (New York: Thomas Y. Crowell, 1946), 88.
8. Deering and Smith, *Committees in Congress*, 3rd ed., 26.
9. Galloway, *Congress at the Crossroads*, 139–144; Goodwin, *The Little Legislatures*, 11–12.
10. George H. Haynes, *The Senate of the United States* (Boston: Houghton Mifflin, 1938), vol. 1, 273–277.
11. Steven Smith and Christopher J. Deering, *Committees in Congress*, 2nd ed. (Washington, D.C.: CQ Press, 1990), 33.
12. Ibid., 42.
13. Randall B. Ripley, *Power in the Senate* (New York: St. Martin's Press, 1969), 23.
14. Ibid., 47.
15. Wilson, *Congressional Government*, 82.
16. Roger H. Davidson, "Subcommittee Government: New Channels for Policy Making," in *The New Congress*, ed. Thomas E. Mann and Norman J. Ornstein (Washington, D.C.: American Enterprise Institute, 1981), 105–108.
17. Deering and Smith, *Committees in Congress*, 3rd. ed., 33.
18. Rieselbach, *Congressional Reform*, 45–46.
19. Norman J. Ornstein, Thomas E. Mann, and Michael J. Malbin, *Vital Statistics on Congress: 1997–1998* (Washington, D.C.: Congressional Quarterly, 1998), 123.
20. Senate Temporary Select Committee to Study the Senate Committee System, *First Report, with Recommendations; Structure of the Senate Committee System: Jurisdictions, Numbers and Sizes, and Limitations on Memberships and Chairmanships, Referral Procedures, and Scheduling*, 94th Cong., 2nd sess., 1976, 6.
21. Deering and Smith, *Committees in Congress*, 3rd ed., 141.

22. Ibid., 78–81.

23. Walter J. Oleszek, *Congressional Procedures and the Policy Process*, 3rd ed. (Washington, D.C.: CQ Press, 1989), 87.

24. Ibid., 88.

25. Melissa P. Collie and Joseph Cooper, "Multiple Referral and the 'New' Committee System in the House of Representatives," in *Congress Reconsidered*, 4th ed., ed. Lawrence C. Dodd and Bruce I. Oppenheimer (Washington, D.C.: CQ Press, 1989), 248.

26. Ibid., 254.

27. Roger H. Davidson, Walter J. Oleszek, and Thomas Kephart, "One Bill, Many Committees: Multiple Referrals in the U.S. House of Representatives," *Legislative Studies Quarterly*, XIII, 1 (February 1988), 4.

28. Oleszek, *Congressional Procedures and the Policy Process*, 3rd. ed., 76.

29. Deering and Smith, *Committees in Congress*, 3rd ed., 201.

30. Smith and Deering, *Committees in Congress*, 2nd ed., 211.

31. Oleszek, *Congressional Procedures and the Policy Process*, 4th ed., 300.

32. Ibid., 301.

33. Roger H. Davidson and Walter J. Oleszek, *Congress and Its Members*, 6th ed. (Washington, D.C.: CQ Press, 1998), 318.

SELECTED BIBLIOGRAPHY

Cooper, Joseph. *The Origin of the Standing Committees and the Development of the Modern House.* Houston: Rice University Studies, 1971.

Davidson, Roger H. "Subcommittee Government: New Channels for Policy Making." In *The New Congress*, edited by Thomas E. Mann and Norman J. Ornstein, 99–133. Washington, D.C.: American Enterprise Institute, 1981.

Davidson, Roger H., and Walter J. Oleszek. *Congress and Its Members.* 6th ed. Washington, D.C.: CQ Press, 1998.

Deering, Christopher J., and Steven S. Smith. *Committees in Congress.* 3rd ed. Washington, D.C.: CQ Press, 1997.

Dodd, Lawrence C., and Bruce I. Oppenheimer, eds. *Congress Reconsidered.* 6th ed. Washington, D.C.: CQ Press, 1997.

Elving, Ronald D. *Conflict and Compromise: How Congress Makes the Law.* New York: Simon & Schuster, 1995.

Endersby, James W., and Karen M. McCurdy. "Committee Assignments in the U.S. Senate." *Legislative Studies Quarterly* 21 (1996): 219–234.

Evans, C. Lawrence, and Walter J. Oleszek. *Congress Under Fire.* Boston: Houghton Mifflin, 1997.

Fenno, Richard F. Jr. *Congressmen in Committees.* Boston: Little, Brown, 1973.

Galloway, George B. *Congress at the Crossroads.* New York: Crowell, 1946.

Goodwin, George Jr. *The Little Legislatures: Committees of Congress.* Amherst: University of Massachusetts Press, 1970.

Haynes, George H. *The Senate of the United States.* 2 vols. Boston: Houghton Mifflin, 1938.

Hinckley, Barbara. *The Seniority System in Congress.* Bloomington: Indiana University Press, 1971.

Katz, Jonathan, and Brian Sala. "Careerism, Committee Assignments, and the Electoral Connection." *American Political Science Review* 90 (1996): 21–33.

Jones, Charles O. *The United States Congress: People, Place, and Policy.* Homewood, Ill.: Dorsey, 1982.

Longley, Lawrence D., and Walter J. Oleszek. *Bicameral Politics: Conference Committees in Congress.* New Haven, Conn.: Yale University Press, 1989.

Maltzman, Forrest. "Meeting Competing Demands: Committee Performance in the Post-Reform House." *American Journal of Political Science* 39 (1995): 653–682.

McConachie, Lauros. *Congressional Committees.* New York: Thomas Y. Crowell, 1898.

McGown, Ada C. *The Congressional Conference Committee.* New York: Columbia University Press, 1927.

Munson, Richard. *The Cardinals of Capitol Hill: The Men and Women Who Control Federal Spending.* New York: Grove Press, 1993.

Oleszek, Walter J. *Congressional Procedures and the Policy Process.* 4th ed. Washington, D.C.: CQ Press, 1996.

Ornstein, Norman J., Thomas E. Mann, and Michael J. Malbin. "Committees." Chap. 4 in *Vital Statistics on Congress: 1997–1998.* Washington, D.C.: Congressional Quarterly, 1998.

Price, David E. *Who Makes the Laws?* Cambridge, Mass.: Schenkman, 1972.

Rieselbach, Leroy N. *Congressional Politics: The Evolving Legislative System.* 2nd ed. Boulder, Colo.: Westview, 1995.

——. *Congressional Reform: The Changing Modern Congress.* Washington, D.C.: CQ Press, 1994.

Ripley, Randall B. *Power in the Senate.* New York: St. Martin's Press, 1969.

Robinson, James A. *The House Rules Committee.* Indianapolis: Bobbs-Merrill, 1963.

Shepsle, Kenneth A. "The Changing Textbook Congress." In *Can the Government Govern?*, edited by John E. Chubb and Paul E. Peterson, 238–266. Washington, D.C.: Brookings Institution, 1989.

Smith, Steven S. *The American Congress.* Boston: Houghton Mifflin, 1995.

Unekis, Joseph K., and Leroy N. Rieselbach. *Congressional Committee Politics: Continuity and Change.* New York: Praeger, 1984.

U.S. Congress. House. Committee on Rules. *A History of the Committee on Rules: 1st to 97th Congress, 1789–1981.* 97th Cong., 2nd sess., 1982. Committee Print.

U.S. Congress. House. Select Committee on Committees. *Final Report of Select Committee on Committees.* 96th Cong., 2nd sess., 1980. H Rept 96-866.

U.S. Congress. Senate. Committee on Rules and Administration. *Report on Senate Operations 1988.* 100th Cong., 2nd sess., 1988. Committee Print 129.

U.S. Congress. Senate. Temporary Select Committee to Study the Senate Committee System. *First Report, with Recommendations; Structure of the Senate Committee System: Jurisdictions, Numbers and Sizes, and Limitations on Memberships and Chairmanships, Referral Procedures, and Scheduling.* 94th Cong., 2nd sess., 1976. S Rept 94-1395.

Reference Materials

How a Bill Becomes Law 163

Political Party Affiliations in Congress and the Presidency, 1789–1997 164

Speakers of the House of Representatives, 1789–1998 166

Leaders of the House since 1899 167

Leaders of the Senate since 1911 169

Recorded Votes in the House and the Senate, 1947–1996 171

Attempted and Successful Cloture Votes, 1919–1996 172

Vetoes and Overrides, 1947–1996 173

Congressional Information on the Internet 174

How a Bill Becomes Law

This graphic shows the most typical way in which proposed legislation is enacted into law. There are more complicated, as well as simpler, routes, and most bills never become law. The process is illustrated with two hypothetical bills, House bill No. 1 (HR 1) and Senate bill No. 2 (S 2). Bills must be passed by both houses in identical form before they can be sent to the president. The path of HR 1 is traced by a black line, that of S 2 by a gray line. In practice, most bills begin as similar proposals in both houses.

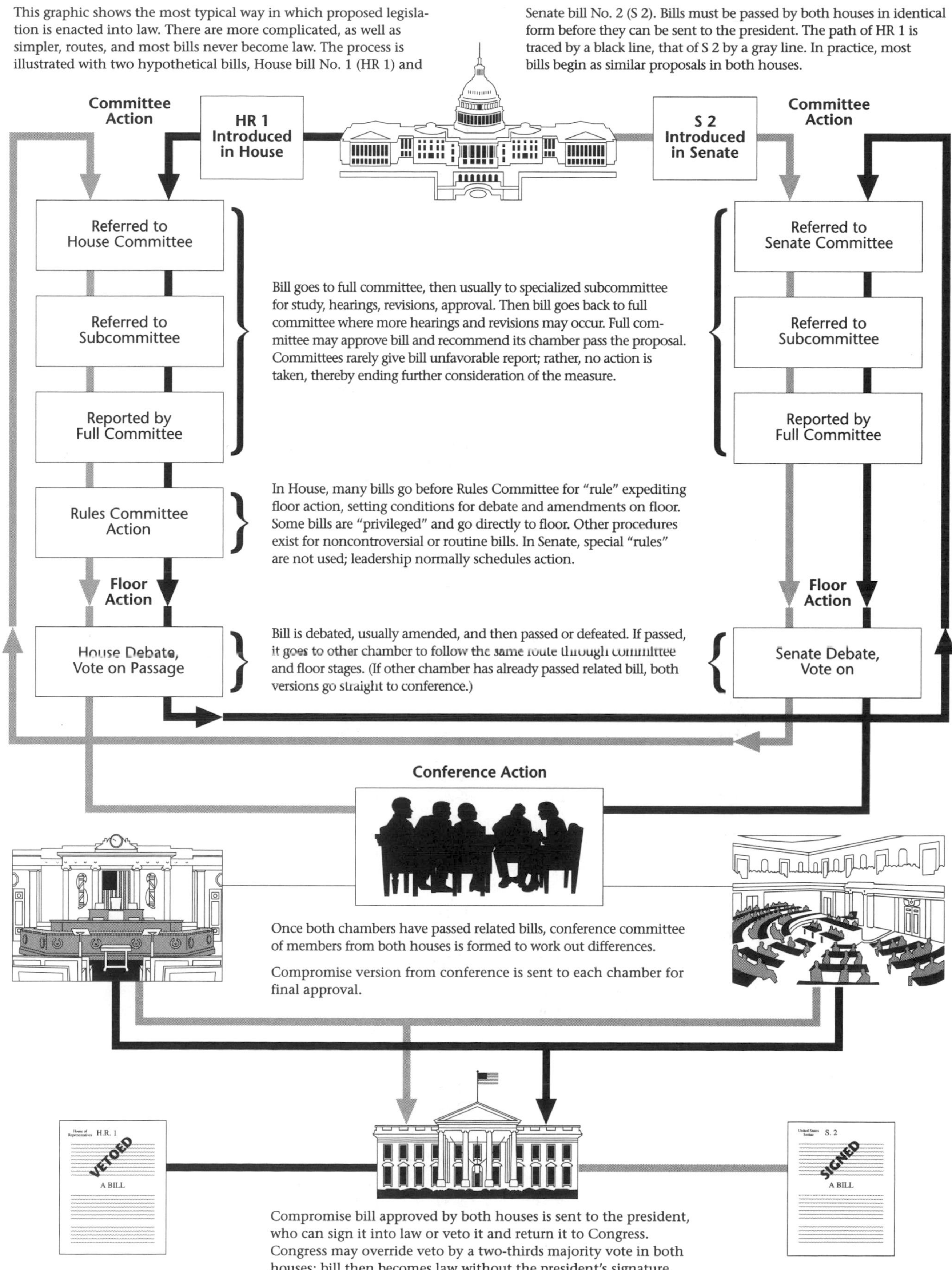

Political Party Affiliations in Congress and the Presidency, 1789–1997

		House		Senate		
Year	*Congress*	*Majority party*	*Principal minority party*	*Majority party*	*Principal minority party*	*President*
1789–1791	1st	AD-38	Op-26	AD-17	Op-9	F (Washington)
1791–1793	2nd	F-37	DR-33	F-16	DR-13	F (Washington)
1793–1795	3rd	DR-57	F-48	F-17	DR-13	F (Washington)
1795–1797	4th	F-54	DR-52	F-19	DR-13	F (Washington)
1797–1799	5th	F-58	DR-48	F-20	DR-12	F (John Adams)
1799–1801	6th	F-64	DR-42	F-19	DR-13	F (John Adams)
1801–1803	7th	DR-69	F-36	DR-18	F-13	DR (Jefferson)
1803–1805	8th	DR-102	F-39	DR-25	F-9	DR (Jefferson)
1805–1807	9th	DR-116	F-25	DR-27	F-7	DR (Jefferson)
1807–1809	10th	DR-118	F-24	DR-28	F-6	DR (Jefferson)
1809–1811	11th	DR-94	F-48	DR-28	F-6	DR (Madison)
1811–1813	12th	DR-108	F-36	DR-30	F-6	DR (Madison)
1813–1815	13th	DR-112	F-68	DR-27	F-9	DR (Madison)
1815–1817	14th	DR-117	F-65	DR-25	F-11	DR (Madison)
1817–1819	15th	DR-141	F-42	DR-34	F-10	DR (Monroe)
1819–1821	16th	DR-156	F-27	DR-35	F-7	DR (Monroe)
1821–1823	17th	DR-158	F-25	DR-44	F-4	DR (Monroe)
1823–1825	18th	DR-187	F-26	DR-44	F-4	DR (Monroe)
1825–1827	19th	AD-105	J-97	AD-26	J-20	DR (John Q. Adams)
1827–1829	20th	J-119	AD-94	J-28	AD-20	DR (John Q. Adams)
1829–1831	21st	D-139	NR-74	D-26	NR-22	DR (Jackson)
1831–1833	22nd	D-141	NR-58	D-25	NR-21	D (Jackson)
1833–1835	23rd	D-147	AM-53	D-20	NR-20	D (Jackson)
1835–1837	24th	D-145	W-98	D-27	W-25	D (Jackson)
1837–1839	25th	D-108	W-107	D-30	W-18	D (Van Buren)
1839–1841	26th	D-124	W-118	D-28	W-22	D (Van Buren)
1841–1843	27th	W-133	D-102	W-28	D-22	W (W. Harrison) W (Tyler)
1843–1845	28th	D-142	W-79	W-28	D-25	W (Tyler)
1845–1847	29th	D-143	W-77	D-31	W-25	D (Polk)
1847–1849	30th	W-115	D-108	D-36	W-21	D (Polk)
1849–1851	31st	D-112	W-109	D-35	W-25	W (Taylor) W (Fillmore)
1851–1853	32nd	D-140	W-88	D-35	W-24	W (Fillmore)
1853–1855	33rd	D-159	W-71	D-38	W-22	D (Pierce)
1855–1857	34th	R-108	D-83	D-40	R-15	D (Pierce)
1857–1859	35th	D-118	R-92	D-36	R-20	D (Buchanan)
1859–1861	36th	R-114	D-92	D-36	R-26	D (Buchanan)
1861–1863	37th	R-105	D-43	R-31	D-10	R (Lincoln)
1863–1865	38th	R-102	D-75	R-36	D-9	R (Lincoln)
1865–1867	39th	U-149	D-42	U-42	D-10	R (Lincoln) R (A. Johnson)
1867–1869	40th	R-143	D-49	R-42	D-11	R (A. Johnson)
1869–1871	41st	R-149	D-63	R-56	D-11	R (Grant)
1871–1873	42nd	R-134	D-104	R-52	D-17	R (Grant)
1873–1875	43rd	R-194	D-92	R-49	D-19	R (Grant)
1875–1877	44th	D-169	R-109	R-45	D-29	R (Grant)
1877–1879	45th	D-153	R-140	R-39	D-36	R (Hayes)
1879–1881	46th	D-149	R-130	D-42	R-33	R (Hayes)
1881–1883	47th	R-147	D-135	R-37	D-37	R (Garfield) R (Arthur
1883–1885	48th	D-197	R-118	R-38	D-36	R (Arthur)
1885–1887	49th	D-183	R-140	R-43	D-34	D (Cleveland)
1887–1889	50th	D-169	R-152	R-39	D-37	D (Cleveland)
1889–1891	51st	R-166	D-159	R-39	D-37	R (B. Harrison)
1891–1893	52nd	D-235	R-88	R-47	D-39	R (B. Harrison)
1893–1895	53rd	D-218	R-127	D-44	R-38	D (Cleveland)
1895–1897	54th	R-244	D-105	R-43	D-39	D (Cleveland)
1897–1899	55th	R-204	D-113	R-47	D-34	R (McKinley)

(table continues)

Year	Congress	House: Majority party	House: Principal minority party	Senate: Majority party	Senate: Principal minority party	President
1899–1901	56th	R-185	D-163	R-53	D-26	R (McKinley)
1901–1903	57th	R-197	D-151	R-55	D-31	R (McKinley) R (T. Roosevelt)
1903–1905	58th	R-208	D-178	R-57	D-33	R (T. Roosevelt)
1905–1907	59th	R-250	D-136	R-57	D-33	R (T. Roosevelt)
1907–1909	60th	R-222	D-164	R-61	D-31	R (T. Roosevelt)
1909–1911	61st	R-219	D-172	R-61	D-32	R (Taft)
1911–1913	62nd	D-228	R-161	R-51	D-41	R (Taft)
1913–1915	63rd	D-291	R-127	D-51	R-44	D (Wilson)
1915–1917	64th	D-230	R-196	D-56	R-40	D (Wilson)
1917–1919	65th	D-216	R-210	D-53	R-42	D (Wilson)
1919–1921	66th	R-240	D-190	R-49	D-47	D (Wilson)
1921–1923	67th	R-301	D-131	R-59	D-37	R (Harding)
1923–1925	68th	R-225	D-205	R-51	D-43	R (Coolidge)
1925–1927	69th	R-247	D-183	R-56	D-39	R (Coolidge)
1927–1929	70th	R-237	D-195	R-49	D-46	R (Coolidge)
1929–1931	71st	R-267	D-167	R-56	D-39	R (Hoover)
1931–1933	72nd	D-220	R-214	R-48	D-47	R (Hoover)
1933–1935	73rd	D-310	R-117	D-60	R-35	D (F. Roosevelt)
1935–1937	74th	D-319	R-103	D-69	R-25	D (F. Roosevelt)
1937–1939	75th	D-331	R-89	D-76	R-16	D (F. Roosevelt)
1939–1941	76th	D-261	R-164	D-69	R-23	D (F. Roosevelt)
1941–1943	77th	D-268	R-162	D-66	R-28	D (F. Roosevelt)
1943–1945	78th	D-218	R-208	D-58	R-37	D (F. Roosevelt)
1945–1947	79th	D-242	R-190	D-56	R-38	D (F. Roosevelt) D (Truman)
1947–1949	80th	R-245	D-188	R-51	D-45	D (Truman)
1949–1951	81st	D-263	R-171	D-54	R-42	D (Truman)
1951–1953	82nd	D-234	R-199	D-49	R-47	D (Truman)
1953–1955	83rd	R-221	D-211	R-48	D-47	R (Eisenhower)
1955–1957	84th	D-232	R-203	D-48	R-47	R (Eisenhower)
1957–1959	85th	D-233	R-200	D-49	R-47	R (Eisenhower)
1959–1961	86th	D-283	R-153	D-64	R-34	R (Eisenhower)
1961–1963	87th	D-263	R-174	D-65	R-35	D (Kennedy)
1963–1965	88th	D-258	R-177	D-67	R-33	D (Kennedy) D (L. Johnson)
1965–1967	89th	D-295	R-140	D-68	R-32	D (L. Johnson)
1967–1969	90th	D-247	R-187	D-64	R-36	D (L. Johnson)
1969–1971	91st	D-243	R-192	D-57	R-43	R (Nixon)
1971–1973	92nd	D-254	R-180	D-54	R-44	R (Nixon)
1973–1975	93rd	D-239	R-192	D-56	R-42	R (Nixon) R (Ford)
1975–1977	94th	D-291	R-144	D-60	R-37	R (Ford)
1977–1979	95th	D-292	R-143	D-61	R-38	D (Carter)
1979–1981	96th	D-276	R-157	D-58	R-41	D (Carter)
1981–1983	97th	D-243	R-192	R-53	D-46	R (Reagan)
1983–1985	98th	D-269	R-165	R-54	D-46	R (Reagan)
1985–1987	99th	D-252	R-182	R-53	D-47	R (Reagan)
1987–1989	100th	D-258	R-177	D-55	R-45	R (Reagan)
1989–1991	101st	D-259	R-174	D-55	R-45	R (Bush)
1991–1993	102nd	D-267	R-167	D-56	R-44	R (Bush)
1993–1995	103rd	D-258	R-176	D-57	R-43	D (Clinton)
1995–1997	104th	R-230	D-204	R-53	D-47	D (Clinton)
1997–1999	105th	R-227	D-207	R-55	D-45	D (Clinton)

SOURCES: *Congressional Quarterly Weekly Report,* various issues; U.S. Bureau of the Census, *Historical Statistics of the United States, Colonial Times to 1970* (Washington, D.C.: Government Printing Office, 1975); and U.S. Congress, Joint Committee on Printing, *Official Congressional Directory* (Washington, D.C.: Government Printing Office, 1967–).

NOTE: Figures are for the beginning of the first session of each Congress. Key to abbreviations: AD—Administration; AM—Anti-Masonic; D—Democratic; DR—Democratic-Republican; F—Federalist; J—Jacksonian; NR—National Republican; Op—Opposition; R—Republican; U—Unionist; W—Whig.

Speakers of the House of Representatives, 1789–1998

Congress		Speaker	Congress		Speaker
1st	(1789–1791)	Frederick A. C. Muhlenberg, -Pa.	53rd	(1893–1895)	Crisp
2nd	(1791–1793)	Jonathan Trumbull, F-Conn.	54th	(1895–1897)	Reed
3rd	(1793–1795)	Muhlenberg	55th	(1897–1899)	Reed
4th	(1795–1797)	Jonathan Dayton, F-N.J.	56th	(1899–1901)	David B. Henderson, R-Iowa
5th	(1797–1799)	Dayton	57th	(1901–1903)	Henderson
6th	(1799–1801)	Theodore Sedgwick, F-Mass.	58th	(1903–1905)	Joseph G. Cannon, R-Ill.
7th	(1801–1803)	Nathaniel Macon, D-N.C.	59th	(1905–1907)	Cannon
8th	(1803–1805)	Macon	60th	(1907–1909)	Cannon
9th	(1805–1807)	Macon	61st	(1909–1911)	Cannon
10th	(1807–1809)	Joseph B. Varnum, -Mass.	62nd	(1911–1913)	James B. "Champ" Clark, D-Mo.
11th	(1809–1811)	Varnum	63rd	(1913–1915)	Clark
12th	(1811–1813)	Henry Clay, -Ky.	64th	(1915–1917)	Clark
13th	(1813–1814)	Clay	65th	(1917–1919)	Clark
	(1814–1815)	Langdon Cheves, D-S.C.	66th	(1919–1921)	Frederick H. Gillett, R-Mass.
14th	(1815–1817)	Clay	67th	(1921–1923)	Gillett
15th	(1817–1819)	Clay	68th	(1923–1925)	Gillett
16th	(1819–1820)	Clay	69th	(1925–1927)	Nicholas Longworth, R-Ohio
	(1820–1821)	John W. Taylor, D-N.Y.	70th	(1927–1929)	Longworth
17th	(1821–1823)	Philip P. Barbour, D-Va.	71st	(1929–1931)	Longworth
18th	(1823–1825)	Clay	72nd	(1931–1933)	John Nance Garner, D-Texas
19th	(1825–1827)	Taylor	73rd	(1933–1934)	Henry T. Rainey, D-Ill.[a]
20th	(1827–1829)	Andrew Stevenson, D-Va.	74th	(1935–1936)	Joseph W. Byrns, D-Tenn.
21st	(1829–1831)	Stevenson		(1936–1937)	William B. Bankhead, D-Ala.
22nd	(1831–1833)	Stevenson	75th	(1937–1939)	Bankhead
23rd	(1833–1834)	Stevenson	76th	(1939–1940)	Bankhead
	(1834–1835)	John Bell, W-Tenn.		(1940–1941)	Sam Rayburn, D-Texas
24th	(1835–1837)	James K. Polk, D-Tenn.	77th	(1941–1943)	Rayburn
25th	(1837–1839)	Polk	78th	(1943–1945)	Rayburn
26th	(1839–1841)	Robert M. T. Hunter, D-Va.	79th	(1945–1947)	Rayburn
27th	(1841–1843)	John White, W-Ky.	80th	(1947–1949)	Joseph W. Martin Jr., R-Mass.
28th	(1843–1845)	John W. Jones, D-Va.	81st	(1949–1951)	Rayburn
29th	(1845–1847)	John W. Davis, D-Ind.	82nd	(1951–1953)	Rayburn
30th	(1847–1849)	Robert C. Winthrop, W-Mass.	83rd	(1953–1955)	Martin
31st	(1849–1851)	Howell Cobb, D-Ga.	84th	(1955–1957)	Rayburn
32nd	(1851–1853)	Linn Boyd, D-Ky.	85th	(1957–1959)	Rayburn
33rd	(1853–1855)	Boyd	86th	(1959–1961)	Rayburn
34th	(1855–1857)	Nathaniel P. Banks, R-Mass.	87th	(1961)	Rayburn
35th	(1857–1859)	James L. Orr, D-S.C.		(1962–1963)	John W. McCormack, D-Mass.
36th	(1859–1861)	William Pennington, R-N.J.	88th	(1963–1965)	McCormack
37th	(1861–1863)	Galusha A. Grow, R-Pa.	89th	(1965–1967)	McCormack
38th	(1863–1865)	Schuyler Colfax, R-Ind.	90th	(1967–1969)	McCormack
39th	(1865–1867)	Colfax	91st	(1969–1971)	McCormack
40th	(1867–1868)	Colfax	92nd	(1971–1973)	Carl Albert, D-Okla.
	(1868–1869)	Theodore M. Pomeroy, R-N.Y.	93rd	(1973–1975)	Albert
41st	(1869–1871)	James G. Blaine, R-Maine	94th	(1975–1977)	Albert
42nd	(1871–1873)	Blaine	95th	(1977–1979)	Thomas P. O'Neill Jr., D-Mass.
43rd	(1873–1875)	Blaine	96th	(1979–1981)	O'Neill
44th	(1875–1876)	Michael C. Kerr, D-Ind.	97th	(1981–1983)	O'Neill
	(1876–1877)	Samuel J. Randall, D-Pa.	98th	(1983–1985)	O'Neill
45th	(1877–1879)	Randall	99th	(1985–1987)	O'Neill
46th	(1879–1881)	Randall	100th	(1987–1989)	Jim Wright, D-Texas
47th	(1881–1883)	Joseph Warren Keifer, R-Ohio	101st	(1989)	Wright[b]
48th	(1883–1885)	John G. Carlisle, D-Ky.		(1989–1991)	Thomas S. Foley, D-Wash.
49th	(1885–1887)	Carlisle	102nd	(1991–1993)	Foley
50th	(1887–1889)	Carlisle	103rd	(1993–1995)	Foley
51st	(1889–1891)	Thomas Brackett Reed, R-Maine	104th	(1995–1997)	Newt Gingrich, R-Ga.
52nd	(1891–1893)	Charles F. Crisp, D-Ga.	105th	(1997–)	Gingrich

SOURCES: *1989–1990 Congressional Directory, 101st Congress* (Washington, D.C.: Government Printing Office, 1989), 520–529; *Congressional Quarterly Weekly Report.*

NOTES: Abbreviations: D—Democrat; F—Federalist; R—Republican; W—Whig. a. Rainey died in 1834, but was not replaced until the next Congress. b. Wright resigned and was succeeded by Foley on June 6, 1989.

Leaders of the House since 1899

Congress		House Floor Leaders		House Whips	
		Majority	*Minority*	*Majority*	*Minority*
56th	(1899–1901)	Sereno E. Payne (R N.Y.)	James D. Richardson (D Tenn.)	James A. Tawney (R Minn.)	Oscar W. Underwood (D Ala.)[a]
57th	(1901–1903)	Payne	Richardson	Tawney	James T. Lloyd (D Mo.)
58th	(1903–1905)	Payne	John Sharp Williams (D Miss.)	Tawney	Lloyd
59th	(1905–1907)	Payne	Williams	James E. Watson (R Ind.)	Lloyd
60th	(1907–1909)	Payne	Williams/Champ Clark (D Mo.)[b]	Watson	Lloyd[c]
61st	(1909–1911)	Payne	Clark	John W. Dwight (R N.Y.)	None
62nd	(1911–1913)	Oscar W. Underwood (D Ala.)	James R. Mann (R Ill.)	None	John W. Dwight (R N.Y.)
63rd	(1913–1915)	Underwood	Mann	Thomas M. Bell (D Ga.)	Charles H. Burke (R S.D.)
64th	(1915–1917)	Claude Kitchin (D N.C.)	Mann	None	Charles M. Hamilton (R N.Y.)
65th	(1917–1919)	Kitchin	Mann	None	Hamilton
66th	(1919–1921)	Franklin W. Mondell (R Wyo.)	Clark	Harold Knutson (R Minn.)	None
67th	(1921–1923)	Mondell	Claude Kitchin (D N.C.)	Knutson	William A. Oldfield (D Ark.)
68th	(1923–1925)	Nicholas Longworth (R Ohio)	Finis J. Garrett (D Tenn.)	Albert H. Vestal (R Ind.)	Oldfield
69th	(1925–1927)	John Q. Tilson (R Conn.)	Garrett	Vestal	Oldfield
70th	(1927–1929)	Tilson	Garrett	Vestal	Oldfield/John McDuffie (D Ala.)[d]
71st	(1929–1931)	Tilson	John N. Garner (D Texas)	Vestal	McDuffie
72nd	(1931–1933)	Henry T. Rainey (D Ill.)	Bertrand H. Snell (R N.Y.)	John McDuffie (D Ala.)	Carl G. Bachmann (R W.Va.)
73rd	(1933–1935)	Joseph W. Byrns (D Tenn.)	Snell	Arthur H. Greenwood (D Ind.)	Harry L. Englebright (R Calif.)
74th	(1935–1937)	William B. Bankhead (D Ala.)[e]	Snell	Patrick J. Boland (D Pa.)	Englebright
75th	(1937–1939)	Sam Rayburn (D Texas)	Snell	Boland	Englebright
76th	(1939–1941)	Rayburn/John W. McCormack (D Mass.)[f]	Joseph W. Martin Jr. (R Mass.)	Boland	Englebright
77th	(1941–1943)	McCormack	Martin	Boland/Robert Ramspeck (D Ga.)[g]	Englebright
78th	(1943–1945)	McCormack	Martin	Ramspeck	Leslie C. Arends (R Ill.)
79th	(1945–1947)	McCormack	Martin	Ramspeck/John J. Sparkman (D Ala.)[h]	Arends
80th	(1947–1949)	Charles A. Halleck (R Ind.)	Sam Rayburn (D Texas)	Leslie C. Arends (R Ill.)	John W. McCormack (D Mass.)
81st	(1949–1951)	McCormack	Martin	J. Percy Priest (D Tenn.)	Arends
82nd	(1951–1953)	McCormack	Martin	Priest	Arends
83rd	(1953–1955)	Halleck	Rayburn	Arends	McCormack
84th	(1955–1957)	McCormack	Martin	Carl Albert (D Okla.)	Arends
85th	(1957–1959)	McCormack	Martin	Albert	Arends
86th	(1959–1961)	McCormack	Charles A. Halleck (R Ind.)	Albert	Arends
87th	(1961–1963)	McCormack/Carl Albert (D Okla.)[i]	Halleck	Albert/Hale Boggs (D La.)[j]	Arends
88th	(1963–1965)	Albert	Halleck	Boggs	Arends
89th	(1965–1967)	Albert	Gerald R. Ford (R Mich.)	Boggs	Arends
90th	(1967–1969)	Albert	Ford	Boggs	Arends
91st	(1969–1971)	Albert	Ford	Boggs	Arends
92nd	(1971–1973)	Hale Boggs (D La.)	Ford	Thomas P. O'Neill Jr. (D Mass.)	Arends
93rd	(1973–1975)	Thomas P. O'Neill Jr. (D Mass.)	Ford/John J. Rhodes (R Ariz.)[k]	John J. McFall (D Calif.)	Arends
94th	(1975–1977)	O'Neill	Rhodes	McFall	Robert H. Michel (R Ill.)
95th	(1977–1979)	Jim Wright (D Texas)	Rhodes	John Brademas (D Ind.)	Michel
96th	(1979–1981)	Wright	Rhodes	Brademas	Michel
97th	(1981–1983)	Wright	Robert H. Michel (R Ill.)	Thomas S. Foley (D Wash.)	Trent Lott (R Miss.)
98th	(1983–1985)	Wright	Michel	Foley	Lott
99th	(1985–1987)	Wright	Michel	Foley	Lott
100th	(1987–1989)	Thomas S. Foley (D Wash.)	Michel	Tony Coelho (D Calif.)	Lott
101st	(1989–1991)	Foley/Richard A. Gephardt (D Mo.)[l]	Michel	Coelho/William H. Gray III (D Pa.)[m]	Richard Cheney (R Wyo.)/Newt Gingrich (R Ga.)[n]
102nd	(1991–1993)	Gephardt	Michel	Gray/David E. Bonior (D Mich.)[o]	Gingrich

(table continues)

Leaders of the House since 1899 ***(continued)***

Congress		House Floor Leaders		House Whips	
		Majority	*Minority*	*Majority*	*Minority*
103rd	(1993–1995)	Gephardt	Michel	Bonior	Gingrich
104th	(1995–1997)	Dick Armey (R Texas)	Richard A. Gephardt (D Mo.)	Tom DeLay (R Texas)	David E. Bonior (D Mich.)
105th	(1997–1999)	Armey	Gephardt	DeLay	Bonoir

SOURCES: Randall B. Ripley, *Party Leaders in the House of Representatives* (Washington, D.C.: Brookings Institution, 1967); *Congressional Directory* (Washington, D.C.: Government Printing Office), various years; *Biographical Directory of the American Congress, 1774–1971*, comp. Lawrence F. Kennedy, 92nd Cong., 1st sess., 1971, S Doc 8; *Congressional Quarterly Weekly Report.*

NOTES: a. Underwood did not become minority whip until 1901. b. Clark became minority leader in 1908. c. Lloyd resigned to become chairman of the Democratic Congressional Campaign Committee in 1908. The post of minority whip remained vacant until the beginning of the 62nd Congress. d. McDuffie became minority whip after the death of Oldfield on Nov. 19, 1928. e. Bankhead became Speaker of the House on June 4, 1936. The post of majority leader remained vacant until the next Congress. f. McCormack became majority leader on Sept. 26, 1940, filling the vacancy caused by the elevation of Rayburn to the post of Speaker of the House on Sept. 16, 1940. g. Ramspeck became majority whip on June 8, 1942, filling the vacancy caused by the death of Boland on May 18, 1942. h. Sparkman became majority whip on Jan. 14, 1946, filling the vacancy caused by the resignation of Ramspeck on Dec. 31, 1945. i. Albert became majority leader on Jan. 10, 1962, filling the vacancy caused by the elevation of McCormack to the post of Speaker of the House on Jan. 10, 1962. j. Boggs became majority whip on Jan. 10, 1962, filling the vacancy caused by the elevation of Albert to the post of majority leader on Jan. 10, 1962. k. Rhodes became minority leader on Dec. 7, 1973, filling the vacancy caused by the resignation of Ford on Dec. 6, 1973, to become vice president. l. Gephardt became majority leader on June 14, 1989, filling the vacancy created when Foley succeeded Wright as Speaker of the House on June 6, 1989. m. Gray became majority whip on June 14, 1989, filling the vacancy caused by Coehlo's resignation from Congress on June 15, 1989. n. Gingrich became minority whip on March 23, 1989, filling the vacancy caused by the resignation of Cheney on March 17, 1989, to become secretary of defense. o. Bonior became majority whip on Sept. 11, 1991, filling the vacancy caused by Gray's resignation from Congress on Sept. 11, 1991.

Leaders of the Senate since 1911

Congress		Senate Floor Leaders		Senate Whips	
		Majority	*Minority*	*Majority*	*Minority*
62nd	(1911–1913)	Shelby M. Cullom (R Ill.)	Thomas S. Martin (D Va.)	None	None
63rd	(1913–1915)	John W. Kern (D Ind.)	Jacob H. Gallinger (R N.H.)	J. Hamilton Lewis (D Ill.)	None
64th	(1915–1917)	Kern	Gallinger	Lewis	James W. Wadsworth Jr. (R N.Y.)/Charles Curtis (R Kan.)[a]
65th	(1917–1919)	Thomas S. Martin (D Va.)	Gallinger/Henry Cabot Lodge (R Mass.)[b]	Lewis	Curtis
66th	(1919–1921)	Henry Cabot Lodge (R Mass.)	Martin/Oscar W. Underwood (D Ala.)[c]	Charles Curtis (R Kan.)	Peter G. Gerry (D R.I.)
67th	(1921–1923)	Lodge	Underwood	Curtis	Gerry
68th	(1923–1925)	Lodge/Charles Curtis (R Kan.)[d]	Joseph T. Robinson (D Ark.)	Curtis/Wesley L. Jones (R Wash.)[e]	Gerry
69th	(1925–1927)	Curtis	Robinson	Jones	Gerry
70th	(1927–1929)	Curtis	Robinson	Jones	Gerry
71st	(1929–1931)	James E. Watson (R Ind.)	Robinson	Simeon D. Fess (R Ohio)	Morris Sheppard (D Texas)
72nd	(1931–1933)	Watson	Robinson	Fess	Sheppard
73rd	(1933–1935)	Joseph T. Robinson (D Ark.)	Charles L. McNary (R Ore.)	Lewis	Felix Hebert (R R.I.)
74th	(1935–1937)	Robinson	McNary	Lewis	None
75th	(1937–1939)	Robinson/Alben W. Barkley (D Ky.)[f]	McNary	Lewis	None
76th	(1939–1941)	Barkley	McNary	Sherman Minton (D Ind.)	None
77th	(1941–1943)	Barkley	McNary	Lister Hill (D Ala.)	None
78th	(1943–1945)	Barkley	McNary	Hill	Kenneth Wherry (R Neb.)
79th	(1945–1947)	Barkley	Wallace H. White Jr. (R Maine)	Hill	Wherry
80th	(1947–1949)	Wallace H. White Jr. (R Maine)	Alben W. Barkley (D Ky.)	Kenneth Wherry (R Neb.)	Scott Lucas (D Ill.)
81st	(1949–1951)	Scott W. Lucas (D Ill.)	Kenneth S. Wherry (R Neb.)	Francis Myers (D Pa.)	Leverett Saltonstall (R Mass.)
82nd	(1951–1953)	Ernest W. McFarland (D Ariz.)	Wherry/Styles Bridges (R N.H.)[g]	Lyndon B. Johnson (D Texas)	Saltonstall
83rd	(1953–1955)	Robert A. Taft (R Ohio)/ William F. Knowland (R Calif.)[h]	Lyndon B. Johnson (D Texas)	Leverett Saltonstall (R Mass.)	Earle Clements (D Ky.)
84th	(1955–1957)	Lyndon B. Johnson (D Texas)	William F. Knowland (R Calif.)	Earle Clements (D Ky.)	Saltonstall
85th	(1957–1959)	Johnson	Knowland	Mike Mansfield (D Mont.)	Everett McKinley Dirksen (R Ill.)
86th	(1959–1961)	Johnson	Everett McKinley Dirksen (R Ill.)	Mansfield	Thomas H. Kuchel (R Calif.)
87th	(1961–1963)	Mike Mansfield (D Mont.)	Dirksen	Hubert H. Humphrey (D Minn.)	Kuchel
88th	(1963–1965)	Mansfield	Dirksen	Humphrey	Kuchel
89th	(1965–1967)	Mansfield	Dirksen	Russell Long (D La.)	Kuchel
90th	(1967–1969)	Mansfield	Dirksen	Long	Kuchel
91st	(1969–1971)	Mansfield	Dirksen/Hugh Scott (R Pa.)[i]	Edward M. Kennedy (D Mass.)	Hugh Scott (R Pa.)/Robert P. Griffin (R Mich.)[j]
92nd	(1971–1973)	Mansfield	Scott	Robert C. Byrd (D W.Va.)	Griffin
93rd	(1973–1975)	Mansfield	Scott	Byrd	Griffin
94th	(1975–1977)	Mansfield	Scott	Byrd	Griffin
95th	(1977–1979)	Robert C. Byrd (D W.Va.)	Howard H. Baker Jr. (R Tenn.)	Alan Cranston (D Calif.)	Ted Stevens (R Alaska)
96th	(1979–1981)	Byrd	Baker	Cranston	Stevens
97th	(1981–1983)	Howard H. Baker Jr. (R Tenn.)	Robert C. Byrd (D W.Va.)	Ted Stevens (R Alaska)	Alan Cranston (D Calif.)
98th	(1983–1985)	Baker	Byrd	Stevens	Cranston
99th	(1985–1987)	Bob Dole (R Kan.)	Byrd	Alan K. Simpson (R Wyo.)	Cranston
100th	(1987–1989)	Byrd	Bob Dole (R Kan.)	Cranston	Alan K. Simpson (R Wyo.)
101st	(1989–1991)	George J. Mitchell (D Maine)	Dole	Cranston	Simpson
102nd	(1991–1993)	Mitchell	Dole	Wendell H. Ford (D Ky.)	Simpson
103rd	(1993–1995)	Mitchell	Dole	Ford	Simpson

(table continues)

Leaders of the Senate since 1911 *(continued)*

Congress		Senate Floor Leaders		Senate Whips	
		Majority	*Minority*	*Majority*	*Minority*
104th	(1995–1997)	Bob Dole (R Kan.)/ Trent Lott (R Miss.)[k]	Tom Daschle (D S.D.)	Trent Lott (R Miss.)/ Don Nickles (R Okla)[k]	Wendell H. Ford (D Ky.)
105th	(1997–1999)	Lott	Daschle	Nickles	Ford

SOURCES: Walter J. Oleszek, "Party Whips in the United States Senate," *Journal of Politics* 33 (November 1971): 955–979; *Congressional Directory* (Washington, D.C.: Government Printing Office), various years; *Biographical Directory of the American Congress, 1774–1971,* comp. Lawrence F. Kennedy, 92nd Cong., 1st sess., 1971, S Doc 8; *Majority and Minority Leaders of the Senate,* comp. Floyd M. Riddick, 94th Cong., 1st ses., 1975, S Doc 66; *Congressional Quarterly Weekly Report.*

NOTES: a. Wadsworth served as minority whip for only one week, from Dec. 6 to Dec. 13, 1915. b. Lodge became minority leader on Aug. 24, 1918, filling the vacancy caused by the death of Gallinger on Aug. 17, 1918. c. Underwood became minority leader on April 27, 1920, filling the vacancy caused by the death of Martin on Nov. 12, 1919. Gilbert M. Hitchcock (D Neb.) served as acting minority leader in the interim. d. Curtis became majority leader on Nov. 28, 1924, filling the vacancy caused by the death of Lodge on Nov. 9, 1924. e. Jones became majority whip filling the vacancy caused by the elevation of Curtis to the post of majority leader. f. Barkley became majority leader on July 22, 1937, filling the vacancy caused by the death of Robinson on July 14, 1937. g. Bridges became minority leader on Jan. 8, 1952, filling the vacancy caused by the death of Wherry on Nov. 29, 1951. h. Knowland became majority leader on Aug. 4, 1953, filling the vacancy caused by the death of Taft on July 31, 1953. Taft's vacant seat was filled by a Democrat, Thomas Burke, on Nov. 10, 1953. The division of the Senate changed to 48 Democrats, 47 Republicans, and 1 Independent, thus giving control of the Senate to the Democrats. However, Knowland remained as majority leader until the end of the 83rd Congress. i. Scott became minority leader on Sept. 24, 1969, filling the vacancy caused by the death of Dirksen on Sept. 7, 1969. j. Griffin became minority whip on Sept. 24, 1969, filling the vacancy caused by the elevation of Scott to the post of minority leader. k. Lott became majority leader on June 12, following the resignation of Dole on June 11. Don Nickles was subsequently elected majority whip.

Recorded Votes in the House and the Senate, 1947–1996

Year	House	Senate	Year	House	Senate
1947	84	138	1972	329	532
1948	75	110	1973	541	594
1949	121	226	1974	537	544
1950	154	229	1975	612	602
1951	109	202	1976	661	688
1952	72	129	1977	706	635
1953	71	89	1978	834	516
1954	76	181	1979	672	497
1955	73	88	1980	604	546
1956	74	136	1981	353	497
1957	100	111	1982	459	469
1958	93	202	1983	498	381
1959	87	215	1984	408	292
1960	93	207	1985	439	381
1961	116	207	1986	451	359
1962	124	227	1987	488	420
1963	119	229	1988	451	379
1964	113	312	1989	379	312
1965	201	259	1990	536	326
1966	193	238	1991	444	280
1967	245	315	1992	488	270
1968	233	280[a]	1993	615	395
1969	177	245	1994	507	329
1970	266	422	1995	885	613
1971	320	423	1996	455	306

SOURCE: Norman J Ornstein, Thomas E. Mann, and Michael J. Malbin, *Vitial Statistics on Congress, 1997–1998* (Washington, D.C.: Congressional Quarterly, 1998).

NOTES: House figures reflect the total number of quorum calls, yea-and-nay votes, and recorded votes, while Senate figures include only yea-and-nay votes. a. This figure does not include one yea-and-nay vote that was ruled invalid for lack of a quorum.

Attempted and Successful Cloture Votes, 1919–1996

Congress		First Session		Second Session		Total	
		Attempted	*Successful*	*Attempted*	*Successful*	*Attempted*	*Successful*
66th	(1919–1921)	1	1	0	0	1	1
67th	(1921–1923)	1	0	1	0	2	0
68th	(1923–1925)	0	0	0	0	0	0
69th	(1925–1927)	0	0	2	1	2	1
70th	(1927–1929)	5	2	0	0	5	2
71st	(1929–1931)	0	0	0	0	0	0
72nd	(1931–1933)	0	0	0	0	0	0
73rd	(1933–1935)	1	0	0	0	1	0
74th	(1935–1937)	0	0	0	0	0	0
75th	(1937–1939)	0	0	2	0	2	0
76th	(1939–1941)	0	0	0	0	0	0
77th	(1941–1943)	0	0	1	1	1	1
78th	(1943–1945)	0	0	1	1	1	1
79th	(1945–1947)	0	0	4	0	4	0
80th	(1947–1949)	0	0	0	0	0	0
81st	(1949–1951)	0	0	2	0	2	0
82nd	(1951–1953)	0	0	0	0	0	0
83rd	(1953–1955)	0	0	1	0	1	0
84th	(1955–1957)	0	0	0	0	0	0
85th	(1957–1959)	0	0	0	0	0	0
86th	(1959–1961)	0	0	1	0	1	0
87th	(1961–1963)	1	0	3	1	4	1
88th	(1963–1965)	1	0	2	1	3	1
89th	(1965–1967)	2	1	5	0	7	1
90th	(1967–1969)	1	0	5	1	6	1
91st	(1969–1971)	2	0	4	0	6	0
92nd	(1971–1973)	10	2	10	2	20	4
93rd	(1973–1975)	10	2	21	7	31	9
94th	(1975–1977)	23	13	4	4	27	17
95th	(1977–1979)	5	1	8	2	13	3
96th	(1979–1981)	4	1	17	9	21	10
97th	(1981–1983)	7	2	20	7	27	9
98th	(1983–1985)	7	2	12	9	19	11
99th	(1985–1987)	9	1	14	9	23	10
100th	(1987–1989)	24	6	20	6	44	12
101st	(1989–1991)	9	6	15	5	24	11
102nd	(1991–1993)	21	9	28	14	49	23
103rd	(1993–1995)	20	4	22	10	42	14
104th	(1995–1997)	21	4	29	5	50	9

SOURCE: Norman J Ornstein, Thomas E. Mann, and Michael J. Malbin, *Vitial Statistics on Congress, 1997–1998* (Washington, D.C.: Congressional Quarterly, 1998).

NOTE: The number of votes required to invoke cloture was changed March 7, 1975, from two-thirds of those present and voting, to three-fifths of the total Senate membership, as Rule XXII of the standing rules of the Senate was amended.

Vetoes and Overrides, 1947–1996

Congress		Total number of presidential vetoes	Number of regular vetoes	Number of pocket vetoes	Vetoes overridden: Total	Vetoes overridden: Percentage of regular vetoes	House attempts to override vetoes	Senate attempts to override vetoes
80th	(1947–1949)	75	42	33	6	14.3	8	8
81st	(1949–1951)	79	70	9	3	4.3	5	5
82nd	(1951–1953)	22	14	8	3	21.4	4	4
83rd	(1953–1955)	52	21	31	0	—	0	0
84th	(1955–1957)	34	12	22	0	—	1	1
85th	(1957–1959)	51	18	33	0	—	1	1
86th	(1959–1961)	44	22	22	2	9.1	5	6
87th	(1961–1963)	20	11	9	0	—	0	0
88th	(1963–1965)	9	5	4	0	—	0	0
89th	(1965–1967)	14	10	4	0	—	0	0
90th	(1967–1969)	8	2	6	0	—	0	0
91st	(1969–1971)	11	7	4	2	28.6	4	4
92nd	(1971–1973)	20	6	14	2	33.3	3	4
93rd	(1973–1975)	39	27	12	5	18.5	12	10
94th	(1975–1977)	37	32	5	8	25.0	17	15
95th	(1977–1979)	19	6	13	0	—	2	0
96th	(1979–1981)	12	7	5	2	28.6	2	2
97th	(1981–1983)	15	9	6	2	22.2	4	3
98th	(1983–1985)	24	9	15	2	22.2	2	2
99th	(1985–1987)	20	13	7	2	15.4	3	3
100th	(1987–1989)	19	8	11	3	37.5	5	4
101st	(1989–1991)	21	16	5	0	—	9	5
102nd	(1991–1993)	25	15	10[a]	1	6.7	3	3
103rd	(1993–1995)	0	0	0	0	0	0	0
104th	(1995–1997)	17	17	0	1	5.9	6	1

SOURCE: Norman J Ornstein, Thomas E. Mann, and Michael J. Malbin, *Vitial Statistics on Congress, 1997–1998* (Washington, D.C.: Congressional Quarterly, 1998).

NOTE: a. President Bush asserted that he had pocket-vetoed S1176, although some members of Congress disputed that on the grounds that bills can be pocket-vetoed only after Congress has adjourned, not during a recess.

Congressional Information on the Internet

A huge array of congressional information is available for free at Internet sites operated by the federal government, colleges and universities, and commercial firms. The sites offer the full text of bills introduced in the House and Senate, voting records, campaign finance information, transcripts of selected congressional hearings, investigative reports, and much more.

THOMAS

The most important site for congressional information is THOMAS *(http://thomas.loc.gov)*, which is named for Thomas Jefferson and operated by the Library of Congress. THOMAS's highlight is its databases containing the full text of all bills introduced in Congress since 1989, the full text of the *Congressional Record* since 1989, and the status and summary information for all bills introduced since 1973.

THOMAS also offers special links to bills that have received or are expected to receive floor action during the current week and newsworthy bills that are pending or that have recently been approved. Finally, THOMAS has selected committee reports, answers to frequently asked questions about accessing congressional information, publications titled *How Our Laws Are Made* and *Enactment of a Law*, and links to lots of other congressional Web sites.

HOUSE OF REPRESENTATIVES

The U.S. House of Representatives site *(http://www.house.gov)* offers the schedule of bills, resolutions, and other legislative issues the House will consider in the current week. It also has updates about current proceedings on the House floor and a list of the next day's meeting of House committees. Other highlights include a database that helps users identify their representative, a directory of House members and committees, the House ethics manual, links to Web pages maintained by House members and committees, a calendar of congressional primary dates and candidate-filing deadlines for ballot access, the full text of all amendments to the Constitution that have been ratified and those that have been proposed but not ratified, and lots of information about Washington, D.C. for visitors.

Another key House site is The Office of the Clerk On-line Information Center *(http://clerkweb.house.gov)*, which has records of all roll-call votes taken since 1990. The votes are recorded by bill, so it is a lengthy process to compile a particular representative's voting record. The site also has lists of committee assignments, a telephone directory for members and committees, mailing label templates for members and committees, rules of the current Congress, election statistics from 1920 to the present, biographies of Speakers of the House, biographies of women who have served since 1917, and a virtual tour of the House Chamber.

One of the more interesting House sites is operated by the Subcommittee on Rules and Organization of the House Committee on Rules *(http://www.house.gov/rules_org/R&O_Reference.htm)*. Its highlight is dozens of Congressional Research Service reports about the legislative process. Some of the available titles include *Legislative Research in Congressional Offices: A Primer, How to Follow Current Federal Legislation and Regulations, Hearings in the House of Representatives: A Guide for Preparation and Conduct, Investigative Oversight: An Introduction to the Law, Practice, and Procedure of Congressional Inquiry, How Measures Are Brought to the House Floor: A Brief Introduction, A Brief Introduction to the Federal Budget Process*, and *Presidential Vetoes 1789–1996: A Summary Overview.*

A final House site is the Internet Law Library *(http://law.house.gov)*. This site has a searchable version of the U.S. Code, which contains the text of public laws enacted by Congress, and a tutorial for searching the Code. There also is a huge collection of links to other Internet sites that provide state and territorial laws, laws of other nations, and treaties and international laws.

SENATE

At least in the Internet world, the Senate is not as active as the House. Its main Web site *(http://www.senate.gov)* has records of all roll-call votes taken since 1989 (arranged by bill), brief descriptions of all bills and joint resolutions introduced in the Senate during the past week, and a calendar of upcoming committee hearings. The site also provides the standing rules of the Senate, a directory of senators and their committee assignments, lists of nominations that the president has submitted to the Senate for approval, links to Web pages operated by senators and committees, and a virtual tour of the Senate.

GENERAL REFERENCE

Information about the membership, jurisdiction, and rules of each congressional committee is available at the U.S. Government Printing Office site *(http://www.access.gpo.gov/congress/index.html)*. It also has transcripts of selected congressional hearings, the full text of selected House and Senate reports, and the House and Senate rules manuals.

An excellent place to explore voting records of individual members of Congress is Congressional Quarterly's VoteWatch *(http://pathfinder.com/CQ)*, a project of Time Warner's Pathfinder and Congressional Quarterly. The site provides voting records for the previous eighteen months and can be searched by the name of the representative or senator, popular bill name, keyword, or subject. The site also has articles about the latest key votes in the House and Senate.

Another Congressional Quarterly site, American Voter *(http://voter.cq.com)*, provides detailed information about individual members of Congress. For each member, it offers a biographical profile, a list of key staff contacts, results of primary and general elections, a record of recent key votes, the text of recent floor speeches, a list of bills and resolutions introduced during the current session, and records of committee votes. The member information can be searched by name, Zip Code, or state.

The U.S. General Accounting Office, the investigative arm of Congress, operates a site *(http://www.gao.gov)* that provides the full text of its reports from 1996 to the present. The reports cover a wide range of topics: aviation safety, combating terrorism, counternarcotics efforts in Mexico, defense contracting, electronic warfare, food assistance programs, Gulf War illness, health insurance, illegal aliens, information technology, long-term care, mass transit, Medicare, military readiness, money laundering, national parks, nuclear waste, organ donation, student loan defaults, and the Year 2000 computing crisis, among others.

The GAO Daybook is an excellent current awareness tool. This electronic mailing list distributes a daily list of reports and testimony released by the GAO. Subscriptions are available by sending an E-mail message to *majordomo@www.gao.gov,* and in the message area typing "subscribe daybook" (without the quotation marks).

Current budget and economic projections are provided at the Congressional Budget Office Web site *(http://www.cbo.gov).* The site also has reports about the economic and budget outlook for the next decade, the president's budget proposals, federal civilian employment, Social Security privatization, tax reform, water use conflicts in the west, marriage and the federal income tax, and the role of foreign aid in development, among other topics. Other highlights include monthly budget updates, historical budget data, cost estimates for bills reported by congressional committees, and transcripts of congressional testimony by CBO officials.

The congressional Office of Technology Assessment was eliminated in 1995, but every report it ever issued is available at The OTA Legacy *(http://www.wws-princeton.edu:80/~ota),* a site operated by the Woodrow Wilson School of Public and International Affairs at Princeton University. The site has more than 100,000 pages of detailed reports about aging, agricultural technology, arms control, biological research, cancer, computer security, defense technology, economic development, education, environmental protection, health and health technology, information technology, space, transportation, and many other subjects. The reports are organized in alphabetical, chronological, and topical lists.

CAMPAIGN FINANCE

Several Internet sites provide detailed campaign finance data for congressional elections. The official site is operated by the Federal Election Commission *(http://www.fec.gov),* which regulates political spending. The site's highlight is its database of campaign reports filed from May 1996 to the present by House and presidential candidates, political action committees, and political party committees. Senate reports are not included because they are filed with the Secretary of the Senate. The reports in the FEC's database are scanned images of paper reports filed with the commission.

The FEC site also has summary financial data for House and Senate candidates in the current election cycle, abstracts of court decisions pertaining to federal election law from 1976 to 1997, a graph showing the number of political action committees (PACS) in existence each year from 1974 to the present, and a directory of national and state agencies that are responsible for releasing information about campaign financing, candidates on the ballot, election results, lobbying, and other issues. Another useful feature is a collection of brochures about federal election law, public funding of presidential elections, the ban on contributions by foreign nationals, independent expenditures supporting or opposing a candidate for federal office, contribution limits, filing a complaint, researching public records at the FEC, and other topics. Finally, the site provides the FEC's legislative recommendations, its annual report, a report about its first twenty years in existence, the FEC's monthly newsletter, several reports about voter registration, election results for the most recent presidential and congressional elections, and campaign guides for corporations and labor organizations, congressional candidates and committees, political party committees, and nonconnected committees.

The best online source for campaign finance data is FECInfo *(http://www.tray.com/fecinfo),* which is operated by former Federal Election Commission employee Tony Raymond. FECInfo's searchable databases provide extensive itemized information about receipts and expenditures by federal candidates and political action committees from 1980 to the present. The data, which are obtained from the FEC, are quite detailed. For example, for candidates contributions can be searched by Zip Code. The site also has data on soft money contributions, lists of the top political action committees in various categories, lists of the top contributors from each state, and much more.

Another interesting site is Campaign Finance Data on the Internet *(http://www.soc.american.edu/campfin),* which is operated by the American University School of Communication. It provides electronic files from the FEC that have been reformatted in .dbf format so they can be used in database programs such as Paradox, Access, and FoxPro. The files contain data on PAC, committee, and individual contributions to individual congressional candidates.

More campaign finance data is available from the Center for Responsive Politics *(http://www.crp.org),* a public interest organization. The center provides a list of all "soft money" donations to political parties of $100,000 or more in the current election cycle and data about "leadership" political action committees associated with individual politicians. Other databases at the site provide information about travel expenses that House members received from private sources for attending meetings and other events, activities of registered federal lobbyists, and activities of foreign agents who are registered in the United States.

Index

A
Abourezk, James, 99 (box), 101
Ad hoc committees, 18, 62, 142, 143
Adams, John, 36–37 (box)
Adams, John Quincy, 20 (box), 36 (box), 38, 109–110
Adjournment
House procedures, 53 (box), 72, 85 (box)
pocket vetoes, 113
Senate procedures, 91, 94
Administrative Review, House Commission on, 133
African Americans, in House leadership, 28, 32
Aging, House Permanent Select Committee on, 144
Akaka, Daniel K., 32
Albert, Carl, 17–18, 123, 129
Albright, Madeleine, 5
Aldrich, Nelson W., 4, 38, 48
Alexander, Bill, 101 (box)
Allen, James B., 91 (box), 99 (box), 101
Allison, William B., 4, 38, 48
Amendment in the nature of a substitute, 67, 80, 86
Amendments. *See also* Germaneness issues
committee action, 66
conference action, 102, 107–109
House floor action, 55, 68 (box), 85–87
in Committee of Whole, 84
degrees of amendment, 86–87
privileged legislation, 66
restricted by the rule, 68 (box), 76, 77, 80–82
recorded votes, 52, 77, 80
Senate floor action, 55, 95, 96–98
Amendments in disagreement, 107, 108
Anderson, Glenn M., 134
Annals of Congress, 100 (box)
Annunzio, Frank, 134
Anthony, Henry, 38
Appropriations bills
committee rivalries, 156
conference action, 107
House origin, 58, 59, 60
line-item veto, 110–111 (box)
nongermane riders, 14, 65, 86, 97
privileged status, 75–76
reports, 67
Appropriations Committee, House
closed sessions, 128 (box)
leadership role, 27, 28, 154
membership, 155
prestige, 151
subcommittee autonomy, 76, 131, 135, 142
Appropriations Committee, Senate
chairmanship challenge, 148 (box), 149
prestige, 151
subcommittees, 142
Archivist of the United States, 104 (box), 113
Arends, Les, 130
Armed Services Committee, House, 149
Armed Services Committee, Senate, 151
Armey, Dick, 27, 28, 30 (box), 106
Aspin, Les, 134, 149
Authorization bills, 60, 67

B
Bach, Stanley, 80, 82
Baesler, Scotty, 71
Baker, Howard H. Jr., 43–44, 64 (box), 89
Baker, Robert G. "Bobby," 40
Balanced budget amendment
"Contract with America," 26 (box), 44–45, 71
discharge petitions, 71
Hatfield vote, 45, 135, 148 (box), 148
Bankhead, William B., 16
Banks, Nathaniel P., 12
Barbour, Philip P., 12
Barkley, Alben W., 4, 39
Barnes, Michael, 135
Bell, John, 12
Bennett, Charles E., 149
Biden, Joseph, 81
Bills. *See* Legislation
Blaine, James G., 10, 11, 21 (box)
Blair and Rives, 100 (box)
Blanket waivers of points of order, 77
Blue slip, 96
"Board of Education," 16
Boehner, John A., 30, 34–35, 106
Boggs, Hale, 18
Bolling, Richard, 13, 20, 123, 126–127 (box), 130, 143
Bonior, David, 28, 32, 106
Bork, Robert H., 63
Boyd, Linn, 10
Brademas, John, 13
Brooks, Jack, 109
Brown, George Rothwell, 9
Brown, William Holmes, 57 (box)
Buchanan, James, 38
Budget Committee, House
budget resolutions, 75, 76
membership, 131, 154–155
majority leader's seat, 27
stripped seat, 147, 148 (box)
term limits, 139
prestige, 151, 156–157
subcommittees, 143
Budget Committee, Senate
prestige, 151, 156–157
subcommittees, 143
term limits, 139
Budget process
budget resolutions, 75–76, 82
budget summits, 157
committee rivalries, 156–157
importance, 52, 54, 59
reconciliation bills, 52, 59, 105, 106, 108
substitute budgets, 76
Burr, Aaron, 21 (box)
Burton, Dan, 30
Burton, Phillip, 13, 20
Bush, George
congressional relations, 5, 23, 24
line-item veto, 111 (box)
Manion nomination, 81
pocket veto, 113
signing statements, 109
tax policy, 34, 42
Byrd, Robert C.
congressional-executive relations, 5, 6
as majority leader, 41–42
paired voting, 81
as party leader, 1, 3
as president pro tem, 37 (box)
Senate floor procedures, 93, 96, 99 (box), 101–102, 112
Senate scheduling, 96
seniority system, 137, 156 (box)
as whip, 41, 47
Byrd Rule, 108
Byrns, Joseph W., 16

C
Cable-Satellite Public Affairs Network (C-SPAN), 6, 63, 64–65 (box)
Calendar of the Committee of the Whole House on the State of the Union. *See* Union Calendar
Calendar of General Orders (Senate), 90, 95
Calendar Wednesday (House), 14, 16, 60 (box), 70–71
Calendars
House scheduling, 67–71
Senate scheduling, 90
Calendars of the U.S. House of Representatives and History of Legislation, 67, 69
Calhoun, John C., 36 (box), 38, 121
Callahan, Sonny, 76
Campaign finance
federal subsidies, 47
investigations, 158–159
reform efforts, 71, 73–75, a44 (box), 96
Campbell, Ben Nighthorse, 148
Campbell, Tom, 159
Cannon, Joseph G., 7, 14, 21 (box), 27, 33, 38
caucus meetings, 33
committee appointments, 125
discharge procedures, 70
Rules Committee, 122, 126 (box)
silent quorum, 11
Cannon's Precedents, 57 (box)
Carlisle, John G., 10
Caro, Robert A., 47 (box)
Carter, Jimmy
congressional relations, 4–5, 6, 36–37 (box), 41
energy policy, 153
ERA time extension, 104 (box)
Social Security, 33
Caucuses, 33, 47–48. *See also* Democratic Caucus, House; Democratic Conference, Senate; Republican Conference, House; Republican Conference, Senate
Celler, Emanuel, 125
Censure, of president by Congress, 105 (box)
Chafee, John H., 135
Chairman's mark, 58
Chairmen. *See* Committee and subcommittee chairmen

Chapman, Jim, 31
Cheney, Richard, 29
Children, 26 (box)
Children, Youth and Families, House Select Committee on, 144
Chiles, Lawton, 41
Chisholm, Shirley, 34
Civil Rights Act of 1964, 62, 93, 153
Civil rights movement, 98–99 (box)
Civility in debate, 65 (box)
Clark, James Beauchamp "Champ," 4, 14–16, 27
Clark, Joel Bennett, 102
"Class of 1974," 18, 115, 129
Clay, Henry, 4, 7, 9–10, 11, 20 (box), 33, 98, 105 (box)
Clean Air Act of 1990, 42, 55
Clean bills, 58, 64–65
Clerk of the House
bill transmission to Senate, 89
election of Speaker, 12, 90 (box)
enrolled bills, 109
legislation introduction, 58
veto messages, 113
voting methods, 79
Clinton, Bill
congressional relations, 5, 23, 25, 44, 53 (box), 56–57
investigations, 5, 30 (box), 46, 104–105 (box), 123, 143, 158
line-item veto, 110–111 (box)
pocket vetoes, 113
Clinton, Hillary, 30 (box), 158
Closed meetings. *See* Open/closed proceedings
Closed rules, 77, 80
Cloture
amendment limits, 97
dilatory tactics, 98–99 (box)
floor debate, 95, 99–100
list of cloture votes, 171
postcloture filibuster, 99 (box), 101–102
Senate rules, 56–57 (box)
supermajority requirement, 60 (box)
Coats, Dan, 135
Cobb, Howell, 10, 12
Cochran, Thad, 45
Coelho, Tony, 13, 22, 28, 32, 47 (box)
Cohen, Richard E., 42
Colfax, Schuyler, 10
College of Cardinals, 76
Collie, Melissa P., 153
Colmer, William M., 123, 126 (box), 129
Commemorative bills, 59
Commerce Committee, House, 136, 151
Committee and subcommittee chairmen
autonomy and power, 76, 115–116
legislative process, 62–63
in seniority system, 17, 33, 51
conference action, 33, 103–104, 106, 140 (box)
as floor managers, 80, 85, 95
procedures, 80, 152–153
role, 62–63, 72, 96
selection
campaign aid potential, 47 (box)
by party caucus, 18, 33, 48, 116–117, 130, 137, 154–155
by presiding officer, 9, 37–38, 121
removal, 134–135
seniority, 124–129, 147–149
subcommittee chair limits, 33, 138
term limits, 139, 146
Committees, House Select Committee on, 133
Committees and subcommittees. *See also* Committee and subcommittee chairmen; Conference committees; specific committees
assignment, 146–147
by party caucus, 35, 38, 48, 116–117
plum assignments, 151–152
by presiding officer, 9, 36 (box), 38, 121
Ways and Means, 15–16, 17, 35
history, 9, 37–38, 115–141
dates of establishment (box), 120
leadership functions, 3
legislative process, 51, 54–55, 58, 115
bill referral, 61–62, 80, 153, 156
committee action, 62–67
discharge, 70–71
hearings, 63, 153
jurisdiction conflicts, 153–157
media coverage, 128 (box)
membership, 121, 154–155
seat guarantees, limits, 33, 116, 137, 138
seniority, 147–150
size, party ratios, 145–146, 149–150
stripped seats, 7, 148 (box)
term limits, 139, 140–141
oversight, 157–159
procedures, 129, 152–153
open meetings, 52, 53, 63, 65–66
proxy voting (box), 132–133
recorded votes, 66, 152
"sunshine" reforms, 128 (box)
reports, 66–67, 152
staff, 108, 117, 129, 130–131, 137, 138
subcommittees, 124, 142–143
autonomy, 52, 118, 131–132
limits, 136, 138, 140
subcommittee bill of rights, 33, 117, 130
types, 141–145
Companion bills, 59
Concurrent referral, 61
Concurrent resolutions, 61, 68
Condit, Gary A., 106
Conference committees
final legislative action, 55, 102–109
House Rules Committee role, 122–123
legislative intent, 67
multiple referral effect, 62, 104, 105
reports, 108–109
blanket waivers, 77
conferee authority, 107
filibusters, 95
order of action, 103, 108
privileged status, 76
Senate appointments, 36 (box)
summary (box), 140–141
"sunshine rules," 52, 53, 128 (box)
"technical disagreement," 107
Conferences, party. *See* Democratic Caucus, House; Democratic Conference, Senate; Republican Conference, House; Republican Conference, Senate
Confidentiality. *See* Secrecy and confidentiality; Open/closed proceedings
Congress, members of. *See also* Committee and subcommittee chairmen; Congressional elections; Congressional ethics; Congressional pay; Term limits; Voting
committee assignments, 116, 146–152
lost positions, 148 (box)
conference committee selection, 105–106
legislative process, 57, 58–59, 80
presiding officers, 90–91 (box)
service records, 125–126
Congress, U.S. *See also* Committees and subcommittees; Congress, members of; Congressional-executive relations; House of Representatives; Legislative process; Senate
information on the Internet 56 (box), 101 (box), 173–174
proceedings reported (box), 100–101
sessions, 53 (box)
terms, 53 (box)
Congressional Budget and Impoundment Control Act of 1974, 59, 75, 158
Congressional committees. *See* Committees and subcommittees; specific committees
Congressional elections
contested elections, 73, 74
privileged status, 75
House, Senate leadership aid, 46–47 (box)
Congressional ethics
House scandals, 23
privileged status of complaints, 75
Speaker controversies, 20–21 (box), 22, 25–26
task force, 145
voting, 79
Congressional-executive relations. *See also* Vetoes
budget summits, 157
caucus nominations for president, 33
censure, 105 (box)
divided/shared control, 4–5 (box), 29, 30
party affiliation (table), 163–164
early Congresses, 8, 37
executive branch oversight, 157–159
impeachment procedures, 60 (box), 104–105 (box)
leadership functions, 6
presidential role in legislation, 55, 58
final action, 109–113
line-item veto, 110–111 (box)
signing statements, 109
vice president's role, 36–37 (box)
Congressional Globe, 100 (box)
Congressional-judicial relations, 67
Congressional pay
pay raise controversies, 22, 106–107
Twenty-Seventh Amendment, 104 (box)
Congressional Record, 79, 81, 86, 100–101 (box)
Congressional Register, 100 (box)
Congressional staff
committee allocations, 108, 117, 129, 130–131, 137, 138
conference reports, 108
floor management of bills, 85
Congressional votes. *See* Voting
Conkling, Roscoe, 38
Consent Calendar (House), 14–15, 16, 69, 122–123
Conservative coalition, 17
Conservative Opportunity Society, 6, 24, 29
Constituents' role in legislation, 57–58
Constitution, U.S. *See also* Constitutional amendments; specific amendments
House, Senate rules, 56 (box), 60 (box), 85 (box)
presiding officers, 2, 8, 36–37 (box), 90–91 (box)
revenue bill origin, 96
voting procedures, 78
impeachment process, 105 (box)
president's role in legislation, 109
veto power, 110–111 (box), 110–112
Constitutional amendments. *See also* Balanced budget amendment; specific amendments
procedures, 60, 60 (box)
discharge petitions, 71
House scheduling, 68
proposed term limits amendment, 82
ratification time limits, 104 (box)
Contempt power, 158–159
Contested elections. *See* Congressional elections
Continuing resolutions, 59, 156

"Contract with America"
bill number assignment, 59
congressional-executive relations, 55–57, 58
Dole support, 44–45
Gingrich leadership, 24, 25
House committee clout, 119
House Republican Conference role, 34
minority leadership, 29, 32
partisan trends, 30 (box)
planks, 26 (box)
balanced budget amendment, 71
line-item veto, 111 (box)
open rules, 80
term limits, 139
Rules Committee, 127 (box)
Cooper, Henry A., 13
Cooper, Joseph, 153
Corrections Calendar (House), 60 (box), 67, 68 (box), 69, 123, 145
Cranston, Alan, 47
Crime bills, 26 (box), 88
Crisp, Charles F., 11, 14
Crockett, Davy, 55
C-SPAN. *See* Cable-Satellite Public Affairs Network
Cummins, Albert B., 148 (box)
Curtis, Charles, 42 (box)

D
Daily Digest, 101 (box)
Daschle, Tom, 1, 43, 48
Davidson, Roger H., 3, 7, 41, 126, 156, 159
Dayton, Jonathan, 8, 31
Debate. *See also* Cloture
House procedures, 68 (box), 77, 74, 84–85, 86
record of proceedings, 100–101 (box)
Senate procedures, 95–96
TV coverage, 64–65 (box)
Declarations of war, 72–73
DeConcini, Dennis, 81
Deering, Christopher J., 119, 121, 124, 126, 142, 145, 156–157
Defense policy
closed sessions, 63
"Contract with America," 26 (box)
Degrees of amendment, 86–87, 97
Delaney, James J., 126 (box)
DeLay, Tom, 5, 27, 30 (box), 32–33, 106
Dellums, Ronald V., 125
Democratic Caucus, House
clout, 115, 116–117
committee assignments, 35, 148–149, 154–155
party ratios, 145
term limits, 139
congressional reforms, 129–136
open meetings, 52
proxy voting, 132 (box)
seniority challenges, 134–135
subcommittees, 143
suspension of rules, 73
history, 16, 33–34
and majority leader, 27
and Rules Committee, 80, 123, 126–127 (box)
select committees abolished, 144
Democratic Caucus, Senate, 38, 39, 41
Democratic Committee on Committees, House, 35, 130
Democratic Committee on Committees, Senate, 39, 48
Democratic Committee on Organization, Study, and Review, 130
Democratic Committee on Party Effectiveness, 34
Democratic Conference, Senate, 48, 135, 137
Democratic Congressional Campaign Committee, 34, 39, 46–47 (box)
Democratic Party
House leadership ladder, 28
House, Senate committee assignments, 154–155
ratios, 145–146
rules evolution, 54
Senate leadership, 38–46
Democratic Policy Committee, Senate, 40, 48
Democratic Senatorial Campaign Committee, 42, 46–47 (box)
Democratic Steering and Policy Committee, House
committee assignments, 15–16, 35, 130, 131, 147
committee system reforms, 117, 134
history, 18, 35
suspension of rules, 73
Democratic Steering Committee, House, 16, 35, 149, 154–155
Democratic Steering Committee, Senate, 39, 48, 121, 137, 149, 155
Democratic Study Group, House, 33, 36, 129
Deschler-Brown Precedents, 57 (box)
Deschler's Precedents, 57 (box)
Dilatory tactics
House, 10–11, 31 (box), 74
Senate, 98–99 (box)
Dingell, John D., 51, 54, 61, 151 (box), 158
Dirksen, Everett McKinley, 39, 43, 47
Disappearing quorums, 10, 11, 14
Discharge procedures
conference committees, 108
House, 16, 67, 69, 70–71, 122
Senate, 93
District of Columbia oversight, 75
Division method of voting, 68 (box), 78
Dodd, Christopher, 43
Doggett, Lloyd, 74
Dole, Bob
congressional-executive relations, 58
government shutdown, 1995, 25
paired voting, 81
as party leader, 1
Senate committee system, 140, 148
as Senate leader, 44–45
tax legislation, 97
Domenici, Pete V., 44, 139
Dornan, Robert K., 74
Douglas, Stephen A., 38, 148 (box)
Dove, Robert B., 41, 100

E
Eagleton, Thomas F., 100
Eastland, James O., 125
Edwards, Chet, 151 (box)
Eisenhower, Dwight D., 5, 40, 111 (box)
Electronic voting, 68 (box), 74, 78, 82 (caption)
Ellsworth, Oliver, 42 (box)
Energy and Commerce Committee, House, 136, 151
Energy policy, 18, 143, 153
Engrossed bills, 87, 89
Enrolled bills, 105 (box), 109
Enzi, Mike, 150
Equal Rights Amendment, 73, 104 (box)
Erlenborn, John, 130, 134
Ervin, Sam, 43, 63
Ethics Reform Act of 1989, 139, 145
Evans, C. Lawrence, 140 (box)
Evans, Daniel J., 54, 81
Evans, Rowland, 40
Executive Calendar (Senate), 90
Expulsion of members, 60 (box)

F
Family policy, 26 (box)
"Fast-track" procedures, 57 (box)
Fazio, Vic, 28, 34
Feingold, Russell, 94 (box)
Filibusters. *See also* Cloture
individual record, 100
Senate floor procedures, 55, 94 (box), 98–102
in morning hour, 93–94
postcloture, 101–102
scheduling, 92 (box)
track system, 90–91
Finance Committee, Senate, 142, 151
Five-minute rule, 68 (box), 84
Flag desecration, 66
Floor leaders. *See* Majority leader; Minority leader
Floor managers, 84, 95, 103
Foley, Thomas
leadership ladder, 28, 32
as party leader, 1
select committees, 144
as Speaker, 22–23, 36
as whip, 13, 19
Follett, Mary P., 8, 9, 10, 12–13
Ford, Gerald
House leadership, 13
as president, 36 (box), 113
as vice president, 28, 36 (box)
Ford, Wendell H., 47
Foreign policy, 5
Foreign Relations Committee, Senate, 151, 152
Frumin, Alan S., 57 (box)
Fulbright, J. William, 63, 151
Fuller, Hubert Bruce, 8, 10, 14

G
Gag rules, 77
Gales and Seaton, 100 (box)
Gallatin, Albert, 8, 37
Galloway, George B., 27
Garner, John Nance, 16, 27
General Accounting Office (GAO), 158
Gephardt, Richard, 1, 6, 28, 30–31, 34, 106
Germaneness issues
conference action, 107, 109
House amendments, 14, 65, 77, 82, 86
Senate amendments, 91, 93, 96–97
budget reconciliation, 108
after cloture, 95, 97
Senate debate, 95
Ghost voting, 79
Giles, William B., 8
Gillette, Frederick H., 13, 16
Gillmor, Paul, 134
Gingrich, Newt
campaign finance reform, 71, 73–75
committee relations, 7, 35, 116, 119, 157
Appropriations Committee, 76, 134
assignments, 147
conference appointments, 106, 140 (box)
oversight committees, 159
Rules Committee, 127 (box)
task forces, 145
congressional-executive relations, 5
"Contract with America," 26 (box), 58, 59
Corrections Calendar, 69
media savvy, 6, 64 (box)
as party leader, 1–2, 3, 7, 8
Dole comparison, 44–45
partisan trends, 30–31 (box)
as Speaker, 20, 23–26
attempted coup, 1997, 20 (box), 27, 28, 35
controversies, 20 (box)
election, 1997, 13, 25–26, 79, 90 (box)

ethics charges, 25–26, 30 (box)
and House Republican Conference, 34–35
as whip, 23, 28, 29–30, 32
Wright ethics charges, 6, 20, 20 (box), 30 (box)
"Golden Gavel," 91
Goldwater, Barry, 81
Gonzalez, Henry B., 85 (box), 155
Goodling, William, 46 (box)
GOPAC, 24
Gore, Al, 36–37 (box), 64 (box)
Gorman, Arthur P., 38–39
Gorsuch, Anne, 158
Gorton, Slade, 81
Government Reform and Oversight Committee, House, 123
Gramm, Phil, 7, 148 (box), 148
Gramm-Latta bill, 29, 83
Gramm-Rudman-Hollings Act, 54
Grant, Ulysses S., 110 (box)
Grassley, Charles, 93
Gray, William III, 13, 28, 32, 34
Griffin, Robert P., 43, 47
Grow, Galusha A., 10, 12, 23
Gun control, 71

H
Hall, Tony, 144
Halleck, Charles A., 13, 28
Hamilton, Alexander, 8, 37
Hansen, Julia Butler, 130–131
Harlow, Ralph V., 8
Hastert, Dennis, 33
Hatfield, Mark O., 45, 135, 148 (box), 148
Hawkins, Paula, 81
Hayden, Carl, 125
Hearings, 63
oversight, 158
procedures, 152, 153
Rules Committee, 76–77, 122
witnesses, 123, 153
Helms, Jesse, 91 (box), 93, 135, 151, 152
Henderson, David B., 14
Herbert, F. Edward, 125, 134
Hind's Precedents, 57 (box)
Hogan, Thomas P., 111 (box)
Holds, 44, 55, 92–93
Hopper, 58
Horton, Frank, 130, 134
House Bank scandal, 23
House Calendar, 67, 68
House Manual, 56 (box)
House of Representatives, U.S. *See also* Speaker of the House; specific committees
committees
list, 120 (box)
membership, 154–155
role, 115
select committees (box), 144
floor action, 67–89
amendments, 55, 85–87
Committee of Whole action, 83–84
debate, 84–85
dilatory tactics, 74
rule adoption, 83
scheduling, 67–83
typical schedule (box), 68
voting methods, 78–79
leadership structure, 2, 26–36
partisan trends (box), 30–31
party caucuses, 116–117
presiding officers, 90–91 (box)
rules, 51–52, 56–57 (box)
seniority system, 151 (box)
supermajority votes, 60 (box)
television coverage, 64–65 (box)
vetoed bills, 111–112
House Oversight Committee, 75, 149, 154–155
House Post Office scandal, 23
House Practice, 57 (box)
House-Senate relations
adjournment, 53 (box)
bill transmission, 89
final legislative action, 102–109
tax legislation, 96–97
unicameral reform, 130, 136
Hoyer, Stenny, 34, 106
Hughes, William J., 144
Humphrey, Hubert H., 42, 98–99 (box)
Hunger, House Select Committee on, 144
Hunter, Robert M. T., 12
Hyde, Henry, 119

I
Impeachment procedures, 60 (box), 104–105 (box)
Incumbents. *See also* Seniority
campaign aid, 46 (box)
committee assignments, 147
committee chairmen, 154–155
Inouye, Daniel, 42, 48, 81
Intelligence Committee, House
closed sessions, 63
majority leader's seat, 27
membership, 143, 144
term limits, 139
Intelligence Committee, Senate
closed sessions, 63
membership, 143, 155
term limits, 139
Internal Revenue Service, 63
Internet
congressional Web sites, 56 (box), 101 (box), 173–174
online voting, 133
Interstate compacts, 68
Investigations
oversight mandate, 157–159
select, special committees, 143
Union Calendar, 67
Iran-contra scandal, 42, 143

J
Jackson, Andrew, 10, 20 (box), 36 (box), 38, 105 (box), 110
Jamieson, Kathleen Hall, 65 (box)
Jefferson, Thomas, 8, 20 (box), 36 (box), 37, 51
Jefferson's Manual, 56 (box)
Jeffords, James M., 135
Johnson, Andrew, 4, 105 (box)
Johnson, Lyndon B.
House campaign aid, 47 (box)
as president, 47
as Senate leader, 2, 4–5, 40, 91–92, 100, 137
as vice president, 36 (box)
"Johnson Rule," 137
"Johnson Treatment," 40
Johnston, J. Bennett, 41, 42
Joint Committee on Atomic Energy, 143
Joint Committee on Printing, 143
Joint Committee on Taxation, 110 (box), 143
Joint Committee on the Conduct of the War, 4
Joint Committee on the Library, 143
Joint Committee on the Organization of Congress, 129, 130, 132 (box), 136, 138–140, 143
Joint committees, 141, 143
Joint Economic Committee, 143
Joint referral, 61, 153, 156
Joint resolutions, 60
Journal (House), 68 (box), 83, 100 (box)
Journal (Senate), 93, 100 (box), 105 (box)
Judiciary Committee, House, 69
Judiciary Committee, Senate, 63
Jurisdiction, 61–62, 80, 153–157

K
Kasich, John, 157
Kassebaum, Nancy Landon, 81, 95
Katzmann, Robert A., 67
Kennedy, Edward M., 41, 47, 133 (box)
Kennedy, John F., 51, 126 (box), 127
Kephart, Thomas, 156
Kern, John W., 39, 42 (box)
Kerr, Michael C., 10
Killer amendments, 55
Kim, Jay, 46 (box)
"King-of-the-hill" rules, 82
Kitchin, Claude, 4, 27
"Koreagate" scandal, 21 (box)

L
La Follette, Robert M., 148 (box)
LaFalce, John, 155
Langdon, John, 37 (box)
Laughlin, Greg, 147, 150
Leadership. *See also* Majority leader; Minority leader; Speaker of the House
functions, 3–6, 46–47 (box)
House committees, 116–117
House positions, 7–36
House scheduling, 69
discharge, 70
privileged legislation, 76
Rules Committee role, 76, 122–123, 126 (box)
structured rules, 82
legislative process, 55
structure, 2–7
Senate positions, 36–48
firsts (box), 42
Senate scheduling, 89–91
task forces, 142
Leadership PACs, 46 (box)
Leadership Task Force on Ethics, 145
Leath, Marvin, 134
Legislation. *See also* Appropriations bills
clean bills, 58, 64–65
commemorative bills, 59
development, 57–67
engrossed bills, 87, 89
enrolled bills, 105 (box), 109
noncontroversial bills, 72–75
omnibus bills, 52, 59, 77, 140 (box), 156
private bills, 69
types, 60–61
Legislative Counsel, Offices of (House, Senate), 57
Legislative intent, 67, 100 (box), 109–110
Legislative process. *See also* Amendments; Budget process; Debate; Scheduling; Vetoes; Voting
anomalies (box), 104–105
committee action, 62–67, 115–119
conference action, 102–109
House floor action, 67–89
dilatory tactics, 74
prying bills from committees, 70–71
how a bill becomes a law (chart), 162
introduction of bills, 58–62
president's role, 109–113
presiding officers, 36–37 (box), 90–91 (box)
record of proceedings, 100–101 (box)
referral, 61–62, 153
rules, 51–57

Senate floor action, 89–102
dilatory tactics, 94 (box), 98–99 (box)
summary, 51
Legislative Reorganization Act of 1946
committee procedures, 152
committee size, 145
committee structure, 119, 124, 125, 142
conference committee authority, 107
jurisdiction conflicts, 153
oversight mandate, 158
Legislative Reorganization Act of 1970
adjournment, 53 (box)
committee procedural rules, 128, 152
committee reports, 66
conference reports, 108
dilatory tactics, 74
House debate on amendments, 86
oversight mandate, 158
proxy voting, 132 (box)
recorded votes, 78–79
"sunshine" reforms, 128 (box), 129
Legislative service organizations, 36
Legislative veto, 159
Lewis, J. Hamilton, 46
Lincoln, Abraham, 4
Line-item veto, 26 (box), 42, 110–111 (box)
Live quorums, 96
Livingston, Robert, 28, 76, 134, 147
Lloyd, Marilyn, 144
Lloyd, Thomas, 100
Lodge, Henry Cabot, 39
Long, Gillis W., 34
Long, Russell B., 47, 135, 137
Longworth, Nicholas, 13, 16, 27, 35
Lott, Trent
on advance notice of amendments, 80
on blanket waivers, 77
congressional-executive relations, 5
House Rules Committee, 127 (box)
as party leader, 1, 3, 31 (box)
passed, unenrolled bills, 105 (box)
presidential censure, 105 (box)
as Senate leader, 45–46, 47, 94 (box)
Lugar, Richard G., 44, 135
Lungren, Dan, 85 (box), 88

M
Mace, 84
MacNeil, Neil, 26
Macon, Nathaniel, 8, 10, 12, 20 (box)
Madden, Ray J., 126 (box), 129
Madigan, Edward R., 29
Madison Amendment, 104 (box)
Madison, James, 4, 9
Majority leader, House
functions, 26–29
leadership ladder, 13, 28 (box)
list, 166–167
Majority leader, Senate
functions, 38–46
list, 168–169
Manion, Daniel A., 81
Mann, James R., 16
Mann, Thomas, 84
Mansfield, Mike, 4, 23, 40–41, 47, 91 (box), 137
Markey, Edward J., 88
Markup, 62, 63–64
Marshall, Thurgood, 125
Martin, Joseph W. Jr., 13, 17, 28
Martin, Thomas, 39, 42 (box)
McCain, John, 94 (box)
McCarthy, Joseph R., 63
McClellan, John, 137
McCloskey, Frank, 31 (box)
McClure, James, 44
McConnell, Mitch, 94 (box)
McCormack, John W., 17–18, 21 (box), 27, 33, 129
McDade, Joseph M., 134
McDermott, James, 30 (box)
McFall, John, 13
McKinley, William, 4, 14, 27
Meehan, Martin, 73
Metzenbaum, Howard, 93, 99 (box), 101
Mica, Dan, 135
Michel, Robert H.
conference relations, 34
and Gingrich, 24
leadership ladder, 13, 27, 28
as minority leader, 21, 29–30, 31 (box)
Mills, Wilbur, 131, 143
Mineta, Norman Y., 134, 151 (box)
Minority leader, House, 27, 29–31
list, 166–167
Minority leader, Senate, 38–46
list, 168–169
Mitchell, George J., 6, 42–43, 47 (box), 48
Moakley, Joe, 31, 123, 127 (box)
Modified rules, 77
Mondale, Walter, 23, 36–37 (box), 41, 44, 99 (box), 101–102
Mondell, Franklin W., 16, 27
Monroe, James, 4
Monroney, A. S. Mike, 129
Moorhead, Carlos, 134
Morning business (Senate), 92 (box), 93, 94–95
Morning Hour (House), 68 (box), 75
Morning Hour (Senate), 93–95
Morse, Wayne, 121
Moses, George H., 37 (box)
Moss, John, 135
Muhlenberg, Frederick A. C., 8
Multiple referral, 61–62, 153, 156
ad hoc committees, 142
amendment control, 80
committee system transition, 118
conference committees, 104, 105, 140 (box)
O'Neill tactic, 19
Muskie, Edmund, 42
MX missile, 19

N
Narcotics Abuse and Control, House Select Committee on, 144
Natcher, William H., 134, 149
National Republican Congressional Committee, 46–47 (box)
National Republican Senatorial Committee, 46 (box), 48
Nethercutt, George, 23
Neumann, Mark, 147
New Deal, 39
News media *See* Television and news media
Nicaragua, 21–22, 31 (box), 42
Nickles, Don, 105 (box)
Nixon, Richard M.
congressional relations, 18, 43
as fiscal guardian, 111 (box)
as vice president, 98 (box)
Watergate scandal, 63, 64 (box), 105 (box)
Nominations and appointments
in adjournment, 60
committee procedures, 152
Senate scheduling, 90
Nongermane amendments. *See* Germaneness issues
Norris, George, 15, 125
Novak, Robert, 40

O
Oberstar, James L., 151 (box)
Obey, David R., 78, 133, 134, 149
O'Konski, Alvin, 130
Oleszek, Walter J.
on committee system, 115, 140 (box), 153, 156, 158, 159
on legislative process, 59, 69, 84, 92
on party leadership, 3, 7
Omnibus bills, 52, 59, 77, 140 (box), 156
One-hour rule, 74
O'Neill, Thomas P. "Tip" Jr.
career, 126 (box)
committee chair challenge, 134
committee jurisdiction, 61–62, 153
partisan trends, 30–31 (box)
as Speaker, 18–19, 20, 21 (box), 24
on Speaker's powers, 6, 7
Open/closed proceedings
caucus meetings, 33, 34
committees, 52, 53, 63, 65–66, 153
conference committees, 52, 53, 141 (box)
Intelligence committees, 63
"sunshine" reforms, 128 (box)
Open rules, 73, 77
Oppenheimer, Bruce I., 77
Ornstein, Norman, 84
Ortega, Daniel, 31 (box)
Oversight, 143, 157–159

P
Packwood, Bob, 81, 96
PACs, 46–47 (box)
Paired voting, 81
Panama Canal treaties, 41
Park, Tongsun, 21 (box)
Parker, Mike, 106
Parliamentarians, 61, 91 (box)
Partisanship
bipartisanship, 5, 89, 91 (box)
House trends, 30–31 (box)
leadership effectiveness, 7
restrictive rules, 80
Senate scheduling, 89
television impact, 65 (box)
Party discipline, 7
Party-switching, 147, 150
Pastore Rule, 95
Patman, Wright, 134
Patterson, Jerry M., 136, 143
Paxon, Bill, 28, 35, 47 (box)
Payne, Sereno E., 26–27
Pearson, James B., 138
Pennington, William, 13, 23, 27
Pepper, Claude, 64 (box), 127 (box)
Perfecting amendments, 85, 97
Peters, Ronald M., 8, 9, 16, 17, 22
Pickering, Thomas, 37
Platt, Orville H., 38
Poage, W. R., 134
Pocket vetoes, 112–113
Political action committees, 46–47 (box)
Political disabilities, 60 (box)
Polk, James K., 10
Polling (committee voting), 133
Postcloture filibusters, 99 (box), 101–102
President pro tempore, Senate
Byrd career, 42
committee assignments, 38, 121
duties, 2, 36–37 (box), 91 (box)
enrolled bills, 109
seniority, 150 (box)
Presidents, U.S. *See* Congressional-executive relations
Presiding officers. *See* President pro tempore,

Senate; Speaker of the House; Vice president
Previous-question motions, 74, 83, 87
Preyer, Richardson, 135
Price, David, 151 (box)
Price, Melvin, 134, 149
Private Calendar (House), 60 (box), 67, 68 (box), 69
Private laws, 69
Privileged legislation, 75–76, 92 (box)
Procedures in the U.S. House Representatives, 57 (box)
Product liability, 26 (box)
Proxy voting, 131, 132–133 (box)
Public Works and Transportation Committee, House, 151

Q
Quayle, Dan, 36 (box), 138
"Queen-of-the-hill" rules, 82
Quillen, James H. (Jimmy), 127 (box)
Quinn, Jack, 158
Quorums
after cloture, 99 (box)
"disappearing" quorums, 10, 11, 14
establishment in House, 78–79, 85 (box)
establishment in Senate, 95–96

R
Rainey, Henry T., 13, 16, 27
Randall, Samuel J., 10
Randolph, John, 9, 20 (box)
Rangel, Charles B., 144
Rankin, Jeanette, 73
Rayburn, Sam
and LBJ, 137
leadership ladder, 27
maxim for members, 52, 127
as Speaker, 2, 16–17, 27
executive relations, 5, 40
Rules Committee enlargement, 122, 126 (box), 129
Ways and Means assignments, 35
Reagan, Ronald
congressional relations, 5, 18–19, 29, 41, 44
line-item veto, 111 (box)
signing statements, 109
Recommittal
to conference, 108, 141 (box)
House floor procedures, 55, 68 (box), 87–89
in Committee of Whole, 84
Corrections Calendar, 69
Senate floor procedures, 98
Reconsider, motions to, 68 (box), 102, 112
Recorded votes
committee procedures, 66, 152
effect on number of amendments, 77
House floor voting, 68 (box), 78–79
in Committee of Whole, 52, 84
forced, 85 (box)
totals, 1947–1996 (table), 170
Reed, Thomas Brackett, 4, 7, 10–11, 14, 27, 33, 74
"Reed Rules," 11
Referral, 61–62, 153. *See also* Multiple referral
Register of Debate, 100 (box)
Reno, Janet, 158–159
Reports Elimination Act, 159
Republican Caucus, Senate, 48
Republican Committee on Committees, House, 15–16, 35
Republican Committee on Committees, Senate, 38, 48, 121, 149, 155
Republican Conference, House
clout, 116–117, 119
committee assignments, 35, 130, 134, 147, 154
Corrections Calendar, 69
history, 34–35
and majority leader, 27
policy committees, 36
suspension of rules, 73
Republican Conference, Senate, 48, 135, 137, 139, 141, 148, 155
Republican Party
campaign aid, 46–47 (box)
House leadership ladder, 28
House, Senate committee assignments, 154–155
ratios, 145–146
rules evolution, 54
Senate leadership, 36–48
Republican Policy Committee, House, 35
Republican Policy Committee, Senate, 48
Republican Steering Committee, House, 16, 35, 117, 149, 154
Republican Steering Committee, Senate, 38, 48
Resolutions, 59–60, 61
Reuss, Henry S., 134
Rhodes, John J., 5, 28
Ribicoff, Abraham, 138
Riddick, Floyd M., 8, 37 (box), 42 (box), 57 (box)
Riddick's Senate Procedure, 57 (box)
Riders, 14, 85–86
Rieselbach, Leroy N., 118, 127
Ripley, Randall B., 16, 29, 37, 42 (box), 124–125
Robinson, Joseph T., 39
Rockefeller, Nelson A., 36 (box), 98 (box)
Rodino, Peter J., 63
Roe, Robert A., 134
Roll-call votes
in committee, 66, 152
constitutional requirements, 78
House procedures, 14, 68 (box), 78–79, 85 (box)
Journal approval, 68 (box), 83
Senate procedures, 79, 92 (box), 96, 99 (box), 102
"sunshine" reforms, 128 (box)
veto overrides, 111
Rolling holds, 92–93
Roosevelt, Franklin D., 4, 39, 48
Roosevelt, Theodore, 4, 14, 38
Rose, Charlie, 30, 134
Rostenkowski, Dan, 23, 90–91 (box), 118, 128 (box)
Rothman, David J., 38–39, 48
Rule X (House), 61
Rule XI (House), 140 (box)
Rule XXII (Senate), 56–57 (box), 60 (box), 95, 98 (box), 98–99
Rule XXIV (House), 75
Rule XXV (Senate), 61, 155
Rule XLVIII (House), 144
Rules
evolution, 52–54
House, Senate compared, 51–52, 56–57 (box)
Rules Committee, House
amendment in the nature of a substitute, 67
as arm of leadership (box), 122–123
relation to Speaker, 10, 14–15, 18–19
conference action, 103, 107, 108, 109
membership, 149, 154–155
assignment, 35
seniority, 126–127 (box)
size, 35, 129
prestige, 151
proxy voting, 132 (box)
rule adoption, 83
scheduling, 68, 68 (box), 69
debate restrictions, 74
discharge, 70–71
major legislation, 76–83
in multiple referral, 156
open rules, 73
privileged legislation, 75–76
report "without recommendation," 62
Rules of the House of Representatives, 56 (box)
Russell, Richard B., 39, 137
Russo, Martin, 32, 156

S
Sabath, Adolph, 126 (box)
Sabato, Larry, 65 (box)
Sanchez, Loretta, 73, 74
Sanders, Bernard, 147
Sanford, Terry, 112
Sasser, Jim, 43
Saulsbury, Willard, 37 (box)
Scalia, Antonin, 67
Scheduling
House floor action, 67–83
discharge, 70–71
privileged matters, 75–76
Rules Committee role, 76–83
typical schedule (box), 68
leadership functions, 6
legislative process, 55
Senate floor action, 89–93
typical schedule, 92 (box)
Schneider, Claudine, 89
Schroeder, Patricia, 125
Scott, Hugh, 43, 47
Secrecy and confidentiality. *See also* Open/closed proceedings
discharge petitions, 70
holds, 92
"sunshine" reforms (box), 128
Secretary of the Senate, 89, 109, 113
Sedgwick, Theodore, 8
Select committees, 141, 143, 144
Self-executing rules, 82–83
Senate Committee System, Temporary Select Committee to Study the, 137, 138
Senate Manual Containing the Standing Rules, 56 (box)
Senate, U.S. *See also* specific committees
committees
list, 120 (box)
membership, 155
role, 115. 136
dilatory practices (boxes), 94, 98–99
floor procedures, 55, 93–102
leadership structure, 2–3, 36–48
presiding officers, 36–37 (box), 90–91 (box)
rules, 51–52, 56–57 (box)
scheduling, 89–93
seniority, 150–151 (box)
supermajority votes, 60 (box)
television coverage, 64–65 (box)
typical day (box), 92
vetoed bills, 112
voting methods, 79
Seniority
benefits (box), 150–151
in committee system, 124–128, 147–149, 150–151 (box), 155
chairmen, 146
House Rules Committee, 126–127 (box)
reforms of 1970s, 33, 134–135, 137
conference selection, 104
restrictive rules, 80
Senate leadership history, 38
Senate presiding officers, 37 (box)
Sequential referral, 61, 153
Sergeant at arms (Senate), 96
Sessions, 53 (box)
Sharp, Philip R., 52
Shays, Christopher, 73

Shelby, Richard, 148
Sherman, John, 12–13, 27
Sikes, Robert L. F., 135
Silent quorums, 10, 11, 14
Simon, Paul, 95
Simple resolutions, 61, 68
Simpson, Alan, 45
Sinclair, Barbara, 24, 32, 106
Skaggs, David, 105 (box)
Slavery, 12–13, 38
Smith, Bob, 151 (box)
Smith, Ellison D., 148 (box)
Smith, Howard W., 123, 126 (box), 129
Smith, Linda, 106
Smith, Neal, 134, 149
Smith, Steven S.
on committee system, 119, 121, 124, 126, 142, 145, 156–157
on legislative process, 52, 64 (box), 80, 82, 92, 101
on Senate leadership, 45
Snell, Bertrand, 29
Snowe, Olympia, 94 (box)
Social Security, 26 (box), 33
Solomon, Gerald B. H., 82, 84, 123, 127 (box)
Speaker of the House
authority, 7–8
committee relationships
ad hoc committees, 143
assignments, 35, 121, 125, 149, 154
bill referral, 61–62, 153, 156
Intelligence Committee, 143
Rules Committee, 10, 14–15, 18–19, 76, 122–123, 126–127 (box), 151
conference selection, 103–104, 106, 140 (box)
Congressional Record, 100 (box)
controversial Speakers (box), 20–21
election, 12, 79, 90 (box)
contests (box), 12–13
leadership ladder, 28, 32
oath of office, 151 (box)
enrolled bills, 109
floor procedures, 136
in Committee of Whole, 84
debate restriction, 74
Journal approval, 68 (box)
suspension of rules, 72, 73
unanimous consent, 72
voting, 78
floor scheduling, 6, 69
Corrections Calendar, 67, 68 (box), 69
Private Calendar, 69
in leadership structure, 2–7
majority leader choice, 27
policy committees, 35–36
list, 165
notable Speakers, 9–26
as presiding officer, 90–91 (box)
voting, 9, 90 (box)
Speaker's Working Group on Policy Development, 36
Special committees, 141, 143
Special interest groups, 57
Special orders, 31 (box), 64 (box), 68 (box)
Special rules, 75, 76–77, 122
Special sessions, 53 (box)
Split referral, 61, 153
Sponsorship of bills, 59
Spooner, John C., 38
Staggers, Harley, 135
Standards of Official Conduct Committee, House, 75, 139, 154
Standing committees, 119–120, 141, 142–143
Starr, Kenneth, 46, 104–105 (box)
Stevens, John Paul, 111 (box)
Stevens, Ted, 44, 47
Stevens, Thaddeus, 10
Stevenson, Adlai E. III, 137
Stevenson, Andrew, 10
Stewart, John G., 40
Striking the enacting clause, 84
Structured rules, 80–82
Subcommittees. *See* Committees and subcommittees
Substitute amendments, 86, 97
Substitute bills, 82
Sumner, Charles, 38
"Sunshine" reforms, 128 (box)
"Super A" committees, 138, 148, 155
Supermajority votes, 60 (box), 69, 99
Supreme Court cases
Burke v. Barnes, 113
Byrd v. Raines, 111 (box)
City of New York v. Clinton, 111 (box)
INS v. Chadha, 159
Pocket Veto Case, 113
Snake River Potato Growers Inc. v. Rubin, 111 (box)
U.S. v. Ballin, 11
Supreme Court decisions
House rules, 11
legislative veto, 159
line-item veto, 42, 111 (box)
pocket veto power, 113
term limits, 23
Suspension of rules
House procedures
noncontroversial bills, 72–75
scheduling, 67, 68 (box), 69
supermajority requirement, 60 (box)
Senate scheduling, 93
Sweeteners, 55

T
Tabling motions, 97–98
Taft, Robert A., 39
Task forces, 32, 35, 143, 145
Tawney, James A., 32
Tax legislation
"Contract with America," 26 (box)
germaneness issues, 65, 96–97
line-item veto, 110 (box)
House origination, 96
supermajority votes, 60 (box)
Taylor, John W., 12
Television
committee hearings, 123 (box), 129
effect of increased coverage, 52
House partisan trends, 31 (box)
House, Senate coverage, 64–65 (box), 100 (box)
leadership functions, 6, 19
"sunshine" reforms, 128 (box)
Teller votes, 78
Term limits
committee service, chairmanships, 139
Foley defeat, 23
House Speaker, 28, 34
proposed constitutional amendment, 82
Senate leadership, 48
Terms of Congress, 53 (box)
Thomas, Clarence, 63
Thomas, William M., 134
Thurmond, Strom, 17, 37 (box), 100, 125–126, 148 (box), 155
Time agreements, 91
Tompkins, David D., 121
Tower, John, 37 (box)
Track system, Senate, 41, 57 (box), 90–91, 101
Transportation and Infrastructure Committee, House, 145, 151
Treaties, 60, 60 (box), 90
Treaty of Versailles, 39, 98
Truman, Harry S., 58
Trumbull, Jonathan, 8
Tuchman, Barbara, 11
Twentieth Amendment, 53 (box)
Twenty-Fourth Amendment, 73
Twenty-one-day rule, 56 (box), 122–123
Twenty-Seventh Amendment, 104 (box)
Two-speech rule, 95
Tyler, John, 109

U
Udall, Morris K., 18
Unanimous consent
House procedures, 72
Senate agreements, 6, 89, 91–92
Underwood, Oscar, 4, 15–16, 27, 42 (box)
Union Calendar, 67

V
V-chips, 88
Vandenberg, Arthur H., 37 (box)
Vander Jagt, Guy, 13
Varnum, Joseph B., 12
Vetoes
final legislative action, 110–113
line-item veto (box), 110–111
list of vetoes, 1947–1996 (table), 172
override votes, 60 (box)
pocket vetoes, 112–113
privileged status, 76
Vice president
committee assignments, 36 (box), 121
as Senate officer, 2, 36–37 (box), 91 (box), 109
voting, 36 (box), 91 (box)
Video conferencing, 133 (box)
Vietnam War, 4, 18, 33, 43
Voice votes, 68 (box), 78–79
Volkmer, Harold L., 71
Voting. *See also* Cloture; Recorded votes; Roll-call votes
committee procedures, 66, 152
House methods, 68 (box), 78–79, 85 (box)
Speaker, 9, 90 (box)
off-site voting, 133 (box)
pairs, 81
proxy voting, 132–133 (box)
Senate
polling, in committee, 133 (box)
vice president, 36 (box), 91 (box)
supermajorities, 60 (box)
whip functions, 32

W
Wadsworth, James W. Jr., 46
War Powers Act, 159
Washington, George, 8
Watergate scandal
Baker, Dole careers, 43, 44
effects on rules, 52
as reform impetus, 18, 128 (box), 129, 131
select committees, 143
television coverage, 63, 64 (box)
Waxman, Henry, 135
Ways and Means Committee, House
closed sessions, 128 (box)
House committee assignments, 15, 35, 130, 131
leadership role, 26–27
membership, 154–155
prestige, 151
privileged legislation, 76
restrictive rules, 80
subcommittees, 131, 142–143

Webster, Daniel, 33, 36–37, 105 (box)
Weld, William, 135, 152
Welfare reform, 26 (box), 55–57
Wheeler, "Fighting Joe," 11
Whips (House), 2, 6, 13, 31–33
Whips (Senate), 46–47
White, John, 20 (box)
Whitten, Jamie L., 126, 149
Whole House on the State of the Union, Committee of the
  floor procedures, 83–84, 97–98
  presiding officers, 90 (box)
  recorded votes, 52, 78–79, 84
  scheduling, 67, 68 (box), 75
Williams, John Sharp, 14
Wilson, Woodrow, 4, 16, 39, 48, 98 (box), 125
Winthrop, Robert C., 9, 12
Witnesses at hearings, 123, 153
Women members of Congress, 34
Wright, Jim
  Gramm's Budget seat, 148 (box)
  on House/Senate rules, 51
  leadership ladder, 13, 27, 28
  as majority leader, 27
  as party leader, 1, 2, 8
  as Speaker, 19–22, 29
    bill number assignment, 59
    ethics charges, resignation, 6, 20, 20 (box), 30 (box)
    House partisan trends, 30–31 (box)
    legislative day, 83
Wyden, Ron, 93

Y

Yates, Sidney, 149, 151 (box)
Yatron, Gus, 135